Samurai and Silk

Haru Matsukata Reischauer

SAMURAI
and SILK

A Japanese and American Heritage

The Belknap Press of
Harvard University Press
Cambridge, Massachusetts
London, England

Library of Congress cataloging information follows the Index.

For my mother and father
to whom I never adequately expressed my gratitude

Miyo and Shokuma, wedding photograph, May 1913

Preface

This book is the product of a search for my heritage—my roots in Japan and America. It is basically made up of the biographies of my two grandfathers and shorter accounts of some of their descendants and relatives. Since both my grandfathers were prominent participants in the building of modern Japan, it also amounts to a personalized family view of modern Japanese history and Japanese–American relations.

The biography of my paternal grandfather, Matsukata Masayoshi, which constitutes the largest part of the book, is based on research I did some four decades ago, together with new materials I have obtained more recently, as well as extensive interviews with uncles, aunts, and friends who knew my grandfather. He was a major architect of the modernized Japan of the late nineteenth century, one of the small group of oligarchs known as the elder statesmen. His greatest achievements were in the field of Japan's financial and economic development, but, with little knowledge in these matters, I must leave it up to specialists to do justice to his financial career. Instead I have concentrated on a personal account of my grandfather, emphasizing the feudal background that formed his character, and on his broad career as a leader in government.

Unfortunately I have not been able to recapture my grandfather as a living, feeling human being. I personally met him only on formal occasions, when he seemed a remote godlike being to a small girl. Even his own sons and daughters regarded him with awe and never felt fully at ease with him. He had been a public figure ever since the oldest of them was born, and he considered himself as belonging more to the nation than to his family. He had grown into a venerable and revered statesman—a figure in history—long before I was born. There was little family lore that brought out his human side, at least as far as I could discover. He left no family letters, probably because he never wrote any. His biographers, as is all too common in Japan, have written pure hagiography or else have simply dealt with his official policies. Except for his own memoirs of his childhood, there is nothing that brings him alive as a person. Still, his life allows a penetrating look into the great transition Japan underwent in the second half of the nineteenth century, and the view of his career from within his family makes the cold facts of history a little more alive through the experiences of real people.

Originally I intended to write only about my Matsukata grandfather, but some ten years ago my uncle Yoneo Arai, then of Greenwich, Connecticut, but since deceased, sent me a copy of a booklet he had privately printed. It consisted of one chapter taken from a larger publication, *East Across the Pacific: Historical and Sociological Studies of Japanese Immigration and Assimilation* (Clio Press, 1972), edited by Hilary Conroy and a personal friend of ours, Scott T. Miyakawa, now deceased, who was a professor of sociology at Boston University. The book is a study of first- and second-generation Japanese in America—the so-called issei and nisei—and the chapter reprinted from it, written by Miyakawa, was about my maternal grandfather, Rioichiro Arai, and some of his issei contemporaries; it was based in large part on my grandfather's letters and documents as well as extensive interviews with my uncle. I remembered my grandfather as a cheerful, wonderfully kind old man, but I had no knowledge of his coming to America in 1876 at the age of twenty to start direct Japanese silk exports to the United States or of his important achievements in the development of economic relations between the two countries. The account of his life was an eye-opener for me, and I readily agreed to my husband's suggestion that I include his biography with that of my other grandfather.

Miyakawa's short biography started with my Arai grandfather's departure for the United States in 1876 and dealt only with his development of the silk trade. My search for background material led me to Hoshino Yasushi, professor emeritus of Tokyo Kogyo Daigaku (Tokyo

University of Engineering), who is an authority on electrical engineering and is known in Japan as the "father of magnetic tape." Professor Hoshino is the grandson of my Arai grandfather's oldest brother, Hoshino Chotaro, and the present head of the Hoshino family. My grandfather was born a Hoshino but had been adopted into the Arai family: hence the different surnames. He started the export of silk to America under the guidance of Hoshino Chotaro, but the two had a falling out, which lasted the rest of their lives. So I grew up knowing nothing about the Hoshino family and met Professor Hoshino for the first time only about ten years ago. He welcomed me with enthusiasm and offered his full cooperation in my undertaking. He also told me of well-kept family records dating back several centuries and of early records of the silk trade, all of which were kept in an old family storehouse in Gumma. He promised to start looking through them and to send me copies of relevant materials. A thorough researcher, he sent most of the documents that enabled me to write the first three chapters of my Arai grandfather's biography. Professor Hoshino realized the historical significance of the documents, which up until then had lain about in a dusty and inflammable storehouse, and has started to have the materials microfilmed, catalogued, and placed in a special archive.

The lives of my two grandfathers dovetailed beautifully, giving a fuller picture of Japan's economic success in the modern world than an account of either could if taken alone. My Matsukata grandfather was the leading figure in establishing modern Japan's financial foundations, but my Arai grandfather typified the private entrepreneurship that took advantage of these foundations to build a thriving economy. Without the foundations the one laid, the success of the other would have been impossible, but without Arai's sort of entrepreneurship, the statesmanship of Matsukata might have created only an empty shell. Their careers represent the two sides of the coin of modern Japanese economic history. They also illustrate the national and international dimensions of Japan's development. Since some of their descendants and relatives further broadened these themes, I decided to include a section on them as well. To help orient the reader I have added an introduction where I briefly recount my own life.

———————•———————

I wish to express my thanks to those who aided me in this project. I am particularly indebted to Professor Yasushi Hoshino for the materials on my Arai grandfather's early life and to my uncle Yoneo Arai, who made available my grandfather's documents, letters, photographs, and personal possessions, which he had kept in storage in his Greenwich home. I feel a great sense of relief to know that all his papers have since been sent to special archives in the University of California at Los Angeles, where they are safely kept with other materials about the early Japanese in America.

My gratitude goes to many of my relatives on both sides of the family and to various friends for providing helpful information, criticism, and aid. My cousin Matsukata Mineo, the present head of the Matsukata family, gave me access to documents, photographs, and personal possessions of my paternal grandfather kept in his country home in Nasuno. I am grateful to Matsumoto Shigeharu, Matsukata Saburo, Ushiba Tomohiko and Nobuhiko, and my aunt Mitsu Arai for the supplementary oral information they all gave me. I have also found helpful the recent publications by some of my informants, such as Matsumoto Shigeharu's *Shanghai Jidai* (Shanghai Period), published by Chuokoronsha, Tokyo, 1975; letters and articles of Matsukata Saburo, compiled and published in several volumes by the Matsukata family; Ushiba Nobuhiko's personal history, *Gaiko no shunkan* (A Moment in Diplomacy), published by Nihon Keizai Shinbunsha, Tokyo, 1984; and the section by Okabe Nagaakira in *Katarizuku Showa shi* (Tales of Showa History), published by Asahi Shinbunsha, Tokyo, 1977. My cousins Matsumoto Shigeharu and Ushiba Tomohiko were good enough to read and correct parts of the manuscript. Albert and Teruko Craig kindly read and commented on the whole text. Finally, my deepest thanks go to my husband for all his encouragement and help. His advice in shaping this book has been invaluable, and I have always been able to count on him for guidance with the historical background and for a great deal of editorial assistance.

H. M. R.
Belmont, Massachusetts

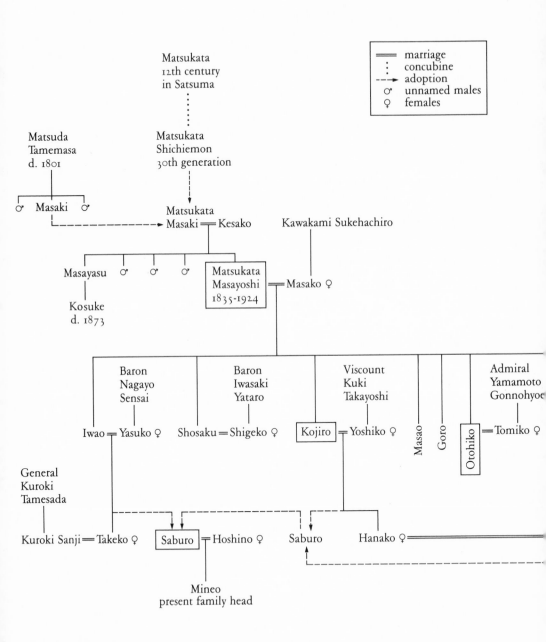

THE MATSUKATA FAMILY

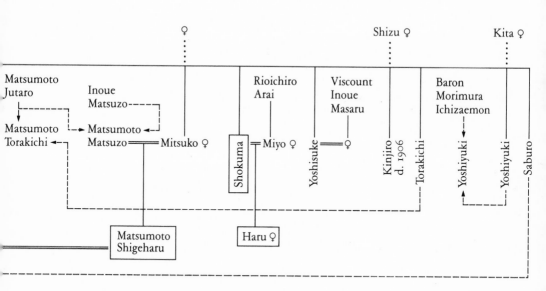

THE ARAI FAMILY

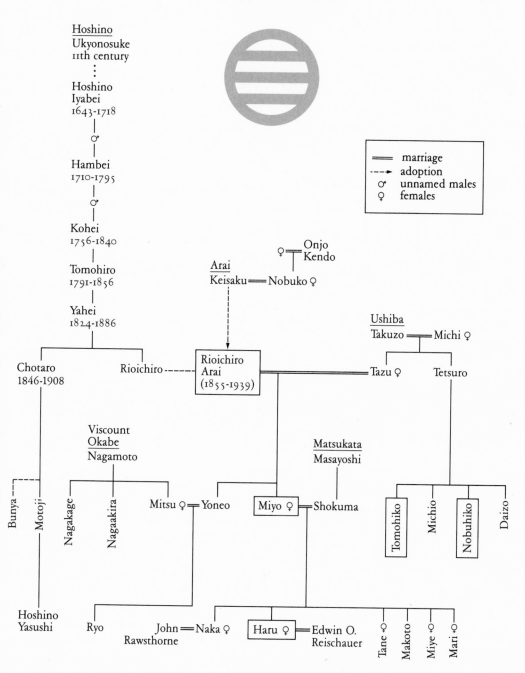

Contents

Introduction: My Dual Background   1

MATSUKATA MASAYOSHI

    A Samurai Boyhood   21

    Satsuma Officer   42

    Imperial Official   64

    Finance Minister   91

    National Leader   113

    Elder Statesman   130

RIOICHIRO ARAI

    A Peasant Background   155

    Modern Student   170

    Emigrating to America   190

    Starting the Silk Trade   207

    New York Businessman   226

    Americanization of the Arai Family   243

DESCENDANTS AND RELATIVES

Matsukata's Sons   263

Matsukata Kojiro   275

Matsukata Saburo   299

Matsumoto Shigeharu   319

Arai Relatives   337

Index   359

Illustrations following pages 108, 236, 332

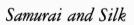

Samurai and Silk

Introduction · My Dual Background

I was born a Japanese citizen in Japan and of purely Japanese ancestry, but there was one thing that set me apart from most of my compatriots. My mother's father, Rioichiro Arai, had gone to New York in 1876 at the age of twenty to set up a business exporting Japanese raw silk directly to the American market, and he lived the rest of his life in the United States, except for annual business trips back to Japan. My mother, Miyo, was born in New York and grew up there and in Old Greenwich, Connecticut, becoming at heart and in her ways much more American than Japanese. But when it came to marriage, Japanese custom prevailed. It was arranged for her to marry Shokuma, a younger son of Marquis Matsukata Masayoshi,* one of Japan's leading statesmen. There was some concession to American ways, however, since my parents had at least a small share in the marriage decision. They had met and were attracted to each other while my father was studying for a short time at Yale, and he was invited on occasion to my grandparents' home in Greenwich.

When my mother went to Japan in 1912 for the marriage ceremony, she was determined to make every effort to adjust to her new life. As she wrote her brother at Harvard, she would do her best "to do in Rome as the Romans do." In the phrasing we see the influence of

---

* The family name always comes first in Japan, and I have followed this practice except for Japanese who became permanent residents of the United States—as did my Arai grandfather—and Americans of Japanese origin.

her American schooling at Miss Low's Finishing School in Stamford. The transition to living in Japan was no easy matter, since life styles in the two countries were vastly different in those days. But she was fortunate in marrying into the Matsukata family, which was somewhat less traditional and formal than most of the other prominent families of the time. Her father-in-law was a broad-minded man who had sent most of his sons abroad to Europe or America for their higher education. He himself was entirely at home in Western clothes, sitting on a chair in a Western-style room or hosting a large dinner party in the occidental manner.

Still, my grandfather was thoroughly Japanese. At home he preferred to dress in a kimono and sit and sleep on the thick tatami mats covering the floor of the one Japanese room in the Western wing of his residence. I remember him as a venerable figure, presiding over a huge patriarchial family. He was in fact one of the last surviving members of the group of young samurai leaders who had been largely responsible for building the new Japan and had come to be known in the West as the "oligarchs" and in Japan as the *genro* (elder statesmen). He had proved the financial genius of the group, serving for more than fifteen years as finance minister and twice briefly as prime minister. As a reward, he had been given successively higher noble ranks. At the time of my mother's marriage, he had attained the second highest rank of marquis, and later he was made a prince.

My grandfather's house, where my mother spent her first married year, had a large staff of more than twenty servants. The unifying force in the household was not my grandfather but his wife, Masako. She brought up the children strictly but with affection, whether they were her own children or the offspring of concubines. She was responsible for creating a warm atmosphere, always comfortable and cheerful. She expected her sons to respect their sisters, and when they married she saw that they treated their wives with consideration and courtesy. It was not without reason that all the daughters-in-law loved Masako dearly.

Masako treated my mother with special understanding and kindness, making no attempt to change her ways and not expecting her to conform to strict Japanese social custom, as she did with her other daughters-in-law. Masako's attitude, together with my mother's conscious effort to conform, greatly eased my mother's transition to her new life. Nevertheless, she found the complex relations within a large aristocratic family quite constraining and unfulfilling. She became determined to bring up her own children to be strong, independent individuals. But this ran counter to the accepted Japanese system of raising children and was no easy task. She had to stand alone to carry out her resolve, with no understanding, much less help, from her relatives, though my father always gave her full and sympathetic support.

Naturally my mother often became despondent, but in 1917, when she was feeling particularly low, two things came into her life which proved a turning point. An American friend, the wife of the American naval attaché in Tokyo, invited her to attend a Christian Science lecture in Yokohama. Greatly inspired by it, she began to study Christian Science and ultimately found in it the spiritual strength with which to carry out her resolve. She became deeply involved in the Christian Science movement in Japan, and a mainstay of the church.

The other factor contributing to this turning point came with the introduction of Florence Boynton into her life. A schoolteacher from California, Miss Boynton had come as a tutor for the children of an American family and stayed on in Tokyo after their departure, teaching English at a municipal middle school. She also conducted private English classes, attended by my sisters and me as well as the children of some family friends. Through these English lessons, Miss Boynton taught us Christian Science. Her house was seriously damaged in the great earthquake of 1923, and my mother invited her to stay temporarily with us. The stay lasted nearly twenty years, and she took charge of the children's education, since my mother found Japanese education completely inadequate for her purpose. Except for a year in a Japanese kindergarten and another as a first-grader in a Japanese school, my whole early education was conducted along American lines under Miss Boynton and Japanese private tutors or at the American School in Japan. Besides Miss Boynton, my mother employed a succession of English governesses to take care of the younger children.

It was not surprising that our relatives gave up trying to influence my mother and her children. They found our family just too eccentric to be amenable to reason. They tended to treat us with friendly aloofness, thus sparing us the intricate relationships and psychological pressures common in large Japanese families of that time. This suited us well, since we had our own circle of friends bound by mutual interests. As time passed, my mother attended fewer and fewer family gatherings, where her sisters-in-law talked incessantly about arranging marriages for their daughters and preparing elaborate trousseaux. My mother scandalized the relatives by insisting that, instead of preparing her girls for early marriage, she would see to it that we received college educations, to prepare us for fuller lives. All six of us children were sent in turn to Principia College, a Christian Science school located in rural Illinois on a beautiful bluff above the Mississippi River, a few miles north of St. Louis. My mother considered education to be of more value to us than any trousseau.

Our upbringing thus made us different from other Japanese in many ways. As a small child I dreaded the daily walks we took around our neighborhood, dressed quite oddly by Japanese standards in sailor suits and high-laced boots and accompanied by a tall, gawky English governess. Foreigners were rare in Japan in those days, and Japanese children would stare at us, sometimes making derisive comments. Still this did not make us insiders at the American School, where we were of course considered "Japanese girls" by the predominantly occidental student body, and the same was true at Principia. The atmosphere there could not have been more cordial, and many of my college friends are still close to me. But we were outsiders—girls from a far and alien land. I had my share of dates and social life, but I remember looking enviously at happy couples among my schoolmates, realizing that their relationships might lead to marriage while I belonged to a different world. At times I felt almost bitter that I had been raised to be so different from other Japanese. Why couldn't I have been brought up the ordinary way, I would think, since being different didn't seem to make me a real American either?

These, however, were not my everyday thoughts. On the whole I was fairly oblivious of being caught between two cultures. My school and college days were for the most part a very happy time. The years at Principia passed pleasantly and with a quickening pace of excitement. The summers I spent with my maternal grandparents and my uncle and aunt and their son in their big comfortable home in Greenwich, overlooking a lovely cove on Long Island Sound.

In the summer of 1936 my one older sister Naka and I had the memorable experience of serving as secretaries to the Japanese delegation at an international conference of the Institute of Pacific Relations held at Yosemite Park. Working with us were two young men, Saionji Koichi, who had been a childhood friend, and Konoe Fumitaka. They were both descendants of the old Fujiwara court aristocracy, which had surrounded the Japanese emperors for more than thirteen centuries. Koichi's grandfather, Prince Saionji Kimmochi, was the emperor's closest adviser and at the time was usually referred to as the last genro. Koichi himself became famous after World War II as a prominent Communist sympathizer and longtime resident of Peking. Fumitaka's father, Prince Konoe Fumimaro, was to serve twice as prime minister between 1937 and 1941, ineffectually trying to reestablish civilian control over the Japanese military and avoid war with the United States. When at the end of World War II he was indicted by the American authorities as a major war criminal, he chose to commit suicide. Fumitaka himself, whom I remember as a dapper Princeton undergraduate addicted to golf and fast cars, was drafted into the Japanese army and at war's end was captured by the Soviet army in Manchuria. He died in 1956, still a captive in the Soviet Union.

But in the summer of 1936 all this lay mercifully out of sight. We were young, happy, and idealistic. The Institute of Pacific Relations, though accused later in the McCarthy period of being a Communist front organization, was in fact devoted to the cause of peace, and the respectable, conservative Japanese delegates to the conference represented those Japanese leaders who truly believed in international friendship and peaceful cooperation. I remember being inspired that summer with the thought that I must somehow dedicate my life to better understanding and peace between my two countries. In particular I dreamed of establishing programs of summertime exchanges between American and Japanese students.

An event the previous winter, however, had thrown a warning shadow across the future. Like most other college students I was too absorbed in my own life to read the newspapers, but I learned through letters from home of a disturbing event that occurred in Tokyo on February 26, 1936, and came to be known in Japan from the date as the 2-2-6 (2/26) Incident. On that snowy day in February certain members of the army's First Division attempted a coup d'état, assassinating some of the more liberal leaders, though failing in their attempt to kill Prince Saionji. The uprising was put down after a few days, but it caused much concern and frightened me greatly. Otherwise the calm and pleasant atmosphere of my college life was untroubled by outside worries at peaceful Principia, deep in the American heartland.

———•———

I graduated from college in 1937 and with two women classmates drove across the country to their homes in California. From there I went back to Japan by ship after four years' absence. It was still the age of leisurely, restful travel by sea, two whole weeks across the Pacific by way of Hawaii. I arrived home full of zeal to do something to further international understanding. But I soon realized the times were out of joint. The ship docked at Yokohama on July 7, the day a small skirmish broke out between Japanese and Chinese troops near Peking: the so-called Marco Polo Bridge Incident. The Japanese had been gradually encroaching into North China, and areas of jurisdiction between the two armies were not clear. The Japanese, hoping for a speedy settlement, called the resulting fighting the China Incident, but it quickly grew into an all-out Sino-Japanese war. In fact, it was the beginning of World War II.

All of my vague hopes for international understanding came tumbling down. Japan was gearing itself up for a decisive war, and the United States was becoming ever more clearly the ultimate enemy. As the fighting spread in China and war then broke out in Europe in 1939, America too began to get ready to fight and Japan, which was allying itself with Germany, was one of the chief foes it had in mind. There was no room for a college girl's naive idealism about Japanese-American friendship. In fact, there seemed no place for me of any sort. Marriage appeared out of the question. My upbringing made me feel that I could never submit to what we would now call the blatant male chauvinism of Japanese husbands. There were few careers open to Japanese women—especially one without a standard Japanese education and with only an impractical American college major in English literature. My happy carefree life was at an end.

The next eight years were the hardest period of my life. The political situation in Japan and the world continued to deteriorate. Informed opinion in Japan held that the war with China would last only a few months at most, but it went on and on. The streets of Tokyo and of every other city, town, and village in Japan were lined with children and women, waving flags and singing war songs as they sent their brothers and sons off to die in battle. Some of our family friends who were knowledgeable about the West and stood for liberal policies had been assassinated in the 1936 attempted coup d'état and in other terrorist acts. Most of the rest, including my own family with its American contacts, were under a cloud of suspicion as secret opponents of war. Faced with a national war hysteria and growing military dominance over the government, the people I knew and admired retreated into cautious silence. Worst of all, Japan and the United States appeared to be moving step by step closer to war.

My younger brother and three younger sisters had left for school in the United States, and my older sister managed to return there to wait to marry her college beau. So I was left all alone at home with my parents, watching my dreams crumble away. The future seemed to hold no hope. Still, one has to do something and I looked around for things to occupy my time. In Japan an unmarried young woman was expected to cultivate one of the polite arts, such as flower arrangement, the tea ceremony, painting, music, classical dancing, or poetry. I knew that my talents and interests did not lie along these lines. I did tutor some of my friends' children in English, but that was not enough to keep me busy. Since I found it impossible to talk with other people about the war or anything that really mattered, I decided to make my own friends by reading books. I began browsing through bookstores, especially the famous second-hand shops of the Kanda district of Tokyo, which stretch for blocks in the neighborhood of some of the major universities.

Remembering how often I had not been able to answer the questions my friends at Principia had asked me about Japan, I decided to learn more about my native land. I was not sure what I was looking for, but today we might say I was searching for roots or identity— something to help me know who I was. I soon found my attention drawn to Japanese history, a subject in which I had first become interested through a course on the Far East I took in college. I began to collect history books and to study traditional Japanese art, assembling a collection of reprints of famous scroll paintings and making translations of the texts that accompanied the pictures. But I had had no training as an historian or student of art, and my efforts were not well focused.

Gradually I realized that it would be interesting to concentrate on a study of my paternal grandfather, since he had been one of the great historical figures of his time. I was eight years old when he died in 1924, and, although I had vague memories of him as a fine, stately gentleman, I had no idea of his accomplishments. Fortunately a two-volume biography called the *Koshaku Matsukata Masayoshi Den* had been published by the Matsukata family in 1935. Compiled by the Committee for the Compilation of the Biography of Prince Matsukata, it was edited by Tokutomi Soho, a journalist and historian who had also edited biographies of other Meiji leaders. The biography was based on all available documents, letters, and previous research on Matsukata, but at its core lay the *Matsukata Masayoshi Kyo Jikki* (The Authentic Record of Lord Matsukata Masayoshi), which my grandfather himself had dictated and edited in his later years. It is a handwritten manuscript in fifty-one handbound pamphlets. I was lucky enough to find the original among my grandfather's books in the library at his country home in Nasuno, and I received permission to use it in my research. In this book I draw most of the information and quotations about my grandfather from these two sources.

Two things impressed me most in my studies of my grandfather. One was the spartan virtues and steel-like willpower of the feudal society that produced him. The other was to discover that in his later years he opposed the aggressive policies toward China of some of his colleagues, whom he condemned as being two-faced in their professed love of China and their actual aggression against it. A scathing document he had written criticizing Japanese policy after he learned of the Twenty-One Demands made on China in 1915 was most revealing. When I remarked that this document should be circulated, I was advised by my family that the time was inappropriate. They were of course right, since the Japanese military leaders certainly would have reacted harshly.

At the same time, I remember feeling somewhat indignant that Westerners seemed to be united in condemning Japan for trying to build the sort of empire the European powers had created for themselves with much glory and self-satisfaction only a few decades earlier. Still, on the whole, I found it hard to grasp the course of Japan's modern development or to understand what was really happening in the world. I didn't seem to fit in anywhere myself, and I was torn by conflicting waves of sympathy for Japan and the United States.

Since I did not have a formal Japanese education and had never studied *kambun,* the Japanized Chinese in which well-educated men of my grandfather's generation wrote, I needed assistance in the translation of his biography. I shall always be grateful to Wakebe Sumi, who transcribed into simple contemporary Japanese those documents and texts that were written in classical Japanese of kambun. With her assistance, I made a complete translation into English of Tokutomi's two volumes and parts of my grandfather's *Jikki.* As a precautionary measure with war impending, I sent a copy of the typed manuscript and other translations I had made to my history professor at Principia College for safe keeping.

My amateurish scholarly endeavors helped me pass several years, not happily but at least tolerably. Through my historical work I managed to shut myself off in part from the distressing world around me. But meanwhile the dreaded event had happened: Japan and the United States were at war. I learned the news from a telephone call while I was still in bed on the morning of December 8, 1941. My first thought was the passage from Job, "The thing I greatly feared has come upon me," and I buried my face in my pillow and wept.

The war soon began to bear down so heavily on our lives that I had to put my books and translations away and struggle simply to survive. By the spring of 1942, less than a half year after Pearl Harbor, food and other shortages had become extremely serious, and the police kept harassing us with questions about our family members in the United States. My parents and I, therefore, decided to leave our Tokyo house and move to our summer place at Kamakura on the beach some forty miles south of Tokyo. We took with us a faithful maid, Tsuru, the daughter of a prosperous farmer. At Kamakura we had ample room to grow our own food and collect sufficient firewood for cooking and heating. Luckily the warm Japan Current keeps temperatures there much milder than in Tokyo. The house faced south directly onto the sea, and it was a comfort to think that only a single, even if broad, stretch of water separated us from our family and friends in the United States.

My father had recently retired, selling his two large sugar companies to Fujiyama Aiichiro, who was to become a postwar foreign minister, and my father, the maid, and I turned ourselves into farmers for the rest of the war. I had always been interested in the work of the gardeners who took care of our grounds in Tokyo, and now I added to this learning by observation a good deal of practical farming experience. In Kamakura we grew all the vegetables we needed and raised chickens, pigs, and a goat, who gave us a steady supply of milk. In time we developed skill in growing sweet potatoes, which were well adapted to the sandy soil of Kamakura. In fact, my father and I were officially appointed municipal sweet-potato experts and went around teaching the real farmers of the region how to increase food supplies through this hardy tuber. This task saved me from being conscripted as a factory worker.

Another three years passed in this way. While all man-made things seemed to be tumbling down or burning up around us, there was great satisfaction in watching nature's spontaneous growth. The hard physical work also kept me busy. But these were sad, hopeless years for me, and I even contemplated suicide. On weekly trips to Tokyo to teach English to a small group of children of our friends, I would think of throwing myself in front of the train as it sped into the station. But of course, I didn't. Suicide is easier to contemplate than to carry out.

By the spring of 1945 the American forces had come close enough to Japan to start a methodical destruction of the cities through massive firebomb raids. The time was clearly approaching when invading American troops would come crashing ashore along our beaches. The long, gently curving beach at Kamakura, so near Tokyo, seemed a likely spot. In early May the navy ordered the whole beach area evacuated by civilians, and it commandeered our house. We were forced to leave with only the clothes and articles we could carry by hand and on our backs. Among these small stores, I remember, was a little bit of sugar from my father's old sugar business and a tiny residue of coffee left us by departing American friends before the war. Both were unobtainable treasures at the time.

We decided to go to Gumma prefecture, north of Tokyo, where my mother's father had been born and lived until he left permanently for America in 1876. The family later had moved to Tokyo and the old house was destroyed by fire, but my grandfather had inherited the property on his father's death and my father looked after it for him. Thus we had connections in the area and were able to rent a room in a farmhouse in the village of Kazuno. The farmers welcomed us but were unable to supply us with food, since they themselves had only subsistence supplies. In May, nothing much was growing in this mountainous area, and we were forced to live on the inadequate government ration of rice, which we made into watery gruel, supplemented only by watercress we gathered from the streams and a little later in the spring by fresh bamboo shoots we dug from the hillsides. The farmhouse where we lived was alive with fleas, which, ignoring my parents' older bodies, fed ravenously on me. Flea bites turned into running sores, which in my undernourished condition would not heal. In desperation, we moved to a storehouse that had belonged to my grandfather's family. It proved to be free of fleas and much more comfortable. In fact, it was so roomy that we brought a friend and her two small boys to live with us, since they were under severe police harassment at their own place.

It was a grim life as we waited for vegetable seeds we planted to bring us a more adequate diet and waited even more desperately for the war to end. Finally on the morning of August 15 (the date was still August 14 in the United States), the elderly postman in making his rounds remarked that the radio had said that the emperor would announce the end of the war at noon. "Who won?" I asked, with tongue in cheek. "I guess we did," he replied innocently. None of us had as yet heard of the dropping of atom bombs, only a new type of bomb of great power. At noon my father and I went down to the house where the village radio was kept to hear the emperor's message. Most of the villagers were unable to understand the formal wording the emperor used in this first direct statement he had ever made to his people, and it was my father who had to explain to them that, instead of calling for a fight to the death, as everyone was expecting, he had announced Japan's unconditional surrender to the enemy.

The villagers could not comprehend the news, since the military propaganda had made them believe that Japan was winning and final victory was near. The enemy forces, it was said, were being drawn closer to Japan so that they could be more easily annihilated. Everyone in the village had been training in the use of bamboo spears against straw dummies in order to learn how to destroy the invading Americans. Of course we knew better. We closed the windows in our storehouse and shouted for joy that finally the senseless war was over and our family might once again be reunited.

———•———

The Americans began landing in Japan in early September, and soon after that word came to us that American friends among the occupation forces were looking for us with news of our family. Since the outbreak of the war almost four years earlier, we had only one communication from them, brought by Japanese who had returned in 1942 on one of the two exchange ships returning diplomats and a few others from both sides. My father and I set off at once for Tokyo to see what we could find. Tokyo and its surrounding towns were a complete wilderness—a vast stretch of more than twenty miles of burned-out ruins, dotted here and there with standing brick chimneys, fireproof storehouses, and iron vaults. Most of the old landmarks had disappeared, and it was difficult to find our way even in neighborhoods we had known all our lives. But finally we managed to reach our old home site. There had been three houses, two of them quite large, surrounded by gardens and trees. We rented one of the houses to the Swedish legation when we fled Tokyo in 1942. The sea of fire from the firebomb raids had swept right up to the property, burning down two of our houses. We could identify the one we had lived in by the metal strings and frames of two pianos, a safe, and heaps of rubble from our smashed porcelain. The third house, still occupied by the Swedish legation, miraculously survived.

We managed to get in touch with the correspondent of the *Christian Science Monitor*, and he took us to Yokohama to meet a former Principia professor who had news of our family in America. My Arai grandfather had mercifully died in 1939 before he saw his whole life's work destroyed, but my grandmother and my uncle and aunt in Greenwich and my brother and four sisters were all well and had been most kindly taken care of throughout the war by American friends. The four girls had stayed at Principia the whole time. My eldest sister, Naka, was still waiting for her American college sweetheart, and he, after four years in the coast guard fighting the Japanese, did return and persuaded his congressman to get a special bill passed permitting their marriage (it was still against the law for a man in uniform to marry an enemy alien). She settled down as a housewife, becoming an American citizen in the process and, now widowed, lives in California. My two youngest sisters had completed college and were thoroughly Americanized. In time they acquired American citizenship, settling down permanently in the United States. Miye, who died in 1981, became a well-known artist in jewelry, with an atelier called Janiye in Boston, and Mari is married to an American and lives in the Los Angeles area.

My next younger sister, Tane, after receiving a master's degree in library science from Columbia University, returned to Japan. She tried to find a job in her field, but with the devastation of the war there were none available, much less an opening for a woman. She turned to education because some Western-oriented mothers were feeling dissatisfied with Japanese education and wanted their children to learn English and a more democratic style of life. They had begun to appreciate my mother's foresight in educating her children and asked Tane to teach their children to develop habits of independent thought that would prepare them to live in the democratic society advocated by the American occupation. Tane started in 1949 with four students in a classroom in a private home, and from this beginning grew the Nishimachi International School, which now has over three hundred students from over thirty countries and is located in our one remaining house and the property around it. The school offers bilingual teaching in English and Japanese, and, while the curriculum is essentially American, students learn to appreciate Japanese culture and to see the world in a thoroughly international way.

My brother, who among us had been given the most Japanese education, taught Japanese at Harvard to American soldiers during the war and at its end enlisted in the army himself, thereby becoming an American citizen. Before long he turned up in Tokyo as part of the American army of occupation and later settled down as an American businessman based in Tokyo. My brother and sisters thus found their niches in the new age of peace and restored Japanese-American friendship. No longer caught between two cultures in conflict, they opted to become Americans or, in Tane's case, the founder of an American-type school in Tokyo. For me too the dark clouds that engulfed me on the day I returned to Japan in 1937 had lifted, and there seemed a faint tinge of light on the horizon of my future. But after eight miserable wartime years in Japan, I was still at a loss about who and what I was.

Despite Japan's utter devastation, hunger, and grinding poverty, however, it was a far more promising country for a person with my background in 1945 than it had been in 1937. Millions of disillusioned Japanese, angry about the disaster into which their military leaders had led them, were demanding that society should become freer, more open, and more democratic—more like the country my American background had taught me to cherish. Under MacArthur, the American occupation authorities were pushing mightily in the same direction. I remember how excited I was over one of the first orders of the American authorities to free all political prisoners, including even the long-oppressed communists. There was also more place for women. Their prospects seemed to be brighter as they were given the vote and legal equality with men and became more forceful in their demands for a role in society. And of course my American background now was no longer a handicap but a distinct asset in a country trying to rebuild itself under American guidance. All this made me feel that I was coming alive again and gave me an indescribable sense of freedom. Not in my wildest dreams had I expected such a complete change for the better.

But I still faced the problem of making a living. We had once been a fairly rich family, but all our money evaporated through the destruction of war, confiscatory laws on land and capital, and a hundredfold rate of inflation. A number of jobs, however, were now open to me because of my bilingual abilities. I decided to accept an offer from the correspondent of the *Christian Science Monitor.* Since he knew no Japanese, I felt that by helping him I could contribute to a better understanding of Japan in the United States. Over the years I held several different jobs. In 1952 I became the permanent local representative of the *Saturday Evening Post,* giving advice to its correspondents who came to Japan from time to time and on occasion even writing articles of my own. This work as a correspondent enabled me to become a member of the Foreign Correspondents Club of Japan, which was quite a well-known institution during the years of the American occupation and the Korean War. For a while I was the only Japanese citizen among its members and one of the few women, and I became both its first woman and first Japanese officer when I was elected secretary of the club in 1954.

I was beginning to find a place for myself, but I still felt ill at ease and uncertain of my identity. My colleagues and friends were mostly

American, but I always felt a gulf between us because of their appalling lack of understanding of Japan. On the other side, I had some Japanese friends and many acquaintances who knew little of the United States and had no understanding of the basically American type of life I was leading. Another problem was that my American friends kept coming and going. After several painful partings from dear friends, I began to shield myself from making close friendships. As the years passed, my sense of aloneness deepened. I was still living in two worlds, even though these worlds were no longer at war and were beginning to become better acquainted.

It was not until I met and married my husband that my two worlds finally came together. Ed, who is more widely known as a scholar, writer, and sometime diplomat under his full name of Edwin O. Reischauer, turned up in Tokyo in the summer of 1955. He had lost his wife of twenty years the preceding winter after a long and terrible illness, and he was physically and psychologically exhausted; his three teenage children were somewhat out of hand. His scholarly life as a Harvard professor had no appeal for me. I had always felt that professors, because of their dullness, and diplomats, because of their stuffiness, were two types of men I could never be interested in.

There was something different about Ed, however. He had been born in Tokyo of missionary parents, and I remembered him as the captain of the basketball team at the American School in Japan the year I had been in the sixth grade there. In many ways he knew more about Japan than I did, especially about its history. He could read difficult things in Japanese I couldn't make out, though my command of spoken Japanese was much better than his. He was as devoted as I to Japanese-American understanding and friendship. In short, he combined my two cultures, though in his own way. He was like the proverbial boy from next door, and after only a few dates we fell in love and were married.

Suddenly becoming at age forty the mother of three teenagers and moving to the United States as a professor's wife posed challenges—but there were rewards as well. We settled into a very happy life until a new twist seemed to throw it all out of kilter again. In the spring of 1960 there had been a blowup in Japanese-American relations over the extension of the security treaty between the two nations. There were massive demonstrations of protest for weeks in Tokyo, and a planned visit by President Eisenhower had to be canceled. Ed and I spent that summer and autumn in Japan, and some other Asian countries as far around as India, in connection with his duties as director of the Harvard-Yenching Institute, and during this time he wrote for *Foreign Affairs* an analysis of the political incident in Japan, entitled "The Broken Dialogue," which attracted considerable attention in both countries. In part because of it, he was quite unexpectedly asked in January 1961 by the new Kennedy administration to go to Japan as the American ambassador.

I was appalled. I had a strong prejudice against diplomatic life, and I couldn't imagine myself being accepted by either Americans or Japanese as the American ambassador's wife. Never before in diplomatic history, we were told, had an ambassador of any country or even a lesser diplomat been assigned to the country of his wife's original nationality. But that was not what bothered me. I was Japanese by race and had been an American citizen for only a year. I just couldn't see the American community in Japan, especially the large military establishment, accepting me as a bonafide American or the Japanese seeing me as anything but a renegade Japanese.

After a few days of desperate protest, however, I saw I had to give in. Ed, in addition to being a scholar of ancient Japanese and Chinese history, had served in both the army and the state department and was something of an authority on American foreign policy in Asia—as he said, it was a case of "put up or shut up." We went to Japan, both of us with considerable misgivings and I in absolute terror.

My fears proved groundless. The Japanese public, excited over the prospect of a Japanese-speaking ambassador and his Japanese wife, gave us an enthusiastic welcome. The American community, and particularly the military, responded to the Japanese enthusiasm by lionizing us. When I went to American military bases to address the various wives' clubs, I was embarrassed to be presented to the audience as "America's first lady in Japan." The embassy work was hard but immensely rewarding for both of us. There was a huge and complex embassy staff, and we lived in a palatial embassy residence. We were busy at least sixteen hours a day, often seven days a week, month after month. It was an exhausting life, but very rich and worthwhile. We were in the best of all possible positions to work for what interested us most—better understanding and friendship between the two countries of our common backgrounds. I felt that I had at last found myself.

Our ambassadorial years were a happy time for both of us, despite Ed's near assassination at the hands of a pitiful, deranged youth—which put him on the sidelines for about six months—and the darkening shadows of the Vietnam War during our final year in Japan. But the pace of work was too strenuous to be continued forever. After five and a half years we felt that the time had come to return to academic life.

The transition back to university life had its difficulties. Harvard offered Ed the special post of university professor, since his two-year leave of absence had long since expired and his old positions were occupied by others. I was relieved to get back to a simpler life, but he found it difficult to get used to the narrower frame of activity and the do-it-yourself style of private life in America. But we managed the transition, and Ed taught for another fifteen years at Harvard until his retirement in 1981. We are now settled into a contented and fulfilling life, still able to play a small but satisfying role in trying to build understanding between our two countries. Recently we have both been busy at our writing, Ed on his memoirs and I on this book. Our three children are married and have families of their own, but family ties remain close. Nine grandchildren—one of them a bright, sturdy Korean adopted grandson—help to enliven things, gathering as they frequently do at our home. And part of what I learned in those bitter war years in Japan has stood me in good stead: my garden thrives.

MATSUKATA MASAYOSHI

Matsukata Masayoshi, keeping the peace in Nagasaki, 1867

A *Samurai Boyhood*

I start with my paternal grandfather, Matsukata Masa-yoshi, because he was twenty-two years older than my mother's father. He was born on the twenty-fifth day of the second month of the sixth year of Tempo, or March 23, 1835, according to the Western calendar. His birthplace was Kagoshima, the capital of Satsuma, a major feudal domain occupying the southern quarter of the island of Kyushu, the southernmost of Japan's four main islands. Located in the latitude of southern Georgia and bathed by the warm Japan Current, Satsuma has an almost subtropical climate, though winter snows are not unknown. The domain centered on its capital Kagoshima, located on a big bay of the same name directly across from the still active volcano of Sakurajima.

Southern Kyushu figures in Japanese mythology as the place where the grandson of the Sun Goddess descended to earth to start the imperial line of Japan, but throughout most of history it has been a somewhat backward part of the country. Its relative isolation may account for the long rule over the region by a single family of lords—in fact, the longest rule of any feudal family in Japanese history. The Shimazu were among the warrior supporters of the Minamoto family, which won control over the country at the end of the twelfth century. The Minamoto and their vassals came from the Kanto Plain in eastern Japan around modern Tokyo, but the Shimazu family was rewarded for its services at this time with the stewardship of an estate in far-off Satsuma. This holding they slowly expanded until they had become the most prominent family of the area and in time a major contender for national leadership.

In the late sixteenth century, after more than a hundred years of incessant warfare throughout Japan, three successive feudal lords from central Japan managed to unify the country once again. This was at the time when firearms, recently introduced by the Portuguese, and castle building on a grand scale had increased the scale and ferocity of warfare. The Shimazu made a bid to gain control over all Kyushu but were forced to submit in 1587 to Hideyoshi, the second of the unifiers, when he invaded Kyushu with an army of 280,000 men. A few years later in 1600—a convenient date to remember—the Shimazu were again on the losing side in a great battle fought at Sekigahara in central Japan against Tokugawa Ieyasu, the third of the unifiers, and were forced to become his vassals.

From their great castle headquarters at Edo, the modern Tokyo, Ieyasu and his descendants fastened Tokugawa rule on all of Japan for the next two and a half centuries. In 1603 Ieyasu took the title of shogun, literally "generalissimo" of the emperor's forces, which had been the traditional term for national military dictators since the Minamoto first adopted it in the twelfth century. The emperors themselves, though in theory the ultimate source of all political authority, were in fact mere puppets, kept by the Tokugawa under careful control in the ancient capital of Kyoto. The Tokugawa continued the feudal division of Japan. They held under their own direct control about a quarter of the agricultural land, centering on the Kanto Plain and the area around Kyoto, as well as all the great cities. The rest of the country they assigned to theoretically autonomous feudal lords (*daimyo*), who remained, however, under the watchful eye of the Tokugawa. They gave some relatively large domains to cadet branches of the family and a great number of small domains to old family vassals—the "hereditary" daimyo. The remainder—more than a third of the country—was left in the hands of so-called *tozama* ("outer" daimyo). Some of these had been allies at the decisive battle of 1600. Others had been enemies but were allowed to survive either because of their remote locations or their continuing capacity to put up at least some resistance.

The Shimazu were lucky to be among the former foes of the Tokugawa who were allowed to continue on, and their Satsuma holdings, though considerably reduced in size, remained the second largest daimyo domain. Their own vassals and samurai retainers, however, had to be accommodated in a smaller area. This gave Satsuma a much higher percentage of samurai in its population than in most of the rest of Japan. In the country as a whole, the feudal military class consisted of some 6 or 7 percent of the population, but in Satsuma it was closer to a third. This meant that all the samurai could not be gathered at the capital castle town, as was usually the situation elsewhere, but had to be spread out over the whole domain. In Satsuma they were in theory scattered among 113 so-called outer castles, but many of these men were no more than farmers, earning their own way by agricultural labor and not supported by stipends from the domain's treasury. Such farmer samurai were known as *goshi* (rural samurai).

———•———

My grandfather's ancestors were such goshi, whose family name was originally not Matsukata but Matsuda. His grandfather, Matsuda Tamemasa, who died in 1801, farmed a small plot of land in the village of Taniyama, along the coast a few miles south of the castle town of Kagoshima, but this patrimony was too small to support his three sons. The younger two had to find a new way to make a living. Masaki, the older of the pair, who was born in 1786 and was my great grandfather, together with his younger brother, turned to trade between Kagoshima and the Ryukyu Islands. The whole Ryukyu chain of islands (largely the modern prefecture of Okinawa) is inhabited by a branch of the Japanese people who had their own kings and long formed a tributary state to China; they were conquered by the Shimazu in 1609 and incorporated into their Satsuma domain. The Ryukyu kings, however, were allowed as Shimazu vassals to continue their tributary relations with China, because the offering of tribute to China was a convenient political cover for an extensive trade that allowed Satsuma to maintain clandestine economic relations with the outside world, despite a strict Tokugawa ban on foreign contacts. The Japanese had withdrawn into almost complete isolation in the late 1630s in order to keep out Christianity, which they regarded as subversive to their feudal system. Trade contacts with the outside world were few, but correspondingly lucrative. Chinese luxury goods, such as silks, lacquer ware, and porcelains, were in great demand in the cities of Japan.

Masaki and his brother happened to enter on their trading venture at a good time. The government of the Satsuma domain was then pursuing a policy of increasing this secret trade with China in order to replenish the domain's treasury, which had been drained by heavy expenditures for reform measures instituted by an overly zealous daimyo. The two Matsuda brothers traded between Kagoshima and Amami Oshima, a large island in the northern part of the Ryukyu Islands. Through this trade Masaki not only became modestly prosperous but began to realize how ignorant most Japanese were about the rest of the world. In 1720 an earlier ban had been lifted on foreign books that did not contain information about Christianity, and a few students had begun to study the Dutch language at the Dutch trading post permitted in the Kyushu port of Nagasaki. Through Dutch books they had learned a little about political and scientific developments in Europe since Japan had secluded itself. But this knowledge, mainly about medicine, gunnery, and a few other scientific subjects, was restricted to a tiny group of scholarly men, and the Japanese populace as a whole continued to have virtually no knowledge of the Western world or even contemporary Asia.

Through his trade contacts Masaki learned something of the industrial and commercial revolutions already underway in the West and of the penetration of Europeans into Asia in search of new markets. He discovered that the Europeans used their superior military might when they could not peacefully win their demands for trade. They had already overrun India and much of Southeast Asia and were now knocking at the gates of China, right next door to Japan. Masaki worried that his own trade ventures would be hurt by the Europeans, and soon he began to fear for the safety of Japan itself: the next advance of the Westerners would probably be to the Ryukyu Islands and Japan.

Masaki, as a successful merchant, had established a comfortable life for himself and his family but, as he thought of the future, he felt it his first duty to give his children a better education so that they could adapt to the changing and troubled times that seemed to lie ahead for Japan. At least these are the motivations attributed to him much later by my grandfather and his biographers. Educational facilities were limited for members of the goshi class assigned to an outer castle. All schools and teachers beyond the elementary level were concentrated in Kagoshima and were open only to those of full samurai rank. Masaki hoped that somehow he could move his family to Kagoshima and raise his social status. Surprisingly enough, despite strict class barriers and severe social controls, he was able to do this. Masaki achieved his ambition through Matsukata Shichiemon, one of his Kagoshima clients.

Shichiemon was of distinguished ancestry, which he could trace back twenty-nine generations to an ancestor who had accompanied the Shimazu family when it first moved to Satsuma from eastern Japan in the twelfth century. In the seventeenth century the heir of the Matsukata family had been sent to Nagasaki at the age of fifteen to learn from the Dutch the manufacturing of guns; ever since then the family had held the hereditary position of supervisor of the gunnery works in Kagoshima. The post was less prestigious than it sounds, because gunnery was held in low esteem and Shichiemon was of relatively low samurai status. Having no sons to continue his line, he decided to adopt an heir, a common practice in Japan, taking for this purpose Masaki, for whom he had apparently developed a high regard. In this way Matsuda Masaki of mere goshi status, who had been living the life of a merchant, the lowest of the four classes according to Tokugawa theory, became the full samurai Matsukata Masaki and inherited Shichiemon's position when the latter died in 1818. He adopted the personal name of Masaki for the first time when he became a Matsukata.*

The shift in residence and status for Masaki had been by no means easy to accomplish. His fellow villagers had raised objections. When he informed the elders of his village of his intention to move to Kagoshima, they were astounded at his flouting of the regulations that prohibited any change in place of residence. They were even more disturbed that the departure of a relatively affluent member of the community would increase their own tax burdens, since taxes were levied collectively on the village. The elders could not dissuade Masaki and finally granted him permission to move, but on condition that he would leave behind all his possessions. He, his wife Kesako, and his children took with them only their clothes and a few personal items

---

* In the Tokugawa period men often changed their personal names several times in the course of their lives, but I shall try to stay with one given name for each person in this account.

when they moved to the home of Shichiemon in Shimo-arata, the area of residency for lower-ranking samurai in the southwestern part of the town of Kagoshima.

Since Shichiemon's annual stipend amounted to only a few bales of rice, the new life for his heir and his family was austere as compared to their former life style as comfortable merchants. Kesako found it difficult to find enough to feed a large and growing family. She seems to have been a remarkable person, strong in both body and character. She was the eldest daughter of a much respected goshi who twice had served as village headman of Masaki's home village of Taniyama. Her father was an ardent Confucianist and had been stricter in the upbringing of his daughters than his sons, since he felt duty-bound to prepare them to be good wives and daughters-in-law. Among the things he taught them were the Confucian precepts from *Onna Daigaku* (The Great Learning for Women) by the Japanese Confucian scholar, Kaibara Ekken (1639–1713). Kaibara's teachings for women helped put much of the steel into the samurai personality, as these excerpts show:

> Seeing that it is a girl's destiny on reaching womanhood to go to a new home and live in submission to her father-in-law and mother-in-law, it is even more incumbent upon her than it is on a boy to receive with all reverence her parents' instructions. Should her parents, through excess of tenderness, allow her to grow up self-willed, she will infallibly show herself capricious in her husband's house and thus alienate his affection . . . Even at the peril of her life must she harden her heart like a rock or metal and observe rules of propriety . . . The great life-long duty of a woman is obedience . . . In the morning she must rise early and at night go late to rest . . . In everything she must avoid extravagance and both with regard to food and raiment must act according to her station in life, never giving way to luxury and pride . . . The five worst maladies that afflict female minds are indocility, discontent, slander, jealousy, and silliness.*

Kesako was married at the age of sixteen, according to the traditional Japanese way of figuring age, in which a child is counted as one

---

* As translated by Basil Hall Chamberlain in his *Things Japanese* (London, 1905), p. 502.

at birth and becomes two at the start of the next calendar year. (Western age counts always run at least a year less, but I shall use the Japanese system throughout the early part of this book.) As was customary, Kesako on marriage shaved off her eyebrows and blackened her teeth. *Ohaguro* (honorable toothblacking) was usually achieved through a preparation based on iron acetate. By the latter part of the eighteenth century, it had become a general custom throughout Japan, intended as a sign of the faithfulness of a wife to her husband as well as an indication of her married status. I remember as a child seeing old friends of my grandmother who still blackened their teeth.

Kesako's upbringing had prepared her well for the new Spartan life style of the Matsukata family. She was frugal and even in the coldest winter days went barefoot, without wearing the customary *tabi* (short socks). Instead of throwing away the velveteen material from worn-out quilts, as most women did, she painstakingly made them into thongs for wooden clogs, which needed replacing often and were expensive to buy. But she was always generous to her friends and neighbors, who admired and loved her, addressing her with great respect as O-Kesa-sama, or "the honorable Kesa."

———— • ————

Masaki and Kesako had four sons and four daughters, but three of the girls died in childhood and the fourth married and left home. When Kesako was about to give birth to another child in 1835, the parents prayed for a daughter. Since it was near the time of the Girls' Festival, Kesako, in anticipation of the birth of a girl, took out the festival dolls of her own childhood and displayed them on special shelves covered with bright red flannel. To her great disappointment, the baby born on March 23, 1835, was a boy.

Kesako, bearing her ninth child, my grandfather, had a hard delivery and was so weakened that she lay almost unconscious on her bed. Masaki, more concerned for her welfare than the baby's, deposited him in a corner of the room and stayed at her side until she revived. When he finally picked the baby up, he found him still alive—a fact they attributed to an act of the gods. Because the preparations Kesako had made to celebrate the birth of a girl were inappropriate, they decided to commemorate the occasion by making a garden in their home, fulfilling a long-cherished dream. They named the baby

Kinjiro, the first of five names my grandfather was to have before finally in 1869 he adopted the name of Masayoshi. As a young child, Masayoshi was very delicate and asthmatic. His mother gave him every available medicine, but to no avail. Only when she took him to soak in the warm waters of a nearby hot spring did he show any signs of improvement. When he was nine, he came down with smallpox, a disease that usually proved fatal, but he recovered and from then on became a strong and healthy child, like his four brothers.

In Satsuma a samurai boy was not just a member of his immediate family but was considered a treasure of the domain. He would grow up to serve his lord and was, in a sense, merely entrusted to the care of his family in the meantime. Thus boys were treated with special deference by their mothers and sisters. They were kept separate from the girls from an early age to ensure that their virility was not sullied. Even the laundry of the boys and men was washed in separate tubs from that for females and hung on separate laundry poles to dry; bedding was marked male or female; even needles used to sew male clothing were kept separate. Girls were confined for the most part to their homes, and on days like the Girls' Festival, when they had their turn to have fun outside, the boys fled to the hills. Brothers and sisters meeting on the street would not speak to one another.

At the age of six, samurai boys in Satsuma started going each day for training in a martial brotherhood, called the *goju* (village fraternity). Its purpose was to keep martial spirit alive by exposing the boys to the discipline of their peers and providing them with physical training, moral guidance, political indoctrination, and some book learning as well. The goju traced its origin to the late sixteenth century, when most of the fighting men of Satsuma were overseas in Hideyoshi's ill-fated campaigns against Korea. The campaigns dragged on from 1582 to 1598, and during this time samurai society at home in Kagoshima became top heavy with women and the aged. The caretaker government of the domain established a fraternity of boys to remove them from female influence and to train them in samurai discipline. It promulgated in 1596 a strict code of conduct, and even after the return of the warriors from Korea the fraternity was continued, coming to be known as the goju in the eighteenth century. Thanks to this institution, the samurai of Satsuma managed to preserve more of their martial traditions than did samurai in other parts of

Japan during the more than two centuries of peace under Tokugawa rule.

The goju of Kagoshima was divided into thirty-three autonomous and competing districts, each with thirty to forty boys and young men, who defended their districts much as American city gangs today protect their "turf." In each district the youths were divided into three groups by age—*kochigo* (small children) for boys from about six to ten, *osechigo* (older boys) for those about eleven to fourteen, and *nise* for youths from about fifteen to twenty-five. Until he became twenty-six, a young man was not considered a full adult member of society and was prohibited from drinking, smoking, or marrying. The youngest group, the kochigo, came under the guidance of a mentor chosen for them from the middle group, the osechigo, and the latter were under the guidance of a member of the older group, the nise, but the nise group chose its own leader, who was responsible for all the boys and young men of the district. Matters of discipline were resolved within each age group and, if this proved impossible, were referred to the next older group. If the nise could not resolve a dispute, they appealed to the *osenshi* (old boys), or recent graduates of the goju.

The code of conduct drawn up in 1596 remained the basic code throughout, but a great many other rules were added to it, regulating most aspects of daily life. Punishments were designed to instill a sense of shame. The lightest punishment, when a boy was found guilty of a slight infraction, such as whistling in the street, quarreling with another boy, or telling a small lie, was to seat him in the middle of the room surrounded by the others, who took turns slapping his cheek. The slaps were not very hard, but the disgrace was galling. A second type of punishment for heavier offenses was to drag the culprit out into the yard and have all the others pile on top of him until he almost lost consciousness. For serious offenses, such as drinking or womanizing, the heaviest penalty was applied, which was ostracism. The guilty member was confined to his home for a prescribed number of days and not allowed to associate or communicate with his peers.

Among the great number of goju precepts and rules, the following few may help show the spirit of the organization:

Honesty is the fundamental principle of samurai conduct.
Loyalty and filial duty are identical.

Respect your elders.
Practice military and literary arts night and day.
Do not associate with members of other goju districts.
Do not associate with females.
Do not enter theaters.
Do not carry money.
Do not go where sake is served.
Do not smoke.
Wear two swords when going a distance.
Do not associate with merchants of the town.

The life of the boys of the goju, however, was not all learning, discipline, and punishments. There was a great deal of fraternal conviviality. Most of the festivals they celebrated together were in memory of war heroes or outstanding leaders of Satsuma. On one of these occasions they would march as a group together the ten miles to the shrine of a renowned hero. Each winter they celebrated the anniversary of the death of the famous forty-seven *ronin* (masterless samurai) who in 1703, after avenging their former lord's death in Edo, all committed suicide. Gathered at the home of one of the members, the boys would read aloud the account of the exploits of the forty-seven, and then the mistress of the household would serve a simple meal of rice, turnip and carrot soup, and rice cookies.

———•———

On the tenth day of the eleventh month of the year after Masayoshi reached the age of five—the number eleven written in Chinese characters can be construed as representing the character for samurai—he was for the first time dressed in a formal kimono bearing the family crest, with the two swords that were the symbol of a samurai stuck in his sash. On normal occasions small samurai boys wore only one sword. Thus attired, he was taken by his father to pray at the local shrines and temples and the graves of his adoptive Matsukata ancestors in order to report his approaching sixth birthday. The tour ended at the home of the leader of the district kochigo group, where his father requested that his son be accepted as a member of the group.

This was the beginning of Masayoshi's life as a goju member. He would get up promptly at six o'clock each morning at the tolling of the temple bells and would start his daily schedule by going to the home of the older boy assigned as teacher to his kochigo group. He would dress himself in a kimono made of rough cotton which barely covered his knees and only reached his elbows. This he tied with a long white sash, and he would then slide his short sword into the sash on his left side. His mother dressed his hair, making sure that the top knot was in place and his forelocks were combed straight. At the front door he tied on his straw sandals and was then ready to start out. Much of the year it was still dark early in the morning, and Masayoshi was too timid to walk alone through the dense forest and cemetery that lay between his home and his teacher's, so his mother would go with him.

The boys would try to arrive at the teacher's house as early as possible, since they had private sessions with the teacher in the order of their arrival. When his turn came, Masayoshi would sit on the floor facing the teacher, who gave him the text for the day. As was the rule in education in both China and Japan at this time, teaching at the goju was by memorizing and reciting texts. Masayoshi would repeat the text after his teacher several times without particular attention to its meaning. The first books he learned in this way were the so-called Satsuma classics. Among these was the *Iroha uta* (Syllabary Poem), which was a poem of forty-seven moral maxims. Each started with a different one of the forty-seven syllabic signs, or *kana,* that constitute the Japanese phonetic writing system, arranged in *i-ro-ha* (a-b-c) order. Another classic was the *Toragari monogatari* (Tale of the Tiger Hunt), relating the feats of a hero in the Korean campaigns of the sixteenth century, and still another was the *Rekidai uta* (Chronicle Poem), a catalogue in poetic form of information about the successive Shimazu lords.

After finishing his turn with the teacher, Masayoshi would return home and work on his study assignment until breakfast. This consisted usually of some pickles and gruel made from rice and sweet potatoes, known in Japan as Satsuma potatoes (*Satsumaimo*). Masayoshi was an earnest student but often fell asleep over his books. To keep awake, he devised a way of pricking the soles of his feet with the sharp point of a knife, until one day his mother saw him doing this and reprimanded him, suggesting that it would be better for him to study on top of a foot stool, so that when he fell asleep he would wake up as he started to fall off.

From eight to ten o'clock the boys would gather outdoors to run races, jump rope, climb hills, fish, or play games, such as "king of the mountain," all under the direction of their leader. The young samurai, though encouraged to be physically energetic, were warned against too much joking and were forbidden to whistle, laugh, or sing in public. Their parents frowned on pointless aggressiveness or mischief but were tolerant of torn sleeves, muddied kimonos, or even broken bones, which they saw as demonstrating the manliness of the boys in their play and mock fighting. On rainy days the time from eight to ten was spent indoors, playing card games of an instructive nature. One such game taught the names of the more than 260 daimyo of Japan and the size of their domains as calculated according to the official estimate of their annual rice yields.

At ten o'clock, the boys would form into two columns and march to the *zamoto,* which was a home selected as their study hall. There were no special school buildings, but the homes of the members of the group were used in rotation. Here Masayoshi and the other kochigo were drilled by the osechigo leader of their group on the text for the day. Then, dividing into pairs, the boys would continue to drill each other. At these sessions the boys were responsible for reporting on one another's failings or misbehavior, and the group would then punish any miscreants. There was also a daily questioning session in which each boy was asked such questions as "Did you whistle today?" or "Have you quarreled today?" or "Have you lied today?" and was expected to answer promptly and honestly. At noon Masayoshi would go home for lunch and then return for a second review session from two to four. For the next two hours, the boys would engage again in physical exercises, such as climbing the surrounding hills, swimming, building moats in the sand along the shore, digging little ponds, and pole jumping, all under the supervision of the older boys. The kochigo were not allowed out of their homes after dark, so this ended their daily schedule.

The boys took great pride in being the sons of full samurai, and some of Masayoshi's group would jeer at him because of his lowly goshi origin and would try to snatch away his books, yelling, "You son of a goshi, you have no right to be studying with us." Masayoshi knew better than to answer back, but incidents of this sort probably made him all the more determined on his course. When later his father wanted him to become an eye doctor—an honorable profession for a younger son of a samurai household—he refused, for he was set on becoming a samurai on active service in his lord's behalf.

Masayoshi must have shown himself to be an outstanding boy. In later life he recalled having overheard a very high-ranking samurai remark, "If this clever boy doesn't go in the wrong direction, he will some day become a man of great distinction." Perhaps this really did happen and the high samurai meant what he said, for he was Kawakami Sukehachiro, who twenty years later gave his only daughter in marriage to this boy of lowly origin. The greatest honor that could be conferred on a small samurai boy was to be invited to attend an audience with the daimyo. Usually this occasion came when boys were more than ten years old, but Masayoshi was asked to attend an audience when he was only eight. This was an important event because through this ceremony a boy was recognized as becoming a samurai in his own right. For this occasion, Kesako made her son a complete set of new clothes, consisting of a crested kimono and a hakama, which is a divided skirt worn over the kimono on formal occasions.

At the age of ten Masayoshi became an osechigo, undergoing in the process the traditional farewell hazing by his comrades. They laid in wait for him and, throwing him to the ground, piled themselves on top of him. They also shoved him into a wooden barrel, which they rolled down the street, inflicting still further bruises. For an osechigo the daily routine was practically the same as for the kochigo, except that Masayoshi now had a third study-hall period after supper under the instruction of the older boys, the nise. This session lasted until eight o'clock, after which time the nise would escort the younger boys back to their homes. Four nights a month the osechigo were also allowed to join the nise in their study of books on the wars and military heroes of Satsuma. The nise would take turns reading these books aloud with clear and proper intonation, and the osechigo would become so familiar with them that they knew them by heart by the time they themselves had become nise. Each of the boys of the goju had a so-called Star Book, in which were recorded his attendance, accomplishments, and punishments. The misdemeanors and punishments were indicated by black stars, which all the boys of course did their best to avoid.

Calligraphy was an important subject in the goju and was practiced daily after the recitation of texts. Good calligraphy was considered the mark of an educated man. The boys would be assigned two or three Chinese characters each day to practice, and these they would write over and over again both at home and at the study hall. Once a month the boys would meet to examine one another's writing and compete for first, second, or third place. As an old man, Marquis Matsukata found calligraphy his greatest pleasure and was intensely proud of his fine classical style. In fact, at the age of sixty he started taking formal lessons again and ten years later received his diploma in the art.

———•———

While Masayoshi was engrossed in the activities of goju life, the fortunes of the Matsukata family took a serious turn for the worse. A relative of the family had illegally made use of a large sum from the domain treasury, where he worked, and in desperation came to Masaki for help. To save the honor of the family, Masaki borrowed money to repay the treasury, thereby incurring a heavy debt. This happened in 1844, and long before the debt could be repaid, Masaki and his wife both died, she in 1845 and he in 1847, when Masayoshi was only thirteen (Japanese count).

The family was left deep in debt under the headship of Masayoshi's eldest brother. Life was very hard during these years. Their diet was largely gruel made of rice and potatoes, and there was scarcely enough money to buy such staples as bean paste, soy sauce, and salt. They could not afford oil for lamps at night, and Masayoshi had to go to a neighbor's home to study his books in the evening.

By this time most of Masayoshi's companions were taking lessons in fencing, or *kendo,* from a fencing master, but he could not join them, lacking the money for such extras. He would watch the master and his class through a window. One day he is said to have been impressed to hear the master say, "The most important thing in fencing is singlemindedness, that is, concentration and the will to do one's best. If one has this, one can get an education even without teachers or books." Inspired by these words, Masayoshi is said to have imbibed the lessons of fencing simply by watching intently and without ever holding in his own hands a practice sword made of oak. (More pliant bamboo is usually used today for this sort of fencing.) The story continues that once an older boy reprimanded Masayoshi for looking at the class through the window, and an altercation broke out, leading to a fencing match between the two. In this set-to, the untutored Masayoshi thoroughly whipped his trained older opponent, thereby so impressing the fencing master that he took Masayoshi on as a pupil without pay.

Skill in swordsmanship was taken very seriously in Japan and was to prove a valuable asset to Masayoshi in the violent times about to visit the country. The style of fencing taught by the master, who was the tenth-generation head of the Jigen-ryu school of Satsuma, emphasized the killing of an enemy in a single offensive lunge. The boys would practice this by striking with their mock swords of oak at thick upright poles set deep in the ground. Later they would get the feel of the real thing by rushing to the body of an executed criminal in an effort to be the first to bloody a sword by hacking off a piece of the corpse.

However practical swordsmanship was when men still carried swords and were prepared to use them, fencing was practiced more as a means of moral training in concentration, discipline, and endurance. In later life Masayoshi credited his moral stamina to his training in fencing. He also practiced other martial arts, such as archery, spear throwing, judo, and horseback riding. A few years later his excellent horsemanship brought him to the attention of Nariakira, who had become the Satsuma daimyo in 1851 and was to prove a great influence in Masayoshi's early career. In later life, after Masayoshi had become an important figure in the national government, he maintained a stable and race track on his property in Tokyo, spending many happy hours riding with his sons, and he bred racing horses on his country estate at Nasuno.

In 1847, at the age of thirteen, Masayoshi entered the Zoshikan, the official school for samurai in Satsuma. Established in 1773, it occupied a spacious enclosure near the castle residence of the daimyo. An imposing Confucian temple was located in its northwestern corner, dormitories for some of the students in the northeast, and a complex of rambling lecture halls in the southeast. A headmaster and a faculty of sixty or more scholars taught a student body of four hundred to eight hundred boys and young men. Like domain schools elsewhere, the Zoshikan basically taught Confucian doctrines through the original Chinese texts. Masayoshi had by this age learned several thousand Chinese characters and could read the Chinese classics, which he had started memorizing in the goju. At school his curriculum consisted of the Confucian classics, including the so-called Four Books and the Five Classics. He also studied Chu Hsi (known as Shushi in Japan), the great twelfth-century Chinese philosopher who helped to rework and round out Confucian doctrines into what is known in the West as Neo-Confucianism. This became the orthodox philosophy for the next seven centuries in China and also in Tokugawa Japan, where, as in China, it was seen as strongly supporting central political authority in a submissive and harmonious society. Masayoshi naturally became an ardent Confucianist and throughout his school days had a portrait of Confucius hanging above his desk.

Despite the strong emphasis on Chu Hsi's interpretation of Confucianism at the Zoshikan, there were some teachers who were sympathetic to other strains of thought, and two of them had a strong influence on Masayoshi. One was the headmaster, Hirokawa Kihei, who considered himself a disciple of Yamazaki Anzai, a seventeenth-century Japanese Confucian philosopher. Anzai had maintained an interest in the native Shinto religion of Japan and equated the Shinto myths with Chinese mythology. In a nationalistic burst of enthusiasm he had even asserted that, if Confucius and Mencius, the two great sages of Confucianism, were to lead an army of invasion against Japan—both had been dead of course for over two thousand years—a good Japanese would have to fight to repel them. Headmaster Hirokawa also was influenced by the teachings of the Chinese philosopher Wang Yang-ming (Oyomei in Japanese; 1472–1529), who represented a sort of revolt against Chu Hsi orthodoxy by emphasizing the importance of intuition, much as in the Zen sect of Buddhism, and the essential unity of knowledge and action. This line of thought produced an activist strain among its adherents, and it is probably no accident that not only my grandfather but a large proportion of the other men who were to end feudalism and create the new Japan had come under the influence of Wang Yang-ming's philosophy.

The other teacher who had a great influence on Masayoshi was Kubota Shintaro. As a scholar of Japanese history, he was well aware of the fact that political legitimacy derived at least in theory from the imperial line and not the Tokugawa shoguns. In teaching his classes,

Kubota used the books officially approved by the Tokugawa, which ended with the beginning of Tokugawa rule in 1600. In fact, it was prohibited to teach history beyond that date. But he took care to emphasize the rightful position of the emperor in Japanese history and in this way undoubtedly contributed to Masayoshi's later enthusiastic support of the imperial cause against the Tokugawa.

Although a student at the Zoshikan, Masayoshi continued as a member of the goju. The younger boys were supposed to have become physically hardened through their studies and martial games, but, before passing on to the senior status of nise at the age of fourteen or fifteen, they had to undergo a special test of bravery. Strings of paper—the sacred *gohei* of Shinto ceremonial—were tied to the ends of bamboo poles stuck in the ground in fearsome places such as execution grounds or deep in the forest, and the boys would have to go alone in pitch darkness to retrieve them. Masayoshi apparently passed this test, and, on the night of the eleventh day after his fourteenth birthday (again the eleventh day was chosen for this occasion since it spelled out the character for samurai), he was summoned to the zamoto, the meeting place of the nise group, to attend his initiation ceremony. On this solemn occasion, his childhood forelocks were shorn and his hair dressed in the nise fashion, combed backward and tied in a bun. He then sat in the middle of the room surrounded by all the nise and read in a loud voice the long list of regulations binding the nise. This was tantamount to taking a solemn oath in front of his comrades of obedience to these regulations.

Masayoshi continued to attend the domain school during the day, but at four in the afternoon he would join the goju group in their athletic exercises and practice of martial arts. At seven in the evening, he would also attend the zamoto sessions, where for an hour he would help some smaller boy review his lessons for the day and then would take him home. After returning to the zamoto, he and the other nise would review and drill one another on their own assignments.

One of the most important aspects of these evening sessions was the *sengi,* a quiz session in which the boys crossexamined one another. This exercise was to sharpen their thinking ability and powers of quick judgment. Their motto was, "Think well, discuss well, and be thorough, without oversight or negligence." It was easier to ask questions than to answer them, and the boys drew lots to be the first to do the questioning. The questions might be either practical or hypothetical and usually involved the position and duties of the boys as future samurai in the service of their lord. The boys were expected to answer promptly and in a manner acceptable to the whole group, and questions would be repeated until a satisfactory reply was forthcoming. This aspect of the educational process in Satsuma was unusual in Japan. In most places little stress was placed on a boy's ability to think. Only memorization was emphasized, and students were taught to accept without question exactly what they were taught. No doubt these evening sessions, with their study of various books about heroes of the past and their rigorous mental exercises, helped to prepare my grandfather and some of the other future Satsuma leaders for the large role they were to play in building the new Japan. The evening sessions ended at ten, but sometimes the boys took long walks together or staged war games in the dark before returning home. All in all, the boys spent very little time with their families, being completely absorbed in their studies at the domain school and their activities in the goju.

Since many of the samurai families were quite poor, boys over fourteen were permitted to work part time in the offices of the domain government to help out with the family finances. Masayoshi began working part time as a clerk accountant in the treasury in 1850 when he was sixteen years old, earning four *koku,* or bales, of rice a year to augment the family income. Since a koku of rice was sufficient for one person's annual consumption, this helped substantially. After seven years of work as clerk at the treasury, by which time Masayoshi had become personally known to his daimyo, he was awarded 130 *ryo* of gold as special compensation for his services. This was a large sum because one ryo was equivalent to a koku of rice. Now Masayoshi was able to pay off the debt his father had incurred before his death. His older brothers were dubious about the desirability of using the whole sum for this purpose, but Masayoshi was determined. After visiting the creditors and handing over the money, Masayoshi visited his father's grave on the way home and reported what he had done. He recalled this incident in later life as one of the most satisfying moments of his whole career.

———— • ————

One of the goju rules prohibited members of different districts from associating with one another, but this regulation had broken down to a certain extent and Masayoshi, who disliked the rule, made an effort to meet boys of other districts. Among his best friends were Okubo Toshimichi and Saigo Takamori of the Kajiya district, although they were five and eight years older than he. Masayoshi's friendship with Okubo and Saigo was to prove extremely important for him, since the two later became the chief Satsuma activists in the movement to restore imperial rule, and he was their trusted assistant.

As in many domains, the samurai officials of Satsuma were divided into progressive and conservative factions. In 1809 the progressives had failed in an effort to take over, and they failed again in 1848 in an incident involving a long-smoldering dispute over the succession to the position of daimyo. They supported the daimyo's able and forward-looking eldest son, Nariakira, while the conservatives favored Hisamitsu, a son by a secondary wife. In 1848 a few of the progressive leaders were executed, and Okubo's father, who belonged to this faction, was exiled to the Ryukyu Islands. Okubo himself was dismissed from his post and confined to his home. Three years later, however, Nariakira did succeed as daimyo through the direct intervention of the shogun, to whom he was related. Nariakira had grown up in Edo, since the heirs and principal wives of all daimyo were compelled to reside permanently at the shogun's capital as virtual hostages; only after his appointment as daimyo did he go for the first time to live in Satsuma, where he was of course little known, except for his reputation as an innovative man. On his arrival in Kagoshima he proceeded with great caution, retaining in office the conservative officials who had opposed his appointment, and, much to the disappointment of the progressives, he failed for some time to pardon those who had taken his side in the 1848 incident.

Nariakira wasted no time on petty internal reforms, for he knew that the country was entering a critical period and there were more urgent needs. Over the past two generations the Western powers had become very active in East Asian waters, and Russian, British, and American ships often approached the shores of Japan. Nariakira realized that Japan's isolation could not last much longer. His keen awareness of the West probably derived in large part from his grand-father, Shigehide (1745–1833), who as daimyo had often visited the Dutch traders in Nagasaki and had become the leading patron of "Dutch learning," the Japanese term for Western science and technology, which they knew only through books in the Dutch language. Shigehide himself studied Western astronomy, medicine, cartography, gunnery, and other sciences. He also studied the Dutch language a little and kept a diary in Japanese written in the Latin alphabet as a means of ensuring its secrecy. He helped to sponsor the first Dutch-Japanese dictionary, which greatly furthered scientific studies in Japan, constructed an astronomical observatory in Kagoshima, and helped in the introduction of vaccination, which reduced the mortality rate from smallpox.

Nariakira, for his part, was greatly interested in Western ships and during his seven years as daimyo threw himself vigorously into the task of building the military strength and technological skills of Satsuma, in preparation for the inevitable confrontation with the West. He strengthened the coastal defenses of his domain and put mines in the sea approaches to Kagoshima. He reactivated the local shipyards in order to produce sailing vessels that could be turned into warships. At first these had to be quite small—an old Tokugawa ban on larger ships remained in force until the year after Commodore Matthew C. Perry came to Japan in 1853 and forced open its doors to Western contact. After that Nariakira was able to build a sailing vessel along Western lines and of larger size. This became the first vessel to fly the Japanese national flag alongside the Western ships that were frequenting Edo Bay. The ships he built, however, were all purchased by the Tokugawa government and thus did not become, as he had planned, the basis for a Satsuma navy.

Nariakira also built experimental Western-style factories and a reverberatory furnace, which was an up-to-date system for converting ores into metal. Some twelve hundred men were put to work in foundries and arsenals, making rifles, swords, and gunpowder. He introduced Western uniforms for some of his soldiers and also accumulated special wartime provisions of food. He experimented with electricity and telegraphy and in 1858 set up telegraph wires within the precincts of his castle, only twelve years after the introduction of telegraphy in Europe. He also experimented with gas lighting for streets. Amazingly, only fifteen years after the invention of photography in Europe in 1839, he managed to take the first photographs in Japan with a camera he himself had made.

Since all this took money, Nariakira put new emphasis on producing goods that could be exported abroad, at first through trade with the Ryukyu Islands and later directly through Westerners. In particular, he developed the production of elaborately decorated, crackled porcelains known as Satsuma ware, which came to be popular in the West, and he also produced a type of ornamental red crystal, said to equal in quality the fine products of this type from Germany.

Nariakira saw the need for a broader, more practical type of education in his domain. To better acquaint his samurai with the outside world, he invited scholars of Dutch learning to lecture at the domain school. He even permitted the open study of the philosophical teachings of Wang Yang-ming, which were banned in most domain schools as subversive. He also started a more intensive military training for his young samurai to better prepare them for confrontation with the West. He initiated a compulsory program of military drill for all samurai boys and young men above the age of seven. The young boys carried mock wooden guns, but the older boys and young men were armed with guns produced by the local arsenals. He trained the young samurai himself for several hours each afternoon until sunset, and he selected a crack team from among them that he personally led.

Masayoshi was among the young men chosen for this group, having attracted Nariakira's attention in 1852 through his skill as a horseman. He fell deeply under the influence of the progressive ideas of his lord, whom he admired intensely. Through his friends, he also came a little closer to the seat of power. Saigo during this period became a trusted aid of Nariakira, who employed him as his gardener in order to have him close at hand; Saigo's relatively lowly birth did not entitle him to a high post as a counsellor. Okubo, who had meanwhile been released from house arrest, also came into occasional contact with the daimyo through Saigo. The years of Nariakira's leadership as daimyo of Satsuma was the time of my grandfather's transition from boyhood to young manhood, and the beginning of the long foreseen confrontation between Japan and the West.

Satsuma Officer

When Commodore Perry sailed his squadron of warships into Edo Bay in the summer of 1853, he posed a great dilemma for the Tokugawa government. Since Japanese guns and ships were no match for Perry's cannon and ships, some of them steam-propelled, it was obvious that the Americans could easily either destroy the capital or cut off its main supply route for food, which was coastal shipping. But to concede to Perry's demand that Japan be opened to normal international relations would be to transgress a basic Tokugawa policy of more than two centuries' standing.

In order to ease the shock and share the responsibility, the shogun's government for the first time in its history consulted outsiders: the imperial court and the whole body of more than 260 daimyo. Nariakira was among the more enlightened daimyo who realized the necessity of at least temporary concessions to the American demands, but the majority as well as the imperial court opposed making any significant concessions. The government in Edo, however, was forced to sign a treaty with Perry when he returned for his answer early in 1854 and had to follow this with similar treaties with the major European nations. This put the shogun in the position of having clearly disobeyed the wishes of the imperial court, from which his legitimacy in theory derived. The act of consulting all the daimyo on the problem had also opened national policies for the first time to nation-wide discussion. During the next few years a debate of growing intensity developed over the great foreign-policy problems posed by the West, and this grew into a questioning of the authority of the shogun and assertions of the sovereign rights of the emperor. Naria-kira, as the daimyo of the second largest domain and a feudal lord of great energy and vision, naturally became a central figure in the tur-moil of the age.

In 1856 the United States sent Townsend Harris to Japan as consul general. Within two years Harris had persuaded the shogun's government to sign a full trade treaty that went far beyond the limited provisions of the treaty Perry had procured. But before signing this new pact, which would put a complete end to Japan's isolation, the Edo government once again consulted the imperial court and the daimyo, and once again drew a largely negative response. A measure of the great changes that had occurred in the five years after Perry was the amount of openly subversive sentiment expressed by extremists intent on preserving Japanese seclusion and transferring at least some political leadership from the Tokugawa shoguns to the imperial court. These two concepts were summed up in the pithy slogans *sonno* (honor the emperor) and *joi* (expel the barbarians), which together became the battle cry of the anti-Tokugawa forces.

The Edo government nonetheless felt compelled to go ahead with the trade treaty with the United States, which once again was followed by similar treaties with the European powers. To push this policy through against wide-spread opposition, the Edo officials selected as their chief minister Ii Naosuke of Hikone, the vigorous and forceful lord of the largest domain among the hereditary house daimyo. Ii cracked down severely on opponents and critics, forcing the imperial court to give its sanction to the treaty and ordering Nariakira and some of the other lords identified with the anti-Tokugawa opposition into confinement within their residences. Nariakira was not one to back down meekly and started plotting to overthrow Ii. For this purpose he dispatched my grandfather's friend Saigo to make secret contacts with like-minded men in other domains, and he threw him-self even more vigorously than before into training his samurai for war. But in his strenuous efforts in the midsummer of 1858, he overtaxed himself, collapsed, and died of heat prostration.

Nariakira's half brother, Hisamitsu, took his place as the leader of Satsuma in behalf of his own young son Tadayoshi, who succeeded as daimyo. Hisamitsu decided to follow a more cautious course, and, when Saigo returned from his mission with a plot for a march on Edo, he was rewarded by being sent into exile in the Ryukyu Islands. This left Okubo as the leader of a group of some forty young samurai, including my grandfather, who had become committed to the pro-imperial, anti-Tokugawa cause. They petitioned Hisamitsu to lead an attack on Edo and, when he refused, began plotting to take action on their own. The plot was discovered, but Hisamitsu dealt leniently with the young hotheads, merely ordering them to bide their time and referring to them as the *Seichu-gumi* (spirited and loyal band), a term by which they came to be known.

The young men did not have long to wait. On March 24, 1860, a group of seventeen samurai extremists waylaid Ii at a gateway to the shogun's castle in Edo and killed him. Most of these men were from the great collateral domain of Mito, showing how seriously divided the Tokugawa supporters themselves had become, but two members of the group were the Arimura brothers of Satsuma, who were members of Okubo's "spirited and loyal band." One of the brothers was the man who actually cut off Ii's head. He made off with it and then kneeling in front of it committed ceremonial suicide, or *seppuku* (belly slitting, commonly known as *harakiri* in the West), before he could be apprehended by the authorities. The other brother managed to make his way back to Satsuma.

Matsukata, as I shall henceforth call my grandfather, encountered the fleeing Arimura brother on the road not far from Kagoshima. Matsukata was part of an advance party of the daimyo's great procession, which was just starting out on its biennial trip to Edo. All daimyo were required to spend alternate years at the capital in attendance on the shogun, and the time had come for the Satsuma daimyo to spend his year in Edo. But Matsukata, learning from Arimura of the assassination and the turmoil in Edo, decided that this was no time for the Satsuma daimyo to be entering the camp of the enemy. He rushed back to meet the main procession, which had stopped to rest at a town, and here he persuaded the chief officer in charge of the young daimyo to stop the expedition and return to Kagoshima on the pretext that the daimyo had fallen ill.

In order to escape reprisals from the Tokugawa government, Hisamitsu ordered the remaining Arimura brother to commit suicide that very night. Arimura's comrades, the spirited and loyal band, pleaded for leniency but to no avail. Arimura, who was only twenty-three, bathed and put on fresh clothing, knelt on the ground facing toward the imperial palace in Kyoto, plunged his sword into his belly, and drew it across his body, performing in perfect fashion the act of seppuku before the eyes of his sorrowing and respectful friends. It was all done according to the samurai code of selfless loyalty to one's lord. Even the mother of the Arimura brothers accepted this fate stoically as fulfillment of the proper role of a samurai.

Ii's assassination shattered the effectiveness of Tokugawa rule, which had lasted for more than two and a half centuries, and the administration in Edo never fully rallied from the blow. Its finances had been in serious disarray for decades, and it had become deeply divided, not just over foreign policy but over the succession to the position of shogun. Now, in addition, it was hopelessly caught between the irresistible demands of the Western powers and the seemingly immovable opposition of conservative Japanese. The leading domains increasingly turned to the imperial court in Kyoto as the new focus of political power. Here isolationist *joi* sentiment and pro-imperial *sonno* enthusiasm were rampant.

In Kyoto, Satsuma and Choshu came to be the two most influential domains. Choshu, which like Satsuma was a large outer domain, was located at the western tip of the main Japanese island of Honshu. Both domains thus were on the western periphery of the country. They also had been foes of the Tokugawa forces at the battle of 1600 and nursed a well-concealed hostility to Edo. They happened to be financially solvent, in contrast to the shogun's government, and able to pay for increased military expenses, including new Western weapons. Satsuma's solvency was the result of rigorous financial reforms carried out in the early 1830s and a monopoly on sugar cane, which could be grown in the Ryukyu Islands.

Satsuma and Choshu were traditionally as suspicious of each other as they were of Edo. In 1861 Choshu made a bid to take the lead by mediating between the imperial court and Edo in an effort to produce a "union of the court and shogunate." Nothing came of this attempt, and the next year Satsuma made its bid for leadership, starting with a trip to Kyoto by Hisamitsu himself. Behind this trip lay a complex story. In 1860 the Satsuma daimyo had failed to go to Edo on schedule because of Ii's assassination, and in 1861, in order to preclude the

45

possibility of his going to Edo, the Satsuma officials burned down the large Satsuma residence there. The shogun's government, however, in an effort to get this important vassal to demonstrate his allegiance, contributed funds for the construction of a new residence. Hisamitsu then hit on the strategem of justifying a trip to the imperial capital by going there to thank the Tokugawa representative stationed in Kyoto. He took with him a force of more than a thousand men, including the original crack brigade of six hundred trained by Nariakira. For my grandfather, who went along as one of this group, it was his first trip outside Satsuma and his first venture into national political affairs.

———•———

By this time Matsukata was a mature samurai and a man of some importance. He had left the goju in 1860 at the age of twenty-six, and in the autumn of that year Kawakami Sukehachiro offered him his eldest daughter, Masako, in marriage. At a time when marriages were arranged strictly between families of equal social rank, this was a most unusual act, for the Kawakami family ranked near the top among samurai families in Satsuma and the Matsukata family near the bottom (and was by blood of goshi origin). But Kawakami, as it will be recalled, had taken an interest in Matsukata since he was a small boy and, no doubt, considered him a promising son-in-law in these disturbed times. Matsukata at first demurred, perhaps out of social propriety but ostensibly on the grounds that he was too poor. This problem was solved when, within a year after his marriage, he was appointed to a relatively important post under the chief minister of the domain.

The expedition to Kyoto in 1862 brought new duties of even greater significance. Just before Hisamitsu reached Kyoto, he learned that a group of pro-imperial samurai, including some men from Satsuma, were planning to attack the Edo officials in Kyoto and capture the Tokugawa castle stronghold in Osaka. Afraid that this sort of ill-conceived coup would ruin his own plans, he dispatched Narahara, one of his trusted retainers and a member of the spirited and loyal band, to find the Satsuma men in the group and dissuade them from their plot. He ordered Narahara to kill the men on the spot if they would not listen to reason. After a long search, Narahara found them at the Teradaya Inn in Fushimi on the southern outskirts of Kyoto next door to the official Satsuma residence. When no amount of persuasion could make the men change their minds, Narahara and his men drew their swords and fell upon the plotters, killing eight outright and wounding more. Matsukata, who was in charge of one of the search parties, consisting of ten foot soldiers (*ashigaru*), reached the Teradaya Inn just at this juncture and was appalled to find one of the spirited and loyal band lying dead among the slaughtered men. He and his soldiers stayed on at the inn to tend to the wounded and bury the dead.

Hisamitsu then displayed the trust and confidence he had come to place in Matsukata by choosing him as his messenger to inform the domain officials back in Kagoshima of his own arrival in Kyoto and the other events. Accompanied by a single foot soldier, my grandfather set off at once by ship from Osaka to a point about midway down the Inland Sea and from there reportedly walked six days and most of six nights to cover the remaining 350 miles to Kagoshima. His unexpected return delighted his wife Masako, who had given birth in his absence to their first child, a son named Iwao. But Matsukata had little time in Kagoshima, being ordered only eight days later to rejoin Hisamitsu in Kyoto.

In the meantime Hisamitsu had won the approval of the imperial court for his proposals for a "union of court and shogunate" and had been appointed to establish order in Kyoto. This was much needed because many extremist samurai had cut their ties with their own domains and thus become *ronin* (masterless samurai) in order to free themselves for violent action. Plots like the one Hisamitsu had just suppressed were rife in the capital. The court also had decided to send an imperial messenger to Edo to order the shogun to Kyoto for consultation with the emperor. All this was unprecedented and shows how much the political climate had changed. Hisamitsu was assigned to escort the imperial messenger to Edo.

Matsukata arrived back in Kyoto to find orders awaiting him to follow Hisamitsu on to Edo at once. He and his attendant foot soldier made the trip by way of the Tokaido, or Eastern Sea Route, the highway between Edo and Kyoto that was always crowded with travelers of all sorts, including many of the great daimyo processions on the annual trip to or from the shogun's capital. The Tokaido was relatively wide and well maintained for the horsemen and pedestrians who used it, but all wheeled vehicles were banned, as on the other highways of Japan. Many rivers were left unbridged, with crossings only by ford or ferry, as a strategic defense against rapid troop movements. The highway for the most part paralleled the Pacific Ocean—hence the name Eastern Sea Route—and it was provided with fifty-three poststations where lodging, food, and relay horses could be obtained. Woodblock prints by Hiroshige of these stations and their surrounding scenery have made the name Tokaido well known in the West and give a good picture of what it looked like when Matsukata made the trip in 1862, for Hiroshige had himself first traveled the road only thirty years earlier.

The Tokaido was about 300 miles long and crossed one stiff mountain range and several lesser hilly areas. Normally it took a good walker at least two weeks, but Matsukata and his attendant covered the distance to Edo in eight days, averaging at least forty miles a day. (Horses were mostly used at this time as pack animals.) On arrival at the Satsuma residence in Edo, which was not far from the present Shinagawa Station, he reported to Hisamitsu, who was happy to obtain the latest news from his domain. The next few weeks of relative idleness in Edo were a welcome respite. Matsukata had been traveling most of the time for the past two months and had covered about 1700 miles on foot.

Edo was an exciting place for a young samurai who until two months earlier had never left his own distant domain. It was one of the largest cities in the world, having reached the million mark well over a century earlier. The great walls and moats of the shogun's castle occupied the center of the city. The inner sections of the great fortification still form the impressive imperial palace grounds at the heart of modern Tokyo. The more than 260 daimyo all maintained residences for their biennial stays in Edo and for permanent occupancy by their chief wives and heirs. In fact, the larger domains maintained more than one residence, capable of accommodating hundreds or even thousands of men. Lesser vassals and retainers had smaller establishments.

About half the population of the city was made up of merchants and other commoners, who were engaged in diverse and often large-scale economic activities. The commoners also patronized Kabuki theaters, restaurants, and pleasure houses. Samurai, with their strict code of conduct, were supposed to be above such diversions, but of course many of them participated surreptitiously. The streets of the city were lined with shops and filled with bustle—daimyo and high officials carried in palanquins, samurai strutting along with their two swords stuck in their sashes, the masterless samurai, disheveled and ready for adventure, priests in their clerical robes, courtesans in elaborate kimonos and hair styles, rich dignified merchants, and craftsmen, artisans, and shopkeepers, each with his distinctive *hapi* coat on which the name of his store or craft was displayed. It must have been a stunning sight to a young man raised in provincial Satsuma.

———•———

The shogun's government accepted the demands and proposed reforms brought by the imperial messenger, which actually consisted of Hisamitsu's plan for a union of court and shogunate. Tokugawa Keiki, from a collateral line, was appointed as guardian of the youthful shogun, and Matsudaira Keiei, a prominent collateral daimyo, was made chief minister. Both men were known to be sympathetic to the imperial cause, and Matsudaira allowed the system of alternate years of residence by the daimyo in Edo to be dropped, thus giving up one of the chief means by which the Tokugawa had controlled the country.

When Hisamitsu, pleased with the achievements of his mission, prepared to escort the imperial messenger back to Kyoto, he appointed my grandfather together with Narahara and two other samurai to be his *kinjuban,* the men assigned to defend his personal palanquin. For Matsukata this was an important promotion, given in recognition of his good work as messenger. To celebrate, Matsukata spent an evening of drinking and festivity with his close friend Okubo, who by this time was a trusted and influential adviser to Hisamitsu.

Hisamitsu started out for Kyoto on September 14, 1862, a beautiful early autumn day. His armed retinue formed a column almost a mile long. Such processions were a survival of the files of armed men who had accompanied their lords to battle in medieval times, but during the peaceful Tokugawa period they had been turned into lavish pageants, demonstrating the rank and status of the traveling lord. The daimyo and high officials rode in palanquins made of lacquered wood and split bamboo, carried on the shoulders of eight to a dozen bearers. The lesser officials, ordinary samurai, foot soldiers, bearers, clerks, servants, and even horsemen traveled on foot. An advance party always went ahead for security checks and to clear the road. These displays provided great entertainment for the townspeople and peasants along the way. They would drop everything and come running to the roadside as soon as they saw a procession approaching. Then, as criers shouted, "Shita ni iro, shita ni iro!" (Keep down, keep down!), they would kneel on the roadside and remain in that position until the procession had passed.

Hisamitsu's entourage was that of a major daimyo, as befitted a man of his power and influence. In the early afternoon of its first day on the road, it was approaching the small village of Namamugi when a historic incident took place. Namamugi was the junction for a branch road to Yokohama, a newly developed port where Westerners had built a settlement in accordance with the provisions of the 1858 treaty. At Yokohama the foreigners were confined in a small area bounded by the sea and canals on three sides and by hills on the fourth, and there were guardhouses at each entrance. The only hotel, called the Anglo-Saxon, provided bowling and billiards for recreation at night, but daytime diversions were limited to taking walks, shooting, and horseback excursions into the countryside around Yokohama. In order to prevent encounters on the nearby Tokaido highway between foreigners and the processions of daimyo, many of whom strongly opposed the presence of foreigners in Japan, the Edo government would give prior notice to the foreign consuls of the schedules of the processions, and the foreigners were supposed to stay away.

Whether or not the foreigners had been informed of Hisamitsu's procession, a small party of Britishers, made up of a merchant called Richardson from Shanghai, a woman from Hong Kong, and two men living in Yokohama, was out riding that day. As the group passed the advance contingents of Hisamitsu's procession, the road was wide enough for them to keep going, but as they came toward the main part of the procession the armed men marching abreast left no room for the Britishers to advance. When the heavily guarded palanquin of Hisamitsu came in sight, the guards shouted in Japanese, "Dismount, dismount!" but the Britishers, not understanding, remained mounted, which was considered an act of great disrespect. The foreigners at this point decided to cut across the procession to the other side of the road, where there was more room. This so outraged

Hisamitsu's retainers that they attacked with their swords, badly wounding Richardson, who toppled from his horse and then was stabbed to death, and wounding the other men slightly, though doing no more harm to the woman than to cut off her fashionable long hair. When Hisamitsu heard the commotion, he lifted the lattice window of his palanquin. Of his four kinjuban guards, only Matsukata was still in place, the other three having rushed after the Britishers. This so impressed Hisamitsu that for the remainder of the trip he had Matsu-kata shifted from the right side of the palanquin to the left, which was a sort of battlefield promotion since the left side was considered more important.

The wounded Britishers fled to the residence of the American consul in the Hongakuji Temple in the nearby town of Kanagawa and from there notified the British consul, who immediately prepared to send his thirty marine guards to find the body of Richardson. When the townsmen of Kanagawa learned of the intended British action, they evacuated their women and children in terror, closed the barricade gates to the town, and waited to warn the British against clashing with the Satsuma force, one thousand strong. The British took the warning and returned to the consul's residence to await the arrival of soldiers from the larger garrison in Yokohama.

The Satsuma officials had decided not to stop in Kanagawa, as they normally would have, and proceeded on to the next poststation for the night. Here they waited on the alert, with pine torches lit, for an attack by the British, but fortunately the latter decided to act through government channels and only the local Tokugawa commissioner turned up, bearing a demand from the British consul that Richardson's assassins be handed over. The angry Satsuma officials treated the commissioner and his request with scorn, declaring that they had done no wrong since it was the law of the land that anyone disrupting a daimyo procession should be killed; it was the fault of the Edo government that foreigners had been on the Tokaido that day.

Narahara, one of the four palanquin guards, was the one who had cut Richardson down and, on hearing the demands of the British, he begged to be allowed to take responsibility for the affair by committing seppuku. But Okubo, his superior officer, would not hear of this and instead commended him for his loyalty. In the morning, the dejected commissioner had to return to Yokohama to report to the

British that they would have to deal with the government in Edo directly.

When Hisamitsu reached Kyoto, he found that a great change had taken place in the political situation there. While he had been negotiating with the shogun's government in Edo, the men of Choshu had taken control of the imperial court and arrested the court nobles who had cooperated with him. Hisamitsu also heard rumors that the British squadron in Yokohama had sailed for Kagoshima, so he left immediately for home, sending Matsukata on ahead to report the incident at Namamugi and alert the authorities to the possible arrival of the British squadron. Matsukata embarked at Osaka, but unfavorable winds slowed the progress of his boat, and in frustration he composed a short poem: "What resentment have the winds toward me, / Knowing my heart is most impatient?" Such poetic expressions were typical of educated Japanese of that time. The samurai, for all their pride in military skills, were equally proud of their literary accomplishments. Matsukata, however, need not have fretted. When he finally reached Kagoshima, he found everything surprisingly calm—there had been no word of the Namamugi affair or any sign of British warships.

Since communications with England took a long time, it was almost a year before the British consul received instructions on what to do about the "Richardson Affair," as the foreigners called it. On the basis of these instructions he presented to the Tokugawa government the following demands: (1) a public apology for the incident, (2) an indemnity from Edo to the British government, (3) an indemnity to be paid by the Satsuma domain for compensation to Richardson's family and the three other Britishers who were injured, and (4) the arrest and execution of the assassins in the presence of British officers. The weak Tokugawa government made a formal apology and promised to pay its indemnity but found itself powerless to force Satsuma either to pay or to hand over the culprits.

After months of fruitless negotiations with Edo, the British decided to take matters into their own hands and dispatched their warships from Yokohama to Kagoshima to negotiate directly with Satsuma. On August 11, 1863, the British squadron sailed up Kagoshima Bay, avoiding by good luck the mine fields Nariakira had laid, of which they were quite unaware. Anchoring in full view of the castle of the daimyo, the British summoned the Satsuma officials to board the flagship and receive their demands.

The Satsuma authorities kept the British waiting for their reply, and, when it finally came, it was hardly satisfactory. They argued that they could not be held responsible for the Richardson affair, since it had been caused by the negligence of the Tokugawa government in failing to include in its treaties with foreigners the Japanese law that a person showing disrespect for a daimyo procession could be killed on the spot. Satsuma, however, did assure the British that an intensive search was being made to find the culprits and that they would be turned over when found. The British put little faith in this promise, for good reason. Narahara, who was known in Satsuma to be the chief culprit, was actually only a few hundred yards away. He and a group of seventy-seven staunch comrades had organized themselves into a suicide squad disguised as peddlers and merchants and, moving among the British ships in sampans, were waiting to be invited aboard to sell their wares. Once aboard, they planned to slaughter the unsuspecting Westerners. The British were much too cautious to permit this, and nothing came of the naive plot.

Frustrated by the obstinacy and delaying tactics of the Satsuma government, the British finally decided to take coercive action. At dawn on August 15 they seized three ships that Satsuma had recently bought from British and American firms. The Satsuma officials interpreted this as an act of war and made preparations for military action, confident that their defenses were adequate to stave off the British. Matsukata, as aide to the young daimyo and Hisamitsu, accompanied them and the government councillors to a headquarters established some way inland. The Satsuma batteries then opened fire on the British ships about noon on August 15. The first shot landed on the deck of the flagship *Euryalis,* lying nearest to shore, instantly killing Captain Josling and Commander Wilmot, who were standing there in conversation with the British consul, Neale.

Taken completely by surprise, the British were slow to fire back. The *Euryalis* in particular had trouble because the door to its ammunition magazine was barricaded by piles of boxes containing Mexican silver dollars, paid as indemnity by the Tokugawa government just before the ship had sailed from Yokohama. A heavy typhoon wind further hampered the British fire, but before long the superior British guns took their toll. They destroyed many of the fragile wooden buildings of Kagoshima, making the streets impassable and starting fires all over town. More than 500 houses went up in smoke, and large areas around the factories and foundries were leveled. The British also looted the three ships they had seized and then set them on fire. The engagement lasted five hours, but the total list of casualties was only 13 dead and 50 wounded on the British side and 10 dead and 11 wounded on the Japanese. Matsukata probably saw the whole of the battle better than anyone else, for his assignment had been to observe the enemy's movements through a telescope placed halfway up the mountain behind the Satsuma headquarters.

The day after the battle, when the typhoon also had abated, the British, satsified that Satsuma had been taught a lesson, quietly sailed out of the bay, again avoiding the unsuspected mine fields. On seeing them depart, the people of Satsuma rejoiced over their glorious victory, but they realized in their hearts the inadequacy of their defenses and the need to make a settlement with the British. Okubo was sent to Yokohama to hold secret negotiations with them and to pay the indemnity, which Satsuma cleverly borrowed from the Tokugawa government. Not having the money itself, Edo in turn borrowed the sum from the merchant firm of Mitsui. Okubo also assured the British that the daimyo would try to find Richardson's assassins, but nothing ever came of this and the British had the good sense to let the matter drop.

———•———

In recognition of Matsukata's exemplary performance of his duties throughout the whole Richardson affair, Hisamitsu rewarded him by appointing him *okanando* (chief steward) to the young daimyo, Tadayoshi. This was one of the highest posts a samurai could occupy, since the chief steward was not only in charge of all the valets, personal servants, cooks, gardeners, stable hands, and the like, of the large household but was also in close contact with the daimyo himself. It had been the post held by the influential Okubo until Matsukata replaced him. From this time on Matsukata came into daily contact with Tadayoshi, now twenty-four years of age, and often was his companion in his favorite sport of *inu ou mono* (dog chasing). This was an old samurai sport, dating back to the twelfth century, in which dogs were confined in an enclosure surrounded by a bamboo fence and were shot with arrows by men riding at a gallop. Matsukata's stipend was also increased to forty-eight bales of rice, an ample amount to support himself, his wife, and his two boys, Iwao and Shosaku.

Matsukata's income now allowed him to establish his own branch family, separate from the main Matsukata line. Actually the main Matsukata line died out not too long afterward, leaving Masayoshi's branch family the only Matsukata family in all Japan. His eldest brother Masayasu had been the thirty-second in the line of heads of the main family, and Masayoshi's two other surviving older brothers had been adopted into other families. Masayasu had died in 1859 and was succeeded by his eldest son Kosuke, the thirty-third family head. One of Kosuke's younger brothers died early, and the other was adopted into the Makino family and died in the rebel cause in the Satsuma uprising of 1877. Kosuke himself as a youth fought as a member of the Satsuma forces in the successful revolution of 1868, then went in 1871 to study in the United States where in 1873 at the age of twenty-three he died heirless at Rutgers College, bringing the main Matsukata line to an end. (Incidentally, his tomb in New Brunswick, New Jersey, was destroyed by anti-Japanese bigots during World War II but was restored after the war by a group of Japanese residents of New York.)

When Masayoshi established his branch family in 1863, he adopted his own *mon* (family crest), which was worn on the back, both sleeves, and two breasts of all formal clothes. The daimyo did him the honor of designing this crest personally. He took the ginger plant (*myoga*) of the original Matsukata crest, which has the same pronunciation as the term for "divine protection," and surrounded it with a wreath of chrysanthemum leaves, one of the crests of the daimyo's own Shimazu family. The original drawing of the crest was kept as a family treasure until it was destroyed in the burning of the family home in 1877, but the crest itself continues in use today.

Matsukata at twenty-eight was an important official in Satsuma and in 1863 was appointed a *giseisho-gakari*, a member of the chief policy-making body of the domain. His rise from humble beginnings and his close association with his daimyo, however, gave rise to envy as well as admiration. In the fall of 1865, on his return to Kagoshima from a month-long visit with the daimyo to a hot-spring resort, he was notified of dismissal from his positions on charges of womanizing and corrupting samurai morals. The daimyo was outraged on hearing this and ordered a retrial, in which it was revealed that some jealous officials had plotted to disgrace Matsukata and remove him from office by bribing a waitress and a foot soldier to give false testimony. After intense questioning, the two confessed, and Matsukata was cleared and reinstated.

———————•———————

The British bombardment of Kagoshima had convinced even the most diehard conservatives in Satsuma of the inadequacy of their outmoded defenses. Their muzzle-loading, round-shot cannon were no match for the new Armstrong guns, which the British had used for the first time in the engagement at Kagoshima. These had long, pointed shells that exploded with devastating force on impact. The encounter also taught the men of Satsuma that the first line of defense for an island country was at sea and that a strong navy was indispensable for its protection, as Nariakira had maintained more than a decade earlier.

Nariakira's death in 1858 had brought the Satsuma shipbuilding program almost to a standstill, but now the domain government hastened to modernize its gunnery and build up a navy. It bought foreign vessels, which it converted into warships; it hired fishermen as sailors and taught them to handle steam-engined vessels; and it recruited officers for the navy from among the samurai youth. A navy bureau was founded in 1866, and Matsukata was appointed assistant commissioner for ships. He was delighted with this new position, for he now could fulfill Nariakira's desire to build a navy.

The education Matsukata had received in the Chinese classics and Japanese history, however, was scarcely adequate preparation for his duties as a naval officer, which called for a knowledge of science and technology beyond his ken. An Institute of Western Studies, called the *Kaiseido,* was established at the domain school in 1864, but Matsukata was at thirty considered too old and important an official to become a student. Again he watched with envy when, the next year, fourteen young samurai from the institute were selected for study in England and, in defiance of the crumbling Tokugawa ban on travel abroad, were smuggled out of the country by Thomas Glover, a prominent Scottish merchant in the port city of Nagasaki. The group was under the leadership of Godai Tomoatsu, who was being sent to

London to purchase spinning machinery and later was to have an important role in the new national government. Among the young students was Mori Arinori, who was to become Japan's first minister to Washington and subsequently the minister of education. Other Satsuma boys and young men were sent to study in Yokohama, where in the foreign community there were many teachers of the English language and Western scientific knowledge. But even Yokohama was too far away from Kagoshima for a member of the policy-making board and a close attendant on the daimyo. It occurred to Matsukata, though, that he might be able to go to Nagasaki to prepare for a naval career. Nagasaki, which had become Japan's chief port of contact with the outside world in the sixteenth century and the center of so-called Dutch learning, was located in northwest Kyushu, only a few days by ship from Kagoshima. Matsukata requested permission to go to study there.

The request was granted, and Matsukata arrived in Nagasaki early in 1867, entering the old Tokugawa Naval School. He found Nagasaki a busy and exciting city, supporting a thriving international trade and full of foreign merchants. After the trade treaties had gone into effect in 1860, the foreigners had first lived in temples or whatever other housing they could find, but by this time they were concentrated in a special settlement provided by the Edo government. The British, who from their experiences in other parts of Asia were adept at making themselves at home in Eastern lands, had already built a church, a hospital, the Nagasaki Club for men, and the Commercial Hotel with bowling alleys. They also published a newspaper, held regattas, had their own fire brigade, and established a semimonthly postal courier service, which took ten days between Nagasaki and Yokohama. Nagasaki was the chief source in Japan for Western ships and weapons, and agents from many daimyo domains thronged here. The city was also full of students from all over Japan, eager to learn Western technology and the English language, which the Japanese had discovered to their surprise was the lingua franca of the foreign traders, not Dutch.

Matsukata found the British to be his most useful contacts in Nagasaki. A cordial relationship had developed between Satsuma and Britain soon after their military encounter. In fact, a few months before Matsukata left for Nagasaki, the British minister Sir Harry

Parkes and his wife had come on a friendly visit to Kagoshima at the invitation of the daimyo and Hisamitsu. Although they were accompanied by two warships, this time there were only exchanges of friendly salutes, and the daimyo sailed out to welcome his guests in a magnificent state barge. There were cordial exchanges of visits and expressions of hope for close relations in the future, and these were followed by five days of banqueting and hunting. During this time, Parkes also had serious talks with the Satsuma leaders and gained an insight into the real political situation in Japan. It became clear to him that the power of the Tokugawa government was waning and that Satsuma and Choshu were rising in strength and influence. The two had achieved a secret alliance in March 1866, negotiated by Okubo and Saigo on the Satsuma side and Kido Koin for Choshu. The call of these two powerful domains for imperial rule in place of continued Tokugawa dominance was gaining in popular acceptance. Henceforth Britain leaned toward the imperial cause sponsored by Satsuma and Choshu, though France, in rivalry with Britain, remained a bitter-end supporter of the Tokugawa.

Thomas Glover, the Scottish merchant in Nagasaki, was particularly helpful to Matsukata. Glover had been instrumental in arranging Parke's visit to Kagoshima and, as we have seen, had helped to smuggle out the samurai youths from Satsuma to England. He had helped other young Japanese get to England to study, including two young Choshu samurai, Ito Hirobumi and Inoue Kaoru, who were later to become leading members of the national government. His home, on a hill overlooking the harbor, is still a show place in Nagasaki and is popularly associated with the Madame Butterfly story. Glover found three Englishmen to teach Matsukata mathematics. He also introduced Matsukata to British naval officers who talked to him about naval training, discipline, administration, ordinance, gunnery, and the storage of ammunition. Matsukata studied naval surveying, but found no place to practice this skill except on the roof of the Satsuma residence in Nagasaki. He felt that he did not have time to learn English, but pursued his studies through interpreters and translations of Western books. He worked diligently over the next several months, managing to absorb a great deal of learning in a short time.

But Matsukata was working against time. Okubo and Saigo in Kyoto had formed the secret alliance with Choshu and, together with the Choshu leaders, were plotting the imminent overthrow of the Tokugawa shogunate. They sent their reports back to Matsukata in Nagasaki, as their trusted liaison with the domain government, and it was up to him to pass on the reports to the daimyo and Hisamitsu. So Matsukata had to interrupt his studies periodically to make trips back to Kagoshima or sometimes go to designated places to meet with Okubo and Saigo. In the autumn of 1867 he met with them in Mitajiri, a Choshu port on the Inland Sea. There the decision was made to proceed at once with the overthrow of the Edo government, and Matsukata was placed in charge of military preparations in Satsuma.

Since Satsuma had only a few warships and the biggest was in drydock, Matsukata took it upon himself to purchase a vessel. The cheapest for sale in Nagasaki cost about 20,000 ryo, but he bought the most expensive, a British paddle steamer of 300 horsepower, 246 feet long and 29 feet wide, with a capacity of 17 knots' speed. It cost the enormous sum of 100,000 ryo, which was about 250,000 in American dollars of that time. He succeeded in persuading a rich Satsuma merchant to pay half the purchase price and got a loan for the remaining amount. Matsukata's fellow Satsuma officials could not believe his audacity and tried to dissuade him from the purchase, but he commented, "If we do not succeed in overthrowing the Tokugawa government, we shall all die together but, if we win, there is no limit to what we will all have." He closed the deal, immediately putting a Satsuma crew aboard the ship and thus forestalling the Westerners from playing their customary trick of replacing the ship's instruments and fixtures with inferior ones.

Matsukata was appointed commander of the ship, renamed the *Kasuga*, and sailed it to Kagoshima, making the trip of slightly over 200 miles in a record-breaking twelve hours. Until then even the fastest ships had usually taken three days. Matsukata had fully expected that the *Kasuga* would be converted into a warship, but when he reached Kagoshima he discovered that the senior councillors had already made the decision to use it for grain transport. Since Satsuma was not self-supporting in rice, it was purchasing rice from Choshu to feed the three thousand Satsuma troops who were about to set out for Kyoto. Matsukata, with the support of the chief elder (*karo*), objected to this use of the *Kasuga,* but the two were overruled. Disappointed in his hopes of becoming a pioneer in a national navy, Matsukata resigned command of the ship and thereafter stuck to a civilian career.

Ironically, only about a month later, when fighting did break out and warships were needed to keep the port of Hyogo near Kyoto from being blockaded by the Tokugawa navy, the *Kasuga* was converted into a warship. The two naval forces finally engaged in battle on January 28, 1868, at Awa at the eastern end of the Inland Sea. The *Kasuga* with its speed of 17 knots showed its superiority over the Tokugawa ships, none of which was capable of more than 12 knots. In this first clash between Western-style warships in Japanese history, the future "father of the Japanese navy," Admiral Togo, was one of the Satsuma gunners on the *Kasuga*. If Matsukata had held out a little longer as commander of the ship, he might well have gone down in history as the creator of the Imperial Japanese Navy rather than as the man who successfully launched the Japanese national economy on an even keel.

Before the civil war broke out, however, Matsukata had been sent back to Nagasaki to purchase arms for the Satsuma army. The Tokugawa government was naturally very suspicious of Satsuma and was watching its every move. The Tokugawa officials in Nagasaki did their best to prevent Matsukata and officials from other domains from making contact with foreign purveyors of arms, but he managed to buy an entire shipment from a foreign vessel. To escape the sharp eyes of the Tokugawa police, he had his stevedores dress in Western clothes, and in the dark of night they transported the boxes containing the guns to shore and then loaded them onto small boats for transshipment to a vessel anchored at sea. The guns arrived in Kagoshima in time to equip the three thousand troops being sent to Kyoto.

———•———

On January 3, 1868 (the ninth day of the twelfth month of 1867 according to the Japanese calendar), the Satsuma and Choshu forces, aided by contingents from some other domains, staged a coup d'état in Kyoto, seizing the imperial palace and announcing the "restoration of imperial rule." The shogun, who was Keiki—the man Hisamitsu in 1862 had gotten appointed as guardian of the shogun—was himself inclined to yield because he had for many years nurtured pro-imperial sympathies, but some of his supporters insisted on putting up a fight.

A battle between the so-called imperial forces and the Tokugawa troops took place at Fushimi, south of Kyoto, and ended in a defeat of the outgunned Tokugawa army. The shogun fled to Edo, where he later surrendered to the advancing imperial forces, though some To-kugawa supporters and the navy continued the fight for another year in northern Japan. The "year period" of the fifteen-year-old emperor who had come to the throne in 1867 was changed to "Meiji" in 1868, and the transformation of the national government that started then came to be known as the Meiji Restoration.

News of the events in Kyoto reached Matsukata in Nagasaki slowly and in garbled fashion. There was a report that the *Kasuga* had been seen fleeing the fire of Tokugawa ships, and a rumor spread that the Tokugawa soldiers in Nagasaki were planning to attack the Sa-tsuma residence. Some of the Satsuma men fled to the hills and others prepared to return to Kagoshima leaving only Matsukata and one gatekeeper. Matsukata felt certain that, if the Satsuma and Choshu coup had failed, pro-Tokugawa forces would already have marched into Nagasaki to reassert their authority, and he began to act as though he were himself in charge of the city. When news of the Tokugawa defeat at Fushimi finally came, Sasaki, a representative in Nagasaki of the Tosa domain, came to Matsukata and suggested that they join forces for an attack on the local Tokugawa commissioner. Fearing that this might lead to a dangerous involvement with the local foreign community, Matsukata persuaded Sasaki to give up the scheme.

The commissioner actually did approach the local British consul on the same day asking for aid in preserving the peace, but the consul refused on the grounds of British neutrality and the readiness of the British warships in the harbor to protect British subjects and property. The commissioner panicked and, stating that he was leaving the main-tenance of peace and order to the domains of Hizen and Chikuzen in north Kyushu, chartered a French ship to take him, his family, and their personal belongings to Edo. The commissioner's own brother, who had switched sides to the imperial cause, informed Matsukata, who dispatched men to board the vessel and seize the public money the commissioner was taking with him. The commissioner meekly handed over 17,000 ryo, of which Matsukata let him keep 3,000 to pay for his passage. Matsukata used this windfall to buy rice and distributed it to the people, who were suffering from a fire that had ravaged the city a few days earlier.

The Tokugawa commissioner was gone, but some five hundred Tokugawa troops remained in the city. Matsukata proceeded to negotiate their surrender, telling Sasaki to take charge while he alone and unarmed went into the enemy camp. After two hours of discussions, he returned at 2 A.M. with a signed agreement that the Tokugawa forces would not put up a fight. As he was met at the door by Sasaki, they heard a gun shot and, dashing out, found the faithful gatekeeper lying dead. He had not been recognized by a Tosa soldier on guard and was shot by mistake. In order to prevent a grave misunderstanding between Satsuma and Tosa, Matsukata asked Sasaki to have the soldier take his own life, and Sasaki ordered the man to commit seppuku. In later years, Matsukata declared that this was one of the most unhappy decisions he had ever made.

A few days later a contingent of three hundred Satsuma troops arrived in Nagasaki, to Matsukata's great relief. Since the daimyo of both Chikuzen and Hizen had refused to substitute for the commissioner, the task of maintaining order in the city had fallen completely to Matsukata and Sasaki. They called a meeting of the resident representatives of fourteen domains and formed a provisional government. It sent a memorandum to the foreign consulates announcing that this newly formed body would be in control of Nagasaki until the arrival of an official from the new government in Kyoto. It also stated that, since it had sufficient troops, it could guarantee the safety of the lives and property of the foreign nationals and that they could continue their trade without anxiety. This document was signed by all the domain representatives, with Matsukata's signature leading the list.

On the day after the organization of the provisional municipal government, Matsukata called on all the consuls, starting with the British, to ask them to continue to pay the usual tariffs at the regular custom house. The British consul recorded in a memorandum dated February 10: "Matsukata the Satsuma agent said they would protect life, property, and trade and would for the present carry on all kinds of public business as hitherto; that they had sufficient troops for any emergency that was likely to occur; and that they had made up their minds to avoid all offence towards foreigners, and in every way to act fairly and honourably by them."* All accepted the proposals except Lequis, the French consul, who refused on the grounds that the French treaty was with the Tokugawa government. He even threatened that the French ships in port would fire on the city, but Matsukata held his ground and advised the French consul to take his protest directly to the new government, since he, Matsukata, was only acting on its orders.

During his calls on the foreign consuls, Matsukata dressed for the first time in Western style, wearing a suit he had a Chinese tailor in the city make for him. He discarded his two samurai swords for the occasion. This was symbolic of the sudden change that the whole imperial faction was making. It had used its slogan of *joi* (expel the barbarians) together with *sonno* (honor the emperor) as rallying cries against the Tokugawa, but the men of Satsuma and Choshu knew full well that they would have to accommodate their policies to the Westerners. Choshu had learned the same lesson at Satsuma when its forts on the Straits of Shimonoseki had been destroyed by an allied naval force the year after the British bombardment of Kagoshima. Once victorious over the Tokugawa, the imperial partisans immediately began to adopt Western models as the only realistic way of building sufficient strength to resist Western domination.

Matsukata was not long in his self-appointed charge of Nagasaki. A governor selected by the new imperial government arrived on March 7, 1868. With him, as his aide, came Inoue, one of the young Choshu samurai whom Glover had helped to go to England and who was to become a close associate of Matsukata as a leading member of the new regime. Though Matsukata remained for a while in various posts in Nagasaki, he now was no longer merely a Satsuma representative but an official of the imperial government.

* M. Paske-Smith, *Western Barbarians in Japan and Formosa in Tokugawa Days, 1603–1686* (Kobe: J. L. Thompson, 1930), p. 179.

Imperial Official

T he disparate imperial forces, made up of men from Satsuma, Choshu, and a number of other domains, faced the problem of creating a national government to replace the collapsing and bankrupt Tokugawa regime. Already in 1868 they made Edo their capital, changing its name to Tokyo (Eastern Capital), and they moved the young emperor from Kyoto to the great Tokugawa castle in Edo, which they transformed into the imperial palace. Under the emperor's putative leadership, they set up a supreme Council of State (*Dajokan*), a name revived from the unified imperial rule of the eighth century, and under it a series of newly created ministries.

The top government posts were occupied by the daimyo of the domains that had led the revolution or senior court nobles who had cooperated with the movement. Such men, however, were largely figureheads, as they had been for much of the Tokugawa period. The chief movers in the new government were the young samurai activists like Okubo and Saigo, and a few of the younger court nobles who together with them had engineered the revolution. These younger men usually held the rank of councillor (*sangi*). Okubo, who was at first in charge of local government, was in a particularly important post, for the men he selected to take over as governors of prefectures, as they called their new units of local government, were crucial to the success of the whole effort. At first the problem was only to take direct control over the cities and the quarter of the agricultural land held directly by the shogun. The domains remained under their autonomous daimyo as before, though in 1869 the daimyo were converted, at least in theory, into governors in behalf of the central government.

Okubo chose his new prefectural governors with care, selecting several men who were eventually to become major figures in the new government. To Hyogo prefecture, the area around the newly opened port of Kobe and not far from Osaka and Kyoto, he sent Ito, one of the Choshu youths Glover had helped get to England and later the chief author of the Japanese constitution. For Kanagawa prefecture, the area including the port of Yokohama near Tokyo, he chose Terashima of Satsuma, who later was to serve as foreign minister. To Niigata prefecture, a port area on the Japan Sea, he sent Saionji, a young court noble, who as Prince Saionji was to become the last of the genro. These areas were all important contact points with Westerners. Okubo appointed Matsukata to a strategically less prominent post as governor of Hita (also commonly called Hida) in northeastern Kyushu.

The town of Hita and its surrounding territory was the largest piece of the Tokugawa realm in Kyushu, occupying a somewhat isolated, largely inland area in what is now the western part of Oita prefecture. It was for the most part a mountainous region with 140 villages centering on Hita, but, because of the protection it had offered by being under direct Tokugawa rule, it had a relatively wealthy community of merchants. Like other parts of the Tokugawa realm, Hita had been administered by a district administrator, or intendant (*daikan*), but with the collapse of Tokugawa authority the area was in a state of confusion. Since the new government, still engaged in fighting against Tokugawa loyalists in northern Japan, was largely dependent for its income on tax returns and contributions from former Tokugawa lands in central and western Japan, it was imperative to restore order in areas like Hita, to resume the collection of agricultural taxes, and to collect special contributions from rich individuals.

Matsukata arrived in Hita on July 30, 1868. In Nagasaki he had been advised to take some troops with him, since the political vacuum created by the departure of the Tokugawa intendant had drawn in forces from neighboring domains, eager to stake out new zones of influence, and this situation had added to the unrest. But Matsukata decided to go to Hita alone, much to the astonishment of the local townsmen. On his arrival, he took over the headquarters of the intendant, thanked the troops from the neighboring domains for their assistance, and then sent them home. The town quieted down. The fact that he was able to do this without force is a good measure of the general expectation of orderly processes resulting from the two centuries of peace Japan had enjoyed under Tokugawa rule, as well as a token of his own strength and will.

Matsukata's chief problem was to win the confidence of the local people. To do this he convened a meeting of local government employees, telling them that, although he was bringing in men from the central government to fill the highest positions, he would retain all of them, thus allaying their fears of losing their jobs. He also decided to break down the barriers that had always existed between officials and commoners. Okubo in Kyoto had set the tone by announcing that the young emperor would come out of seclusion and mingle with his subjects like a Western monarch. Before this, the intendant in Hita had acted as a lofty official, greatly feared by the people and hardly ever seen. When he passed in the street, they had to prostrate themselves on the ground. At his headquarters his office was closed to the public, and only high officials were allowed to enter. Matsukata chose the room closest to the entrance for his office and kept the door open for anyone to come in and talk with him. He placed a suggestion box outside the building to receive petitions, complaints, and suggestions, making only the stipulation that each document should bear the signature of the writer. He abolished the age-old custom of present giving, which had become a great burden on people forced to deal with the officials, and announced that neither he nor any of his officers would accept gifts of any kind. To break down class distinctions, he even initiated town wrestling matches in which he and his staff took part with merchants, artisans, and peasants.

In a short time Matsukata had established order in Hita and won the confidence of its inhabitants. So when he called together the rich men and urged them to come to the assistance of the new government by making loans, the response was good. The merchants wanted him to determine the amounts to donate, but he left it up to them to decide. The following day the richest merchant was the first to deliver his contribution of 50,000 ryo in copper coins—it weighed 400 pounds—and he was followed by others who together gave another 50,000, for a total of 100,000 ryo ($250,000). This was a sizable amount, not only in value but in weight and bulk. Matsukata had the money placed in two large chests slung on poles, which were carried on the shoulders of eight bearers the whole five hundred miles to Kyoto. This contribution was a welcome boost to the finances of the new government, and Matsukata received a commendation from Okubo.

———— • ————

Hita was a flourishing town with many restaurants and geisha houses catering to the pleasures of rich men. Sexual mores were notoriously loose, resulting in an unusual number of illegitimate pregnancies. Although abortion and infanticide were common practices throughout Japan at that time, used as ways to hold the population in check, Matsukata did not like these practices. He realized he could not stop abortions and infanticide by fiat and at first tried persuasion by lecturing townsmen, doctors, and midwives. When this proved fruitless, he took some funds collected from sympathizers and built the Yoikukan, a nursery for illegitimate children. He promised to remunerate doctors and midwives if they reported the names of women they knew who were pregnant out of wedlock, and more money if they could persuade these women not to have abortions. He also promised to give financial aid to the women and to care for their unwanted infants if they would bring them to the Yoikukan.

No babies were brought at first, until it was announced that women could come at night and leave the babies at the front door of the nursery without being seen or asked questions. This proved successful and many babies were brought, until there were over 150 infants, including orphans and legitimate babies whose parents could not support them. Baskets made of woven bamboo were used for cribs, hung in rows from the ceiling. A pull on a main rope that tied them all together rocked all the baskets in unison. When the babies became too many for the supply of wet nurses, Matsukata, having heard that Western babies were fed cow's milk, bought cows in Nagasaki and at the suggestion of the French consul there got milking equipment from Shanghai. The Japanese of the time did not eat meat and abominated milk. In fact, Matsukata himself never drank it his whole life, but he managed to overcome the local prejudice in the case of the babies. They thrived on cow's milk and were found to be healthier than the babies in respectable families who drank only mother's milk. The children of the Yoikukan came to have such a good reputation that childless families began to adopt them.

Matsukata took a great interest in these babies and spent many hours in the nursery. He was aided in this work by his wife Masako, who, together with their four children, had joined him in Hita. Matsukata personally named all the nursery children, at first including in their names Matsu (pine tree) from his own surname. He was very strict with the nursery workers, telling them that they were not there merely to feed and care for castaways but should treat the babies with tenderness and love. The children had great affection for their foster father, and some years later in 1883, when Matsukata toured Kyushu as finance minister, ninety of them, now all sturdy teenagers and adopted into families, called on him. Some of them continued to keep in touch with him throughout his life.

Matsukata found his office employees lacking the qualities that would make them good public servants working in behalf of the people of the prefecture. He persuaded a locally famous scholar of Chinese philosophy, Hirose Ringai to train them. Hirose used to have a school in which he taught the Chinese classics to more than two hundred students from surrounding regions, but he had disbanded the school because of the political disturbances. Matsukata induced him to lecture several times a month at the prefectural office and, whenever he himself felt overburdened and weary, would call on Hirose for relaxing conversation. Matsukata also became friends with a Zen priest, Gogaku, who was an accomplished poet and landscape painter in the Southern Chinese style, and from him learned to appreciate art.

In Nagasaki, Matsukata had come to know a Satsuma merchant who was studying English with Guido Verbeck, a Dutch American who was to become an important adviser to the new government. The merchant and Verbeck had compiled an English-Japanese dictionary, but it could not be printed for lack of funds. Now the merchant came to Matsukata to seek funding, which Matsukata was able to provide. Printed in Shanghai and called the *Satsuma jisho* (Satsuma Dictionary, presumably because of Matsukata's connection with it), it sold well: this was a time when learning English had become almost a necessity for ambitious young men.

Matsukata traveled extensively in Hita to learn how best to increase the productivity of the area. He developed irrigation projects and reclaimed waste lands. Since the terrain and climate were suitable for a lumbering industry, he initiated programs of reforestation. He showed farmers living in the mountain areas how to increase their incomes by grazing sheep on the hillsides and planting mulberry trees in order to feed silkworms. Since transportation facilities were poor, he started road and bridge construction. In order to finance these programs, he established a special office to provide capital loans.

One of the more interesting of his many projects was the construction of the harbor in Beppu on the northeast coast of Kyushu, along the one short stretch of shoreline in Hita prefecture. On visiting the town of Beppu for the first time, Matsukata was forced to wade ashore through heavy surf because there was no harbor or dock. He spoke to the men of the town about his undignified manner of arrival and pointed out that they could make Beppu, with its many fine hot springs, a prosperous resort to attract people from all over Japan. They received his suggestion with enthusiasm and immediately started to raise money for the harbor; finding their funds still insufficient, they came back to ask for a loan of 15,000 ryo ($37,000). Matsukata did not have the cash available but provided them with a loan of 20,000 ryo in national certificates, and the port was built. A stone memorial inscribed with Matsukata's calligraphy still stands at the entrance to the harbor, and Beppu today is the most famous hot-spring resort in Japan.

Matsukata showed surprising energy and wisdom in tackling the many problems he faced as prefectural governor. He had had little background for this sort of work and was in Hita for only a little over two years, but he claimed that he got his inspiration from his former lord, Nariakira, who in turn had derived many of his ideas from the teachings of Sato Nobuhiro (1769–1850), a well-known philosopher and agricultural economist. Born in Akita in northern Japan, Sato came from a family that had lost its samurai status in the seventeenth century and for four generations had been first doctors and then agricultural experts. Sato's grandfather and father deplored the poverty of the peasantry and the prevalence of infanticide, especially in the two northern provinces of Dewa and Mutsu, where 70,000 children were said to be killed annually. They traveled extensively throughout Japan, becoming experts on agriculture, forestry, and mining, and they advocated various programs for the development of resources. Sato

69

inherited their attitudes and expanded his skills by studying astronomy, geography, military science, agriculture, and water control with scholars of Dutch learning in Edo. He wrote many books on a wide variety of subjects from Western history to sea defense and agricultural administration. Nariakira had been one of Sato's ardent disciples in Edo and, after going as daimyo to Satsuma, had based many of his policies on Sato's teachings.

Among the ideas Sato advocated were the abolition of the four traditional social classes and the formation of a one-class society; selfless service for the people by the rulers; education for all children regardless of class; the abolition of abortion and infanticide and the establishment of charity organizations to take care of orphans; the development of natural resources in mining, forestry, and agriculture; the development of transportation to facilitate commerce; and the establishment of a national financial agency to provide loans for the development of new enterprises. One can see a reflection of Sato's ideas in many of Matsukata's activities in Hita. Matsukata had read several of Sato's books and, together with Okubo and other friends, had frequented the home of one of Sato's disciples who lived in Kagoshima. Okubo was attempting to apply some of Sato's teachings in the central government, and Matsukata's adoption of them in Hita fitted in well.

Although Matsukata's duties were in theory limited to Hita, he was sometimes called on for tasks outside his prefecture. One such case arose from the discovery that there were some clandestine Japanese Christians in the Nagasaki area. Christianity had been first introduced in Japan in 1549 by the Portuguese Jesuit missionary, St. Francis Xavier. Christians in Japan in the early seventeenth century may have numbered as many as 300,000, constituting a far higher percentage of the population at that time than they do today. The Tokugawa authorities, fearful of the possible political threat of people with such alien loyalties, stamped out the religion ruthlessly. The climax came with the destruction in 1638 of some 37,000 embattled peasant Christians who had based themselves in an old castle at Shimabara, southeast of Nagasaki. Thereafter suspect Japanese were routinely required to trample on a Christian icon, a practice known as *fumie* (picture treading), to prove that they were not believers.

Some small communities of peasants or fishermen around

Nagasaki had maintained their faith in secret. Emboldened by the new treaties with the West, a group from the farming village of Uraga—now part of Nagasaki and ironically near the point where the second atomic bomb was dropped in 1945—attended a service in 1865 at what was known as the French Church, recently established in Nagasaki by French Catholic missionaries. One of the women in the group whispered to the French priest, "The heart of all those present is the same as yours." Clandestine Christians had been ferreted out several times before in the Nagasaki area, and the new government felt it should take action in 1868 about those discovered three years earlier, since the ban on Christianity remained in force. Rumors circulated that the Christians would all be executed, but Western leaders remonstrated in the name of humanity. Okubo, alarmed by the foreign involvement, sent Matsukata from Hita as his personal representative to help the governor of Nagasaki and Okuma Shigenobu, who had been put in charge of the case and was soon to rise fast in the new government. From the domain of Hizen in north Kyushu, Okuma had been a student of Verbeck's in Nagasaki and collaborated with Matsukata in the takeover of the city in 1868.

Sir Harry Parkes, the British minister, had come from Tokyo in an attempt to handle the matter locally, but his first meeting with the governor and Okuma had produced no results. Matsukata was not at this meeting, but the others agreed that at the second he should do the talking. In response to Parkes's demands, Matsukata asked if Parkes should not instead be dealing with the Ministry of Foreign Affairs in Tokyo, since he himself and his colleagues were merely representatives of the central government and bound by its decisions. Parkes realized that he had been outmaneuvered and returned quickly to Tokyo.

The central government sought to solve the problem by scattering throughout the country the 150 Christians who had been discovered. When the ships on which they were loaded cleared port, Matsukata composed a poem to express his relief that the crisis was over. Since the Christians locally were called "blacks" and the non-Christians "whites," he wrote: "The mountains in all directions are blanketed in white./The snow that falls today is the spirit of the gods."

Although the Japanese had refused to give way on the old ban against Christianity, they learned how delicate an issue religion was in their relations with the West. They made no effort thereafter to prevent new conversions in the port cities, where missionaries were already active. After a large delegation of government leaders—the Iwakura mission—returned from abroad in 1873 with a clear realization not only of the military strength of the Western nations but also of the strength of their feelings about their religion, the ban on Christianity was quietly dropped. One night in March 1873 the public notice boards that for two hundred and thirty years had proclaimed throughout Japan the outlawing of the religion were quietly taken down, and Christianity was tolerated in Japan.

Another special problem assigned Matsukata concerned the circulation of counterfeit currency bills in Kyushu. The government's paper money, known as *Dajokan-satsu,* was printed so crudely that it was easy to forge. The counterfeit bills in Kyushu were traced to the great Chikuzen domain of Fukuoka, whose lord, now called governor, was a relative of the Shimazu of Satsuma. Okubo, afraid of stirring up animosities between Chikuzen and Satsuma, assigned Matsukata to look into the matter, even though the seat of the problem was outside the reach of his authority and in a large and still virtually autonomous domain. When Matsukata began to probe into the counterfeiting plot, the people of Fukuoka, resenting his activities in their city, threatened several times to kill him, but he pursued his search and to his amazement discovered that the printing presses were actually in the daimyo's castle. The more than seventy men who were doing the work were kept prisoner in the castle, being allowed to go back to their homes only once or twice a year.

When Matsukata reported his findings to Okubo, he was ordered to proceed with the greatest caution and in no circumstances to involve the daimyo-governor. In order to arrest the workers and seize the machinery, Matsukata dressed policemen in uniforms of the imperial army and sent them into Fukuoka as if they were on their way back to the capital and were merely spending the night there. Then in the morning they entered the castle, made known their identity, arrested the workers and the officials in charge, and dismantled the presses. The governor was not arrested but resigned his position shortly thereafter.

While still governor of Hita, Matsukata also responded to a request made of all the important government officials to submit memorials expressing their personal opinions on domestic and foreign policies. In this document he clearly demonstrated a statesmanlike combination of idealism and common sense. He pointed out:

> The West is advanced because it has been developing for many centuries, and it would be a mistake if we should try in a hurry to become a great nation. We must first consolidate the nation and then, little by little, take what is good from the Western countries and eliminate what is bad. The country must not be shortsighted and only think of its own benefits, for a nation that thinks merely of its own good attains only 50 to 60 percent greatness . . . As a basic policy for diplomacy, it must make fidelity, sincerity, and reasonableness the foundations . . . In order to negotiate with a foreign nation, the country itself must be in good order, with plenty to eat and plenty of soldiers.

In contrast to this general advice to go slow, Matsukata also made some specific proposals for immediate sweeping changes. He eagerly outlined his views on land-tax reform and fiscal policy and advocated the complete abolition of the feudal structure and the unification of Japan under the rule of the emperor. When Matsukata's memorial came to Okubo's attention, Okubo became fearful for Matsukata's safety. Such ideas were dangerously premature. He warned Matsukata to keep his ideas to himself, although he confided that he and others shared them and this was the course that would eventually have to be taken. Such ultimate objectives, however, had to be kept in complete secrecy until the proper groundwork had been laid. The daimyo had no intention of giving up more than they already had, and, if it became known that the domains were to be abolished, they would no doubt put up armed resistance and plunge the nation into civil war. Okubo added that Hisamitsu would oppose this move more than any other daimyo and, should he find out that Matsukata, one of his trusted retainers, harbored such ideas, Matsukata would certainly lose his head.

The daimyo had been persuaded in 1869 to return their domains to the emperor and were appointed governors, but it was not until the summer of 1871 that the central government felt secure enough to take the big step of eliminating the domains. On August 29 it suddenly announced that the whole country was being divided into three urban and seventy-two rural prefectures. (The number was gradually reduced to the present forty-seven.) The night before the momentous announcement, Okubo celebrated by inviting Matsukata, who by then had been transferred to Tokyo, to accompany him for a festive evening on a boat on the Sumida River, and on this occasion Matsukata thanked Okubo for his advice against speaking out prematurely.

———— • ————

The new government was not merely concerned with establishing its direct rule over all Japan. It was attempting to develop communications by building telegraph lines, improving port facilities, starting a mail service, building railway lines, and sponsoring the development of modern Japanese shipping lines. In 1871 it adopted a new currency system, making the yen the chief monetary unit, with a value that varied between a half and full American dollar during the next few decades. The same year it created a ministry of education, which embarked on an ambitious plan for the education of all youth. During these years it sent young students abroad to learn new skills and brought to Japan many expensive European and American experts to establish advanced schools and instruct Japanese in Western technology. It also established many pilot plants in textile, glass, brick, and other manufacturing enterprises. In 1873 the government shifted the country to the Western calendar, making the third day of the twelfth month of 1872 the first day of January 1873. A few days later, it presaged the abolition of the whole feudal class system by instituting compulsory military service for all Japanese men, in place of the samurai army of the past.

Okubo was a prime mover in many of these reforms, especially the economic ones, and he used the finance ministry as the means through which to carry them out. This he staffed with men he believed had the right progressive ideas. In 1871 he made Okuma of Hizen vice-minister, under a figurehead minister, and he appointed Ito of Choshu the chief of taxation, with Inoue, also of Choshu, and Matsukata as his principal assistants. Matsukata, who had been brought from Hita to Tokyo and designated assistant home minister on November 26, 1870, transferred his activities to the finance ministry and succeeded Ito as chief of taxation when Ito went abroad with the Iwakura mission in November 1871.

The Iwakura mission was named for its leader, a court noble who had taken a large role in the imperial restoration and was now foreign minister in the new government. With him went Okubo, the chief Satsuma representative in the government, Kido, his counterpart from Choshu, and other prominent but slightly younger leaders like Ito. The group went first to the United States and then to Europe, not returning until September 1873. The chief objective of the mission was to persuade the Western nations to revise the unequal treaties forced on Japan during the last years of the Tokugawa regime. Like those earlier imposed on China, these treaties gave the Western nations special privileges. Their nationals had the right of extraterritoriality, which meant that they were subject only to their own laws even when resident in Japan. The Western nations were also permitted to station their own military forces in Japanese ports, and they controlled Japanese import tariffs through treaties. This made it impossible for Japan to protect traditional products and its new infant industries from the competition of cheaper, machine-made Western goods.

The mission's secondary objective was to study the West. Along with it went 154 young people for more lengthy study abroad. Those who were assigned to study in the United States came under the supervision of Mori, one of the young samurai sent from Satsuma in 1865 to study in England. He had gone from there to the United States, where he spent a year at the communal retreat in upstate New York of an American spiritualist, Thomas Lake Harris. Mori now at the age of twenty-four was the Japanese minister in Washington. By this time there were altogether some two hundred young Japanese, all on Japanese government fellowships, studying in American institutions. Quite a few of them were at Rutgers in New Jersey because Verbeck, the influential American missionary, had connections with this institution through the Dutch Reformed Church. One of the students who went with the mission and ended up at Rutgers was Matsukata's cousin Kosuke, whose untimely death in 1873 I have already mentioned. He was one of eleven Japanese who died in an influenza epidemic. Among the other students on the mission were five girls between the ages of eight and fourteen. The youngest, Tsuda Ume, after long years of study in New England and then at Bryn Mawr College near Philadelphia, returned to Japan to found Japan's first school of higher education for women, known as Tsuda College for Women.

75

Although the mission was warmly received in Washington and Europe, it failed entirely in its efforts to persuade the Western powers to revise the treaties. Yet it proved extremely educational for the Japanese leaders. They realized how far behind the Occident the Japanese were in technology and modern institutions. They saw that it would take a long time and great effort before they could begin to catch up and then expect the West to change its attitude toward Japan. At times Okubo almost despaired. As one of the senior government leaders, he felt himself at the age of forty-two already too old for the task and wrote in a letter to Matsukata, "An old man like me cannot do anything for the future. As I travel in these Occidental countries, I see I cannot keep up with all the progress, and I am greatly troubled for the future of our country." But Okubo was in fact indefatigable and wrote enthusiastically from England that the group had seen "courts, prisons, schools, trading firms, factories, shipyards, iron foundries, paper plants, wool and cotton spinning and weaving factories, silver cutlery and glass plants, coal and salt mines, not to speak of castles and cathedrals . . . There is nowhere we haven't been." Okubo was much impressed with England, where he stayed for four months. He was even more inspired by his contacts with Bismarck. Noting that Prussia too had been a late starter in industrialization, he became convinced that Japan also could become a world power if the people were prepared to expend the necessary effort and make sacrifices. It is worth noting that his younger colleague Ito, a decade later, chose Prussia as the chief model for the constitution he was then preparing for Japan.

———•———

The three most influential leaders of the new government, Iwakura, Okubo, and Kido, had gone abroad on the mission, leaving behind a curiously ill-assorted trio in control. Matsukata's old friend Saigo and Itagaki Taisuke of the Tosa domain on Shikoku were the leading generals in the fighting that brought the new government to power but had been less involved in the reform efforts since then; Okuma of Hizen was perhaps the most iconoclastic of all the leaders. The departing statesmen made their stay-at-home colleagues promise not to make any great changes during their absence, but the unstable situation made innovations constantly necessary. In fact, two of the most important of the early reforms—universal military conscription and a new land ownership and taxation system—were inaugurated in 1873 before the mission's return in September of that year. Matsukata as chief of taxation was the prime mover in the tax reform.

Agricultural land had theoretically belonged to the shogun and daimyo, though for all practical purposes it was in the hands of the peasants, who constituted about 80 percent of Japan's population. They paid taxes in kind to their respective lords. Tax rates differed from place to place, though they averaged between 30 and 40 percent of the yield, and there were in addition various forms of special money requisitions and corvee labor. Tax returns naturally varied greatly from year to year, depending on the size of the harvest and the price of rice. This uncertainty made government budgeting almost impossible. Obviously much had to be done to determine just who owned each piece of land, to equalize tax burdens and to make tax yields more consistent and predictable.

Matsukata as governor of Hita had become familiar with the problems of land ownership and taxation and had made suggestions in the memorial he had submitted in 1869. Some of his specific proposals were that farmers should be free to buy and sell land and to decide what crops they would plant; that certificates of land ownership should be issued to the farmers; that taxation should be constant and based on the value of the land, instead of varying according to the size of the annual crops; that for this purpose there should be a survey of all agricultural land followed by a fixed rate of taxation; and finally that grains should be freely imported and exported. In conformity with these concepts formulated three years earlier, a law on title deeds was adopted in 1872, permitting the sale and purchase of land and making the person who had been paying the land tax the owner of the land. The law thus established that the peasants themselves, and not the feudal lords, were the landowners. This freed Japan from the whole problem of continuing feudal estates that still plagued much of Europe in the nineteenth and twentieth centuries. The law also recognized that considerable land was being farmed by tenants for richer farmers, who were the taxpayers of record and therefore now the recognized owners. This set the stage for the later growth of tenancy into a serious social problem. Again in conformity with Matsukata's original pro-posals, the land tax was set in July 1873 at 3 percent of the assessed value of the land, to be paid not in produce but in money.

The new system was not to go into effect fully until 1875 because it involved a great deal of work to establish land values. It aroused the vehement opposition of the peasants, who were deeply suspicious of almost any innovation. Matsukata felt the implementation of the land-tax reform was so difficult that it should not be simply an additional task for the finance ministry to handle. So he proposed to the top leaders, who had just returned from the Iwakura mission, that the work be assigned to a special office of land-tax reform. The suggestion was approved, but neither Iwakura nor Kido, who were suggested for the presidency of the new office, would accept the post, and Matsukata felt that Okuma, whose name was also mentioned, was too indecisive for such an assignment. Finally Okubo agreed to take the position, but only with the understanding that Matsukata, as chief of taxation, would do all the work.

The reforms were carried through successfully despite many problems. The budgetary procedures of the government became more orderly. The clear establishment of the peasant's ownership of his land eventually gave the Japanese farmer an increased sense of dignity and independence as well as an incentive to increase the productivity of his land. The 3 percent rate of taxation proved too high and was reduced to 2.5 percent in 1876, just at a time when a serious inflation was beginning, which reduced the actual value of the taxes still further. The result was unprecedented prosperity for the farmers. This per-mitted them to make still heavier investments in land improvements, which in turn contributed to a rapid increase in agricultural produc-tion.

The evaluation of all agricultural property brought to light many old abuses of concealment or underestimation of production, which, when discovered, stirred up bitter resentment against the local tax officials. This discontent came at a time when Itagaki of Tosa, who had left the government over a policy dispute with his colleagues, was starting a movement for rights and a share in political power for the people. Disturbed by these signs of popular opposition, reactionaries in the government, such as Hisamitsu, Matsukata's former feudal master, who occupied one of the highest posts, demanded that the private ownership of land be rescinded. Matsukata stuck by his guns, declaring, "At a time when we are racing to attain equality with the Occidental nations, it is an absolute necessity for us to establish the spirit of independence and individual initiative. Should we abolish the private rights of land ownership, this will again enslave the people, the fields will become barren, and it will be a disaster for the nation."

In 1874 Matsukata presented a memorial to the government, "Internal Tax Reform." He pointed out that rising inflation had produced a budget deficit of over six million yen and that additional types of taxation were needed. He stressed that it was most important for the government to give close consideration to the entire problem of taxation, since, except for farmers, Japanese had not been accustomed to paying taxes. As he wrote, "The people will put up strong opposition because they will not consider it their duty to pay taxes. They are servants of custom and since time immemorial have associated taxes only with farmers and farm fields . . . In order to put through new taxation the government will have to proceed cautiously and slowly, investigating the tax systems of other countries as well as considering carefully what commodities will be fair to tax without favoring the rich or putting more burdens on the poor." It was suggested that a tax should be placed on textiles, but since cloth was a necessity for all the people, the decision was finally made to tax only sake and tobacco.

In 1876 Okubo established the Bureau of Industrial Promotion to oversee the implementation of the many programs for economic development, and he appointed Matsukata as its head. This was an enormous job. The office for a while absorbed over half of the government's budget and employed more than five hundred high-salaried Western experts. A few months later Okubo appointed Matsukata to head still another bureau, the Jusan kyoku, which had been set up to help destitute samurai find employment in industry and agriculture (their hereditary stipends were being terminated with small lump-sum payments). Matsukata, who already felt overburdened with his taxation and industrial jobs, and was suffering chronic stomach trouble from overwork, pleaded that a third major job would kill him. Okubo replied in true samurai fashion, "Even if you die, your work will live on."

The creation of a major office to help destitute samurai was a response to growing samurai unrest, which was a far more serious threat to the new government than the opposition of the generally meek peasantry. The trio left in charge when the Iwakura mission went abroad had even laid plans for a war with Korea, ostensibly to avenge insults from the Korean government but really to give employment and honor to the depressed samurai. The plan was overruled in 1873 by the returning members of the mission, who now realized the weakness of Japan in comparison with the West and the folly of such an adventuristic foreign policy. In pique, Saigo and Itagaki withdrew from the government. Itagaki developed into the leader of a "freedom and people's rights movement," made up largely of ex-samurai from his native domain of Tosa. Saigo returned to Satsuma, where he devoted himself to opening schools to train military officers; this attracted a following of dissident samurai from all over the country. In the meantime, samurai uprisings began to break out in various parts of the country. These culminated in a great rebellion in 1877 in Satsuma, where close to 80,000 samurai under the leadership of Saigo rose against the Tokyo government that Saigo had done so much to establish.

The revolt was a major test for the new government and its army, consisting largely of peasant conscripts with samurai officers. Lasting from January to September 1877, it is usually called the Satsuma Rebellion in English but is known in Japanese as the Southwestern Rebellion (*Seinan-no-eki*). Okubo moved to Kyoto to be nearer the scene of battle, but Matsukata stayed at the capital, working at the finance ministry on the problem of paying for the war and reporting regularly to Okubo on the state of the government in Tokyo. He spent his nights in the imperial palace in order to look after the safety of the emperor in a city stripped of troops. When the war at one point seemed to be going adversely for the government, he prepared to use the city fire brigades and to call for volunteers to protect the palace. He is said not to have returned to his home even once until the uprising finally collapsed and Saigo took his own life. The rebellion was a deep personal tragedy for many of the government leaders, particularly Okubo and Matsukata, who had been close friends of Saigo since childhood. Matsukata always felt that Saigo was a great patriot and had been forced into his unhappy final role. Much later, at the time of the promulgation of the constitution in 1889, it was largely through Matsukata's efforts that Saigo was cleared of the charge of rebellion and awarded posthumous honors.

During the fighting in the Satsuma capital of Kagoshima, fire destroyed much of the town, including Matsukata's old home, where his family was still living.* Matsukata's wife Masako managed to rescue their seven children from the conflagration and also the *Yoyoki,* a record of his life between 1835 and 1865, and the diary he kept from 1861 to 1868. These are the only extant records of his early life. After the fire Matsukata moved his wife and children to Tokyo to a home in Sendaizaka in Azabu, reuniting the family for the first time in six years—but not for long. Only a few months later he embarked on his first trip abroad.

———— • ————

With the quelling of the Satsuma Rebellion, the new government was now safe from internal challenge. By the autumn of 1877 Matsukata's land-tax reforms had been virtually completed, and he experienced for the first time a respite from pressing national duties. Persuading Okubo to make good on a promise of long standing to send him abroad, he got himself appointed to head the Japanese delegation at the Paris International Exhibition, which was to take place in the fall of 1878. International exhibits had become major world events ever since London's Crystal Palace Exhibition in 1851. Japan's first participation in one was at the Paris exhibition of 1867, a year before the Restoration. Japan then was represented by two separate exhibits, one by the Tokugawa government and the other by the "Nation of Satsuma and the Ryukyu Islands," which presented Napoleon III with a decoration bearing the Satsuma crest. The Meiji government, intent on increasing Japanese exports, took a great interest in international expositions. It won several prizes at the Vienna exposition of 1873 and made a particularly large effort at the American Centennial Exposition of 1876.

The position of head of the Japanese delegation at the Paris exhibition was of some importance, but Matsukata's chief reason for

* After World War II, when the city was again destroyed by fire, the area around the homesite was converted into Matsukata Park, where Ed and I planted a memorial tree while he was ambassador to Japan.

going was to learn more about industry, commerce, and agriculture in the West, especially about financial institutions, in order to prepare himself for his position as head of the Bureau of Industrial Promotion. To ensure time for these studies, he planned to spend several months in Europe in advance of the actual opening of the exhibit. Before departing, he paid a call on Okubo. Taking with him a book of poems written by his friend Gogaku, the Zen priest of Hita, he asked Okubo to inscribe a farewell message in it. In his beautiful calligraphy, Okubo wrote four Chinese characters, *dai kan sai ron,* taken from one of the priest's poems and meaning "broad observation and detailed discussion." Matsukata treasured this for its relevance to his trip, and almost four decades later, in 1916, he wrote the same four characters on a decorative inscription he presented to Okubo's heir.

On a month-and-a-half journey on a French ship via the Suez Canal to France, Matsukata had his first opportunity in several years to do extensive reading. He took piles of books with him, mostly translations of European and American books on history, economics, and business. He also included law books and special reports on constitutions, a subject that was now much on the minds of the Japanese leaders.

To most Europeans, Japan was still an unknown country; many thought of it as an appendage to China. Hoping to use the exhibition to inform foreigners about Japan as well as to promote the sale of Japanese goods, Matsukata before his departure had commissioned an account of Japan's two-thousand-year history and then had it translated into French. On his arrival in France, he discovered that ignorance about Japan was so abysmal that he had a huge map of Asia made, accompanying it with charts and statistics on Japan. This he placed in the entrance hall of the Japanese pavilion for all visitors to see before they entered the exhibit rooms. The Japanese exhibition featured lacquer ware, porcelain, cloisonné, bronze ornaments and vases, painted screens and fans, and such handicrafts as bamboo baskets. It was well attended, and the French and other European newspapers gave it favorable coverage.

It was customary at the close of international exhibits to sell off the displays to dealers, but not many Japanese goods were sold. A few Britishers bought some, but the French were unwilling to pay more than $100 for any one item. Matsukata's staff urged him to dispose of the remaining articles at any price so that they would not have to go through the trouble of repacking and shipping them home. But Matsukata thought it would be unfortunate to give foreigners the impression that the Japanese would cut prices if buyers held out long enough. He called in carpenters to estimate the cost of crating the goods, and, when rumors of this spread around town, the dealers came rushing back and bought up every item at the asking price.*

Matsukata had arrived in Paris in March 1878, and the exhibition did not open until November. This gave him time to study in Paris and travel around Europe. Soon after his arrival, he visited the French Tobacco Monopoly Bureau, which was under the management of the finance ministry. He figured out the industry's daily production by determining the output of each workman, but when he later took his figures to the bureau office he found that there was a discrepancy between them and the official statistics. Although he had to communicate through an interpreter, he deluged the officials with questions until he was fully satisfied about the reasons for the difference. This was reported to Léon Say, the finance minister, who became curious about this man from Japan who was such a keen observer. Say asked Matsukata to call on him, and this was the start of a pleasant and educational relationship. Say became Matsukata's "financial teacher" and gave him a desk in his private office for the duration of his stay in Paris.

As a fledgling financial official, Matsukata was very fortunate to come under the wing of this great financial statesman. Léon Say (1826–1896) was elected in 1871 to the National Assembly and was six times finance minister of France. For many years he was the autocrat of French finances. He was the grandson of Jean-Baptiste Say (1767–1832), a disciple of Adam Smith and a strong exponent of free trade, and was himself well known for his "law of markets," which postulated that supply creates demand. Throughout his career he was an indefatigable writer and lecturer on economics, and in this he exerted far wider influence than in politics.

---

* On a visit to the Ethnological Museum in Leiden in 1982, I saw three large, handsome Buddhist idols displayed in a special room. The curator remarked that, at the time they were bought at the 1878 Paris exposition, Holland was a rich country and could afford such purchases.

83

Matsukata had known of Say and read his works in translation even before he came to France. In a memorial in 1874 he referred to Say's raising of French tariffs to pay off the idemnity incurred in the Franco-Prussian War of 1870. Matsukata's argument had been that Japan must have the same right to control its own tariffs in order to lessen its unfavorable balance of trade. Japanese exports had increased sevenfold between 1860 and 1870, but imports continued to rise still faster and could only be held down by higher tariffs. As Matsukata remarked to Say in 1878, he was a great admirer of Adam Smith's laissez-faire economics and hoped that the day would come when Japanese industry would be strong enough to make those policies feasible in his country—but protectionism was more appropriate for Japan at that time. In fact, throughout his life Matsukata often referred to the protectionist policies of the German economist Friedrich List as more suitable then for Japan than Adam Smith's ideas.

Say was interested in the reports on Japan's finances that Matsukata had brought with him. The sharp changes in government income from year to year especially caught his eye, giving Matsukata a chance to explain the traditional Japanese system of basing taxes on percentages of shifting rice yields and the tax reforms he himself had made to correct the fluctuations. Say, who was then trying to get a tax-reform bill through the French assembly, was so impressed that he asked Matsukata to send him a fuller report after his return home. The original Japanese draft of this report is to be found in the seventh volume of the *Matsukata jikki*.

Say was also interested in the Japanese banking system, which in 1871 had been set up on the American model: each bank could set its own interest rates and issue bank notes up to 80 percent of its deposits. With a rapid increase in the number of banks in Japan, the financial situation was becoming chaotic. Say urged Matsukata to shift to the European system of having one central bank as the sole issuer of notes and having strong control over the other banks. On Say's advice, Matsukata studied European banking systems, and eventually in 1882 he did create the Bank of Japan, with the Belgian Central Bank as its model.

One thing that astonished Matsukata was the railroad system. Remembering his days of walking the length of Japan, he marveled at the ease and speed of travel in Europe. He also realized the vital role railways played in economic development. Horse-drawn carriages and stage coaches were beginning to replace travel by palanquins in Japan, and in 1871 a foreigner in Yokohama, by using light bicycle wheels, invented for the use of his invalid wife a newfangled "man-drawn cart," or *jinrikisha,* which came to be known in the West as a rickshaw. But there were still few railways. The first one constructed in 1872 between Tokyo and Yokohama was only 18 miles in length and the second, completed in 1877 between Osaka and Kyoto, not much longer. Japan had a total of only 50 miles of track, as compared with the 10,000 miles in France alone.

The general commissioner of the 1878 exhibit was Jean Baptiste Krantz, a politician who had spent more than twenty years in developing the French railway system, and from him Matsukata received much advice. The two studied the topographical maps of Japan, and Krantz suggested that the first major undertaking should be a line from Tokyo to Osaka, running through the mountainous center of the country, and the next a line between the west coast port of Niigata and Aomori in the far north of Honshu. These lines would develop the mountainous inner regions, leaving marine transportation to service the coastal areas. A line hugging the coast, as the Tokaido highway did, would be vulnerable, Krantz said, to enemy fire in case of war. He also warned Matsukata to anticipate opposition from the people through whose holdings the new lines would cut. He further suggested that double tracking would be advisable, though a narrow gauge, like England's, would be best for a small island country; costly bridges and tunnels should be minimized; foreign financing and control should be avoided if Japan were to retain its independence; and the government should finance the construction but have private firms do the actual work. With the exception of the mountainous routes of the first long lines, much of this advice was indeed followed as Japan rapidly expanded its rail network in the following decades.

In Europe Matsukata was not completely absorbed in problems of economic development. Ito had specifically asked him to collect materials pertaining to imperial succession, the sovereignty of rulers, systems of organization for imperial households, the disciplining of government officials, and the problem of impeachment. The Japanese had noted the wide discrepancy between the American system, in which even the president could be impeached, and the British, in which the sovereign could do no wrong.

Matsukata's letters to his friends were full of the exciting experiences he was having in Europe. He wrote to one, "I seem to be a great curiosity here in Europe, and I am summoned each night to dinner parties. I feel like a first-class geisha, going to and fro between Shimbashi and Yanagibashi, but I hope I have made these occasions profitable for our country by helping to promote better trade relations." One important outcome of Matsukata's trip was to make him feel at home in Western society—he remained at ease with Westerners for the rest of his life, though he never learned to speak or read a European language. Ever since the court had adopted Western ceremonial dress in 1871, and frock coats, morning coats, Prussian hats, and French shoes had come into vogue, government officials dressed in the Western manner. They also abandoned the traditional samurai hairdress in favor of Western haircuts. But it was only in Europe that Matsukata acquired a taste for Western food. He was accustomed to eating pork, because Satsuma was famous for its pork dishes, but bread, butter, and beef were unfamiliar.

Before his departure from Paris, Matsukata hosted a dinner to show his gratitude to those who had shown him hospitality. At the dinner table he seated Krantz and Viscount Ferdinand de Lesseps, the builder of the Suez Canal, side by side, unaware that the two, once good friends, had recently had a falling out. To everyone's surprise, this innocent faux pas resulted in a happy reconciliation.

The dinner table was decorated not with the usual floral centerpiece but with an arrangement of fruit. In an after-dinner toast, Matsukata commented, "As you can see, I purposely avoided having flowers on the dinner table this evening and instead have fruit. My observations during this trip to Europe have shown me the beautiful flowers of Western civilization. Most people become impressed only with the magnificence of these flowers, not giving thought to the good seeds that were planted earlier to bring forth such blossoms. This fruit contains the seeds of a glorious civilization, which I shall take back with me, and we shall then plant and cultivate them so that we too in time can have the grandeur and beauty you have today. I know the task will not be easy, and we shall not be able to accomplish our objectives overnight, but I look forward to the day when I can welcome you to my country, which will then have as beautiful a civilization as yours."

————•————

Matsukata sailed from Marseilles in December but did not reach Yokohama until March 1, 1879. During the year he had been away, he had kept in close touch with news at home by letters and sometimes by telegraph. In May 1878 he was stunned to learn of Okubo's assassination in revenge for Saigo's death. It happened as Okubo was getting out of his carriage on the way to his office. If Matsukata had been home, he too might have been killed, since it was customary for Okubo to pick him up each morning on the way to work. Okubo's death deprived Matsukata of his last close childhood friend. The power vacuum created by Okubo's death was filled by Ito, who, after Kido's death from illness in 1877, had become the leading member of the Choshu clique. Okuma, remaining as finance minister, was probably the second most influential official, and Matsukata took up his former post under him as chief of the Bureau of Industrial Promotion.

Matsukata had learned a great deal about modern agriculture and industry in Europe, and he immediately set about finding ways to apply his new knowledge. In the early 1860s, a silkworm blight in Europe had crippled silk production in France and Italy and opened a good market for Japanese silk and silkworm eggs, producing a favorable balance of trade for a few years. But Matsukata noted in Europe that Japanese silk was selling for about half the price of European silk because of its inferior quality—it was considered even worse than Chinese silk. The latter point was true also of Japanese tea, which was the second largest export item. Something needed to be done about the quality of both silk and tea. Matsukata encouraged unemployed samurai as well as farmers to go into sericulture. Since he had witnessed in Europe the effectiveness of competitive exhibits for improving quality, he introduced them to Japan. The first exhibit in Yokohama in 1879 resulted in a meeting of silk merchants interested in organizing a company to specialize in exporting silk directly abroad, a development that, as we shall see, had a bearing on my other grandfather's career.

Since foreign cotton yarn and cloth constituted over a third of

Japanese imports, Matsukata while in Manchester bought two hundred spindles for spinning cotton, and he also purchased machinery for weaving wool and linen. With this new machinery the government set up three additional pilot textile plants in or near Nagoya in central Japan. Not long afterward, however, private industry began to prove more efficient than the various government efforts in creating a modern textile industry. In 1881, Shibusawa Eiichi, a remarkable man of peasant origin who had managed before the Restoration to become a samurai in the service of the Tokugawa and then served in the Meiji government, founded the Osaka Spinning Mill. It was the first plant large enough in scale and with sufficient technical know-how to become truly competitive with Western factories.

During the Tokugawa period, Satsuma, with its control over the subtropical Ryukyu Islands, enjoyed a sugar monopoly in Japan, but the Satsuma supply of cane was inadequate to meet the rising demand for sugar, which had become a major import item. So, Matsukata purchased a sugar-beet refinery in Europe, since sugar beets could be grown much more widely in Japan than sugar cane. The pilot factory was also placed in Nagoya, but later the industry was transferred to the northern island of Hokkaido, where the climate was better suited to sugar beets. My father was to continue this aspect of my grandfather's activities, devoting his business career, beginning in the early 1900s, to the production of beet sugar in Hokkaido and cane sugar in Taiwan.

Matsukata was astonished to find out in Europe how backward the Japanese economy was in comparison with the leading Western nations. He noted that the per capita value of exports was 130 times higher in France than in Japan and was still higher in England and the United States. He realized that Japanese farmers would have to break with traditional practices and follow more scientific agricultural techniques. For this purpose he founded a bureau to collect and translate Western books on agriculture and animal breeding and to spread this knowledge among farmers.

With its meager exports, Japan was ill prepared to pay for the imports it required to modernize, and the government was forced to finance itself through the excessive issuance of paper currency. This resulted in the depreciation of paper money and the hoarding of solid currency. By 1877 the value of paper was only two-thirds the value of silver coins, and prices were half again as high as they had been a decade earlier. Accustomed to horrendous rates of inflation in more recent times, the contemporary reader may not be impressed by such figures—but in the nineteenth century they were shocking, and in any case Japan was facing an increasingly difficult problem in its balance of payments.

Since 1871 Matsukata had worked basically on economic and financial matters in the finance ministry under the supervision of Okuma and Ito and with men like Inoue and Shibusawa as his colleagues. The ministry had accomplished great things. It established a new national currency, a new tax system, and a new budget system and sponsored extensive industrial development. But there had been problems. The samurai revolts of the 1870s were a serious drain on government finances. It proved necessary to reduce the land tax from 3 to 2.5 percent in 1876, just before inflation began to become serious. The growing imbalance in foreign trade created a dangerous situation. The transmutation of all the traditional samurai stipends into lump payments of cash or government bonds, which was in effect by 1877, placed an even heavier burden on the treasury. The more affluent samurai were encouraged to pool their lump payments in order to form national banks. Matsukata had proposed in 1876 that the former daimyo, who had been generously paid off by the new government, should be allowed to form a national bank with their funds. The next year this idea was accepted in the founding of the Fifteenth Bank, which served as a source of funds to suppress the Satsuma Rebellion. Between 1877 and 1880 a total of 193 national banks were founded, with more than 70 percent of their capital coming from daimyo and samurai. The Fifteenth Bank towered above the others, with 17 million yen in capital compared to a total of 25 million yen for all the others combined. Many of the samurai banks fared poorly. These institutions, with their right to issue bank notes, also added to the inflation, and proved financially disastrous for their inexperienced samurai managers.

Okuma had been forced as early as 1873 to borrow 2.4 million pounds sterling from England at 7 percent interest. He was reluctant to borrow more the next year, when the government found itself in a double financial bind because of a samurai revolt in Hizen, his old domain, and an expedition sent against the aborigines of Taiwan. This overseas venture was ostensibly in retaliation for the deaths of some mariners from the Ryukyu Islands, but in reality it was to placate by a smaller venture those members of the government who had been advocating a war with Korea as a means of recouping the fortunes of the samurai. In a quandary, Okuma threatened to resign, but Matsukata managed to help solve the financial problem temporarily by having the beginning of the fiscal year shifted from January to June, a trick he had learned from his study of Western fiscal policies.

By the late 1870s, however, Japan was in even more serious financial straits, and Okuma had no answer to the problem except to advocate increased borrowing from abroad. In this he was supported by Parkes, the influential British minister we have met before. Parkes advised that an Englishman named Robertson be hired to form a central bank and float foreign loans, preferably from England. But many of the government leaders, including Matsukata, preferred a more conservative financial policy. Before long this difference of opinion with Okuma, combined with other more serious clashes over policy, resulted in the dismissal of Okuma from the government and the appointment of Matsukata as finance minister in his place.

Finance Minister

The shakeup of the Japanese government in 1881 centered on a dispute over the adoption of a constitution. For some time the leaders had been thinking about creating a constitution and an assembly to give the people a voice in the government. Such institutions seemed to contribute to the strength of the most advanced Western nations and should, it was thought, impress them favorably. There was also popular demand for a representative body, started by the former government leader Itagaki when he withdrew from the governing group in 1873. Vague promises about a constitution and national assembly had been made at various times, and in 1879 the emperor requested each of the councillors to submit his personal views on the matter.

Okuma's memorial, which was not handed in until 1881, made the radical suggestion that the complete British parliamentary system be adopted within two years. His colleagues were flabbergasted, and Ito in particular was outraged. Okuma had become his chief rival for top leadership, and Ito feared that this proposal was a stratagem Okuma was using to get control of the government by appealing to the populace. The cleavage between Okuma and his colleagues over financial policy also played a part. Another factor was Okuma's recent accusations of corruption leveled at Kuroda Kiyotaka, a former Satsuma samurai who was in charge of the Hokkaido Colonization Agency; Kuroda had been proposing the sale at extremely low prices of money-losing government properties on that northern frontier island. The support that the rising newspapers gave Okuma on this issue did not endear him to his colleagues, who thought this might lead to undisciplined mob rule.

Okuma had always been a semi-outsider in the government, which was dominated by men from Satsuma and Choshu. By this time he was the only high official from a different place, the domain of Hizen in northern Kyushu. He was by nature an iconoclast, fascinated by the civilization of the West, and little interested in the traditional martial and literary arts that Matsukata and the others had been raised on. He had learned English under Verbeck, founded an English school in Nagasaki, and served as the trade representative of his domain in that city. There he had come to the attention of the central government through Inoue of Choshu, who had gone to Nagasaki in 1868 as an aide to the first governor. In Tokyo, Okuma rose rapidly through sheer ability, but he always needed the backing of leaders from either Choshu or Satsuma. At first he was a protégé of Kido of Choshu and then of Okubo, after breaking with Kido in 1873. It is said that Kido and Okubo, having some doubts about Okuma's financial judgment, had purposely placed the more reliable and conservative Matsukata in the finance ministry to keep him in check. With both Kido and Okubo gone, Okuma now stood on a footing of equality with Ito but he stood alone.

The effect of Okuma's 1881 memorial was to consolidate the Satsuma and Choshu leaders against him. Matsukata, not yet a councillor, was urgently recalled from a trip to Hokkaido, where he and Okuma had been in attendance on the emperor. After a series of meetings at Kuroda's home in Tokyo, the Satsuma and Choshu group went out to Senju, a town north of Tokyo, to meet the emperor returning from Hokkaido and get his approval for the decision they had made. The next day, October 12, 1881, an imperial decree was issued promising a constitution and the convening of a national assembly by 1890. Kuroda's plan for the sale of the Hokkaido properties was dropped, and on October 21 Matsukata was appointed a councillor and concurrently finance minister in Okuma's place.

These moves marked a turning point in Japanese history. A cautious, somewhat conservative approach to representative government had been decided upon in place of Okuma's proposal for full and immediate parliamentary rule, and a financial policy more conservative than Okuma's was adopted. The leadership also contracted into a fairly clear-cut Satsuma-Choshu oligarchy, which was soon to be called by its enemies the "Sat-cho clique." In this group, which was later given the informal name of *genro* (elder statesmen), were three Choshu men (Ito, Inoue, and Yamagata Aritomo, the builder of the Imperial Japanese Army) and four men from Satsuma (Matsukata, Kuroda, Oyama Iwao, and Saigo Takamori's younger brother Tsugumichi). While Ito and Yamagata later emerged as the strongest members of the group, among the four Satsuma men Kuroda at first was considered the most prominent, though Matsukata soon took his place.

Meanwhile the opposition to the Sat-cho clique had also consolidated. Okuma, now out of office, immediately set about starting a popular political party and in 1882 founded a school, later known as Waseda University, where he hoped to train future leaders outside of the government university system. Itagaki, who had left the government in 1873, also renewed his political efforts, founding in 1881 the Liberal Party—a name still used by the ruling Liberal Democratic Party.

———•———

The four years following Matsukata's appointment as finance minister were the high point of his career, when he took the leadership in turning around Japan's financial system. Through a severe program of financial retrenchment, he halted inflation, balanced the budget, reversed the adverse balance of trade, and established a sound monetary policy. These years are known in history as the period of *Matsukata zaisei* (Matsukata's financial policies). Through them, in a sense, he completed the work of the 1868 Restoration by creating a firm economic foundation for the great political and social changes it had inaugurated.

Matsukata's sharp retrenchment of government spending and his tight money policy naturally brought severe economic distress to the people and certain risks for the nation. A deep economic depression settled over the country, causing countless bankruptcies. Matsukata was well aware of the situation. During these years, instead of taking his usual pre-breakfast walk in his garden, he would ride horseback through the business districts, observing sadly the increasing number of "To Let" signs on the doors of business establishments. The depression, it was feared, would lead to public disorder. Naturally there was strong opposition from the business community and the common people, and meetings condemning Matsukata's policies were held all over the country. Opposition even came from same of his colleagues, including Inoue, who favored Okuma's policy of seeking foreign loans.

But Matsukata had anticipated several years of turmoil before his policies would take effect. He had the strong backing of Ito and most of the other leaders, who knew him as a man of few words and one of iron will. He obtained their agreement to his austerity program in advance and their promise to back him up with military force in case of public rioting. He also took care to obtain the emperor's specific support. He sought an audience for this purpose in the company of the two leading court nobles, Iwakura and Sanjo, and obtained the emperor's promise that, no matter what troubles might arise, Matsukata's policies would not be abandoned midstream before they had a chance to take effect.

Matsukata also had some support from prominent private citizens. Among them was Yamamoto Kakuma, a man Matsukata always considered one of his economic mentors. Yamamoto had been a samurai of the Aizu domain, which had remained loyal to the Tokugawa, and was blinded in fighting for its cause in the battle near Kyoto in 1868, but went on to play a prominent role in the founding in that city of the Christian institution that became Doshisha University. Matsukata, when starting on his financial reforms, surprised everyone by going to Kyoto to consult with Yamamoto, instead of summoning him to his own office in Tokyo. Yamamoto, while approving of Matsukata's policies, specifically warned that he was courting assassination by pursuing them.

Even before becoming finance minister, Matsukata was a vehement opponent of Okuma's policy of borrowing from abroad, warning that this could "inflict on our country a wound so deep that it might take a hundred years to heal." He had in mind the semi-colonial status into which Egypt had fallen as the result of defaults in the high interest payments on foreign debts. One of Matsukata's first acts as finance minister was to call on Parkes to explain why he was unwilling to float a foreign loan and to outline his determination to restore public confidence in paper currency by accumulating specie through an increase in exports. He planned to stimulate exports by giving special discount rates for bills against export shipments, in what would now be called an export subsidy program. Parkes expressed doubt that Matsukata would succeed in these plans, but, before leaving Japan in 1885, he visited Matsukata to admit his error and offer congratulations.

As part of his plan to increase exports, Matsukata assigned to the Japanese consuls in New York, London, Lyons, and other cities the function of looking after exported goods not yet delivered or paid for. For this purpose, he took care to see that suitable men were selected for the posts. He also sought to increase the variety of Japanese exports, pushing the sale abroad of Japanese minerals and also rice, which had won recognition in Western markets for its quality. Today the export of such food and raw materials from Japan sounds strange, but at the time Japan was what we would now call a developing nation. As it turned out, rice and seaweed during the 1880s did join silk and tea as leading export items from Japan.

The other side of Matsukata's policy was a vigorous retrenchment of government spending. This involved the cutting of government budgets, the virtual elimination of expensive foreign advisers, and a thorough execution of the policy already embarked upon of selling off government-owned development projects and industrial plants not involved in strategic military production. These sales could only be made at comparatively low prices because the government properties were all in the red and money was very tight under Matsukata's deflationary policies. The financial drain on the government, was stopped, however. The private entrepreneurs who at this time acquired these government properties at bargain prices were able in many cases to make them financially profitable when Matsukata's policies began to take hold and when the boom in cotton spinning after Shibusawa's success with the Osaka mill brought improved economic conditions. Some of these businesses in time grew into the great family enterprises known as the *zaibatsu,* and it is often asserted that the Meiji government purposely created this group of big financiers and businessmen. But such thoughts were far from Matsukata's mind. He was simply cutting government expenses in every way possible.

Another aspect of Matsukata's effort to establish a sound financial system in Japan was banking reforms. In this he was at last able to carry out Say's recommendation for a central banking system to replace the diffuse American system, in which more than 150 national banks, all permitted to issue bank notes, had contributed to the inflation. In his memorial proposing a central bank he pointed out that, though "government should not take immediate concern in trade and business matters . . . financial matters which have direct bearing on the well being of the community at large . . . must be undertaken by the government . . . The establishment of a central bank is just such a policy."

The Bank of Japan, modeled as we have seen on the Central Bank of Belgium, was founded in October 1882, just a year after Matsukata took office. Three years later it was able to issue convertible ten-yen notes, to be followed later by convertible notes of one hundred yen and five yen. Recognizing his debt to Say for this banking system and for much else in the hard money policies he had been following, Matsukata not only wrote Say expressing his gratitude but in 1883 had the First Class Order of the Rising Sun conferred on him by the emperor. It was the highest civilian decoration in Japan, the same one that had been conferred on Matsukata himself in 1881.

By 1885 Matsukata's reforms had clearly succeeded. There had been much economic suffering at first, but no great civil disturbances; wholesale prices had declined by 25 percent and the price of rice by half; Japan's export balance had shifted from a deficit of 8.2 million yen in 1880 to a surplus of 7.7 million yen in 1885, the highest so far in its history; the country had adequate specie reserves; and paper currency, which had fallen to a low of 58 percent of the value of silver coins, had returned to equality. Japan was able to allow full convertibility of paper money in January 1886 and to go officially on the silver standard. Best of all, business was booming.

Matsukata had reason to feel satisfied with his accomplishments. He was showered with plaudits, and the press throughout the world commented favorably on his achievements. American Minister John A. Bingham, in a laudatory letter in 1885, compared him to Alexander Hamilton. The emperor personally expressed his gratitude in 1886 and gave Matsukata a special gift of 5000 yen. Two years earlier, when Ito created a new nobility in preparation for the establishment of a house of peers in the promised national assembly, Matsukata together with Ito and a few other of the former samurai leaders had been given the third highest rank of count. The two higher ranks were still reserved for the more prominent of the former daimyo and high court nobles.

———•———

While Matsukata had been engaged in his financial reforms, Ito had been busy preparing for the constitution and national assembly promised in 1881. He had gone on an eighteen-month trip to Europe to study constitutions, concentrating on the conservative German and Austrian systems and consulting with the leading German constitutional authority, Rudolph Gneist. During this period Ito kept up an active correspondence with Matsukata, informing him of his thoughts and findings and receiving in return reports on financial and political developments in Japan. Neither showed much regard for the ousted Okuma. Ito wrote of him, "How pathetic is the movement of Mr. Reformist . . . I can assure you no form of government like the parliamentary government he envisages . . . will ever be established; it is too unsuited to our country."

Ito was scornful of the republican government of the French, writing that their "minds have been poisoned by the mistaken views of Rousseau," and even of the British he wrote, "In the matter of royalty alone, there is a heaven and earth difference between the British and us, and their government could never be applicable to our people." He much preferred Gneist's advice to keep the national assembly weak and not give it full financial power. He quoted Kaiser Wilhelm I as saying to him, "For the sake of the emperor, I do not rejoice in the opening of a national assembly in your country."

Though personally well received, Ito was shocked to discover the contempt Europeans had for Asians. He wrote Matsukata, "Since arriving in Europe I have been taking great pains to discern the feelings Europeans harbor toward us, and I am coming to the conclusion that, from the point of view of both feeling and reason, there is more bad feeling than good toward us . . . As individuals, when it does not concern their interests, they seem to be kind and cordial, but it goes little beyond that . . . Should something occur between the Occident and the Orient, all the countries of Europe will consolidate against us in an attempt to override and isolate Japan. The cause lies in differences in race and religion. The morality of Europe is founded on Christianity, and all feel like brothers. They have no intention of sharing their civilization and morality with those of other religions." The German kaiser told Ito that, without Christianity, Japan would never become a truly civilized land. Ito was also distressed at the rapid colonial expansion of the European nations in the Middle East, Indochina, and even in China itself and wrote Matsukata that for Japan's security "complete military preparations must be accomplished during peace time against any eventualities."

Despite his indignation, which he kept well concealed from the Europeans, Ito pushed ahead with his constitutional studies. After returning to Japan, he started to create and experiment with institutions he expected to make part of the constitutional system. In 1884 he set up a new peerage made up of the old court nobles, the former daimyo, and the samurai leaders of the new government. As we have seen, he and Matsukata became counts. In December 1885 Ito instituted a cabinet system on the German model. The cabinet, made up of a prime minister and the heads of the nine government ministries, became, under the symbolic sovereignty of the emperor, the supreme organ of government, replacing the old Dajokan, which had been headed by figurehead personages drawn mostly from among the court nobles and former daimyo. Ito himself became the first prime minister, with Matsukata a member of the cabinet in his continuing role as finance minister. The first cabinet had four men each from Choshu and Satsuma, establishing the precedent for a balance between the two groups, and there were in addition two "neutrals," who were from the domain of Tosa and the old Tokugawa administration.

In the same month of December 1885, civil-service regulations, again on the German model, were adopted and became the basis for the development of the modern Japanese bureaucracy. In 1888 a Privy Council was established, though without clearly defined duties. Work was also started on drafting the constitution itself. Ito again took the lead, but several of his colleagues assumed reponsibility for sections of the constitution in their particular areas of competence and for supplementary legislation. Matsukata naturally took over all financial, tax, and budgetary matters. Specifically he supervised the drafting of chapter 6 of the constitution on finance, consisting of articles 62 through 72, and the Laws of Finance that supplemented this section.

Finally on February 11, 1889, the constitution was promulgated in a magnificent ceremony in the presence of the emperor and empress. They and all the dignitaries attending were dressed in formal Western style, with the one exception of Hisamitsu, Matsukata's former lord who, now called Prince Shimazu, had become a notorious conservative. The constitution was signed by the emperor and his ministers of state. Matsukata signed twice, as finance minister and also as acting home minister in the absence of Yamagata, who was in Europe studying local government.

Despite Ito's disillusionment with the attitude of Westerners, he and the others realized that the approval of the West was essential if Japan were to rid itself of the unequal treaties and gain legal equality. In fact, one of the major reasons for having a constitution was to win Western respect. Ito and Foreign Minister Inoue also felt that the imitation of Western social customs would help. Ever since the Restoration there had been a craze for Western things among many Japanese, and with official sponsorship this craze reached a peak in the early 1880s. The symbol of the age was the Rokumeikan, or Pavilion of the Deer's Cry, a two-story brick building in Italian style on the old site of the Satsuma daimyo's residence in Hibiya. Completed in 1883, it had rooms for card playing and billiards, and there were frequent balls and dancing every Sunday starting in the summer of 1884.

The whole Rokumeikan experiment did not last long and in retrospect seems almost ludicrous. A grand masquerade ball in 1887, at which Ito, Inoue, and other dignitaries appeared in fancy dress, proved to be the last straw. Such Western ways ran counter to the basic concepts and customs of the Japanese leaders themselves, and there was widespread popular disapproval of such goings on. Wives had no social life outside of their families, as the terms for wife implied: *kanai* for one's own wife or *okusama* for another man's wife both mean "person of the interior." For Japanese who went abroad for the first time, perhaps the greatest cultural shock was to find women participating in society with men. In samurai society the sexes had been completely segregated, and there were no social occasions that included respectable women. Social dancing seemed the strangest of all the Western customs. As one member of the first Tokugawa mission to the United States in 1860 noted in his diary, "It was, of course, with no small wonder that we witnessed this extraordinary sight of men and bare shouldered women hopping around the floor, arm in arm, and our wonder at the strange performance became so great that we began to doubt if we were not on another planet."*

* *The First Japanese Embassy to the United States of America* (Tokyo: American-Japan Society, 1920), p. 43.

I find it hard to think of my grandfather and grandmother, he dressed in Western formal evening attire, she in high Victorian decolletage, arriving at the Rokumeikan by carriage with liveried footmen and dancing the evening away. The picture just does not fit the two venerable, sober, and very Japanese figures I knew as a small child, and it is even harder to visualize after having immersed myself in the accounts of their upbringing. But it all happened. My grandmother and the wives of other government leaders did abandon the kimono for the latest Western styles, gathered at the Rokumeikan to learn Western social dancing from a German teacher, and then tried to put their new skills into practice in the arms of Western diplomats at regularly scheduled Rokumeikan balls.

Following the 1887 fancy-dress ball, there was revulsion against close mimicry of Western ways, but the modernization of technology and society continued. The elite Tokyo club, modeled after a Western men's club and designed for the social mixing of Japanese and European men, fared better than the Rokumeikan and is still in existence. The Japanese were elated when they were admitted into the International Red Cross in 1886. It seemed a sign that they were being accepted into the international community. There had, in fact, been a debate in the Red Cross as to whether non-Western countries should receive its assistance. The wives of the Japanese government leaders had already organized a Volunteer Lady Nurses' Association under the honorary chairmanship of the empress. My grandmother was one of the prime movers and served as executive secretary.

Bazaars were held at the Rokumeikan to raise funds for the support of charity hospitals. Commenting on such an event, Clara Whitney, the young daughter of an American teacher, wrote in her diary in 1884, "The bazaar came off successfully and the energetic Japanese ladies took a net amount of 10,000 yen at the sale of their things. I went to the Rokumeikan . . . and was much pleased at the success of the novel enterprise . . . The prices were, of course, very ridiculously high and many complained of being made dupes of, but it was really a very pleasing affair all around."* The Japanese Red Cross

---

* Clara A. N. Whitney, *Clara's Diary: An American Girl in Meiji Japan,* (Tokyo: Kodansha International, 1978), pp. 331-332.

proved itself an efficient organization of lasting importance, and it became a tradition for upper-class ladies to do volunteer work.

My grandfather took great interest in the Japanese Red Cross, and he served as its president from 1903 for ten years, after retiring from active participation in the government. During the Russo-Japanese War the Red Cross was very active; Japanese women proved their competence as nurses and volunteers; and several thousand of them ministered to over a million Japanese and Russian wounded soldiers and prisoners. For the assistance given the Russians, the tsar in 1909 awarded a Red Cross decoration to my grandfather.

———— • ————

One clear sign of the changing times was the greater ease with which the emperor, once secluded in his Kyoto palace, now moved about among his people. Starting with a visit to Prime Minister Ito's residence in 1885, the emperor and empress began making visits from time to time to the homes of the leading ministers, honoring Matsukata, Yamagata, and Kuroda in this way in 1887. These imperial visits were grand occasions. The emperor would be accompanied by a retinue of imperial princes, chamberlains, and the minister of the imperial household and his higher subordinates. The host would provide elaborate entertainment as well as a sumptuous dinner, and the emperor would give him in return a set of silver sake cups with the imperial crest, a larger gift of an art object, and a thousand yen.

When the emperor and empress visited Matsukata's residence on a beautiful autumn day in 1887, they first were ushered into the large living room in the Western wing of the house, where eleven of my grandfather's children were lined up to greet their majesties, the girls in kimono and the boys in their natty Peers School uniform of navy blue with red piping. My four oldest uncles were away at school in Europe or the United States, but my father was present, only a first-grader. Each child was given a package of red and white sugar-coated bean cakes in the shape of the imperial crest. The tradition and form of these cakes never changed. I remember receiving them in my childhood and at the time of the state funeral for my grandfather in 1924, and, when my husband and I were at the American embassy, we got them when we attended the annual palace reception on New Year's Day.

During the afternoon of the emperor's visit in 1887, he strolled through the garden and was taken out on the pond in a small boat to see the giant golden carp. Later he watched horsemen riding with traditional Japanese saddles on the horsetrack my grandfather had laid out at one end of the estate. The emperor himself was an avid horseman and was said to ride two days out of three. Then he and the empress watched entertainers brought from Kagoshima play Satsuma musical instruments and perform Satsuma dances. After a Western-style banquet in the large dining room, the imperial couple returned to the palace at 9:30, a late hour in Japan at that time.

Except for his financial reforms, what is probably best remembered by Japanese about my grandfather is an incident that took place during the emperor's visit. Seeing eleven of my grandfather's children and knowing there were more, the emperor asked him how many children he had. My embarrassed grandfather asked for a day to look into the matter. There was reason for his hesitation. At least one child had died in infancy and another one or two, who were the children of concubines, were probably not living at home then.

Concubinage had been an established practice among the families of the rich during the Tokugawa period, but the new legal system, which was still being developed in the 1880s, did not give it official recognition. Concubines were considered desirable by those who could afford them to ensure the continuation of the family line without resorting to adoption. Mothers were looked on as little more than human incubators. A common saying was, "The womb is a borrowed thing." Concubines also solved the eternal problem of the wandering eye of the aging male. Another solution was provided by geisha and women of lesser repute in the so-called amusement quarters of the cities. Several of the Meiji leaders were notable patrons of these quarters. As Ito wrote in a poem, "Asleep with one's head in the lap of a beauty, one awakens at dawn to resume the mantle of empire."* Prominent men frequently married geisha, as did Kido and Katsura, but there was a great difference between even the higher-ranking geisha and concubines. Geisha normally came from impoverished

* Albert M. Craig, "Kido Kōin and Okubo Toshimichi: A Psychohistorical Analysis," in Albert M. Craig and Donald H. Shively, eds., *Personality in Japanese History* (Berkeley: University of California Press, 1970), p. 264.

families, which sold them into establishments where they were trained to become professional entertainers. Concubines, on the other hand, were usually from respectable families, willing to let their daughters assume this secondary role in a more prominent family.

My grandfather differed from other Meiji leaders in two ways. One was that he had a large family. Masako bore him eleven children, eight boys and three girls, ten of whom survived infancy. It was not until after their birth, when he was in his late forties and was finance minister, that he started taking concubines. The other difference was that he recognized the eight offspring of his three successive concubines as his full legal children. The children of the first two concubines were brought into the family when they were a few years old and were raised by Masako, who treated them as if they were her own. They felt no sense of distinction from the other children and called Masako by the Satsuma term for mother, *okakasama*. The children of the last concubine, born when Masako felt herself too old to raise them, were put in the care of other members of the family, but they enjoyed the same legal position as the others.

All three of Matsukata's concubines came from the Kansai area around Kyoto. Whether he felt it more discreet to have them away from Tokyo is a point of conjecture. Little is known about the first concubine. None of my relatives remembers her name, and the only information about her I could get was that she was a very gentle, refined person who entered a monastery and became a Buddhist nun after she gave birth to a daughter and two sons, one of whom was my father. From the elegant looks of her daughter, one can easily imagine that she was beautiful. The second concubine, Shizu, also had two sons and a daughter. One of the sons was sent to America to study at the Naval Academy in Annapolis, but after several years there, he contracted influenza in 1906 and died. Shizu herself was subsequently adopted into a prosperous merchant family in the Kansai area and, as their daughter, was married to an Osaka industrialist. The third concubine, Kita, was a daughter of a Kyoto family that owned a store selling accessories for the ancient court dances, *Bugaku*. Kita also had two sons and a daughter, and one of her sons became heir to the Matsukata family. Kita remained with my grandfather as his housekeeper at his villa in Kamakura, a seaside resort near Tokyo. In order to observe the proprieties, Masako never permitted her to come to the

main residence in Tokyo or to travel in the same train as my grandfather. She always followed on the next train.

The story about my grandfather's not knowing the number of his
children is usually told as an amusing anecdote, but it actually had a
deeper significance. The emperor was surprised to see so many strong,
vigorous children; he himself had fathered twenty, but most of them
had died at birth or shortly thereafter. Even those who had survived
were frail and not as healthy looking as my grandfather's sturdy lot.
This explains why my grandfather wished to check his records to see
how many of his own children had died. As a result of this incident,
the emperor was persuaded to shift from oldfashioned Japanese doctors
to physicians who had been trained in Germany or England. Matsukata's longtime doctor, Takaki Kenkan, was one of the early
foreign-trained physicians. He was an old friend of the family, having
come from Satsuma, and he was not only the family doctor but also
advised them on diet. He taught them that barley with a small
amount of rice was a much more healthful staple than the polished
white rice Japanese love to eat. He also advised the family to eat a lot
of meat. This diet probably accounted in part for the fact that most of
Matsukata's children lived into their eighties—the last one died in
1978—while few of his colleagues' children even reached maturity. In
any case, Takaki became famous as the chief surgeon of the Imperial
Japanese Navy who eliminated beriberi through diet.

———— • ————

When Matsukata moved his family to Tokyo following the destruction of their home in Kagoshima in the Satsuma Rebellion of
1877, he settled them in small house on an extensive piece of property
of about twenty-two acres at Sendaizaka in Azabu ward (formerly
belonging to the Nabeshima domain). On this land, then known as
Matsukata-yama, or Matsukata Hill, he carried out numerous agricultural experiments. In the 1930s the property was broken up into
modern housing lots and sold, except for an area where one of my
uncles had his residence (after World War II it became the headquarters of the South Korean mission in Japan).

Not long after moving his family to Tokyo, Matsukata established a new residence across the valley on a hill in Mita in Shiba ward.
The house was large enough to accommodate his seven boys and three

girls, though the boys actually had a separate little house of their own. The property in Mita had been the residence of Matsudaira Sadanobu, a prominent daimyo who carried through a great financial reform of the Tokugawa government between 1786 and 1793, thus having been in a sense my grandfather's most recent predecessor as a successful financial reformer for the nation. When Matsukata decided to buy the property, his friends could not understand why he would want such an overgrown, unkempt place. It had, though, a famous garden laid out in the seventeenth century by the Buddhist monk Takuwan, who is better known today for having bequeathed his name to a still popular type of pickle. It was in this garden that the famous forty-seven ronin, whose story Matsukata had learned in his youth, had committed suicide in 1703. Their venerated graves are located in the grounds of a nearby temple. Matsudaira Sadanobu's residence was no longer standing, but the garden had a small nine-story pagoda and paths that wound through man-made hills, all centering on a beautiful pond. When Matsukata restored this garden to its original design, it became one of the most famous private beauty spots in Tokyo. I still have a clear picture in my mind of the times when, as a youngster, I would visit my grandparents and see the well-kept lawns sloping down to the pond and the bronze storks standing on one leg along its edge.

The Japanese house Matsukata built had many large straw-matted rooms with sliding doors. For big family gatherings, some of these doors could be taken out to make one impressively large room overlooking the garden. In the spring and summer the house was comfortable, but in winter it was freezing cold, with no central heating. Each person was provided with a charcoal brazier by which to warm his hands. The roadway from the original wooden gate led to this part of the house, where shoes and wooden clogs were removed before entering.

Matsukata also built a Western-style wing made of brick especially to receive the emperor and empress when they visited him in 1887. By then the imperial family lived in Western style, and it seemed more appropriate to receive them in a manner they were accustomed to. The builder of the Western wing was a brilliant young British architect, Josiah Conder (1852–1920), who designed two landmarks that typified the age—the famous Rokumeikan hall in 1883 and the blocks of Victorian red-brick buildings for the Mitsubishi Company in the Marunouchi district of Tokyo, which were not torn down until 1970.

The first floor of the Western wing of Matsukata's house, which had a large parlor, living room, and dining room, was used for entertaining foreign visitors, and the second story had a study and a Japanese-style room for Matsukata's personal use. The Western part of the house was approached through a new main gate of iron and a winding driveway leading up to an impressive porte-cochere, where carriages and later automobiles could discharge their passengers elegantly and without fear of the weather. Everything about this structure was Victorian. The rooms were enormous, with high ceilings and heavy drapes that made them dark and cold-looking even at noon. They were filled with solid heavy furniture, all imported from England. When my uncle, who was my grandfather's heir, moved out of the house to a smaller residence, following the failure in 1927 of the Fifteenth Bank of which he was the president, my parents were given the immense oak dining-room table, because they were the only branch of the family living in Western style and with enough members to make good use of it. The house was destroyed in the American air raids of March 1945, but the Italian embassy today occupies its old site.

Matsukata left the running of his large Mita residence entirely to Masako. Most of his adult life he devoted practically all his waking hours to affairs of state, leaving little time for his home or family. As he rose in importance in the government, he increasingly became a public man, appearing always as a stately gentleman in Western clothes, which he wore with great dignity. In time he became entirely comfortable in full Western evening dress or his official uniform, which had a handsome gold-braided coat. Very few people, not even his colleagues in official life, had the opportunity to know the private man. Even his sons and daughters looked on him with awe of a sort due more a public figure than a father. This Matsukata regretted, and once, when my mother talked to him about a problem my father was having, he remarked that he wished his sons would discuss their problems with him rather than merely report some good news. Matsukata was his complete private self only with Masako and perhaps one or two close secretaries, and then only after he returned home, took off his Western clothes, donned his kimono, and relaxed comfortably on the tatami floor. In his own house he lived a simple life, as his strict samurai upbringing had accustomed him to.

As a proper wife of a samurai, Masako took complete control not only of running the large household but also of caring for the children. His friends often spoke of Matsukata as the finance minister of Japan and Masako as the finance minister of the Matsukata family. Masako was a remarkable person in her own right. She was a small woman, barely reaching the shoulder of her five-foot six-inch husband, and was quite plump, at least in later life. As will be recalled, she was the eldest daughter of one of the highest-ranking samurai of Satsuma. Married by her father to the still quite lowly Matsukata, she had accepted her reduced circumstances and looked after the family finances with meticulous care. Both she and her husband throughout their lives adhered to samurai values and maintained a personally austere life style, keeping careful records of even the smallest expenditures. Matsukata insisted that all bills should be paid daily and in cash and that the books should be balanced every night. My mother remembers that, no matter how late it was, Masako never retired until the account books were in order and had been tallied with the cash kept in an old wooden box in her room.

Overseeing the running of the Mita establishment was no small task. Besides the main residence, there was a dormitory for the boys and a house for the men servants. In addition to the large family, there were several dozen servants—almost always twenty maids, mostly country girls, two cooks, one each for Japanese and Western cuisine, and their assistants, three gardeners, two men to cut firewood, rickshaw pullers, coachmen, and the like. There were also always several *shosei* (student assistants), promising young men whom Matsukata was helping with their education. Mostly students at the nearby Keio Gijuku school, the forerunner of the modern Keio University, they would answer the door, run errands, and perform other odd jobs. Several of them grew up to become prominent men and lifelong associates and friends of my father and his brothers. In fact, they almost felt themselves to be members of the family.

Despite all the work of running this large household, Masako found time to be a companion to her husband, taking daily morning walks with him. They would rise between 4:30 and 5:00 on summer

107

mornings and around 6:00 in the winter. Both loved nature and enjoyed walking together in their garden in Tokyo, in the woods on their Nasuno estate north of Tokyo, or along the beach at their seaside summer homes. Both loved flowers, and, after the children were grown, Masako built a large greenhouse on the horsetrack and raised a great variety of flowers. They both had their artistic pastimes as well. Masako liked to paint water colors in the Japanese style, some of which she mounted on delicately embroidered silk backgrounds she herself made. I have already mentioned that my grandfather was proud of his calligraphy and that, under the influence of the priest Gogaku in Hita, had become interested in art. He built up a large collection of Japanese paintings, said to have been second only to that of Inoue among the elder statesmen. His tastes were broad, ranging from the medieval landscapist Sesshu (1420–1506) to the more recent Okyo (1733–1795), who showed the strong influence of Western perspective. Gogaku had told Matsukata that the hereditary Kano painters were not sufficiently appreciated and urged him to acquire paintings of this school. A pair of six-paneled screens bearing the inscription that they were painted by Kano Tanyu, the greatest master of his day, in the sixty-ninth year of his life, which was 1670, was given to my parents at the time of their marriage and eventually came to my husband and me.

Masako created a pleasant hospitable atmosphere throughout the household. The servants adored her for her understanding and kind treatment, though she was very strict and demanded the best of each of them. Foreign guests were often invited to dinner, and, although Masako did not speak English, she made them feel at home. She always remembered kindnesses and warmly thanked senders even for the most trifling gifts.

For all her outstanding qualities as a household manager and wife, Masako is best remembered as having been a wonderful mother. She had been raised in the strict samurai code of regarding jealousy as the worst of all feminine vices, and she lavished on the children of her husband's concubines the same love and care she gave her own children. I cannot remember my father or any of the other children of the concubines ever having spoken of her except with the greatest respect and affection. Yet she was a strict mother, though she exercised her discipline in a gentle way, never scolding or showing anger. In accor-

Hiroshige's woodblock print of Nihonbashi, the "Bridge of Japan," at the start of the Tokaido highway in Edo

Payment of indemnity to the British after the killing of Richardson, 1863. From Ishin to Satsuma

The daimyo of Satsuma, Shimazu Nariakira, makes his own camera, 1854. From Ishin to Satsuma

Samurai outside Shimazu's palace, Edo, 1867

*Matsukata at age
forty-eight, 1882*

Matsukata Masako, seated third from left, with her Red Cross volunteers, 1887

The Matsukatas at their Nasuno estate, c. 1920

The Matsukata residence in Tokyo

Golden Wedding anniversary, 1910

Prince Matsukata

Masako dressed for Hirohito's coronation, 1912

The last three genro, 1920:
Saionji Kimmochi,
Matsukata (age eighty-six),
Yamagata Aritomo

Matsukata and his eldest
son, Iwao, 1922

dance with samurai custom, she was harder on the girls than on the boys. She had them perform menial jobs, such as polishing the floors of the long wooden hallways with bags of rice bran or cleaning out toilets, all to help prepare them to become good housewives.

The size of the family was a help in a way because the children could play together and the older ones took care of the younger. Although by this time the traditional samurai concept of keeping brothers and sisters separate had been abandoned, the boys enjoyed having their own quarters, where they could rough-house as well as study. All the children particularly enjoyed summers at Tomioka on the beach south of Tokyo, studying in the mornings and swimming and playing in the afternoons. The daily *o-sanji,* or three-o'clock tea with cakes and candies, was an especially happy memory. All the members of the family, including my grandfather and grandmother, definitely had a sweet tooth, though my grandfather was unusual in not having much of a taste for tobacco or sake and other alcoholic beverages.

Some of the daughters after marrying found their lives hard to bear because of difficult mothers-in-law and the problem of being accepted in their new households by longtime servants; they often returned in tears to Masako. Although she comforted them, she sent them back with the admonition that it was up to them to make an effort to win acceptance and respect in their new families.

Masako joined her husband in insisting that their sons treat their wives with respect. My mother remembered once when after a family gathering one of the boys climbed into his carriage before his wife, Masako pulled him out and insisted that his wife enter first. All of Matsukata's children loved Masako dearly and when possible came to visit her weekly throughout her life. Not surprisingly, they all felt much closer to her than to their father. Affairs of state naturally took him away a great deal, and, as is still common among urban Japanese families, the mother was very much the center of the family.

———— • ————

The feelings generated by the Rokumeikan fancy-dress ball of 1887 and the imitation of Western social customs was only part of a general anti-Western mood that was setting in at that time in Japan. As one newspaper editorial cynically observed, "Who does the government think most important—the foreigners in the country or the Japanese? It seems that everything is done for the benefit of the foreigners." Underlying this reaction was frustration over the failure to persuade the Western powers to relinquish the unequal treaties dating from Tokugawa times. Inoue as the foreign minister took responsibility for this failure and resigned, but there was rising dissatisfaction with Ito's leadership as prime minister. In December 1887 the government sought to strengthen its position by creating more stringent controls over the press and publications and by issuing a severe Peace Preservation Regulation, limiting political agitation and giving the authorities the power to send troublemakers away from the capital—a weapon they immediately used on several hundred political activists.

Kuroda, who had been somewhat discredited in 1881 by the scandal over the sale of the properties of the Hokkaido Colonization Agency, returned to a place in the cabinet and did not hide his desire to succeed Ito as prime minister, replacing his Choshu government with a Satsuma one. For the ticklish post of foreign minister, he wanted Okuma, who had a large popular following. Since Okuma had been thrown out of the government in 1881 in part because of his condemnation of Kuroda, it was no easy matter to persuade him to serve under Kuroda. Much of the negotiations was carried on at *machiai,* the houses where geisha met with their patrons. This gave rise to the characterization of the politics of the time as "machiai politics."

Kuroda finally succeeded Ito as prime minister on the last day of April 1888, with Okuma as his foreign minister, but the new cabinet had little success. Okuma early in 1889 concluded a treaty with the British, providing for mixed courts that would include foreign judges to sit on cases involving foreigners. This treaty also would permit Westerners for the first time to own land outside the prescribed foreign settlements. When the treaty was published by *The Times* of London, there was an uproar of protest in Japan over these humiliating halfway measures for ending the extraterritorial privileges of foreigners. The cabinet too was divided over them, and Ito, removed from active politics by having been made president of the Privy Council, resigned this post in order to fight the new treaty. In this he had Matsukata's backing.

Both sides were eager to win the support of Yamagata, who was just then returning from his protracted study trip abroad. Matsukata and a few others took a small boat out to meet Yamagata's ship the night before it docked in order to explain the situation. A series of meetings in the emperor's presence followed, and Yamagata finally came down on the side of the opponents of Okuma's treaty. The intensity of public feeling on the issue was revealed when an extremist threw a bomb at Okuma's carriage as he was returning from the last of these meetings, shattering one of his legs, which had to be amputated. Earlier the same year, a fanatical Shinto priest had assassinated Minister of Education Mori, who earlier had been the first Japanese minister in Washington.

The rejection of Okuma's foreign policy and treaty and the attack on his life led to Kuroda's resignation as prime minister. Yamagata was persuaded to take his place in December 1889, despite his stated reluctance as "merely a soldier" with little knowledge of politics or diplomacy. As in the Kuroda cabinet, Matsukata continued as finance minister, but he and his colleagues soon faced new problems that were to make Japanese politics and especially the post of finance minister quite different from what it had been. In keeping with the new constitution, a national parliament, or Diet as the Japanese call it in English, was elected on July 1, 1890, and a favorable vote by both of its houses was henceforth required to pass new tax laws or adopt a budget. Ito and his assistants in drawing up the constitution had been persuaded by German political theorists that they could keep the purse strings out of the hands of the Diet by stipulating that, if it failed to adopt a budget, last year's budget would continue in effect. But there was a flaw in this reasoning. In a rapidly growing economy, last year's budget was never enough.

While the House of Peers, made up as it was largely of conservative noblemen and a few imperial appointees, could normally be counted on to support the cabinet, the three hundred members of the House of Representatives were a different matter. Although the electorate at this time was limited to a mere 460,000 higher taxpayers out of a population of some 42 million people and therefore was decidedly conservative by modern standards, it leaned more to the Liberal Party of Itagaki or to Okuma than to the Sat-cho clique in control of the cabinet. Representing the major taxpayers, it was also quite understandably interested in low taxes and therefore low budgets.

When Matsukata presented the budget to the Diet for the first time, the legislators promptly proceeded to slash it by 8.8 million yen, which was a trifle over 10 percent. The government leaders were appalled. Several wished to strike back by dissolving the Diet and starting over again with new elections, which would drain the finances of the politicians and teach them a lesson. A few, including Kuroda, even argued for dropping the whole experiment of a national assembly as having been a mistake. But Yamagata, Matsukata, and Ito refused to admit defeat. They feared the scorn of the Western powers if Japan should so obviously fail in its first try at representative government on a national scale. (Local elected assemblies with very limited powers had been in existence for a decade.) Compromise seemed the only solution, and after long negotiations with Itagaki and his supporters, a budget reduced by 6.3 million yen was finally accepted.

Yamagata soon wearied of dealing with the obstreperous Diet and resigned, proposing Inoue or Ito as his successor. Inoue flatly refused, and Ito suggested it was Satsuma's turn to provide the prime minister. Matsukata and Saigo's younger brother Tsugumichi were both proposed, and, after each had modestly declined, the choice finally went to Matsukata, who became prime minister on May 6, 1891, at the age of fifty-six. This passing of the position of prime minister back and forth between Choshu and Satsuma men—called in Japanese *tarai-mawashi* (passing the bucket)—was the rule for the first seven prime ministerships. The position had been occupied in turn by Ito of Choshu, Kuroda of Satsuma, Yamagata of Choshu, and now Matsukata of Satsuma. After Matsukata resigned in August 1892, Ito and he passed the post back and forth three more times until 1898.

National Leader

Matsukata's 1891 cabinet differed from earlier ones in that the other elder statesmen did not join it but left the troublesome cabinet posts to their younger, more energetic protégés. But Matsukata had persuaded the genro to promise behind-the-scenes support. Thus the cabinet came to be known as the *kuromaku* or wire-pulling cabinet, *kuromaku* being the name for the black-hooded stagehands or puppeteers of the Japanese theater who manipulate the puppets or props in supposed invisibility. It was also called the "natural-calamity cabinet" because it encountered a series of catastrophes.

Only five days after Matsukata took office, a near calamity, though not a natural one, occurred. While Matsukata was announcing the formation of his cabinet to the emperor, a telegram arrived reporting an attempt in Kyoto to assassinate Nicholas, heir to the Russian throne. He later became Nicholas II, whose execution in 1918 brought an end to the line of tsars. Nicholas, who with his cousin Prince George of Greece was in Japan on the last leg of a grand sightseeing tour of Asia, was riding in a rickshaw when a policeman, after saluting him, drew his sword and attacked him. Nicholas managed to scramble out of the vehicle, and his assailant was wrestled down by the rickshaw men.

Nicholas escaped with only some cuts about the neck, but the Japanese government was humiliated by the incident and feared serious diplomatic consequences, if not worse. An imperial prince, accompanied by our old family friend Takaki and another doctor, were sent at once to Kyoto to attend the patient. The emperor himself followed the next day, but by then Nicholas had boarded a Russian warship, canceling his intended visit to Tokyo. The emperor, against the advice of his attendants, accepted Nicholas' invitation to lunch with him aboard ship, but the question remained of how to deal with the would-be assassin.

According to Japanese law, an unsuccessful attack on a member of the imperial family brought the death penalty but only indefinite imprisonment if some other person were attacked. Matsukata wished to have the death penalty applied to appease Russian feelings. He argued, "There is no reason why laws are greater than a nation. When the very existence of a nation is at stake, one cannot cling to the letter of the law." But Kojima, the president of the Supreme Court, showed that he had learned the Western concepts of law and adamantly refused to alter the verdict. Some high officials suggested that the way out of this impasse was to hire an assassin to do away with the culprit, but this oldfashioned remedy was not adopted. The Russians were satisfied when the trial revealed that the attack had been the act of a single fanatic without accomplices, and Kojima's steadfast adherence to the law won respect for the Japanese judicial system.

A real natural calamity befell Japan later in the year, on October 28. This was a great earthquake centering on Gifu prefecture a little east of Kyoto. The toll of people killed or injured was 25,248. Matsukata went to the scene three days later to inspect the damage and oversee relief measures. Dealing with the Diet, however, proved to be the most serious problem. Despite his financial acumen, Matsukata was no politician like Ito. Six years his junior, Ito adapted quickly to the problems of working with an elected assembly, but Matsukata had no stomach for parliamentary maneuverings and remained true to the original concept of the framers of the constitution that the members of the cabinet should stay above Diet politics and act as the emperor's faithful servants. Where Ito could treat the emperor quite informally and more as an equal, Matsukata showed the influence of his more thorough samurai upbringing in his awe for the emperor and his unquestioning loyalty to imperial wishes. Where Ito learned to bargain with the Diet, Matsukata viewed with repugnance the development of political parties and the eagerness of the lower house of the Diet to challenge the authority of the emperor's ministers. The intransigence of the politicians, he felt, threatened the sovereignty of the emperor. In short, he was no champion of democracy but a transitional figure who found it difficult to adapt the feudal concepts of his youth to emerging trends toward parliamentary government.

No one doubted that the second session of the Diet, which Matsukata now faced as prime minister, would be even stormier than the first and would probably end in dissolution. Yamagata, who shared Matsukata's views, told him that he had learned from a study of Western historical precedents that dissolutions were frequent in the early days of a parliament's existence. He said that it would probably take two such dissolutions to force the parties to knuckle under and that, if they got by with only one, they would be lucky. As it turned out, elder statesmen were to dissolve the Diet five times before they themselves in 1901 gave up the unpleasant job of facing it as prime ministers.

Unfortunately for Matsukata, his cabinet was disunited. Mutsu Munemitsu, the foreign minister, had taken it upon himself to try to strengthen the cabinet by a secret agreement that its members would speak and act in unison and by creating a Department of Political Affairs within the cabinet that would coordinate statements and speeches by the various ministers. This scheme he cleared with Ito before presenting it to Matsukata and the others, and he himself assumed the presidency of the new body. But his high-handed acts in this position so angered some of his colleagues that the cabinet split into two factions, one led by Mutsu and Goto Shojiro, with Ito's backing from outside the cabinet, the other by Shinagawa Yajiro, the home minister, with Yamagata's backing. Shinagawa was very much Yamagata's man. The two were related by marriage, and Shinagawa had been made a member of the cabinet at Yamagata's insistence. Thus Matsukata faced an unruly Diet session with a cabinet divided into two factions that looked either to Ito or Yamagata rather than to Matsukata for leadership.

The Diet, as expected, attacked the proposed budget, especially the navy and army appropriations, even more violently than the year before, and when the navy minister appeared he was greeted with cat calls and shouts of "The country today exists solely for the benefit of the Sat-cho clique." When he argued back, he caused pandemonium on the Diet floor and embarrassment to his cabinet colleagues, who did not find this a dignified way to handle the situation. The Diet made revisions in the budget, but on December 24, 1891, the day before it was to be presented for a final vote, Matsukata dissolved the Diet. Thus he refused to accept open defeat but settled instead for the previous year's budget.

The special election for a new Diet, which followed on February 15, 1892, was the most violent and corrupt in Japanese history. Matsukata gave a free hand to Shinagawa, who as home minister had jurisdiction over elections and the police. Shinagawa, though an honest man, was harsh by temperament and felt it his duty to suppress the parties and win majority support for the government by fair means or foul. In order to harass the opposition politicians, he had the police use to the full the various restrictive laws on political activities, and he provided secret funds to the prefectural governors for bribing voters. The parties fought back as best they could, using ruffians to counter police violence. There was turmoil throughout the country, houses were burned, and more than twenty-five persons were killed and hundreds injured. Despite all the efforts of the government, the opposition won 163 to 137, the government further lost the confidence of the public, and the cabinet became even more deeply split.

In this predicament Matsukata called on the other senior statesmen to make good on their promises of backstage support. The seven genro started meeting together on February 23 but almost at once fell into disagreement. Ito wanted the dismissal from office of those responsible for the repressive actions during the recent election, meaning Shinagawa in particular. The rest felt such action too extreme, whereupon Ito took umbrage and threatened to resign once again from the presidency of the Privy Council. Shinagawa, getting wind of Ito's stand, decided to resign, but Matsukata, backed by the other genro, refused to permit this. Then Mutsu and Goto threatened to resign if Shinagawa did not. In the end, Shinagawa and Mutsu did resign their posts as home and foreign ministers, and Ito quit the Privy Council for a second time.

The third session of the Diet, which convened in May, attempted to present a memorial to the emperor censuring the cabinet for its actions in the election and, when this failed, tried to impeach the cabinet directly. Matsukata countered this move by bluntly telling the Diet that it could do this only through the courts. Otherwise the session proved more peaceful than the first two had been. The main budget had already been decided on by the adoption of the previous year's, and the Diet was willing to go along with almost all of Matsukata's plans for an extension of the railway system, which was still only 1600 miles long.

Matsukata continued to have serious problems with his cabinet. The army and navy ministers threatened to resign because of the behind-the-scenes activities of the genro. Then the justice minister did resign when it was discovered that he, together with the president of the Supreme Court and other justices, had participated in an unseemly way in a gambling game during the trial of Nicholas' assailant. Matsukata finally gave up the post of prime minister in disgust and, after eleven straight years as finance minister, resigned that position too.

———— • ————

Through a series of meetings of the elder statesmen Ito was chosen on August 8, 1892, to head the government for a second time. Saddled with the job of dealing with the Diet, he used his political skills to persuade the politicians into compromises on the budget, but even he was forced to crack down on the Diet by dissolving it twice in 1894. Meanwhile, Matsukata was able for two years to lead the simple life he preferred, devoting most of his time and energy to developing a tract of some 4000 acres of wasteland, which he had earlier acquired at Nasuno in Tochigi prefecture, north of Tokyo. It cost him only 11 yen per acre, not much more than five dollars.

Matsukata had always been interested in land reclamation, and his attention was drawn to the Nasuno area in 1882, when Dutch engineers were hired to draw water from Lake Inawashiro through a mountain range to help create an extensive area of paddy fields in Miyagi prefecture just north of Nasuno. In developing his estate, Matsukata did not merely play the gentleman farmer but enjoyed working side by side with his help. He had the area cleared of poisonous snakes and over the years developed 50 acres of rice paddy and 73 acres of other cropland, where some forty farmers were settled. Much of the rest of the area he turned into pastures for sheep, cattle, and horses. He was particularly interested in sheepraising, which was new to Japan, and bought his breeding stock of sheep and horses from Australia. It had been assumed that sheep could not thrive in Japan because of a fatal hoof disease brought on by a too warm and damp climate, but in France Matsukata had discovered that the problem was more one of diet. He succeeded quite well with the sheep, and they became his pride and joy. Domestically produced wool actually provided the uniforms of Japanese soldiers through World War I, though since then the scarcity of land in Japan and the growth of international trade has virtually eliminated sheep from the Japanese economy. A large tract of his land Matsukata devoted to raising corn, hay, and other fodder for the animals, and he imported farm machinery from America to cultivate and harvest the land. In a sense, he was the first person in Japan to engage in mechanized farming.

At Nasuno Matsukata showed the same enthusiasm for reforestation he had displayed as governor of Hita. He planted eight million seedlings of cryptomeria, a Japanese cedar, and of *kunugi,* a type of oak used to produce high-quality charcoal, which was still the main fuel for cooking and the heating of homes. Charcoal production actually paid 70 percent of the expenses for operating the whole farm. Hunters had almost depleted the Nasuno forests of bird life, so hunting was banned. The first stork was observed there only three years later, and before long more than fifty species of birds had been counted.

Matsukata built a big Victorian summerhouse on a part of the property that had a large stand of red pines, from which he derived the name Senbon-matsu, or Thousand Pines, for his estate. In 1905 while the crown prince, the future Taisho emperor, was visiting at Thousand Pines from the nearby imperial villa in Nasuno, a telegram arrived announcing the decisive victory of the Japanese navy over the Russian fleet in the the battle of Tsushima, and everyone present shouted out "Banzai!" Because of this incident, the name of the house was changed to the Banzai-kaku, or the Banzai Pavilion, but the name Thousand Pines is still used for the pasture area, where experiments in cattle breeding and the production of dairy products are still conducted.

When I was a small child, my family often visited my grandparents at Nasuno. The house was very large, with Western rooms on the ground floor and a second story consisting of Japanese matted rooms, which very unconventionally had fireplaces. A big glass-enclosed porch overlooked a panorama of pines and a beautifully kept lawn, over which flocks of sheep wandered each morning. I also remember Nasuno for my first experience in horseback riding. My career as a horsewoman ended abruptly when the horse threw me.

Although the agricultural lands of the Matsukata estate became the property of resident farmers through the land reforms initiated by the American occupation following World War II, the forest lands and house, now in considerable disrepair, are the property of the heir of the direct line of the family, my cousin Matsukata Mineo, an executive of Japan Air Lines. He recently added a modern touch by converting the house into a tennis club. During World War II, all of my grandfather's valuable documents, including the *Matsukata jikki,* were stored in Nasuno. I went there with my father once during the war to check over the documents, and again in 1976 when I resumed this project and persuaded my cousin to bring these valuable documents back to Tokyo for safe keeping. I personally would like to see the house restored and some of its former contents reassembled so that it could be made into a public museum to preserve a phase in Japan's modern history that is being rapidly buried under factories, highways, housing developments, and hamburger joints.

———•———

Matsukata had been happily engrossed in his projects at Nasuno for only two years when national events forced him to return to Tokyo in June 1894. Ever since Japan had forced a modern treaty on Korea in 1876, much in the manner of the Americans with Japan in 1853–54, there had been a strong rivalry between China and Japan over their smaller neighbor. China claimed it as a tributary state, as it had been for many centuries, and Japan maintained that Korea was now an independent country. China stood for the status quo in Korea, while various Japanese groups urged the Koreans to modernize their country as Japan was doing. A rebellion of the Tonghak religious sect in southern Korea in 1894 induced the Korean government to ask China for troops to suppress the uprising. The Chinese complied, informing the Japanese of what they were doing in accordance with an 1885 agreement between the two countries, and then Japan also decided to dispatch forces to the peninsula.

On returning to Tokyo, Matsukata was appalled to discover that Ito seemed to have no clear strategy in mind. Matsukata urged that

Japan avoid interfering in the internal affairs of Korea and merely take a stand in favor of Korean independence. But Ito sent the Chinese a list of proposals for reforms in Korea to be jointly sponsored by the two countries. Before seven o'clock on the morning of June 22, Ito hurried to Matsukata's residence by carriage and informed him that late the night before he received word that the Chinese had rejected his proposals and were preparing for war. Matsukata, despite his disapproval of Ito's policy, agreed that Japan must prepare for war too. At Ito's insistence he joined a conference in the imperial presence,* in which he was the only person present not in an official post. This meeting confirmed the decision to prepare for war. At its close the emperor drew Matsukata aside and demanded that he stay in Tokyo and attend strategy meetings.

A few days later, on June 30, Ito informed Matsukata that an inquiry had just been received from Britain regarding the reforms Japan had proposed for Korea, and a threatening message had come from Russia stating that, since the Tonghak insurrection had already been quelled, Japan and China should simultaneously withdraw their troops. Matsukata chided Ito for not having informed the British from the beginning, and he advised a flat rejection of the insulting Russian demand. Relations between China and Japan continued to deteriorate, and Matsukata was surprised when the cabinet meeting of July 11 did not make the decision to go to war. He reproached Ito for his indecisiveness, but Ito replied that Japan lacked an adequate casus belli. The more forthright Matsukata, however, insisted that China's continuing refusal to abandon its traditional suzerainty over Korea was ample cause for war and that withdrawal of the Japanese forces would be a national disgrace. If Ito did not listen to him now, he threatened, he would never speak to him again or engage in political life. Perhaps influenced by Matsukata's belligerency, Ito went to Mutsu, once again the foreign minister, to tell him of his decision to take a strong stand. An ultimatum was sent to China, and on July 23 the Japanese forces in Seoul, the Korean capital, seized the king and installed a pro-Japanese

---

* The emperor did not take part in the discussions but merely validated the decisions made by the fact of his presence. Such meetings were officially known as "conferences in the imperial presence" (*gozen kaigi*).

cabinet, which demanded the withdrawal of the Chinese forces. By August 1 the war was on.

Finances, of course, were the area in which Matsukata had the most influence during the Sino-Japanese War. At the outset he discovered that Ito was embarrassed by a lack of funds for buying ships for transport service. He easily solved this problem by informing Ito of a special fund he had had the Bank of Japan build up in London for just such an emergency. He also discovered that Ito feared that the floating of national bonds "would invite apprehension in people's minds" and that he was expecting to finance the war on a budget surplus of 25 million yen plus donations of 15 million from rich individuals. Matsukata pointed out that the Satsuma Rebellion in 1877 had cost 40 million and that vastly more would be needed for the present overseas war. Public donations, he assured Ito, would never meet such demands. Ito then sent Inoue, who was better versed in financial matters than the prime minister, to argue the point with Matsukata, but Matsukata won Inoue over to accepting the need for financing the war through national bonds, and an issue of 50 million was decided on by August 13. Matsukata was asked by the finance minister to help in raising the money. He won the support of the business community first in Tokyo and then in Kyoto and Osaka. The 50 million issue proved a great success, being oversubscribed by 27 million yen.

The governments of England, France, and Germany also offered to loan Japan money for the war. Knowing that Matsukata would be opposed to this, Ito tried to bypass him by going directly to Kawada, the governor of the Bank of Japan. Matsukata naturally was held in great respect at the bank as its founder, and the successive governors always stood at attention when Matsukata spoke to them. When he let Kawada know of his opposition to the foreign loans, the governor flatly turned down Ito's suggestion. Instead, a second domestic bond issue was floated, and in October the Diet, in a frenzy of patriotic fervor, accepted a war budget of 150 million yen without a single dissenting vote.

Matsukata was distressed to discover that Western news correspondents were writing articles largely favorable to the Chinese side and were paying little attention to the Japanese point of view. He asked Ito what was being done about this, and the answer was "nothing." Matsukata preached to Ito on the importance of "honor" in a

foreign war, pointing out that Japan's honor was staked on guarantee-
ing Korea's independence. He urged Ito to make this clear to the
representatives of the foreign powers and to explain Japan's "righteous
cause . . . a conflict between civilization and barbarism, between an
old conservative policy and a progressive one." Matsukata admitted
that a propaganda campaign would be costly but felt it would be
worth the expense. Mutsu later told Matsukata with enthusiasm that
the cabinet had decided to follow his advice. How successful it was is
open to doubt, but this must have been one of the earliest programs of
international public relations anywhere in the world.

The war progressed more than satisfactorily for the Japanese, and
the terms of victory soon drew the attention of the government leaders. Here too Matsukata had his ideas, which he energetically pushed.
He was in favor of a policy of "guarding the north and advancing
southward." Specifically, he advocated the seizure of Taiwan (then
usually called Formosa in the West) and the nearby Pescadores Islands
to forestall their annexation by a Western power and to open the way
to further southward expansion. Even before the end of 1894 he wrote
a long and eloquent justification for this course of action, addressing
his statement to the vice-chief of the army general staff. When the
Chinese sued for peace in March 1895, he bitterly opposed the army's
demand for the annexation of the Liaotung Peninsula, the southern tip
of Manchuria, because of the danger that the Western powers would
not permit this, and, when the decision went against him, he expressed his disapproval by leaving the imperial headquarters in
Hiroshima, whence the war had been directed.

The wisdom of Matsukata's view was soon revealed after the
signing on April 17 of the peace treaty. It clearly established Korea's
independence from China, provided Japan an indemnity worth 32.9
million pounds, and gave Japan Liaotung as well as Taiwan and the
Pescadores. Just six days later, however, Russia, Germany, and France
sent identical notes to Japan demanding the return of Liaotung. The
Japanese government, despite the xenophobic clamor of the public,
felt it must yield to this humiliating "triple intervention" and accepted in place of Liaotung an additional 4.9 million pounds of indemnity. Only three years later, the intervening powers on flimsy
pretexts seized pieces of Chinese territory. The Russians added to the
indignation and frustration of the Japanese by taking for themselves

the Liaotung Peninsula, which they had long coveted for its ice-free ports. These two incidents marked in a way the highpoint of nineteenth-century imperialism in Asia. They were bitter lessons for the Japanese that may have contributed to their own imperialistic acts in later years.

———•———

In the concluding days of the war, Matsukata had been asked to rejoin the cabinet and became finance minister once again on March 20, 1895. Japan's financial situation was much strengthened by the Chinese indemnities, but the government also faced a great increase in military expenditures. Western imperialism threatened East Asia more than ever. The Russians were expanding their military potential in the Far East by the construction of the Trans-Siberian Railway, and their hostility to Japan as a rival imperial power was clear. Western navies were growing fast. Racial animosity toward Asians was rising in the West and was highlighted by exclusionist policies in the United States, Canada, and Australia and the fulminations of the German kaiser about the "yellow peril." The Japanese government felt the need for a large expansion of both army and navy. In fact, the army budget was raised from 15 million yen in 1893 to 53 million in 1896. New industries were also needed to support the military expansion, the railway and telephone systems required extension, and other expensive economic projects were necessary.

Matsukata wanted a special Diet session to discuss these matters, but Ito and Mutsu suspected that he might use it to attack them for their mismanagement of the Liaotung issue. Angered by these unfounded suspicions, Matsukata withdrew from the cabinet after only four months, but his successor got his ambitious budget safely over the Diet hurdle. This was possible because of Ito's political skill. Realizing that, with the war over, the cabinet could no longer depend on xenophobic popular support, Ito won the cooperation in the Diet of the Liberal Party by making a deal with its leader, Itagaki, the man who had broken with the other leaders in 1873. In April 1896 Itagaki joined the cabinet in the key post of home minister, and for the first time a peacetime cabinet had substantial party backing in the Diet. The support of the Liberal Party, however, was not an unmixed blessing. It made the other parties all the stronger in their opposition. As a result, Ito soon gave up the prime ministership, and since it was Satsuma's turn, Matsukata was chosen by his fellow genro to succeed him.

Matsukata assumed the post of prime minister on September 18, 1896, the second man to have a second term in this top position. He also took over once again his old function as finance minister. This time he showed a little more political acumen than he had in 1892. He followed Ito's precedent by bringing into his cabinet a representative of the political parties. He chose for this purpose Okuma as his foreign minister, and Okuma's political following, the Progressive Party, then gave its support to the cabinet.

This had not been easy to arrange. There were many old animosities between Matsukata and Okuma. Matsukata had long served under Okuma in the financial field, and relations between the two had never been cordial since he had replaced Okuma as finance minister in 1881. Even in 1896 it was no small matter for Okuma to accept a status of subordination to Matsukata. The two were also very unlike in personality. Okuma, like Ito, was garrulous and sociable, while Matsukata was taciturn and sober. In policy the two had often been bitter opponents. Okuma had made himself the champion of parliamentary supremacy, which was anathema to Matsukata, and he had favored borrowing from abroad, which Matsukata opposed. Matsukata had also been among Okuma's chief critics on the question of treaty revision and the mixed courts in 1889.

Despite all these difficulties, a reconciliation between Matsukata and Okuma was worked out by their mutual friends. The final agreement between the two came at a meeting in Kyoto arranged by Iwasaki Yanosuke, the brother of Yataro (1834–1885), founder of the great Mitsubishi zaibatsu empire and the father-in-law of Matsukata's second son, Shosaku. Matsukata conceded to Okuma's conditions, including greater freedom of speech, press, and association, as well as greater emphasis on "careers open to talent," instead of the near monopoly the genro had kept on appointments to high office. Behind this personal reconciliation one can discern a more basic convergence of interests between the two men. Okuma's party was supported by business firms that profited from the sudden economic expansion produced by the Sino-Japanese War, while Matsukata had by now developed the firm reputation of an able administrator of national finances in whom the business community could have full confidence. The cabinet was formed in September 1896 and came to be commonly known as the Matsukata-Okuma Cabinet.

Back in the prime ministership and in charge once again of the finance ministry, Matsukata proceeded to put Japan on the gold standard, as he had earlier put it on the silver standard. The gold standard was being adopted by many countries in Europe, and it seemed advisable for Japan to adopt the same monetary system because of its growing trade with the West. The Chinese war indemnities, moreover, had given Japan the means whereby to carry out this reform. Matsukata had induced Ito to specify at the peace conference with China that the indemnity be paid, not in Chinese silver taels, but in corresponding British gold pounds—37.8 million pounds for 230 million taels—and deposited in London, where it could serve as the monetary reserve to support Japan's gold standard. When Matsukata in September 1896 presented his monetary reform bill, the emperor approved it, though he admitted that "he did not fully understand the details" but accepted them because of his confidence in Matsukata.

The bill to adopt the gold standard had no difficulty in the lower house of the Diet because of the support of Okuma's party, but it did encounter some resistance in the House of Peers. There was strong opposition to Matsukata's reform in many influential circles, largely because of Japan's lack of gold mines. Yasuda Zenjuro, the founder of another of the great zaibatsu enterprises, had his doubts about the proposal, joking that he would erect a statue of Matsukata in gold if it succeeded. Another opponent was Fukuzawa Yukichi, a man of tremendous prestige. His writings in the 1860s and 1870s had been a major source of knowledge about the West, and the educational institution he founded even before the Restoration grew into prestigious Keio University. Because of Fukuzawa's influence, Matsukata spent a long evening with him and won him over. Ito and Inoue were also critics of the reform. Ito pointed out Japan's lack of gold mines or reserves, but Matsukata contended that "overseas trade goods are our real gold mines," a prophetic statement. There were also reasonable fears that many Japanese silver coins had found their way abroad and their return for conversion into gold would prove too burdensome. Matsukata's studies, however, indicated that many of these coins had been melted down in China into bullion and that only about 10 million yen in coins would be returned for conversion—an estimate not far from the actual figure of 10.8 million.

The reform drew considerable favorable attention in Europe and much interest in the United States, where the debate over the gold standard or bimetalism was always a lively issue. In response to the foreign interest, the finance ministry in 1899 published an English version of its official report, entitled "The Adoption of the Gold Standard." On the whole, the shift to gold, which went fully into effect in December 1898, was accomplished smoothly and probably did contribute to a stabilization of fluctuating prices as well as to the expansion of trade with the West.

After the end of the tenth Diet session, the Progressive Party under the leadership of Inukai Tsuyoshi demanded further concessions from Matsukata for continuing its support of the cabinet. Matsukata secretly agreed to their demands but was infuriated when the party, hoping to see that he would live up to the agreement, published the agreement in the newspapers. He responded by condemning the party soundly for interfering in government affairs. Matsukata also fell out with Okuma over an increase in the land tax needed to help cover the expansion of the overall budget from 80 million yen before the Sino-Japanese War to 200 million yen in 1896–97. The upshot was that Okuma resigned and the Progressive Party withdrew its support of the cabinet. Matsukata reconstructed his cabinet largely with protégés of Yamagata in place of men close to Okuma. He lacked majority support in the Diet, however, and it proceeded at the next session to pass a motion of nonconfidence in the government. Matsukata was prepared for this move, having brought with him an imperial edict dissolving the Diet. After issuing this, he himself resigned the prime ministership on December 28, 1897, and retired to his seaside villa at Kamakura.

———•———

Ito, representing the Choshu faction, took the position of prime minister for a third time on January 12, 1898, but he found a united opposition in the Diet, where the parties had joined to form the Constitutional Party (Kenseito). All Ito's financial bills were voted down. The important land-tax bill initiated by Matsukata went down to defeat, 247 to 27. It was obviously becoming impossible to rule without Diet support, and Ito decided that the only solution was to form his own parliamentary party. Yamagata and Matsukata were appalled at the idea, believing that the government ministers should rule in behalf of the emperor and should find means to force the Diet to conform. At a conference in the imperial presence, Ito was denied permission to carry out his scheme, but none of the other genro was willing to replace him as prime minister. Finally, at Ito's suggestion, Okuma and Itagaki, the two members of the early leadership who had broken away to form popular parties, were selected to lead a joint cabinet.

Matsukata missed this meeting because floods had blocked the railway line, but on his arrival in Tokyo he made a secret agreement with Yamagata that the latter should become the next prime minister. The two did not have long to wait. The third Ito cabinet had lasted only five months, and the new one, with Okuma as prime minister and Itagaki as home minister, lasted only four. Okuma and Itagaki and, still more, their respective followers could not get along, and the bureaucracy, particularly the army and navy, was not at all cooperative in this premature experiment in party government. By November 8, 1898, Yamagata had been selected as prime minister on the recommendation of Matsukata, who himself once again became finance minister, though for the last time.

The new cabinet was admittedly antiparty and conservative, determined to restore the prerogatives of imperial rule—or more accurately the prerogatives of the emperor's self-selected ministers. Still, support in the Diet was a necessity. Yamagata managed a compromise with the politicians whereby they got certain concessions and Yamagata got their support for much of the cabinet's program. Despite difficulties, Matsukata got his budget and financial bills through the two Diet sessions held during the tenure of this second Yamagata cabinet, but he found difficulties in raising adequate funds for the great military expansion that was taking place. He therefore reversed his earlier stand against foreign loans, feeling it was now safe to do so, since the extraterritorial privileges of the Western powers were by then a thing of the past. In 1894 the British had agreed to give up these privileges in 1899, in return for the granting to foreigners of the right to purchase property outside the old treaty settlements. The other Western powers made similar agreements. Japan was also regaining control over its tariffs, completing the process by 1911. Thus Japan was no longer as vulnerable to foreign intervention, and Matsukata found himself able to increase tariff rates to cover foreign interest payments. In these circumstances a loan for 100 million yen was floated in England. The fact that it was fully subscribed within a week shows the confidence the world had come to have in Japan's finances.

In the summer of 1900 a popular disturbance in China, the Boxer Uprising, threatened the legations in Peking and the foreign concessions in Tientsin. Remembering the triple intervention of 1895, the Japanese government was nervous about playing too large a part in the military intervention planned by the foreign powers. Matsukata himself felt Japan should do more, but Yamagata hung back because of Ito's disapproval. However, after the first international force dispatched proved inadequate and the German minister and a Japanese official were killed by the insurgents in Peking, the Japanese government decided to supply two divisions. Thus the Japanese provided roughly half of the total international force, which by August 14 had relieved the attack on the Peking legations. While many of the European troops did much pillaging, the Japanese soldiers conducted themselves in exemplary fashion and were widely praised.

Not long after this international triumph for Japan, Yamagata resigned in a huff on September 26. His foreign minister, a trusted protégé from Choshu and an experienced foreign-policy expert, had become worried about the growing rivalry with Russia over control of Korea. On his own authority he had instructed the Japanese minister in Berlin to sound out the kaiser regarding Germany's attitude if Japan were to go to war with Russia. When he was assured that Germany would remain neutral, he memorialized the throne to advocate immediate war with Russia, without even informing Yamagata. Yamagata, now sixty-two, had long been disgusted with parliamentary politics and irritated at the growing independence of the younger generation of bureaucrats. He wanted no more of front-line political life. With the demise of the Yamagata cabinet in 1900, Matsukata's long career of almost fifteen uninterrupted years as finance minister also came to an end.

Ito now was given a chance to try his political skills as a party leader. He had received permission to organize a party, the Seiyukai, which he formed by merging his following with Itagaki's. The Seiyukai party was to remain the majority or at least plurality party most of the time, until the fading of all parties with the military takeover of government leadership in the 1930s. It was revived after World War II as the Liberal Party, becoming in 1955 the largest element in the Liberal Democratic Party, which is still in power. But Ito himself had only a brief career as a party politician. He became prime minister on October 19, 1900, for the fourth and last time, with a cabinet that had several party men but no other genro. He soon tired of the heavy responsibilities of the position, resigning as prime minister in May 1901 and as party president in 1903. Since none of the genro, all now feeling their age, was willing to take on the hurly-burly of political infighting with an obstreperous Diet and a proliferating bureaucracy, they chose a man of a slightly younger generation, General Katsura Taro, a protégé of Yamagata's from Choshu, to be Ito's successor as prime minister. This ended the long period of genro domination of the cabinet and the nation.

Elder Statesman

Ito's resignation as prime minister in 1901 marked the permanent retirement of the seven original genro from day-to-day politics. None ever again occupied the post of prime minister. Only Okuma of their generation remained in the political forefront, taking the prime ministership between 1914 and 1916. But he had been dropped by the group in 1881 before it was fully consolidated. The genro themselves after 1901 served only behind the scenes as advisers and as the interpreters of the "imperial will," especially in the choice of a new prime minister.

It was only after 1901 that the group came to be generally known as the genro, the elder statesmen. Actually, the more correct term for them is *genkun* (veteran statesmen). This title had been conferred by the emperor first on Ito and Kuroda in 1889 and subsequently on the others. Matsukata received it in December 1896, after resigning from his second term as prime minister. At that time the emperor presented him with a set of gold sake cups, which came to my branch of the family on his death. Unfortunately we were forced to "donate" these gifts to the government in the autumn of 1939, when the war with China was underway, along with all other objects of gold, including my mother's wedding ring and the gilded tops of pages in fine editions of books.

The genro were gradually reduced by death, until in 1916 only Yamagata and Matsukata remained. Yamagata died in 1922, Matsukata two years later. But meanwhile another genro had been added. This was Saionji, the court noble whom we first met as governor of

Niigata in 1868. He was from the old court nobility, had cooperated with the Satsuma-Choshu group in the overthrow of the Tokugawa, and then, after his stint as governor of Niigata, had studied in France and England from 1871 to 1880. On his return to Japan he taught French law at a university and worked as a newspaperman before being persuaded by Ito to return to government service. He joined Ito in forming the Seiyukai party in 1900, succeeded him as its president in 1903, and subsequently served twice as prime minister. Saionji survived as the so-called last genro until his death in 1940.

Although Matsukata had already been eager in 1892 for a respite from public life, he did not relish complete retirement after 1901, despite the fact that he had spent more than four decades in arduous service first for Satsuma and then for the imperial government. He felt that, with a younger generation of leaders taking over the main administrative posts, his responsibilities as adviser to the emperor were all the more important. He did in fact play a part in the formation of the Katsura cabinet in 1901. When Yamagata had been prime minister, he secretly promised Katsura that he would make him his successor, but instead Ito was chosen in 1900. Since this led to a cooling of feelings, in 1901 Yamagata asked Matsukata to negotiate with Katsura in his behalf.

The chief problem the new cabinet faced was a growing confrontation with Russia over Korea. Ito and Inoue strongly advocated an alliance with Russia as the best way to solve the problem, but, when the British showed interest in an alliance with Japan, the genro at a secret meeting convened by Katsura on August 4, 1901, decided that nothing could be better than a British alliance. However, at a second meeting of the genro on December 7, Inoue in behalf of the absent Ito expressed doubts about a British alliance. Matsukata strongly supported Katsura on the proposal, and the pact was concluded and made public early in 1902. The Anglo-Japanese Alliance was the first equal treaty ever made between an occidental power and a non-Western nation. The British wanted it because they found themselves stretched thin in their worldwide rivalry with Russia and felt the need for an ally in distant East Asia. For the Japanese it meant that, if Japan were to fight Russia, the European powers would not conspire against it, as they had in the triple intervention of 1895, because Great Britain would join Japan if any other power supported its opponent.

———•———

Matsukata was eager to visit the West again, not having been abroad since 1878. Because the Anglo-Japanese Alliance appeared to give Japan at least temporary security, this seemed a good time to refresh himself on developments in the West and to reassess Japan's position in the world. He particularly wished to observe the West's industrial and economic progress in the intervening quarter century since his trip and to gather new ideas for Japan's own further development. The emperor gave him permission for a six-month absence abroad, and Matsukata proceeded at once to select his staff. He chose Megata Tanetaro as his chief aide and official interpreter. Megata, who was from Satsuma too, had gone to the United States for study in 1870, remaining there for seven years and becoming the first Japanese graduate of the Harvard Law School in 1874. In 1902 he held Matsukata's old post of chief of the bureau of taxation in the finance ministry and was the ministry's official representative in Matsukata's party. Writing in 1926, Megata claimed that Matsukata's advice to Americans during this trip to establish four national banks was influential in the subsequent creation of the twelve federal reserve banks. Another member of the party was Fukai Eigo, who had long been Matsukata's private secretary but now represented the Bank of Japan, of which he became president in 1924. For his private secretary Matsukata took his fifth son, Goro, who was the first of his sons to graduate from a Japanese university, Tokyo Imperial University.

Matsukata sailed from Yokohama on March 11, 1902, seen off by some five hundred government officials, diplomats, family members, and friends. He kept a journal of the trip, which was later copied into the *Matsukata jikki*. His ship, captained by an American, was owned by the principal Japanese shipping company, Nippon Yusen Kaisha, or N.Y.K. When the weather cleared after some stormy days, his son Goro came up on deck with surveying instruments to calculate the ship's position, and Matsukata was reminded of his own efforts at surveying on the roof of the Satsuma residence in Nagasaki some thirty-five years earlier.

In this second trip abroad, Matsukata now came as a world-famous statesman and everywhere was given splendid treatment and much press attention. After suitable formal greetings in Victoria,

British Columbia, and Seattle, Washington, he boarded the private train of James Jerome Hill, president of the Great Northern Railway, to ride in luxury, with a private bedroom, bath, living room, and dining room, halfway across the continent to St. Paul, Minnesota. There he was joined by his sixth son, Otohiko, then a freshman at Harvard. After attending elaborate social functions held in connection with the wedding of Hill's daughter, the party went on to Chicago, where it saw the grain exchange, the slaughter houses, and an Italian opera. Then it proceeded to Niagara Falls, still popular with Japanese visitors to America, and finally on to New York City.

In New York the person who most impressed Matsukata was the steel magnate Andrew Carnegie, who came of similar humble origins and had the same birth date of 1835. The sixty-seven-year-old men apparently held forth to each other about their respective philosophies of life. Matsukata told Carnegie that the martial spirit of the Japanese accounted for their military success, but that as businessmen their greed for money and lack of trust made them inferior to Chinese businessmen. Carnegie confided that any personal wealth beyond three million dollars became a handicap and should be given away.

From New York Matsukata went to Boston, where he toured the historic sites associated with the American revolution, visited his son's classes and room in Harvard Yard, and was entertained at a large banquet by President Charles W. Eliot. Then he went to Washington, where he was received by President Theodore Roosevelt and visited Mount Vernon. On the whole he was favorably impressed by the United States, which he was visiting for the first time, and somewhat revised his opinion expressed to his sons that America was a new country and that they should all also visit Europe as the home of "real civilization."

Matsukata continued on to Europe, where he visited seven countries: England, Belgium, France, Germany, Italy, Austria, and Russia. In each he was received in audience by the chief of state, and all bestowed high decorations on him. At Plymouth in England, Matsukata was joined by his second son, Shosaku, who was a member of the Japanese foreign ministry and serving as chargé d'affaires in Brussels. Matsukata received a warm welcome in London, where he was well known. The recently concluded Anglo-Japanese Alliance was an added reason for the cordial attitude, and he gained the impression that the racial and religious prejudices he had felt in Europe had diminished over the last twenty-five years. He was received at Buckingham Palace by Edward VII, was banqueted by Lord Landsdowne, the foreign secretary, was entertained at the Rothschild estate in Cambridge, and had long discussions with economist Alfred Marshall. Oxford University conferred on him the honorary degree of doctor of civil law. At first when the degree was offered, he replied in embarrassment, "I am sure you have come to the wrong person. I can neither read nor write your horizontal writing, nor am I a scholar." Matsukata also inspected the Clyde dockyards in Glasgow, the Armstrong arms factory in Newcastle, the Vickers steel foundries, and the Liverpool dockyards and storage facilities.

Before Matsukata left London, Valentine Chirol, chief of the foreign department of *The Times,* informed him that arrangements had been made for the paper's foreign correspondents in each city to call on Matsukata to brief him on the local situation—but that in Paris Henri de Blowitz, who had been *The Times*'s chief foreign correspondent since 1873, made it a rule never to call on government officials or diplomats. On Matsukata's arrival in Paris, however, Blowitz did invite him to dinner. Fukai relates about this evening that Blowitz, after remarking how people had been showering Japan with praise, told Matsukata, "You must not be pleased by all this praise, for none of it is genuine. The fact is they are still treating your country as a child. When someone truly attains greatness, people do not go about telling him to his face that he is great. Who says that the British navy or the German navy is great? . . . Take my word, as long as you are treated as a child, things will go easily for you, but, when you grow to adulthood and become really great, things will become difficult."* On their way back to the hotel, Matsukata remarked to Fukai that Blowitz had given him the most valuable assessment of Japan he had heard in his entire trip.

Throughout Europe Matsukata was much impressed with the great progress made since his visit in 1878. For example, he noted that Belgium, although the size of the single Japanese island of Kyushu and with only six million people, a seventh of Japan's population, produced as much wealth as the whole of Japan. A question by a

---

* In Fukai's memoirs, *Jimbutsu to shiso* (People and Ideas; Tokyo, 1939), p. 363.

Londoner had suggested to him one reason for Japan's relative poverty: "In a country like yours where there are so few people of wealth, what kind of a race are you that you spend so lavishly?" Embarrassed, Matsukata replied about the age-old Japanese disdain for money and the wild spending habits of peasants and merchants who for the first time found themselves with excess funds. He saw that most Europeans lived frugally and placed strong emphasis on savings, encouraged by the government. He was particularly impressed by the British emphasis on postal savings, a system of private savings accounts set up in each post office. Matsukata noted that even on the high seas there were provisions for British sailors to deposit their pay in savings accounts and that in Russia every station on the Trans-Siberian Railway had a savings bank. He came to the conclusion that, if Japan were to put more emphasis on savings, the country would find the resources for rapid industrial development without loans from abroad.

All this may sound quaint at a time when much of the Western world stands in awe of the savings rate of the Japanese. Actually a postal savings system had been started in Japan as early as 1875, but it attracted few depositors and little money. An improved system initiated in 1898 brought a marked change, and by 1906 there were six million participants in the system, with 56 million yen on deposit, a figure that doubled in the next three years. Postal savings did catch on in Japan, and I can remember how as a highschool student in the 1930s I faithfully saved my allowance and felt great satisfaction in seeing my postal savings grow.

In Europe Matsukata was struck by the great number of industrial schools. He also noted that university graduates averaged in age in the early twenties, whereas in Japan, because of delays in education caused by the insufficiency of highschools, they tended to be close to thirty. Whether or not his reports on these matters had any influence, educational reforms soon did increase the number of industrial schools in Japan, and the average age for graduates from university was reduced to around twenty-four.

In Berlin Matsukata had an interesting audience with the kaiser, who was well briefed and told him that the German decision to maintain the gold standard, despite strong opposition from the landed aristocracy, had been encouraged by Matsukata's having put Japan on the gold standard. In St. Petersburg he had a long discussion with

Finance Minister Serge Witte, who like Matsukata had played a major role in reforming his nation's finances. Count Witte told Matsukata that, in putting Russia on the gold standard, he too had been influenced by Japan's success. Matsukata also had a cordial audience with Nicholas II, who seemed to harbor no ill will because of the attack on him in Kyoto during Matsukata's first prime ministership. From St. Petersburg Matsukata returned to Japan by the Trans-Siberian Railway and a Japanese warship, arriving in Kobe on August 30, 1902.

After returning, Matsukata gave a series of lectures in his native Kagoshima, which were published under the title of *Shoko kunron* (The Homilies of Lord Matsukata). He held up the life of Andrew Carnegie and his establishment of libraries throughout the United States as an ideal for young people to emulate. Speaking to audiences of highschool girls, he extolled the virtues of upper-class British women, whom he described as gentle and faithful wives, refined and well-mannered, and not like some foreign women who were known for their wild and extravagant tastes. He also praised British ladies for their bravery and endurance as volunteer Red Cross nurses in time of war. To a businessman's group, he returned to the subject of women, but in a different context. He urged this audience to make greater efforts to export silk, since all European ladies were beginning to wear silk undergarments.

———— • ————

The year after his return, Matsukata was appointed to the Privy Council. Since this exalted body had only ill-defined duties, appointment was often considered being "kicked upstairs" or, as the Japanese say, "enshrined alive." Matsukata's appointment resulted from a clash between Ito and his successor as prime minister, General Katsura. Ito had continued on as the president of the Seiyukai party he had founded in 1900, and Katsura, declaring that this put him in an untenable position, tendered his resignation late in June 1903. Yamagata and Matsukata then demanded that Ito resign the party presidency and again assume the presidency of the Privy Council. Ito was finally persuaded to do so, but only with the understanding that Yamagata, Matsukata, and Inoue would join him in the council. Inoue refused, but the other two accepted, becoming privy councillors on July 13.

Now a much more serious crisis was brewing for Japan. Ever

since the end of the Sino-Japanese War in 1895, Japan had been engaged in a duel with Russia over Korea. The Japanese were particularly disturbed at the failure of the Russians to carry out their promised withdrawal of troops from Manchuria on Korea's northern border following the Boxer Uprising. There were lengthy negotiations, but the Russians seemed determined to be dilatory.

On February 4, 1904, a note was received from the Russians showing no change in their uncompromising stand, and on the next day a meeting of the genro and key members of the cabinet was called to decide whether Japan should go to war. Matsukata, who all along had been demanding a firm stand, persuaded Katsura to draw up in advance of the meeting a clear statement of the reasons why Japan should resort to war. Matsukata himself brought this document to the meeting and asked all those present to sign it. Only Ito refused, displaying what Matsukata considered to be Ito's typical vacillation in the face of a real crisis. On February 6 the same group met with the emperor to formalize the virtually unanimous decision for war made the day before. To Matsukata's surprise, Ito argued that Japan was financially unprepared to go to war and stated that at the time of the Sino-Japanese War, Kawada of the Bank of Japan had taken charge of financing the war, but this capable man was no longer with them to perform the crucial task. Matsukata was furious and replied that Ito knew perfectly well that it had been he, Matsukata, who had stood behind Kawada in his work to finance the war in 1894, and he was prepared to do the same again for Kawada's successor. He argued that shortness of funds was no reason for deciding against war.

Diplomatic relations with Russia were broken that very day, and on February 8 the Japanese navy launched a successful surprise attack on the Russian fleet anchored at its base at Port Arthur, at the southern tip of Manchuria. Two days later, Japan formally declared war. This was the first case in modern times of the commencement of a major war by a surprise attack—a technique that was to become the rule rather than the exception. Meanwhile the finance minister, who had been put in a humiliating position in the argument over finances between Ito and Matsukata, had tendered his resignation, but Matsukata insisted that he continue in his post because a resignation now would be interpreted as a sign of weakness.

When the finance minister presented Matsukata with the proposed war budget, Matsukata chided him that 300 million yen could maintain only nine divisions. The war budgets were finally increased to 1.5 billion yen, and nineteen divisions were put in the field. War funds were raised domestically through increasing taxes and floating war bonds five times. Despite all this, the funds were insufficient and it became necessary to raise money through foreign loans. For this purpose Matsukata was in daily communication with his protégé, Baron Takahashi Korekiyo, then president of the Yokohama Specie Bank and later a prime minister. All during the war, Takahashi when in Tokyo never failed to visit Matsukata each day at his residence in Mita and usually stayed for dinner.

Takahashi was not the only caller at the Mita house, which every day from early morning on was deluged with official visitors. Frequently Matsukata had little time to eat his breakfast and would swallow a few egg yolks, giving the whites to the children. In the evenings groups of callers often stayed for dinner, and each group would be served separately in a different room. All this entailed a great deal of cooking and work for the staff. Masako always had her daughters serve the dinners to the guests, not allowing the maids to perform this task. Umeko, the youngest of the daughters, recalled how as a young girl she would be made to bathe immediately after returning from school and then get dressed for the evening in order to serve her father's guests.

During the course of the war Takahashi was sent to London to raise a loan, but he found the British uncooperative. Fortunately, he befriended Jacob Schiff while there, and after a few meetings Schiff agreed to float a loan for six million dollars in New York. Schiff was the son of a prominent German financier in Frankfurt and had come to America in 1864 as a young man; three years later he established his own brokerage firm in New York. He became one of the most prominent financiers in the city and in 1904, when Takahashi met him, was at the peak of his career. Schiff's interest in helping did not stem from any love of Japan but from an intense hatred of imperial Russia for its antisemitic policies and pogroms. At first, the financiers Schiff called on in New York to take part in the loan were reluctant, claiming that the chances of Japan's defeating Russia were remote. But Schiff persuaded them, and J. P. Morgan of the First National Bank, John D. Rockefeller of the National City Bank, and other financiers agreed to participate. In all, Schiff raised $30 million for Japan, which proved crucial to Japan's ultimate victory.

In the fighting, Japan piled up a list of unbroken victories over Russia, which, despite its much greater size, had difficulty supplying its armies over the lengthy single-track Trans-Siberian Railway and was in addition plagued by revolutionary disorders at home. The Russian Baltic fleet, denied the use of the Suez Canal and British ports, overcame incredible difficulties in sailing halfway around the globe, only to be waylaid and virtually annihilated by the Japanese navy on May 27 in the Straits of Tsushima between Japan and Korea. This naval disaster sealed Russia's defeat, but the war had proved costly to Japan in men and resources. It was on the verge of exhaustion and, after carefully feeling out the United States, formally requested President Roosevelt on May 31 to act as a mediator in ending the war.

Peace negotiations commenced in August at Portsmouth, New Hampshire, chosen to avoid Washington's summer heat, and the peace treaty was signed there on September 5. The Japanese had set their hearts on a war indemnity as part of the settlement, as in the Sino-Japanese War, but the Russians were determined not to undergo this indignity. The Japanese government, realizing its inability to continue the war or to strike at Russia's real seat of strength in Europe, finally contented itself with Russian acceptance of Japan's complete control over Korea, the transfer to Japan of the Russian lease of the Liaotung Peninsula at the southern tip of Manchuria, the transfer to Japan of the southern half of the railways the Russians had built in Manchuria, and the cession of the southern half of the large island of Sakhalin.

The Japanese public, which did not realize the nation's precarious position, was outraged at the failure to win an indemnity and broke out in wild protest, burning police stations and attacking the homes of government leaders. Roosevelt was blamed for the unsatisfactory treaty terms, and there was strong anti-American feeling. The government, however, appreciated Roosevelt's aid, and it also expressed its gratitude for Jacob Schiff's financial assistance by inviting him to Japan. Schiff was received at the palace by the emperor, who conferred on him the highest order of the Sacred Treasure and invited him to lunch, the first time a foreign private citizen was thus honored. The emperor also expressed his gratitude to Matsukata for his wartime contributions and personally conferred on him the Grand Order of the Chrysanthemum. Since normally such high awards were made by the prime minister in the emperor's name, Matsukata jokingly commented to his family that he had received an honor higher than that of Admiral Togo Heihachiro, the celebrated victor of the battle of Tsushima. Later in 1905, he was promoted from count to marquis and presented with 20,000 yen (then $20,000) by the emperor.

———•———

The solidarity of the genro began to break up after the Russo-Japanese War. The deaths of Kuroda and Saigo Tsugumichi had already reduced them to five, and now Ito went off to Korea to serve as resident general in virtual control of that country; he was assassinated by a Korean in Manchuria in 1909. Oyama, who died in 1916, considered himself merely a soldier and did not pay much attention to political matters. Inoue, who died in 1915, was mostly concerned with private economic development and had become closely associated with the Mitsui zaibatsu interests. This left Yamagata and Matsukata as the only genro broadly involved in national affairs, though Matsukata's interests ran largely to economic matters and Yamagata exerted far greater political influence.

The unpopularity of the Portsmouth peace treaty forced Katsura to resign the prime ministership, and on Yamagata's recommendation Saionji succeeded him in January 1906. Saionji as prime minister was in a rather ambiguous position, being both a party president and a high court noble. Yamagata saw to it, though, that he had a quite traditional cabinet made up of four men from Choshu, three from Satsuma, and only two from Saionji's party, including Hara Takashi, who in 1918 became the first true party prime minister. Saionji had absorbed liberal ideas during his studies in Europe and a socialistic leaning toward government control of key industries. He favored a government takeover of the private railway lines and was backed in this by Matsukata and Yamagata. Matsukata had been won over to this policy during his second trip to Europe. The bill for government ownership of the railways passed the Diet, giving the government control over nine-tenths of the 5000 miles of railways Japan then had.

When Saionji resigned the prime ministership in 1908, in part because of opposition by Matsukata and Inoue to his plan to increase currency supplies to cover revenue deficits, Yamagata selected Katsura to replace him. Yamagata was at the height of his influence and only held pro forma consultations with the other genro on this important step. Even on the momentous decision to annex Korea outright, he conferred only with Ito, Katsura, and the foreign minister. After Ito's death, and only two months before the actual annexation took place in August 1910, Matsukata and Inoue were informed of the decision as an "already fixed policy" to which they were to give their approval. Incidentally, no foreign government made the slightest protest at this imperialistic move by Japan, which all had already accepted as inevitable.

On November 22, 1910, Matsukata and his wife Masako held in Western style a celebration for their golden wedding anniversary. This was a gala occasion, as befitted a man considered the second-ranking civilian subject of the realm. He presented elaborate gifts to the emperor and empress, the crown prince and princess, and other members of the imperial family and received comparable gifts from them in return. The celebration was held on the grounds of Matsukata's Mita residence and was attended by several hundred guests. The family was there in full force, and I treasure the anniversary photograph showing them together, more than fifty strong, the men and boys all in Western attire and the women in formal Japanese kimonos. Around the venerable couple, then seventy-five and sixty-five respectively, are grouped their eleven sons and six daughters as well as various spouses and grandchildren. My father is there, but still without a wife.

The Meiji emperor, who had been the central symbol of the whole great transformation of modern Japan, died on July 12, 1912, to the great sorrow of his people. General Nogi Maresuke, the hero of the Russo-Japanese War, and his wife committed suicide by seppuku in their home as the emperor's funeral was being held, thus living up to the archaic feudal tradition of following one's master in death. Both their sons had died in the war with Russia. Mrs. Nogi's death at her own hand by a short sword reminds me of an incident near the end of World War II. One day, when I visited the home of one of my aunts, I noticed a short sword on top of a bookstand and inquired about it. She told me she had it in readiness for her own suicide if the actions of the expected American invaders made this necessary.

———•———

The Meiji emperor was succeeded by his son, who is known by the name of his year period, Taisho. I was born during his reign and always speak of myself in Japanese as having been born in the fourth year of Taisho (1915). Taisho was less capable than his father and in time became mentally unbalanced, putting greater burdens on the genro to make decisions for him.

Early in the new reign a major political crisis arose, usually called the Taisho Political Change. Katsura had returned the prime ministership to Saionji in August 1911, and when the army, dissatisfied with the proposed military budget, withdrew its minister from the cabinet, Saionji was forced to resign in December 1912. This gave rise to a popular outburst against the army, called the Movement to Preserve Parliamentary Government. Efforts were made to persuade Matsukata as a relatively neutral figure to resume the prime ministership, but he was quite unwilling because of his age and the strong popular feeling against the old Satsuma-Chosu oligarchy. After fourteen meetings of the genro in a twelve-day period, Katsura was reappointed prime minister. But he proved unable to win Diet support and was forced to resign in February 1913, dying soon thereafter a broken man. Matsukata again was asked to become prime minister but steadfastly refused, suggesting Admiral Yamamoto Gonnohyoe of Satsuma in his place. Yamamoto was an honest and able man and incidentally the father-in-law of Matsukata's sixth son, Otohiko.

The Yamamoto cabinet lasted only a little over a year. With no Satsuma or Choshu men available for the task of prime minister, the genro turned to their opponent Okuma. Soon a squabble broke out between the genro and the new foreign minister, Kato Takaaki, who was the president of the Diet party supporting Okuma. Shortly after the outbreak of World War I in Europe, Japan declared war on Germany in order to live up to its obligations under the Anglo-Japanese Alliance and, more significantly, to avail itself of the opportunity to seize the German holdings in China and the North Pacific. At this juncture Kato, who was a product of the new educational system and a longtime foreign-ministry bureaucrat, persuaded Okuma to promise that during the war there would be no meddling by the genro in the cabinet's foreign policies. When word of this came to Matsukata, he was outraged. An all-day meeting was held at Inoue's home on September 24, 1914, between the genro and Okuma and Kato. Kato was forced to promise to show the genro all important communications concerning foreign negotiations and consult with them on key decisions. It was also agreed that the Japanese policy toward China should be to dispel the distrust toward Japan on the part of the Chinese people and government and to refrain from international rivalries in China.

Despite this agreement, after Japan had completed its seizure of the German held port of Tsingtao in Shantung province in China and the various German islands in the North Pacific, Kato proceeded to exploit the situation further without informing the genro. He secretly presented to the Chinese government on January 18, 1915, a series of "requests," which have come to be known as the Twenty-One Demands. These were designed to ensure Chinese acceptance of the transfer of German rights in China to Japan, the consolidation and extension of Japan's economic position in Manchuria and certain other parts of China, and, in the fifth group of "requests," to make China a virtual Japanese protectorate. Word of this leaked to Matsukata who, recovering at age eighty from a near fatal illness, wrote heatedly in protest to Yamagata. The Chinese also leaked the Japanese terms to the world, and international indignation, especially in the United States, helped to blunt the Japanese pressure. A meeting including the genro was held on May 4 but produced no clear agreement. Eventually, after long negotiations with the Chinese government and discussions with its own allies, the Japanese government withdrew the offensive fifth group of demands.

Kato, in an effort to restore his relations with Matsukata, made a call on him, but the old gentleman, without allowing the younger bureaucrat a chance to speak, gave him a thorough tongue lashing. Speaking of diplomacy, he is recorded as having said:

> Its cardinal principle is to abide by justice and to perfect international faith . . . To lose Chinese confidence in our country for the sake of temporary convenience is to sow the seeds of evil for the future. Good relations with China are the key to the maintenance of peace in East Asia. There is no road of self-preservation for Japan other than this . . . No matter what clever strategem you may have, it is difficult to succeed if you lose the world's faith in you. From the very beginning, the basis of internationalism has been faith and the sharing of profits . . . Our policy toward China

is not one toward a single country, but it is one vis-à-vis the whole world. Notwithstanding this, in your dealings with Peking you concealed from our allies the fifth group [of demands], thus slighting international faith in us and bringing international disgrace on us through the censure of the whole world.*

In this declaration, we hear the echo of nineteenth-century concepts of the consort of powers in China, but we also see an expression of an international ideal that might have spared both Japan and China the tragedies of the 1930s and 1940s. Kato was left speechless and did not dare call again on Matsukata for several years, even though the families were related through the Iwasaki family (Kato and Matsukata's second son were both married to daughters of Iwasaki Yataro, the founder of Mitsubishi). However embarrassing the rupture with Matsukata, Kato's falling out over the incident with Yamagata was to prove more politically costly because Yamagata blocked his subsequent consideration for appointment as prime minister, a post Kato was not to attain until 1924, two years after Yamagata's death.

The elderly Okuma resigned the prime ministership because of ill health in October 1916, and Yamagata chose one of his own protégés, a Choshu general, Terauchi Masatake, to succeed him. Matsukata at once presented to Terauchi a lengthy statement on China policy, which is worth quoting at length because it shows the relatively enlightened and perspicacious views he held on international affairs and Sino-Japanese relations:

> Ever since the Restoration, the fundamental principles underlying Japan's foreign policy have been . . . to follow the highway of justice, build up national good faith, and place Japan in a stable position like Mt. Fuji in the world . . . So far we have not taken advantage of the weak but have advocated walking in the traditional and only path of upholding justice in foreign policy. Despite disparities in race, religion, customs, living, and ideals, we have acted in harmony with the powers and have thus gained a sound and stable position internationally . . .
>
> However, our recent policy toward China has overthrown this

* Tokutomi Iichiro (Soho), ed., *Koshoku Matsukata Masayoshi den*, vol. 2, pp. 919–920.

fundamental policy and through temporary chicanery has become the source of ill effects for years to come . . . The policy toward China of territorial integrity and equal opportunity has already been established by the world powers . . . Japan's policy toward China for this reason cannot be an independent, separate one . . . but must be decided on from the broader point of view of a Japanese world policy . . .

The problem is how Japan, as the leader of the yellow race, can execute her heaven-bestowed duty. The crux of this problem lies in the establishment of good Sino-Japanese relations, since China is the greatest power outside of Japan in East Asia. Good Sino-Japanese relations not only will maintain peace in East Asia and save China but are the path of self preservation for Japan . . . Japan will become the leader of East Asia, first guarding China and then the other countries of East Asia, gradually letting East Asia govern East Asia and making unnecessary the interference and pressures of the white race . . .

However, the recent Sino-Japanese policy of our country has been to take advantage of our strength and China's weakness . . . This has resulted only in making China hate Japan . . . Our unprincipled, aimless policy toward China has resulted in our tearing down with our left hand what we have built with our right hand . . . Is Japan's policy toward China going to be to weaken it, extinguish it, and annex it? Or is it Japan's policy to treat China like a brother and lead it well and thus establish our influence as a means to attaining self-rule for East Asia? . . . If we are to gain the real heart of China, there is no other way than to tread the path of mutual interests . . .

Sino-Japanese relations mean Japan's relations to the world. Behind and around China are the world powers. The Japanese position in China can never be considered safe unless we are at least to satisfy these foreign powers . . . The policy of China to be on good terms with distant states and to attack neighbors will always be the policy of a weak nation. That she should ally herself with America to try to frustrate Japanese plans . . . is but a symptom of the suffering of a weak nation . . . It is for us not to be angry with her but to have sympathy for her . . . There are people who should be called Japanese pirates, disturbing the peace of China and bringing shame to Japan. Spreading evil in this way, they inevitably will isolate Japan and make her the focus of hatred of the world powers . . . Unless Japan takes a big ax to this problem and makes fundamental reforms, the future dangers for the nation are incalculable. (Tokutomi, vol. 2, pp. 923–930)

In May 1917 Matsukata was appointed Lord Keeper of the Privy Seal, or Inner Minister (Naidaijin) as the post is known in Japanese. Though largely symbolic, this position was considered to be one of the highest in the whole government and it did have a special significance in Japan, where even today seals are normally used on official documents in place of signatures. I can remember in my younger years handling my mother's banking simply by using her seal, and there are endless stories of families or businesses being ruined by unscrupulous persons who got control of their seals. But Matsukata's status as genro remained far more significant than his new post. By now there were only three genro: Matsukata, Yamagata, and the newly added Saionji.

The Russian revolution of 1917, the victory of the Communists that autumn, and the withdrawal of Russia from the world war all greatly disturbed the Japanese government and occasioned many meetings between the cabinet ministers and the genro. One problem was a proposed expedition to Siberia to bolster an eastern front against Germany. The army was eager to fish in the troubled waters of the Russian revolution, but the civilian leaders were more hesitant. Eventually an expedition, largely made up of Japanese soldiers with a few Americans and other allies, was dispatched to Vladivostok in 1918. It produced nothing but problems for Japan and was finally withdrawn in 1922.

More than a doubling of the cost of living during the war years had led to rice riots in Japanese cities, and Terauchi, unable to handle the situation, resigned the prime ministership in September 1918. Saionji refused to take on the job again and persuaded a reluctant Yamagata to accept Hara, Saionji's successor as president of the Seiyukai, as a frankly party prime minister. Hara was a man of relatively high samurai birth but, since he came from northern Japan, he had been forced to fight his way to power as a party politician, opposing the Satsuma and Chosu oligarchy. He had been baptized a Christian in 1873 and thus was the first Christian as well as the first strictly party man to serve as prime minister. Matsukata's approval of Hara had been even harder to win than Yamagata's was, not because of Hara's party affiliation but because Matsukata preferred a different Seiyukai leader.

When Hara became prime minister, he let it be known that political decisions would be the province of his cabinet, while decisions regarding the court would be left up to the genro. One problem that soon arose was over the fiancée of Crown Prince Hirohito, the present emperor. He became engaged in 1916 to Nagako, a daughter of Prince Kuni, the head of a branch of the imperial family, but in 1920 rumors began to circulate that there was hereditary color blindness in Nagako's mother's family, the Shimazu of Satsuma, and that therefore the engagement should be canceled. Prince Kuni refused to accept this, and the court divided over the question. The three genro unanimously opposed the engagement, though Matsukata, as a former samurai and a close friend of the Shimazu family, remained discreetly in the background. But when the minister of the imperial household resigned in protest against the genro's stand, Matsukata took the lead in selecting Makino Shinken as a compromise successor to the post. Makino was by birth the second son of Matsukata's old leader Okubo but had been adopted by another prominent Satsuma family. He had gone to the United States with the Iwakura mission in 1871 and stayed on to study in Philadelphia. When Matsukata and Yamagata, to reinforce their stand on the marriage question, resigned from the Privy Council and offered to relinquish all other posts and honors, Makino tactfully managed to persuade the two crotchety old men to continue in their positions, even though he insisted that the marriage be carried through. Nagako today sits beside Hirohito on the Japanese throne, and, so far as we know, none of her children or grandchildren has proven to be color-blind.

Another prolonged wrangle at court was over a proposed trip by the crown prince to Europe. The three genro had originated the idea because they were convinced from their own travels abroad that the future emperor of Japan should also see the outside world. Their proposal was twice turned down on the grounds of the emperor's incapacities and, when the public became aware of the idea, there was an outburst of violent opposition from rightist groups, who criticized the whole concept of the divine leader of the "land of the gods" defiling himself by going to barbarian countries. There was also widespread fear about the safety of the prince if he were to go abroad.

Toward the end of 1920 the worsening condition of the emperor made the genro realize that Hirohito might soon have to take over his father's duties by becoming the prince regent so, if he were to go abroad, it would have to be then or never. Matsukata made a third appeal on behalf of the genro directly to the empress, concluding his presentation with the old Japanese adage, "Let your darling child travel." The empress finally agreed, and the tour was announced in January 1921. This produced a new rightist outburst, with threats on Matsukata's life and an attempted attack on Saionji Hachiro, the son-in-law and heir of Saionji and a close friend of my father's, who had been chosen to accompany the prince. In fact the whole trip went off smoothly. Hirohito "studied" briefly at Oxford and traveled in France, Belgium, and Italy, returning to Japan in September 1921.

While the crown prince was away in Europe, the empress was much pleased with the favorable reports she received of his trip and showered Matsukata with gifts for having insisted on it. When she received news that the prince had boarded a Japanese warship in Naples for the voyage home, she sent to Matsukata's residence a huge banquet prepared in the palace. The food was so abundant that he invited all the members of the family in the Tokyo area to participate. I was still too young to be included, but my cousin Matsumoto Shigeharu tells me that the repast was so sumptuous that even he and his school-age cousins could not make much of a dent in it.

Shortly after Hirohito's return, Matsukata decided that it was time for him to assume the position of prince regent, taking over the duties of his now incapacitated father. On this occasion Matsukata received a letter of appreciation dated November 27 from Yamagata, who was seriously ill. Of all the many letters he received from Yamagata, this was the only one not written in his own hand, but the old man had at least been able to sign it.

———— • ————

Prime Minister Hara proved a strong leader as well as an able politician, but he was assassinated by an ultrarightist on November 4, 1921. The three genro gathered at Yamagata's bedside—this probably was the last time they ever met together—and chose as Hara's successor Takahashi Korekiyo, who had so ably handled the foreign loans during the Russo-Japanese War and had been a staunch party supporter of Hara. Takahashi proved a less capable prime minister and resigned the post in June 1922. Since Yamagata had died on February 1 and Saionji was ill, the choice of a new prime minister fell to Matsukata. A lengthy call by Kato Takaaki—the first since their falling out in 1915—gave rise to rumors that Kato, as the leader of the opposition party, was to be chosen as prime minister but Matsukata, after consulting with various government leaders, chose instead Admiral Kato Tomosaburo, recently returned from heading the Japanese delegation to the Washington disarmament conference.

This was a lonely time for Matsukata, for he was now the last surviving member of the original genro and of the group of men who had shaped the new Japan between 1868 and 1890. His greatest loss was that of his wife and lifelong companion, Masako, who had died on September 13, 1920, at the age of seventy-five. He repeatedly asked to be allowed to retire, and his third request, made directly to the prince regent in September 1922, was finally accepted. On the occasion he was promoted from marquis to prince, the highest noble rank, and given a lump-sum pension, which he divided equally among his five daughters.

In 1922 Matsukata, according to the East Asian way of counting age, was eighty-eight years old, a very special age because the characters for 88 can be compressed together to form the character for rice. Thus it is known as the "rice age," or *beiju*. My grandfather's friends formed a committee of forty-seven members to organize a celebration and collected 180,000 yen. Getting word of this, he asked them not to use the money for a bronze statue or some similar memorial but to use it to encourage the study of agriculture and the Chinese classics, the latter in order to strengthen the moral character of young Japanese. He was thinking of how important the Chinese classics had been in his own education. The money was accordingly given to the Peers' School.

Despite his resignation from official posts, Matsukata was still one of the two remaining genro. When Prime Minister Kato Tomosaburo died in August 1923, he and Saionji, after consultations with various government leaders, chose Admiral Yamamoto, who had been the prime minister in 1913, to serve once again. However, at noon on September 1, the day before Yamamoto assumed the post, the so-called Great Kanto Earthquake destroyed much of Tokyo, Yokohama, and surrounding areas. It took probably more than 100,000 lives and set back the Japanese economy severely. Japan was forced to float a foreign loan of 200 million yen; because of the world's confidence in the nation, the loan was oversubscribed within hours. The American Red Cross and other American institutions immediately sent generous assistance, including food, clothing, and prefabricated housing. My memory of the next year is of endless meals of tapioca and American canned pork and beans, for which I still have no great liking.

At the time of the earthquake Matsukata was at his Kamakura seaside residence, south of Tokyo and close to the epicenter of the earthquake. He was pinned under a beam of his collapsed house, unable to move. Some of the servants who had been able to scurry outside found my grandfather and managed to cut him free with a saw. All communications in the Kanto area had been severed, and rumors spread throughout Japan that Tokyo had been completely destroyed. Newspaper specials were issued stating that Matsukata had perished in his home. Matsukata Kojiro, his third son, who lived in Kobe and was then head of the Kawasaki dockyards, immediately organized in the Kansai area a collection of food, clothing, and other necessities to send to the victims of the quake; he loaded them on a ship together with his own Buick and a coffin for his father. He found the port of Yokohama destroyed but managed to unload his Buick nearby and drove it to Kamakura. On arrival he found, to his great joy, his father alive and being well cared for by family and friends.

I was eight at the time and happened to be in Kamakura too, at our summer home on the beach not far from my grandfather's villa. When the earthquake struck, I was walking down a narrow lane between stone walls on my way to a friend's house to pick up a book. Seeing the stone walls falling on both sides, I scrambled out to a wider street, only to see big cracks open up and terrified people falling into them. I tried to make my way home but found the streets blocked with houses that had collapsed under their heavy thatched roofs. Finally I managed to get out to the beach. As I came in view of my home, my father dashed out to me, grabbed my hand, and raced with me inland away from the sea, for he had noticed that the ocean water was withdrawing in preparation for a tidal wave (*tsunami* as we now call it even in English). I remember the huge wave crashing ashore and hissing after us as we ran desperately ahead of it. We escaped un-harmed, but the wave greatly damaged the village of Kamakura and the whole shoreline.

The second Yamamoto cabinet did not last long after this. On December 7, 1923, an anarchist attempted to assassinate the prince regent, and the prime minister, taking the blame for his act in the Japanese manner, resigned the next day. The aged Matsukata la-mented the degenerate times that had produced such a shocking event. Though both he and Saionji were too ill to meet, they conferred through intermediaries and chose a conservative bureaucrat, Kiyoura Keigo, to be the new prime minister.

Matsukata had recovered sufficiently from the ordeal of the earth-quake to compose in the spring of 1924 a memorial for the new prime minister, aimed at the economic problems of the time. While men-tioning the vast destruction of the earthquake, he blamed the eco-nomic ills of the country in true Confucian fashion on the moral weakness of the Japanese people and their "serious malady of indul-gence in luxury and frivolity." He called for the further development of the economy, especially export industries. The way to increase exports was to produce "cheap but high-quality products" which would "establish a good reputation for the country." He argued that protective tariffs should be reinstated, but the chief means for rein-vigorating the Japanese economy, he insisted, was by a lowering of interest rates, to be achieved through the Bank of Japan.

This memorial was Matsukata's last formal effort to participate in affairs of state. By the late spring of 1924 his health started to fail. His mind continued to be alert, and he was still concerned for the future of his country. He had come to accept the political changes brought by the popular movement in Japanese politics, and he realized the neces-sity of broader popular education. One of the last things he said to a close friend was "use all your influence to make schools and univer-sities into factories, not storehouses." He passed away peacefully on July 2, 1924, at the age of eighty-nine, Western count.

The Diet in deference to Matsukata's status as a genro voted to give him a state funeral and appropriated 50,000 yen for the purpose. The funeral ceremonies were held in the garden of his residence. A Shinto shrine was erected so that the ceremonies could be conducted according to Shinto rites, which was appropriate for a high courtier (most Japanese have Buddhist funeral ceremonies). On both sides of the walkway leading to the shrine, canopies of black and white bunting were raised to shield the invited guests from the hot July sun. Over a thousand persons came to pay their last respects, including representatives of the imperial family, government officials, foreign dignitaries, and Japanese from all walks of life. The priests and attendants taking part in the ceremony were attired in ancient costumes. So too were my uncles and aunts and even my mother, who was dressed like the others in a costume made especially for the occasion. The women's long hair tied at their necklines flowed down their backs. My mother's curious costume was what impressed me most about the funeral. The men wore black lacquered headgear appropriate for the occasion. As the funeral procession moved slowly toward the shrine, it was like a scene taken from an ancient scroll. In the background could be heard the ancient court music, and the sad, eerie sounds produced by the reed instruments and the chanting of the priests created an unreal world. Only the presence of soldiers, dressed in modern uniforms and standing at attention before escorting the coffin procession to the crematory, gave a sense of the present.

Matsukata's life had spanned nine decades, a time when Japan had grown from a feudal to a modern nation. He had actively participated every step of the way, helping to bring his country out of the chaos of the last years of feudalism through the national reconstruction of the Meiji period and three wars to the position of a world power. As he rose to the status of senior statesman, Japan kept evolving along democratic lines beyond the system of government he had helped to create and operate. Matsukata had been the product of an extraordinary period of transition, but he himself was becoming an anachronism left over from a passing era. There was much he could take satisfaction in, however. He left behind him a large family that could continue the work of building a new Japan. Most important, he more than any other single person had laid the solid foundations of financial stability for the further economic growth and prosperity of his country.

RIOICHIRO ARAI

Rioichiro Arai, young man on Broadway, c. 1880

A Peasant Background

My two grandfathers had sharply contrasting backgrounds and careers. Rioichiro Arai was born twenty years later than Matsukata Masa-yoshi, representing a new generation raised not in purely feudal days but in the period of transition after the opening of Japan to the West. He was of so-called peasant stock, as opposed to Matsukata's higher social status as a member of the ruling samurai class. Despite his supposedly humble rank, however, Arai actually came from a family of considerable wealth and broad economic activities; Matsukata, for all his samurai pride, was raised in comparative poverty. Arai was born in the *tenryo* (heavenly realm) of direct Tokugawa rule, which was economically and socially more advanced than peripheral Satsuma, where earlier feudal attitudes and ways were more fully preserved. In the shogunal tenryo, loyalty to the Tokugawa ran deep, and the Satsuma and Choshu samurai who took over the central government were viewed as interlopers. Whereas Matsukata quite naturally found himself on the inside track of the new government, Arai, as a non-samurai from the Tokugawa area, was an outsider who found his road to success in private business, spending most of his life in the United States as an importer of Japanese silk. Despite their very different lives, though, the careers of my two grandfathers as financial reformer and businessman fitted neatly together, illustrating well the reasons for Japan's economic success in modern times.

Arai was born in 1855, two years after the appearance of Commodore Perry's ships signaled the approaching end of the feudal age.

His birthplace was the small village of Mizunuma in the hills on the northwestern edge of the Kanto Plain around Edo. Today Mizunuma is merely a hamlet, or unofficial community, though it serves as the central point in the larger administrative village of Kurohone. It is located in the northern part of present Gumma prefecture, which in premodern days was the province of Kozuke. In ancient times Kozuke was a local cultural and political center. The lower slopes of the mountains that surround it on three sides have numerous prehistoric sites dating from the preagricultural period, but later the people moved down into the marshy valleys and plain to cultivate rice. They built numerous burial mounds for their leaders during the mound-building age in the fifth and sixth centuries and subsequently constructed Buddhist temples in the style of the eighth-century Nara period. Kozuke thus was a major eastern outpost of the culture of the capital area in western Japan.

Mizunuma literally means "marshland," a name presumably derived from the once marshy terrain of the narrow valley in which it is nestled. It lies along the Watarase River, which leads up into the mountains to Ashio, the site of one of Japan's largest copper mines, not far from the mausoleums of the early Tokugawa shoguns at Nikko. The road that went through Mizunuma to the Ashio mines continued over the mountains to Nikko and was considered the "back road" to this important place. Over this road passed a number of travelers who brought a breath of the outside world to the otherwise isolated mountain village of Mizunuma. The Watarase River in modern times became famous for the pollution it brought down from the Ashio mines onto the Kanto Plain. The popular agitation and lawsuits this produced in the 1890s are known as Japan's first great ecological dispute.

The montainous fringes of the Kanto Plain were a relatively poor part of Japan. Little rice could be grown, and the inhabitants subsisted largely on sparse crops of barley, wheat, and millet, grown in narrow fields on the steeply terraced hillsides. The average holding of a peasant family was only a half acre, which might produce five koku of grain. Since a koku was considered the amount needed to keep one person alive for a year, this was marginal existence for a family with many mouths to feed. The peasants got by with the aid of a variety of supplementary work, such as lumbering in the surrounding mountains, charcoal making, and hiring out as laborers or transport workers in more prosperous areas.

The most important side industry was sericulture: mulberry trees can be grown along the borders of fields and on the poor soil of the mountainsides, and mulberry leaves form the main diet of silkworms. The worms were raised on wicker trays placed on shelves in the upper portions of farmhouses. Sericulture was heavy seasonal work, especially for women. The worms had to be fed constantly during the spring and summer months. No one who has heard the sound will ever forget the low, all-night roar created by the munching of thousands of voracious silkworms in a Japanese mountain farmhouse. Until a system of preserving silk cocoons was discovered, they had to be unspun into individual filaments soon after they were formed. A cocoon produces from 2000 to 3000 feet of filament—about half a mile—and four to eighteen of these tiny strands have to be twisted together to make a silk thread strong enough to use. One cocoon thus provides the material for about 200 feet of thread. The period of unwinding the cocoons and reeling the thread was a time of particularly concentrated labor for women. Because of the seasonal nature of the work, a single farm household produced no more than about four pounds of silk thread a year.

After the closing of Japan to most foreign contacts in the late 1630s, Chinese silks could no longer easily enter Japan, and Chinese silk thread was officially banned in 1685. This made native production much more important than before, and sericulture grew into a major industry in mountainous areas all over Japan. But the greatest silk-producing area of all was the mountainous borders of the Kanto Plain. Kiryu, a town on the plain a little south of Mizunuma, became Japan's most famous producer of silk cloth, though Kyoto remains even today the center of production for fine silk textiles.

Despite sericulture and other supplementary industries, Mizunuma and the region around it were poor even by premodern standards. I remember the four months I lived in the area before the end of World War II, when wartime deprivation worsened the natural poverty of the area. The peasants lived hard, frugal lives even compared to ordinary Japanese rice farmers. I would watch men, women, and children trudging each morning and evening through the valley on their way to and from work. Because they were too poor to own horses, and wheeled vehicles could not negotiate the steep hillsides, they walked along with their backs bent double under bamboo baskets loaded with tools, fertilizer, wood, or crops. They worked from dawn to dusk on tiny patches of land, often located miles apart. They ate a simple fare of boiled barley, buckwheat noodles, and pancakes made of wheat and millet, all garnished in the summer months by fresh vegetables and in the winter by pickled vegetables, but with almost no meat or fish. Their chief source of protein was soy beans, made into *shoyu* sauce, fermented *miso* paste, or *tofu*. They lived in flimsy wooden houses, with heavy thatch roofs and sparse furnishings. In the colder months the one cheerful spot was the sunken hearth in the center of the main room, where the family members could gather to warm themselves and talk. Since there was no chimney, the smoke from the twigs and sticks they burned filtered out through holes in the eaves. The charcoal they made was sold to more affluent areas, being too expensive for their own use. Even as late as the 1940s it was a life of grinding poverty, but the farmers quietly accepted it with dignity and self-respect, treating one another with decorum and courtesy.

———•———

Arai was not my grandfather's original surname. He was born into the Hoshino family but was given as an adopted son to carry on the Arai family, which had no heirs. Despite this, my grandfather throughout his life remained a Hoshino at heart, having this family as his main support and the economic base for his career in the United States. There are Hoshino family records dating back to the sixteenth century in the village temple, the Jokanji, dedicated to Kannon, the Buddhist goddess of mercy, and built in 1559, but oral family tradition goes back much farther. The Hoshinos are said to have originated in the old capital district around Kyoto and moved to the Kanto area in the tenth century as followers of Fujiwara Hidesato from the great Fujiwara clan of court nobles. Hidesato is known in history for his defeat in 940 of a rebel chieftain in the eastern part of the Kanto area, and he was the ancestor of the powerful Fujiwara family that settled in Mutsu, the northernmost province of Honshu. Here the Japanese slowly rolled back the frontier against the Emishi, the earlier inhabitants of this area and possibly the ancestors, at least in part, of the modern Ainu of Hokkaido.

The authority of the central government was not well established in this distant border area, and great families fought among each other for control, often in the name of the imperial court. In one such contest, which lasted from 1055 to 1063, the rising Minamoto family invaded Mutsu and destroyed the ruling Abe family. The Abe leader was killed, and his younger brother Muneto was captured and exiled to the extreme west in Kyushu. His followers accompanied him on his march into banishment, but along the way some decided to become *ochido* (dropouts), abandoning their lord and settling down in the area around Mizunuma. Three Hoshino brothers were said to have been among them.

Two of the three Hoshino brothers were swordsmiths, or *kajiya*. In early times this was an important and honorable profession, because these smiths not only made the swords the warriors treasured but looked after and repaired all of their lord's weapons. The younger of the swordsmith brothers, Sakyonosuke, settled on the northwest side of Mount Akagi at a place that came to be called Kajiya in honor of his profession. The older brother, Ukyonosuke, settled in Mizunuma, east of Akagi. An anvil used by his branch of the family was preserved for centuries, until it was lost in the disturbances at the time of the Meiji Restoration in 1868. When Ukyonosuke came to Mizunuma, most of the arable land had already been appropriated by earlier settlers, but as a swordsmith he did not need much space. He built his home and smithy on a narrow strip of land between the river and the mountain rising behind it. Today this is the site of the Kurohone village office.

At the edge of Mizunuma lies the community graveyard. In it a small flat stone measuring only 5 by 5 by 15 inches is thought to be the gravestone of Ukyonosuke himself. Time has erased its inscription, but it is of a style used in the eleventh century. Such small grave slabs are called *seoi* (carry on the back) because they were light enough to carry away if a family was forced to flee from its enemies. By the late sixteenth century the Hoshino grave plot was the largest and most imposing one in the cemetery, showing that they had become the most prominent family in the village. The earliest of the inscribed Hoshino graves is dated 1591 and is for Seikoin, the thirteenth-generation ancestor of the present head of the family. For him and the next six generations of family heads, only posthumous family names and death dates are recorded. Recent research, however, has revealed approximate birth dates for these early Hoshinos. Most seem to have lived past seventy and one to the age of eighty-five. The present head of the family, as I have mentioned, is Hoshino Yasushi, my grandfather's great nephew by blood.

When the Hoshinos first settled in Mizunuma in the eleventh century, Japanese feudalism was in its early days and the line between warrior and peasant was not sharply drawn. Most warriors were at the same time farmers, supported by their own pieces of agricultural land held in fief from their lords, and many peasants were armed and often formed a major part of a lord's fighting forces. With the political unification of the country in the late sixteenth century, however, a clear class line was artificially drawn between the samurai and the common people, who, in descending order of public status, were peasants, artisans, and merchants.

Hideyoshi, the second of the three great unifiers of the time and himself of peasant-soldier origin, decreed this division of classes, perhaps in an effort to cut down on the overabundance of fighting men in a now pacified country. In 1587, the year he achieved suzerainty over all of western Japan by winning the submission of Satsuma, he ordered the peasants to surrender their arms in what has been called the "great sword hunt." He also required all lesser landowners either to give up their lands and follow their lords to their castle towns as professional samurai soldiers or else to give up their military status and stay on their lands as demilitarized peasants. It is not surprising that among the less prominent warriors it was often the poorer ones who chose to become salaried soldiers and the more affluent who stayed as peasants on their lands.

This situation gave the Japanese countryside a class of former gentry warriors, who became proud village leaders. With the samurai class congregated largely in castle towns, these villagers enjoyed a great deal of autonomy. They were required to pay heavy taxes in kind to the local lord, to preserve peace and order in the village, and to observe the numerous laws and regulations of the political authorities, particularly the sumptuary laws that put strict limitations on clothing, housing, or any unseemly display of wealth. Within these bounds, however, villagers ran their own affairs, and the leading families were people of considerable prestige and constituted for all practical purposes the lowest stratum of officialdom.

The relatively high status of rich peasants was particularly marked in the broad Tokugawa realm. Whereas the reduction of the Satsuma domain had compressed many retainers of the Shimazu lords into a relatively small area, thus producing a high proportion of samurai in the population, the expansion of the Tokugawa realm after their triumph in 1600 had resulted in a relatively low ratio of samurai to commoners and therefore a greater role for peasant leaders. In the course of the Tokugawa period, the spread of a money economy, especially in the Tokugawa realm, also enhanced the status of the richer peasants because it lead to greater discrepancies between the rich and the poor in rural society. The history of the Hoshinos of Mizunuma, who from the start were among the local leaders, clearly shows these tendencies. Though classified as peasants in the strictly divided society of Tokugawa times, they served in fact as semi-government officials in the seventeenth century, and they steadily increased their wealth.

In 1667 the Hoshinos were made the hereditary village headmen of Mizunuma, serving under the supervision of the local intendant, or representative of the shogunal government, who oversaw the taxation of a large area with the help of such peasant administrators. Though requiring governmental approval, headmen in many cases were elected by their fellow villagers. They kept records of births, marriages, deaths, and land titles and were responsible for the payment of the village's share of taxes. When peasants could not pay their taxes, the Hoshinos would lend them money guaranteed by mortgages on their fields and, if the peasants defaulted, would acquire title to these lands. In this way, they became over the next century and a half one of the largest landholding families in the area.

———— • ————

Iyabei (1643–1718), the fourth generation of recorded Hoshinos in Mizunuma, added another semiofficial position. He was appointed by the shogunate to supervise the Ashio mines. Since copper had become the principal Japanese export in the restricted Chinese and Dutch trade at Nagasaki, and Ashio was the largest copper producer, this was a position of considerable importance. It was probably at this time that the Hoshinos gave up their original profession as swordsmiths to concentrate on their functions as village administrators, pawnbrokers, moneylenders, landowners, and mine operators.

The golden age of the Hoshino family started with the sixth family head, Hambei (1710–1795), who was nicknamed *ogosho-sama* (the emperor) because of his wealth and prestige. The family land, which had been only a half-acre in 1667, had increased by 1771 to seventeen acres, farmed by tenants. The Hoshinos received a percentage of the produce as rent and were also entitled to the mulberry leaves grown on the margins of their tenants' fields. Their production of mulberry leaves increased at this time from twenty bales to 315. The silk cocoons spun by the worms fed on these leaves was processed into silk thread by the womenfolk of the tenant households and then sold by the Hoshinos, who thus became silk merchants along with their various other activities.

Not all Japanese prospered as the Hoshino family did. The increase in nonagricultural production and the monetization of the economy, which moved inexorably ahead throughout the Tokugawa period, helped city merchants and the richer members of the peasant class but had adverse affects on poorer peasants and the warrior class as well. Prices rose but not the incomes of the samurai or their lords, which were tied to taxes based on rice production. The shogunate, already feeling the financial pinch in the second half of the seventeenth century, settled five of its higher retainers, known as *hatamoto* (standard bearers), in the area near Mizunuma and eighty-nine more in the nearby Kiryu region, where they were to be self-supporting from the lands allotted them. The shogunal realm had in all some five thousand hatamoto, who ranked between the daimyo, or enfeoffed lords with domains producing ten thousand or more koku of rice, and the various categories of samurai below the hatamoto, who had lesser salaries.

Before long the hatamoto who had settled near Mizunuma fell into debt to the Hoshinos, as did some of the lesser daimyo located in Kozuke. The five local domains that figure in our story were, in descending order of size, Maebashi, Takasaki, Tatebayashi, Numata, and Annaka, the last being the birthplace in modern times of Niijima Jo, the ex-samurai founder of Doshisha, the Christian university in Kyoto. The Maebashi domain is recorded in 1735 as borrowing from the Hoshinos 50 ryo, a not inconsiderable sum in those days, (a ryo was roughly equivalent in value to a koku of rice). The Hoshinos' activities as moneylenders illustrate the topsey-turvey economy of the late Tokugawa period, when feudal lords and lesser warrior aristocrats fell into debt not just to city merchants but even to peasants.

The country as a whole also underwent periods of famine. While that of 1732–33, caused by insect pests, affected southern Japan for the most part, the protracted famine conditions of 1783–1787 were worst in east and northeast Japan. Whole villages were wiped out, and cases of cannibalism were reported. Kozuke was particularly hard hit because Mount Asama, Japan's largest active volcano, located on the western border of the province and looming above the modern summer resort of Karuizawa, added to the woes of the people by erupting disastrously in 1783. Villages were swept away, rivers boiled, and ashes buried much of Kozuke and some other provinces to a depth of several feet, destroying all the crops. My husband and I remember well that around Karuizawa, where we both spent many of our childhood summers, the mountains and valleys lie buried several feet deep by a layer of scoria, a kind of pumice stone from this eruption. What fascinated us as children was not the geological history of these stones but the fact that they are so perforated with holes that they float. More than a million people are reported to have died from this great erup-tion and the more widespread famine. Rice prices soared sixfold, and, because of the disastrous fall in rice production, daimyo, hatamoto, and samurai fell further into debt. The Hoshinos, however, had ade-quate stores of food on hand to survive these hard times, and their ledgers show a thriving business in pawnbroking and moneylending.

Following the famine of the 1780s, the shogunate reacted with a renewed effort to enforce sumptuary laws and return to the austere ways of an earlier day. Although such attempts have always been lauded by traditional historians, it was improved weather conditions rather than governmental moralizing that led to a return of prosperity. The shogun's court, the daimyo, and their samurai retainers quickly resumed the spendthrift ways that were to plunge the whole feudal establishment ever deeper into debt.

Hoshino Kohei (1756–1840), the eighth generation of recorded Hoshino family heads, was in control of its fortunes during the time of restored prosperity. He found he had more accumulated wealth than he could easily invest locally and went in search of new economic opportunities. He proceeded to the Nambu domain in northern Honshu, the present Iwate prefecture, where the shogunate was opening new gold, silver, and copper mines, and also to the northern tip of Honshu, where he invested in coastal shipping as well as horse breeding. Despite his entrepreneurial daring, however, these enterprises proved unprofitable and Kohei returned to the traditional family activities in Kozuke. By then the family had 124 acres of land spread throughout a number of villages around Mizunuma. Of this only 20 acres was arable land, half of which he rented out to tenants. The rest he farmed himself with hired workers, adding temporary help at peak seasons. In 1816 the household living in the family compound consisted of twenty-one persons—six members of the Hoshino family, seven hereditary servants, and eight hired servants.

During Kohei's time a revolutionary innovation took place in sericulture. Around 1830 a process was developed for the drying and preserving of silk cocoons so that the reeling of the silk could be done during the slack period of winter and not in the peak work season of summer. This greatly increased the productivity of each woman reeler. By this time records show the Hoshinos producing as much as 1451 bales of mulberry leaves on their own lands in a single year. They also bought cocoons from merchants in the nearby town of Numata, which had developed into a center for the silk trade. In a good year the Hoshinos would spend more than 2000 ryo on such purchases. These together with the cocoons produced on their own lands were dried and stored until winter and then doled out in sixteen-pound bags to their tenants and other peasant families in Mizunuma and neighboring villages; the women of these households would spend the winter months turning the cocoons into silk thread. Wages were paid in advance. The contents of the bags would be dumped into huge iron pots of water in which the outer protective membranes of the cocoons were boiled away. The ends of the silk filaments would then be painstakingly located from the mass of silk thread that made up the bulk of the cocoons and would be passed through tiny holes in porcelain cylinders onto hand-operated reels where the thread was wound. These reels the Hoshinos would collect in the late winter and early spring months for sale as raw silk to merchants and weavers of Kiryu. Some they even sold as far away as Kyoto. A 1793 entry records 85 ryo worth of silk bound for Kyoto.

———— • ————

Because of the prominence of the family, Tomohiro (1791–1856), the ninth-generation family head who had taken over the headship of the family from the still-living Kohei, was elevated in 1830 to quasi-samurai status. This was called *myoji taito* (surnamed and sword-bearing). Commoners generally were not allowed to have family names, though those of higher background and wealth obviously did. I am not certain whether the name Hoshino was adopted at this time or had been used surreptitiously all along. In any case Tomohiro, even after being elevated to surnamed and sword-bearing status, is referred to in the official documents simply as Shichiroemon, which was the formal personal name used by each family head from the fourth through the tenth generations.

With his new officially recognized position, Tomohiro was expressly assigned the duties of collecting and delivering the taxes of the local area, preserving the peace, settling disputes, and arresting and punishing lawbreakers. The Hoshinos by this time, though still classified as peasants, were clearly local government officials. To perform his peacekeeping functions, Tomohiro built a wooden prison on the present location of the village office below his own home. Here culprits were held until retainers of the lord of the nearby Numata domain, who served as the local shogunal intendant, came to take them away. Tomohiro also maintained a storehouse stocked with bows, arrows, pikes, armor, helmets, firearms, and three hundred swords. The swords were kept in a large specially constructed sword chest (*katana-dansu*). The chest still remains, but the swords were donated to the government during the Russo-Japanese War.

To prevent rich commoners from amassing too much wealth, the Tokugawa government from time to time would drain off some of their money through especially assigned duties. For example, when it was decided to rebuild the Hommaru, the central part of the great Edo castle which had been destroyed by fire in 1829, the authorities ordered two of the richest commoners in Kozuke to supply the necessary lumber. The two men were Kabe Yasusaemon and Hoshino Tomohiro, and the undertaking lasted most of 1834 and 1835, costing a total of 5215 ryo. A strict time limit was set, and a failure to meet it could result in the loss of all one's wealth. Even daimyo who failed in such assigned tasks might be stripped of their domains and transferred to some other part of the country.

The Hoshinos owned extensive forests of *keyaki,* a tall hardwood tree commonly used for construction, but the trees were in inaccessible areas deep in the mountains. To build the necessary roads and bridges and drag out the great logs required considerable manpower as well as organizational skills. The Hoshino family still treasures a six-hundred-page document and a scroll painting eleven meters long which describe and illustrate the great undertaking. The first scene on the scroll shows lumbermen chipping a groove around the trunk of a tree near its base. The next shows them fanning the flames in this groove made by oil-soaked charcoal set on fire, which gradually burned through the trunk and toppled the tree. Other scenes show the construction of roads, the building of bridges over ravines, the plaiting of ropes, the skidding of logs down steep slopes to the river below, the binding of the logs together in great rafts to float down the Watarase River to the large Tonegawa River in the environs of Edo, and a government receiving station, where the logs were numbered and recorded. Above the station float banners displaying the red sun of the later national flag of Japan and characters reading *goyo* (honorable use), meaning service to the government.

Just when the Hoshinos were reaching their peak of prosperity and local prominence, Japan was subjected once again to prolonged famine. Starting in 1832, the so-called Tempo famines, named for the year period, lasted through the decade, producing much suffering and rioting. The most serious uprising, which occurred in the large city of Osaka, was led by a samurai named Oshio Heihachiro and had revolutionary overtones—but the smaller riots, called "smashing," which broke out all over the country, were merely desperate efforts by peasants and townsmen to seize food and have their debts canceled. In 1836 several hundred hungry peasants, after ravaging the town of Omama just south of Mizunuma, started marching toward the Hoshinos' land. To fulfill his official duties, Tomohiro donned his armor and helmet and, mounted on a black steed, led a large contingent of villagers he had armed with swords, pikes, bows and arrows, and even firearms to meet the approaching mob. Confronted by this formidable force, the rioters turned and fled.

Tomohiro himself had sufficient food and with his fifteen-year-old son, Yahei (1824–1886), went among the villagers to deliver food and medicine. After the famine ended, the villagers in gratitude organized a large labor force to dig out the hill above the Hoshino house, making a broad level space. On this Yahei constructed what was called his "upper residence." On the original lower level, he left quarters for his servants and employees and his stables. In front of the upper level was an impressive stone wall with a heavy tile-roofed gateway, decorated and reinforced with wrought iron. In addition to the residence, the upper level also had five storehouses for grain and valuables. Under the storehouses ran a secret escape passageway that led out onto the mountainside. In short, this "peasant" home was very reminiscent of a feudal stronghold. The front wall and gate still stand, but behind them the once beautiful garden and buildings are in a state of disrepair. Only two of the storehouses remain, crammed until 1983 with old family possessions and valuable documents, deep in dust.

The Tempo reforms of 1841–1843, which followed the famines of the preceding decade, did little to halt the financial decline of the shogunate, the domains, and the whole warrior class. As the commercial money economy continued to grow, the ruling class found itself receiving less and less of the economic pie. It lived off the taxes on agriculture, which remained fairly constant, as the economy as a whole kept growing, prices rose, and living standards improved. Reforms aimed at restoring frugal ways of life had no chance of success. Domain monopolies on some local products gave some respite, but only in a few areas. Currency debasement simply hastened the upward spiral of prices. The cutting of samurai stipends to salvage shogunal or domain treasuries made warrior indebtedness all the more inevitable and undercut the loyalty on which the whole feudal political structure rested. To keep going financially, the shogunal government in Edo, as well as most domains, exacted from their merchants forced loans, euphemistically called "funds for honorable use" (*goyokin*), and individual samurai added to their personal debts to moneylenders at an ever-increasing rate.

While the samurai and feudal lords were becoming the debtor class, city merchants and rich peasants like the Hoshinos were becoming the creditor class. During the first half of the nineteenth century, in the time of Tomohiro and his successor Yahei, these conditions reached their peak. Many local hatamoto, officials of the shogunal government, and nearby daimyo fell deeply into debt to them. By 1832 they had 8526 ryo out in loans and investments, some 30 percent to hatamoto alone. Their annual income from pawn brokerage was 333 ryo and from interest on loans 525 ryo. These high levels were maintained for the next two decades. When you remember that a ryo was equal in value to a koku of rice, that the smallest daimyos were by definition possessors of domains that produced 10,000 koku of rice, and that the income of a daimyo, which included all the expenses of government, was derived from the percentage of the rice yield gathered as taxes, you can see that the Hoshinos were about as well-off as the average small daimyo. It is no wonder that Yahei was promoted by the shogunal government to the prestigious posts of local elder (*toshiyori-yaku*) and county administrator (*gun torishimari-yaku*).

There was a flaw in the situation, however. The Hoshinos' prosperity depended on the solvency and cooperation of their debtors. As the economic conditions of the warrior class continued to deteriorate, they increasingly defaulted on their loans, and by the 1850s the Hoshinos' revenues from this source had dropped to less than 30 percent of what they had been. At times the Hoshinos found themselves so overextended with bad loans that they were forced to borrow money themselves in an effort to keep their aristocratic debtors afloat. Because of the drastic decline in income from moneylending, they had to fall back on their agricultural holdings. These by now were considerable, for they had 176 tenants on their land.

The turmoil that followed Perry's arrival in Japan in 1853 only worsened matters for the warrior class but, when the commercial treaties negotiated by Townsend Harris went into effect in 1860, they brought sudden prosperity to Japanese silk producers. A silk-cocoon disease had broken out in 1852 in southern France and in a few years worked its way northward, all but destroying the French silk industry. By the early 1860s, the blight had spread to Italy, the other major European silk producer. As a result, British merchants rushed to Japan from Hong Kong and Shanghai and eagerly bought up all the silkworm eggs and raw silk they could find. The European silk blight thus pushed Japan rapidly into world trade and gave it for a few years a favorable balance of trade.

Louis Pasteur, however, eliminated the silk disease, and by the 1870s European silk production was restored. This caused a momentary setback for Japanese silk, but the industry had established a place for itself in the world silk market. The demand for silk grew, and prices skyrocketed. Fortunes in a silk-producing area like Kozuke were made almost overnight. One would have expected Yahei to have ridden the wave of this new prosperity, but he was what might be called loan-poor as well as land-poor. His capital was tied up and not available for extending his operations in silk. Nevertheless, as Japan entered the new age, he remained the most prestigious figure in his corner of Kozuke.

Modern Student

My grandfather was the sixth son of Hoshino Yahei, the tenth generation of recorded heads of the family. He was born on the nineteenth day of the seventh month of the second year of Ansei, which was August 31, 1855, in the Western calendar. It was two years after the coming of Perry's ships but before the shock of the opening of Japan had reached the mountain village of Mizunuma. At first his education was quite traditional. At six he began his studies with a tutor who came to the house. Two years later he started studying the Chinese classics under a Confucian scholar, who for some unknown reason had renounced his samurai status in the Omura domain in distant Kyushu and settled down in Mizunuma. He also took lessons in the martial art of kendo from a samurai of the nearby small domain of Annaka.

At the age of twelve he was adopted by Arai Keisaku (also known by the name of Denemon, which was the *shumei,* or succession name, of the eldest son of the Arai family). Keisaku's own son had died at a young age, and in order to have a successor he had adopted in succession two other Hoshino boys, both of whom had also died. It was at the time of his adoption that my grandfather's original name of Ryosuke was changed to Rioichiro, a name signifying a first son. According to the standard form of *Romaji* (Roman letters), the system for writing Japanese in the Latin alphabet, the name should be spelled Ryoichiro, but I shall respect my grandfather's own practice by rendering it Rioichiro.

The Arais were the leading residents of Kazuno village, some two miles back in the hills from Mizunuma. They were large landowners, but their principal business was wholesale dealing in silk for the silk-weaving industry in Kiryu. The name of their company was Yamaguchi-ya. *Yama,* meaning mountain, is often used as the equivalent of forest, and the company name derived from an earlier time when the family had dealt in instruments connected with forestry work, such as hatchets, axes, and saws. The company trademark, which includes the character for mountain, is to be found on the large storehouse that still stands in the village: 𡶠

The Arai family lived in the largest house in Kazuno, surrounded by a lovely garden. The storehouse for silk is a beautifully built two-storied structure, with huge beams, broad polished floorboards, white plastered walls, and a tile roof. It was in this spacious and sturdy building that my parents and I spent the last few months of World War II, and today it is the base for a small summer camp of my sister Tane's Nishimachi International School. When I lived there, the main residence was gone, destroyed by fire. The villagers would reminisce nostalgically about it and their former leading family. Incidentally, almost all of them had adopted the surname of Arai themselves when they were allowed to take family names shortly after the Meiji Restoration.

After the death of his first wife, and after my grandfather had left the Kazuno-Mizunuma area to make his way in the world, Keisaku married Nobuko, who was twenty years his junior. She and her mother moved to Tokyo after Keisaku's death, and I have childhood memories of both of them. Nobuko I called Kazuno no Obaasan, or Kazuno grandmother, and her mother, Onjo no Obaasan, Onjo grandmother, a name derived from her married name. Whenever Nobuko and her mother came to see us, they would arrive with many gifts, including Nagasaki *kasutera.* The name *kasutera* is said to be derived from Castile and designates a type of cake much like a pound cake; it is a specialty of Nagasaki, where the Japanese supposedly learned how to make it from the Portuguese or Spanish before these Europeans were expelled from Japan in the first half of the seventeenth century.

My Onjo grandmother had a fascinating background. Her husband, Onjo Kendo (1823–1910), had been a low-ranking samurai footsoldier (*ashigaru*) in the service of Ii Naosuke, the daimyo of Hikone, who was the shogunal prime minister who made a valiant effort to restore Tokugawa authority, only to be assassinated in 1860. Onjo's devotion to his lord was so great that he vowed to serve his memory the rest of his life. He resigned his samurai status to become a Buddhist priest and lived in the Gotokuji temple near Edo in order to care for Ii's grave. On his own death, gravestones were erected for him near the stones for Ii Naosuke in Hikone and at the Gotokuji, and a large stone tablet recounting Onjo's story was also raised at the temple.

The Gotokuji remains a beautiful place of solitude, now engulfed by the suburban sprawl of Tokyo's Setagaya ward. It is well known both as the site of the impressive graves of the Ii family and as the origin of the popular figure of the "beckoning cat," which has one paw lifted in a beckoning gesture. The cat is believed to be an incarnation of Kannon, the goddess of mercy. According to tradition, in the seventeenth century a cat saved the life of the head of the Ii family by beckoning him into the temple grounds, saving him from being killed by a thunderbolt that stuck at the spot he had just left. Pottery beckoning cats are still popular all over Japan.

When Onjo took Buddhist orders, he renounced his wife and three children, making his wife a virtual widow. In order to support her children, she moved to the town of Takasaki in Kozuke to work in the silk industry, which was prospering because of the strong demand for Japanese silk in Europe. When the government built a silk factory in 1872 in Tomioka about ten miles southwest of Takasaki, she was hired to instruct the young girls in silk reeling. Keisaku, who was a widower, frequently visited Tomioka in connection with his work and met her daughter, Nobuko, whom he eventually married.

———•———

By the time of Rioichiro's adoption, Japan was in a revolutionary uproar caused by the impact of Western military power and trade. Because of this and in order to give Rioichiro the companionship of his natural brothers, he was not moved to his adoptive home but continued his education in the Hoshino household. In fact, he never did live with the Arai family. As political order in Japan kept deteriorating, a famine struck in 1867. The people of Kozuke were particularly hard hit, since in this silk-producing region many farmers had converted grain fields to mulberries. Food prices soared, sometimes as much as threefold. Once again the "smashing" type of riot broke out through the countryside and enveloped the nearby town of Omama.

Yahei, who was determined to protect the eighteen villages over which he now held jurisdiction, prepared to take the offensive. He provided his people with food from his own storehouse and supplemented this with imported Chinese rice. He also organized a military force under the command of his eldest son, Chotaro (1846–1908), who was Rioichiro's oldest blood brother and in time became the eleventh generation of family heads. Chotaro in traditional armor and helmet and riding a black horse, as had his grandfather in 1838, led his men out to the borders of their territory. There they found that the peasants of other villages had buried their valuables, boarded up their houses, and posted large signs reading, "We surrender." Chotaro chided them for their cowardice and ordered them to join his band to protect their villages. Thus strengthened, he proceeded and, when he encountered the rioters, quickly routed the unruly mob, taking many of them prisoner and confining them in a nearby Buddhist temple.

The Meiji Restoration of the next year brought further disorders to the Mizunuma area and near disaster to the Hoshinos. The so called imperial forces, led by samurai of Satsuma, Choshu, and other western domains, seized the imperial palace in Kyoto, defeated the Tokugawa army in a battle outside of the city, marched on Edo, and after some fighting there received the capitulation of the Tokugawa—but some Tokugawa loyalists fought on. Among them, the most determined were the men of the relatively large collateral domain of Aizu, which occupied basins in the mountainous region northeast of Mizunuma. For two centuries they had provided the shogunate with guards for the imperial palace in Kyoto, and they were furious at being displaced by rank outsiders from distant Satsuma and Choshu. They looked on these men from western Japan as simple rebels and, despite the shogun's surrender, were determined to put up a last-ditch stand at their castle headquarters in Wakamatsu.

Itagaki of Tosa, whom we have already met as one of the early Meiji leaders and later the founder of a popular opposition movement against the new government, was the general of the imperial forces dispatched to subdue Aizu. The Aizu forces were being surreptitiously supplied by daimyo and rich individuals in surrounding areas. Itagaki was informed by one of the rioters whom Chotaro had captured and confined the previous year that the Hoshinos were among these supporters of Aizu. Even though the Hoshinos no doubt were Tokugawa sympathizers, that charge was not true; but they had no way to prove it. Itagaki, terming the outside support Aizu was receiving "the roots of the rebellion" and declaring that "if we destroy the roots, the branches will whither," dispatched to Mizunuma a force of two hundred soldiers, armed with guns and dressed in new Western-style uniforms with leather boots.

Yahei, confident that he would be cleared of the false charges, ordered his villagers to welcome the soldiers, but Itagaki's men ignored the peasants and marched directly to the Hoshino residence. With fixed bayonets they stomped in their muddy boots into the house and rounded up all the members of the household, then numbering thirty-six. After some interrogations, they arrested only the family members, including thirteen-year-old Rioichiro, and threatened them all with execution. With swords pointed at their throats, they were dragged by the soldiers to the village prison, which Yahei's father had himself constructed. The trembling village barber was forced to shave the right eyebrow and the right half of the head of all the members of the family to mark them as criminals, a procedure called *katabin* (half-shorn). Then, with ropes around their necks, they were paraded around the village as enemies of the imperial cause. The Hoshino lands and belongings were confiscated and placed under the custody of the local Jokanji temple. Yahei in prison stubbornly maintained his innocence, declaring he would stand his ground even in the face of execution. Even then, only the intercession in his behalf by the daimyo of the nearby Tatebayashi domain, with which the Hoshinos had had close economic ties, induced the court noble Iwakura, the commander-in-chief of the imperial forces, to order his release.

Yahei had suffered great humiliation and, after returning home, he vowed in fury that he would never again live in such an ill-omened house where the tatami floors had been desecrated by the muddy boots of soldiers. (Japanese even today do not wear any outdoor footgear when walking on tatami floors or, for that matter, in any part of a Japanese house.) Yahei ordered his men to destroy the house and himself started cutting down the pillars of the storehouses and setting them ablaze. When he had destroyed two of the storehouses in this way, *metsuke,* who were the government spies of the old Tokugawa system, arrived and ordered the destruction stopped. Today only two of the storehouses survive. It was in this terrifying manner that my grandfather was introduced to the new age of imperial rule.

————•————

The new government busily set about liquidating the old feudal system. The daimyo were paid off with government bonds, and the stipends of the hatamoto and samurai were reduced and finally in 1876 commuted into relatively small cash payments. This economic decline of the warrior class meant almost complete ruin for the Hoshinos. Their extensive loans to daimyo, hatamoto, and samurai, on which the rate of defaults had been steadily mounting, now had to be written off completely. Despite their inauspicious start with the new government, however, Yahei's son Chotaro was appointed in 1869 chief accountant of the newly created prefecture of Iwahana. In contrast to Matsukata's small prefecture of Hita, Iwahana was an area that produced over 500,000 koku of rice.

Rioichiro saw how pleased his brother was by such public recognition, and he began to think about his own future in this strange new age. He was determined to get away from Mizunuma and learn something of the world. Perhaps he also felt that he was no longer obligated to succeed his adoptive father in the family business in Kazuno because the so-called Charter Oath, which the new leaders had had the boy emperor issue in the spring of 1868, had specifically stated that everyone "will have a chance to fulfill his just aspirations." He decided that he would go to Tokyo, as Edo had been renamed, to discover for himself what opportunities there were. This was a daring decision for a fourteen-year-old, but his two sets of parents gave their consent. Yahei arranged for Rioichiro to live with a family friend, a samurai who had gone to Edo to teach the Chinese classics. Thus in late 1869 he set off by foot for Tokyo, some 65 miles away as the crow flies but considerably more by road. He carried only a small bundle of clothing and a few books wrapped in a *furoshiki,* a square piece of cloth that is still used in Japan as a useful carry-all.

Tokyo was in a sorry state. Parts of the city had been damaged by the fighting in 1868, and the population had dropped sharply after many of the daimyo and their retainers had left their residences in Edo, following the abandonment of the system of alternate years of residence in the capital. But to a wide-eyed country boy it must have seemed a wonderful place. It was a huge city. Even in 1700 it had a population of around a million and was probably the largest city in the world for a century or more. In Mizunuma there were almost no stores, but in Tokyo they lined both sides of most downtown streets and were overflowing with wondrous merchandise.

Tokyo was crammed with fierce-looking soldiers from Satsuma, Choshu, and other western domains. Many of them had bayonetted guns and were dressed in newfangled occidental uniforms like those worn by the soldiers who had stomped into the Hoshino house. The streets were crowded with grandees in palanquins, men on horseback, sword-bearing samurai, peddlers hawking their wares with lacquer boxes on their backs or baskets slung on poles, and artisans and merchants, dressed in their distinctive blue costumes decorated with the trademark or name of their companies and often carrying huge packages on their backs. Because of the unsettled times, there were many beggars in filthy rags, huddled under bridges or in dark corners.

In the center of the merchant quarter of the city stood high, curving Nihonbashi, the Bridge of Japan, from which all the main highways of Japan were measured and where, in the clean air of that time, one could see Mount Fuji on the horizon. In front of the bridge stood an imposing wooden billboard set on a stone foundation and sheltered by a tile roof. It announced the centuries-old prohibition of Christianity: "So long as the Sun shall warm the earth, let no Christian be so bold as to come to Japan; and let all know that the King of Spain himself, or the Christian's God or the Great God of all, if he violates this command, shall suffer for it with his head." Despite this stern warning, there was a French hotel and other Western buildings in the foreign settlement in Tsukiji on the waterfront not far away. Here could be seen the blue-eyed, red-haired, and red-bearded Westerners, dressed in strange apparel. For all East Asians, accustomed only to jet black hair and brown eyes, hair of any other color always seemed red and eyes blue, the colors commonly used in East Asian art to depict demons.

Inland from the merchant quarters and on higher ground were the huge residences of the daimyo, now being converted into government offices and homes for the new officialdom. At the center of this part of the city stood the great castle of Edo. Its mammoth stone walls were capped by white walled guardtowers and were surrounded by broad moats with steep embankments. Here, where the Tokugawa shogun had lived for more than two and a half centuries, the young emperor was now ensconced.

Rioichiro may have dreamed of becoming an official and playing a large role in government, as my other grandfather was starting to do, but if he did entertain such thoughts they probably would have led only to frustration. Some able men from the shogun's realm and from domains all over Japan were brought into the new government, but the important places belonged to the samurai from Satsuma and Choshu, who with their protégés were to dominate Japan's political life until the early twentieth century. Rioichiro probably could see that for him, a peasant boy from a commercially oriented family in the shogun's realm, private enterprise held more promise than government service. It was even clearer that Chinese classical studies offered little and that the new knowledge from the West and a command of English, which some described as the "intellectual currency of the commercial world," were the paths to success. He decided that he must master English.

Before Rioichiro could get really started on his English studies, he was recalled to Mizunuma by Chotaro, who was by now taking the lead in family planning in place of the aging and less adaptive Yahei. Iwahana prefecture, like Hita, had been created in June 1868 out of pieces of the shogun's realm, but when all the domains were abolished in November 1871 the prefectural system was completely reorganized to incorporate the whole country; the province of Kozuke was made into the new prefecture of Gumma. With the disappearance of Iwahana, Chotaro's position with the prefectural government came to an end, and he decided that the whole family would have to make a fresh economic start by immersing itself in the booming silk industry. He wanted Rioichiro back in Mizunuma so that he too could learn the business.

Since the start of trade with the West in 1860, Kozuke, now Gumma prefecture, had become the largest producing area of silk, which together with tea were Japan's chief exports. As a result Gumma prospered greatly. For example, the small Maebashi domain had been bankrupt in 1860, with its daimyo living in debt-ridden poverty, but the domain did so well in the silk trade over the next few years that he could build himself a new castle and the samurai of the domain were rescued from destitution. The process of reeling by hand, however, limited production and produced silk of inferior quality because of its lack of uniformity. Since Western reeling machines could overcome both problems, the Maebashi domain in 1869 hired Swiss technicians to set up a Western-style silk-reeling factory. This was the first factory of its kind in Japan, though it is less famous than the one established in Tomioka in 1872 by the central government.

Chotaro soon came to realize that, without modernized production techniques, he could not produce silk in adequate quantity or quality to meet the demands of the foreign market. He decided to go to Maebashi to learn the Western machine techniques for reeling. He turned over the management of the family's farmlands to one of his younger brothers and became an apprentice at the Maebashi factory. There he came under the supervision of Hayami Kenso, then the leading Japanese expert in machine reeling and silk production in general. After finishing his apprenticeship, Chotaro returned to Mizunuma and built a small reeling factory run by power from a wooden waterwheel on a small stream running through the compound of the Hoshino residence. He lacked the ready capital to pay for the imported machines, but the central government, interested in promoting Japan's most promising export industry, lent him 3000 yen without interest, repayable in five years.

———•———

When Rioichiro returned to Mizunuma, he set about learning the silk business, but he also started to study English, late in 1871, since the family intended to get into the export business. He went to an English school in the nearby Takasaki domain. The daimyo of Takasaki was a strong promoter of education and established several domain schools for various subjects. In 1855 he founded a school to teach his samurai Western military techniques and another school for Japanese poetry and literature. Shortly before Rioichiro returned to Mizunuma, the daimyo had started the Takasaki Domain English School (Takasaki Han Eigo Gakko), for which fifty promising young samurai were chosen as the first students. Among them were Uchimura Kanzo, who was to become a leading intellectual and Japan's most famous Christian leader. Rejecting the sectarian divisions of the

Protestant missionaries and any formal ecclesiastic organization, he started what was called the "no-church" movement. Another samurai student was Ozaki Yukio, who became one of the great liberal politicians of Japan and the Tokyo mayor who presented the city of Washington with its glorious cherry trees.

It was this group that Rioichiro joined, even though he was a "peasant" and from outside the domain territory. But there seems to have been no particular prejudice against him, which is hardly surprising given the long economic contacts of the Hoshino family with the nearby domains. In fact, one interesting comment on Rioichiro from this time shows quite a different attitude. Ozaki wrote in his autobiography:

> Arai Rioichiro was a surprisingly handsome young man. When I was a child I used to be called a "demon child" because I looked so much like one. The holes of my nose were turned upward, and on rainy days one would have expected raindrops to fall right into them—though I don't recall that they actually did—and my teeth jutted out. I was famous in the neighborhood as the "ugly boy," much to my parents' embarrassment, especially my poor mother's. I longed to become like the unmatchably handsome Arai, and I thought if I tried hard enough to look better I could change my looks somewhat. So, with Arai as my model, I did my best, and today I feel certain that it was because of this that my physiognomy did improve.*

When the capital of Gumma was moved from Takasaki to Maebashi in 1872 and the English school in Takasaki was closed soon thereafter, Rioichiro decided to join some of his schoolmates in following their best teacher, Koizumi Atsumi, to his new assignment to start an English school in distant Yamada in Ise, near the great Ise Shrines southeast of Kyoto. Rioichiro and the other students set off together with Koizumi. On this second trip away from Gumma, Rioichiro did not have to carry his own baggage. A transport company using hand-drawn carts had been organized to carry freight and the travelers' *kori,* which were convenient basket-type trunks that expanded or contracted to fit the contents. The party walked to Tokyo,

* *Godo jiden* (Tokyo: Osaka Jiji Shimposha, 1947), pp. 9–11.

then took the newly completed train line the eighteen miles to Yokohama—surely an exciting experience for any Japanese at this time—and from Yokohama it went by steamship to Ise.

The English school at Yamada was set up in the Miyazaki Library (Bunko), located in the outer precincts of the Ise Shrines and established in 1648 for the training of Shinto administrators. It was an odd place for an English school. The shrines are Japan's most holy spot, housing the sacred mirror that symbolizes the Sun Goddess and serves as one of the "three imperial regalia" of the emperors. Though suffering from neglect at various times in Japanese history, the Ise Shrines were now once again the focus of national attention as a link between the new imperial government and Japan's ancient traditions. Normally the shrine buildings were reconstructed every twenty years, in faithful imitation of the simple, austere architecture of the fifth century. Though far from imposing structures, they invoke even today a sense of worshipful awe in their setting of natural beauty among great towering trees.

Rioichiro was in Yamada from November 1873 until May 1874, paying tuition of 24 yen for that half-year period. He then decided to return to Tokyo to continue more advanced English studies. Many schools had been set up by foreigners in Tokyo and Yokohama to teach English, and it was clear that there was more to be learned at the capital than in remote Yamada. In 1873 Rioichiro had passed hurriedly through Tokyo, but in 1874 he got a much fuller impression of the city. It had changed greatly in the five years since his first brief stay there in 1869. The population was returning to what it had been before the collapse of the Tokugawa. The destruction of the 1868 war had been repaired. Many daimyo mansions had been torn down to be replaced by new government buildings in semi-Western style. Here the officials now sat on chairs and worked at desks instead of sitting on the floor, as had always been the custom in Japan. The streets were cleaner, and some even had gas lighting. Palanquins had virtually disappeared, and rickshas and carriages dominated traffic. The billboards banning Christianity had been removed. Few oldfashioned samurai with their two swords were to be seen, and instead there were many soldiers wearing Western uniforms and armed with rifles. There were policemen also in Western uniforms. Most samurai topknots had disappeared, and cropped haircuts in the Western fashion were the style. Barbershops had sprung up all over the city, and a Western haircut was regarded as a symbol of modernity. Western hats were to be seen everywhere, even if the man below the hat might still be wearing Japanese clothing. Most high government officials were dressed fully in Western style, and there were stores selling foreign goods of all sorts.

The Charter Oath of 1868 had stated that "absurd customs and practices of the past shall be discarded," and indeed many old customs were being abandoned. Upper-class married women were less frequently shaving off their eyebrows or blackening their teeth, though I remember my grandfather's mother and grandmother by adoption did continue these practices to the end. Abortion, infanticide, mixed bathing of the sexes, mixed wrestling, tatooing, and the sale of pornographic books were all banned as "absurd" relics of the uncivilized past. Although the eating of the meat of any four-legged animal had been abhorred by Japanese for centuries, daring young men were experimenting. The prejudice against the eating of meat had arisen from the Buddhist condemnation of the taking of any life and had probably been strengthened by the lack of space for raising animals for food. Now beef eating was suddenly fashionable and praised as highly nutritional. It was at this time that some medical students are said to have invented sukiyaki.

Whereas only a few years earlier the battle cry of the imperial forces had been *sonno joi* (honor the emperor, expel the barbarians), the new slogan was *bummei kaika* (civilization and enlightenment). Now the barbarians were looked on with great respect, and their science, technology, and ways of doing things were what was meant by "civilization." The words of the 1868 Charter Oath—"wisdom and knowledge shall be sought from all over the world"—were being put into practice with enthusiasm. Westerners were avidly sought as teachers, and their books were translated and eagerly read. The Tokugawa government had a translation bureau for foreign books, but the new government in 1869 established a much larger bureau for this purpose. The translation efforts of private individuals, however, had an even greater popular impact. One relatively obscure English book had a particularly deep influence. This was *Self Help* by the Englishman Samuel Smiles, published in Japan in 1870 as *Saikoku risshi,* which might be rendered "The Establishment of Will Power in the West."

The translation was by Nakamura Masanao (1832–1891), a former Confucian scholar of the old shogunate official school, who later became a Christian. It expounded Western ethical principles of self-reliance, hard work, and upright character.

The most important figure in the "civilization and enlightenment" movement, and a man who greatly influenced Rioichiro, was Fukuzawa Yukichi (1835–1901), whom we met earlier as a critic of Matsukata's economic policies. Fukuzawa was a samurai from the relatively small north Kyushu domain of Nakatsu. He had gone as a student to Edo where, on the opening of trade with the West in 1860, he learned to his chagrin that English, rather than the Dutch he had been studying, was the language of the traders coming to Japan. He accompanied the first Tokugawa mission to America in 1860 and traveled twice more in the West. Shortly before the Restoration he founded a school in Edo that eventually grew into Keio Gijuku University. Keio ranks today with Okuma's Waseda University as one of Japan's two leading private universities. In 1866 Fukuzawa started issuing pamphlets, collectively called *Seiyo jijo* (Conditions in the West), which played a major role in informing Japanese about the West, though to many what he wrote seemed like "curious tales from dreamland." In 1872 he started a new pamphlet series called *Gakumon no susume* (The Encouragement of Learning), which is said to have sold millions of copies. In it he expounded Western concepts in his own terms, writing, for example, "Heaven does not create men over men or men under men. All men are created equal without distinction as to high or low, noble or humble."*

Because Fukuzawa was concerned with the common man, he avoided the usual artificial literary style, which used obsolete grammatical forms and was heavily larded with Chinese idiom and vocabulary, writing instead in the spoken language. He also wrote for women and children and believed strongly in the necessity of educating women as the people who would raise the next generation. He sent his own wife and daughters to learn English under American teachers at the Christian school established by Nakamura in Yokohama. In 1874, the year the Meiji political leaders established their Western social

* As quoted in Chitoshi Yanaga, *Japan since Perry* (New York: McGraw-Hill, 1949), p. 132.

hall, the Pavilion of the Deer's Cry, Fukuzawa and nine other leading intellectuals founded a group misleadingly called the Meirokusha, or Society of the Sixth Year of Meiji (1873). It was modeled after the literary and scientific societies of the West and was designed to enlighten Japanese on the new concepts and train their leaders in public discussion and debate, which had never been much practiced in Japan.

As feudalism collapsed and the old Confucian orthodoxy became discredited, Japanese intellectuals reached out for something to take the place of Confucianism. Many of them found this in the Protestant ethic of men like Smiles and the American missionaries. English-language textbooks used in all the schools were mostly American and deeply implanted in Japanese minds mid-nineteenth-century American ideals, as well as George Washington and Benjamin Franklin as heroes of world history. The emphasis on strength of character, uprightness, and public service in the new Christian ethics was not very different from some aspects of the old Confucianism, but it was free from the traditional Sinocentric and Japanese feudal concepts of the past.

For the men from Choshu and Satsuma, like my Matsukata grandfather, who were engrossed in building a new Japanese state consistent with their own ideas of imperial unity, this foreign philosophy had less significance, but for many of the outsiders who were being frozen out of the new leadership it was more appealing, and they embraced it eagerly. They were the avid learners of English and of new commercial ways, and many of them seized on Christianity as being the essence of the new civilization and a satisfying substitute for the discredited Confucian-feudal ethics. Young samurai from Kanto domains, such as Uchimura and Niijima of Gumma, became the leaders of a strong Japanese Christianity, which was fiercely independent of missionary domination and provided an alternative value system to the emperor-centered thought of the Satsuma-Choshu clique. Others, like Inukai, though not necessarily adopting Christianity, became the leaders of the democratic opposition to the government's authoritarian centralism. Still others made their way in the world as private businessmen and entrepreneurs. Together these outsiders formed a second, balancing side to Japan's modernization, to which Rioichiro naturally belonged as a double outsider—a youth with a peasant-commercial

183

background from the shogun's realm—just as Matsukata, a Satsuma samurai, naturally belonged to the side of authoritarian, emperor-centered government.

———•———

In May 1874 Rioichiro entered the Kaisei Gakko, a government school for the teaching of English, which was to become a part of Tokyo University when it was founded in 1877. The Kaisei Gakko had been started under the leadership of the Dutch-American mission-ary Verbeck. Okuma had brought Verbeck to Tokyo from Nagasaki in 1869 as a government adviser and to convert the old official Tokugawa school into a better institution for teaching English. Recruiting an adequate teaching staff had been a problem, and the bottom of the barrel was scraped to find enough persons who met the one essential qualification of being able to speak English. As a result, the instruc-tors included many unsavory or at least unsuitable characters, such as failed adventurers who had started out to make their fortunes in the fabled China trade, sailors who had jumped ship in Yokohama, or simple drifters. Verbeck got rid of these men and in 1872 invited a professor from Rutgers College in New Jersey to review the Japanese educational system and make recommendations for reform. The fol-lowing year David R. Murray, a mathematician also from Rutgers, was appointed superintendent of educational affairs, a post he held for five years. Japan was divided into eight university districts, under which 32 middle-school districts and 210 elementary-school districts were established.

The Kaisei Gakko was the first of the proposed universities, and in 1874 it was the outstanding school for the study of English. It was located in Owaricho, which today is the main intersection of the famous Ginza in downtown Tokyo. Rioichiro learned the Spencerian form of penmanship and the composition of letters in English, aided by a book of sample letters that Sugenoya, a close friend at the school, gave him. In presenting this book Sugenoya wrote in tortured En-glish, "I suppose myself this volume is one of the most indispensable for young ladies and gentlemen who desire to learn how to concise elegant sentences of their letters. It contains tolerably easy words while it appears a very beautiful eloquent expressions. I am sure that when you studied it very well, you are soon able to express your good ideas on your coming letters, without picking up some sentences from a book as you wish." During these early years, students of English commonly used it to write letters to each other.

In March 1875 Chotaro completed the Western-style factory on his property. It had thirty-two reeling machines, and he avoided the difficulty of finding female operators locally by hiring several from the Hokkaido Colonization Agency, which was later to figure in Matsukata's replacement of Okuma as finance minister. Within a few months, Chotaro produced his first batch of silk thread for export and consigned it to the *ninushi,* a local merchant who collected silk from the producers for sale to foreign merchants in Yokohama. Chotaro had high expectations and was devastated when he learned that his shipment had been sold at a loss because, though its quality was highly praised, the quantity was too small for a satisfactory financial transaction. Chotaro took his next shipment himself to Yokohama, avoiding payment of a high commission to the ninushi, and sold it directly to an English merchant for a good price. But after paying for the high transportation costs to England and the export tariff, he found that he had made very little profit.

These two experiences with foreign trade taught Chotaro that producers like himself could never be successful under existing conditions, since all the profits went into the pockets of the foreign traders. He realized firsthand what he had heard Fukuzawa emphasize in his public speeches: Japanese themselves must engage in foreign commerce, and the foreign merchants were "parasitic middlemen" who should be driven out of the country if foreign trade were to be profitable for Japan. Local merchants organized into foreign-trade companies knew nothing about trade beyond the treaty ports themselves. Whenever a Japanese attempted to find out about where his goods were shipped or their selling price, the Western merchant would refuse to divulge the information or show him the monthly commercial journals by which Westerners were kept informed of market conditions abroad. In fact, very few Japanese had direct contact with the foreign merchants themselves, since the foreigners kept aloof from the Japanese merchants, using Chinese middlemen to deal with them. It was only by accident that Hayami Kenso, the leading silk authority, found out through a copy of *The Times* of London that higher prices for Japanese silks were being quoted in the European markets than by the foreign merchants in Yokohama.

On the way back from Yokohama, Chotaro stopped in Tokyo to talk with Rioichiro about his disappointing experiences and his determination to go into direct trade abroad. He was glad that Rioichiro was learning English, but he wanted him also to get some knowledge about Western commercial practices. It happened that in Asakusa, only a few miles from where they were talking, frantic preparations were being made to open Japan's first commercial school. This school was the brainchild of Mori Arinori, the American-educated former minister in Washington. In 1872 Mori, who had been in charge of more than two hundred students sent to the United States, visited the Bryant, Stratton and Whitney Business College in Newark, New Jersey, to see how one of his students, Tomita Tetsunosuke, was getting along. Tomita later became the first consul in New York. Mori was greatly impressed with the director of the school, William C. Whitney, and he decided to hire him to establish a similar institution in Japan. Whitney was delighted and signed a five-year contract at a salary of $2500, a good salary in those days but much less than the Japanese government was paying to foreign technicians and advisers.

Mori found on returning to Japan that the finance ministry had already established a training section for banking and that the government was unwilling to finance Mori's commercial school. This left him in a quandary when Whitney arrived in Yokohama with his wife, son, and fifteen-year-old daughter Clara, whose diary I have quoted from. Fortunately, Mori had a wide circle of influential friends, some of whom believed as strongly as he in the need for a commercial school, and they came to his rescue. Among them were Fukuzawa, Shibusawa Eiichi, the great financier and industrialist, and, most helpful of all, Katsu Kaishu, the former Tokugawa official who had negotiated the surrender of Edo castle in 1868. Fukuzawa in a prospectus for the school wrote:

> The Western nations as a rule have commercial schools for the training of businessmen, just as we in feudal times had places where a samurai could learn the martial arts. In a military struggle one does not proceed to the battlefield without having first

learned the art of swordsmanship. By the same token we cannot take on our foreign opponents in commercial warfare without prior study of commerce. The man of commerce must ever keep his eye fixed . . . on the trade struggle in which our entire nation is engaged.*

The Whitney family was appalled to discover that the plans for the school had fallen through and that they did not even have a place to live. Clara recorded in her diary on September 5, 1875: " 'Thus we cried unto the Lord in our trouble and he delivered us out of distress.' Mr. Katsu . . . sent $1,000 for our benefit as a donation to the business college we came to establish!" Katsu also lent the Whitney family a house in his own compound and treated them as members of his household. Incidentally, Clara eventually married Katsu's son by a mistress, after she and her mother had converted the young man to Christianity. The school, the Shoho Koshujo (Short-Term Commercial Training School), soon opened its doors. As Clara wrote in her diary, "Our business college underway Thursday, September 16: Our business college is getting along fine, God grant it may be a success. We have already eight or ten young Japanese men, besides one American boy named George Bachelder, whose mother called yesterday."

Rioichiro enrolled in the school in October, the second month of its existence. The school had two entrance requirements: a student must know English, since all instruction was in English, and he must be fifteen years or older. Rioichiro joined the first class, which by then had twenty-three students. Because of lack of government funds, the school had financial difficulties, but in time it became a government school. It changed names four times before becoming Hitotsubashi University in 1949. (Hitotsubashi today is considered Japan's leading university in the field of economics and business and is ranked with four or five other national universities at the top of the educational pyramid.) Rioichiro studied bookkeeping, using *Bryant and Stratton's Bookkeeping and Commercial Arithematic* as his textbook. His personal account books show that he shifted at this time from the use of Chinese characters for numbers to Arabic numerals. He also studied Wayland's *Elements of Political Economy,* but he found it very difficult.

* Ivan Parker Hall, *Mori Arinori* (Cambridge: Harvard University Press, 1973), p. 257.

———•———

Rioichiro was determined to prepare himself for trade abroad, but he had no idea how to break into foreign trade, which was held as a tight monopoly by the foreign merchants. Back in Mizunuma his older brother Chotaro was equally determined and equally baffled. To make matters worse, economic conditions in Japan were deteriorating seriously as Japan sank into the great inflation of the late 1870s. Increased imports of Western machinery as well as cheap manufactured consumer goods, for which the Japanese public was beginning to develop a taste, combined with the costs of liquidating the old feudal system and building up a modern state, were bankrupting the government and the whole nation. Japan in the early years of commerce with the West had a favorable balance of trade because of silk. But exports between 1868 and 1875 increased only 20 percent while imports grew 180 percent. Specie was being drained from Japan, and the country was being flooded with all sorts of imported goods—cotton and woolen textiles, sugar, flour, tobacco, salt, alarm clocks, and even celluloid kewpie dolls, which had caught the fancy of the young. When I was a child, these pudgy, naked pink dolls, with their outstretched arms, round faces, blond hair, dark lashes, and blue eyes, were still very popular.

The Japanese government could not stem this flood of imports because its tariffs were fixed at low rates by treaty, and the Western powers were still quite unwilling to give up this unfair advantage. The only solution was to increase exports, but the question was how. The government tried every means it could. This was why it was willing to lend money to Chotaro on easy terms to build his small silk-reeling plant. It also attempted to explore markets abroad. When the United States announced the Philadelphia Centennial Exhibition in 1876, the Japanese government seized on this as a good opportunity to send a mission to study the American market and display Japanese goods.

Among the members of the mission sent to America was Hayami, the silk expert. Accompanied in his travels by Tomita Tetsunosuke, who by then was the consul in New York, he took with him samples from the government's Tomioka silk mill. He found about thirty silk mills on the eastern seaboard of the United States, with the machine-operated ones using the thinner machine-reeled Italian silk and the hand-operated mills utilizing domestic or Chinese hand-reeled silk, which was less uniform and thicker. He also learned to his surprise that the sericulture industry of the United States had a long history. It dated back to the encouragement by James I of silk production in Virginia because of his great dislike for tobacco. Later the British government gave a special bonus of forty pounds of tobacco for every two hundred pounds of silk thread produced, but the great impetus for silk production came after American independence, when the Congress put an import tax on raw silk. Production increased greatly in Pennsylvania, New York, and New England, and in the 1830s there was a silk boom in New England. The New England Thread Company at its height produced over two hundred pounds of silk thread a week. After the Civil War the American market for silk continued to expand, but farmers found wheat and other crops more remunerative. Production stagnated, though the demand for silk thread increased. This made the United States a promising market for Japanese silk thread, and Hayami found the Tomioka silk he had brought compared well with imports from Italy.

At home government officials and private leaders were eager to expand Japanese exports. Fukuzawa, who was a great admirer of British theories of free trade, constantly emphasized the need to increase exports, arguing that this was necessary if Japan were to preserve its independence, and he himself founded a trading company, Maruzen, which is still in existence. At his school, the future Keio University, he urged his students to go into business as a patriotic duty, and he did his best to break down the old Confucian prejudice of the samurai class against commerce as being unworthy of educated men. The government established a Trade Encouragement Bureau (Kansho-kyoku) in the home ministry to encourage both production and foreign trade. The journal it published, *Kansho nippo,* informed would-be traders of opportunities and tried to encourage a competitive spirit that would break the foreign monopoly in international trade.

The problem still remained how to get started. Rioichiro and Chotaro were not the only people at a loss. The government made an attempt at direct silk trade with the United States, but it ended in failure. The whole country faced a crisis in trade, with a threat of national disaster. Matsukata's financial reforms were to prove part of the answer, but another part was to be provided by a breakthrough in the silk trade in which Rioichiro played an important part—though at first under the guidance of another young man, Sato Momotaro.

Emigrating to America

While Rioichiro was studying English and business in Japan, Sato Momotaro was acquiring practical experience in the United States, and it was his self-confidence and experience that opened the way for Rioichiro. Sato's pioneering role has been largely overlooked in accounts of the development of Japan's foreign trade, and he deserves more credit for his achievements. He was born in 1854 in Sakura, not far from Edo. His family for generations had been physicians. The best-known member of the family was his grandfather, Taizen (1804–1872), who was an ardent advocate of Western medicine, the physician for a while to an important daimyo named Hotta, and the founder of the Juntendo in Sakura, Japan's first private hospital and medical school. In 1853 his son moved the Juntendo to Edo (Tokyo), where it still exists. When Momotaro was eleven years old, his father sent him to live with his grandfather in Yokohama to learn English and receive a Western education. Though he was the oldest son, he was not expected to follow the family profession of medicine, since the tradition was to adopt a young man with special medical talents as the successor.

Momotaro's grandfather on retirement had moved to Yokohama to be close to James C. Hepburn and other foreign friends. Dr. Hepburn and his wife were American Presbyterian missionaries who arrived in Japan in 1859. He had served as a doctor in China for many years before coming to Japan, and, since the proselytizing of Christianity was still banned, he opened a dispensary and medical clinic. He was also a linguist, inventing the standard system for Romanizing Japanese names and words, which still bears his name. He also started home classes in English with another missionary, James Ballagh of the Dutch Reformed Church. These classes were attended by many Japanese and eventually evolved into Meiji Gakuin University in Tokyo. Mrs. Hepburn had similar classes for girls, and in 1870 these became Ferris Seminary, which still exists in Yokohama.

Sato Momotaro, while living with his grandfather, learned English from Dr. Hepburn and was constantly exposed to his grandfather's American, Dutch, French, and other Western friends, absorbing considerable knowledge about Western society and culture. Hepburn encouraged Momotaro's parents to send him to study in America, and the boy left in 1867 at the age of thirteen for San Francisco, where he chose to concentrate on commerce instead of medicine. He attended a business school and after graduation worked in a general merchandise store to learn its business methods. Later he subleased a section of the store to start his own shop, in which he sold Japanese green tea and other Japanese goods, such as lacquer ware and paper umbrellas. From the beginning of foreign trade and up until the 1880s, green tea was Japan's chief export item to America, amounting to as much as eight to nine million pounds annually. Two years before Sato's arrival, the Western merchants had made San Francisco the main transit port for all tea bound for America, replacing Shanghai and Hong Kong.

In 1871 Sato was granted a Japanese government scholarship to continue his business education. He went to Boston to attend the Boston Technical School, the forerunner of the Massachusetts Institute of Technology. The school was then located at the corner of Boylston and Newbury streets in the building today occupied by Bonwit Teller. The following year, during the stay of the Iwakura mission on the east coast, Sato served as one of the interpreters. After that, he settled in New York, where Tomita Tetsunosuke, a co-passenger on the ship that had brought Sato to America in 1867, had become the first Japanese consul.

In New York Sato operated a small store selling general merchandise and some Japanese articles, but he gradually came to realize that there were possibilities for developing a much greater market for Japanese goods and decided to start an importing company of his own.

He went back to Japan in 1875 to organize the company and also to bring back with him a group of young men to start similar enterprises. He was still only twenty-one years old and already had eight years of education and practical experience in America. Under the new Meiji government the country had changed drastically from the feudal land he had left. He was distressed by its economic problems, but the new government's policy of increasing exports made him realize that he had returned at a propitious time.

Sato first called on his family's friend, Fukuzawa. Fukuzawa listened attentively to his account of his adventures and education in America and commended him on his enterprising spirit. Fukuzawa also told Sato how he had been preaching to his students for some time that it was their patriotic duty to go into foreign trade. He gave Sato enthusiastic support and promised to find suitable men to accompany him back to America. On Fukuzawa's advice, Sato informed various businessmen of his plans. When he met with Hayami Kenso, Hayami immediately spoke of Hoshino Chotaro and his strong desire to start the direct export of silk to America. Sato, Hayami, and Hoshino met in late November 1875 in Kumagaya, midway between Mizunuma and Tokyo. As the three sat huddled around the charcoal brazier on the tatami floor and Hoshino listened to the young man from New York, just a year older than his own younger brother, he saw the possibility of his dreams coming true. Rioichiro was already prepared to enter trade in the United States, and Hoshino made up his mind on the spot to send him with Sato to New York.

Hoshino immediately wrote Rioichiro about the meeting and in his eagerness sent him another letter on December 6:

> I sent a letter to you the other day from Kumagaya. Concerning Sato's store in New York, he will need a young man who has some knowledge of a foreign language, and he is leaving it up to me to take charge of this. I have consulted your parents and your adoptive family, and they are all in agreement to respond to this request by sending you. If you do go, you must go with great patriotic enthusiasm for the sake of your country and do your very best, entering into your activities without thought of returning to your country, even if the work does not go well. Whether you are in agreement with us or not, in either case come back at once

to discuss this matter at Mt. Akagi [Mizunuma]. Although we ourselves know something about the West, it is nothing compared to your knowledge. Should you decide to go, you will be expected to leave on a ship some time in February. In the meantime continue to study diligently. I will write you again later.

Rioichiro, of course, responded enthusiastically to his brother's proposal, and Hoshino wrote him again on December 12:

With regard to your decision to go to America, I am sending you a letter of introduction to Sato Momotaro, on whom you will be calling. When you sail in February we shall come to see you off. But your mother of your new home wants to see you before you go, and, if there is any time later in December after your classes are over, you should plan to come back home for a while, at least before February. However, in the meantime I implore you to study diligently for your future success.

It should be recalled that Rioichiro had only started his studies at the Whitney business school in early October. So the next few months were a crucial time in which to learn as much as he could before his departure. Unlike the government officials, who were then wearing Western clothes and shoes, Rioichiro, like most Japanese students, still dressed in the traditional kimono, *hakama* (divided skirt), and wooden clogs, so he had to acquire a completely new wardrobe. His brother wrote that he should "purchase for yourself four sets of Western-style suits—a coat, vest, and pants—and pay not more than three yen for each. Kinsuke [a relative] has gone to Yokohama as a [silk] thread merchant, and you can get credit from him."

The well-to-do had their Western suits custom-made by Chinese tailors who had opened up shops in Tokyo, but, for a poor boy like Rioichiro, the only thing to do was to buy secondhand suits in Yokohama. He was able to acquire them for less than the three-yen limit his brother had set. In his account book there is a notation of the purchase of a Western suit in December for 2.14 yen. The yen at that time was slightly double the value of a dollar. Nevertheless this was a bargain compared to the 2.10 he paid for an American history book when he entered business school. After slight alterations, the suit fitted him handsomely. He already had a Western haircut, but he now grew sideburns and looked very stylish.

The Meiji government had issued regulations in 1869 requiring all travelers to obtain documents before going abroad. Sato's adopted brother, who had been chosen to continue the family's traditional medical practice, had received the first of these documents when he went to Germany to study medicine. Since then quite a few students and government officials had gone abroad, and the number on Rioichiro's document was 1833. It was, however, one of the first issued to a Japanese going abroad as a businessman.

Hoshino in Gumma was busy making financial and travel arrangements for his brother. To pay the trans-Pacific fare and living expenses in New York, he estimated that he needed to raise $750, a large amount at a time when business was bad. He had counted on some government assistance, but, when this failed to materialize, he wrote his brother, "As far as expenses are concerned, whatever the officials say, we expect to pay for it ourselves." Hoshino could not afford to have his brother travel first class, as did all the government-sponsored students. Rioichiro would have to go in steerage at a cost of 270 yen.

Although the expedition to America was delayed until the beginning of March 1876, Rioichiro was so busy with his studies and preparations for the trip that he was reluctant to take a few days off at the end of February to make his farewells in Mizunuma and Kazuno and pay his respects to the governor of Gumma prefecture (then known as Kumagaya prefecture). Hoshino insisted that he visit the governor, who had been a strong supporter of the development of silk for export, had enthusiastically endorsed Hoshino's decision to start direct exports to America, and had also finally helped to obtain some government funds for Rioichiro's expenses. When the two brothers called on Governor and Mrs. Katori, she left the room for a moment and returned bearing a long object wrapped in lavender silk brocade. She knelt on the floor in front of Rioichiro and placed the object before him. Removing the wrapping, she revealed a gleaming short sword, which she explained had belonged to her late brother, Yoshida Shoin (1830–1859), and had been given to her as a keepsake.

Yoshida Shoin was one of the most famous imperial loyalists of the pre-Meiji period. He was a samurai of the Choshu domain and as a boy had been sent to Choshu to study Western learning in Nagasaki and Edo. He developed into an expert in military tactics and became convinced that, in order for the country to survive, it would have to become militarily strong and more centralized under the direct rule of the emperor. He felt he must learn more about the West by going abroad. Defying the laws of the time, he smuggled himself aboard one of Perry's ships in 1854, only to be apprehended and sent back to Choshu as a prisoner. After he was transferred to house arrest, he started a private school, where he ostensibly taught Western learning but clandestinely imbued his students with his own ideals of loyalty to the emperor. He greatly influenced some younger Choshu samurai, such as Ito and Yamagata, who were to become the main builders of the new imperial Japan. He himself did not live to see this happen, since he was arrested in 1859 for attempting to assassinate the shogun's representative in Kyoto and was executed, becoming a great martyr-hero of modern Japanese nationalism.

Rioichiro was overwhelmed with Mrs. Katori's gift, but she explained to him that it embodied her brother's soul (*tamashii*), which would only be put at rest when it crossed the Pacific to America, as Yoshida had planned to do. Rioichiro accepted the sword reverently and promised to prove himself worthy of the trust put in him. When I was a college student and visited my grandparents in Greenwich, Connecticut, my grandmother showed me the sword, which is a superb example of the swordsmith's art, signed by the maker Kunitomi and dating from the fifteenth or sixteenth century. It is about fourteen inches long and has a gold-decorated lacquer scabbard. Today it is in the possession of my cousin Ryo Arai, who lives in California. Short swords, or *tanto,* were used to take one's life when a samurai found this necessary to preserve his honor.

———•———

While Rioichiro was making his preparations, Sato was scurrying around the country convincing producers of the profitability of exporting their merchandise for sale at his store in New York. Although he had no capital of his own, he did have the backing of his prestigious family, which pledged its assests as security on a large share of the 26,000 yen in merchandise he collected on credit to start his store.

Recruiting young men to return with him was made easy for Sato by Fukuzawa's recommendations. There were four others besides Arai (as I shall henceforth call my grandfather) who responded to the opportunity. Including Sato, this made a group of six young men, who came to be known as the "Oceanic group" from the name of the ship on which they crossed the Pacific. The four other recruits were Date Chushichi in the field of ceramics and art goods in behalf of the Mitsui family, Masuda Rinzo in tea, Suzuki Toichi in pharmaceuticals and general merchandise, representing the Maruzen company of which Fukuzawa was one of the founders and directors, and Morimura Yutaka, also in general merchandise. Arai was to develop close relations both in business and private life with Morimura, who was familiarly known as Toyo rather than Yutaka. The relationship between the two later deepened through the Matsukata family, when one of Matsukata's sons married Rioichiro's daughter, my mother, and another married Matsuko, the only daughter and heir of Ichizaemon, the head of the Morimura family. I have vivid and happy recollections of our association with the Morimuras during my childhood. I especially remember the annual all-day parties at their residence at Takanawa in Tokyo, where there would be food stands scattered about the garden, serving a wide range of special delicacies, while acrobats, dancers, musicians, and sporting events would provide the entertainment.

The Morimuras were an old merchant family that dealt largely in armor and weapons. Morimura Ichizaemon VI (1839–1919) was already the head of the family when the commercial treaty with America went into effect in 1860, and, as the official shogunal party was preparing to go to Washington to exchange ratifications, he was commissioned to select suitable gifts for the president and forty other American officials and their wives. For the ladies he selected handsome black lacquer boxes with designs in gold and filled them with woodblock prints, combs, and ornamental hairpins inlaid with shell. Each gift cost 25 ryo.

Ichizaemon was also assigned the task of obtaining Mexican dollars for the trip, which were the international currency in East Asia at that time. Japanese coins were not negotiable in America. Morimura went to Yokohama, accompanied by a well-guarded procession of men on foot carrying thirty heavy boxes each containing one hundred ryo in gold and silver coins. Arriving at the Ame Ichiban (American Number 1) Company, he trusted the American merchant there to give him the correct exchange. He suspected he had been cheated when he was given coins that looked like Japanese silver coins of the 1830s in exchange for his gold coins. Actually the American had taken advantage of the discrepancy between gold and silver exchange rates in Japan and the rest of the world. In Japan the ratio was between 8.5 and 10 to 1 and in the outside world between 14 and 16 to 1. This difference gave foreign merchants huge profits and produced a damaging gold drain in Japan.

Ichizaemon became aware of the situation and called on Fukuzawa to voice his concern. He had first met Fukuzawa at the Tosa mansion, where Fukuzawa was a frequent visitor, and was impressed to hear Fukuzawa addressed respectfully as an honored teacher, *sensei,* and invited to sit in conversation in the same room with the senior councillors, despite the fact that he was in origin a footsoldier, the lowest rank among the samurai. Fukuzawa was amazed at the astute observation about gold and silver exchange rates by the twenty-one-year-old merchant and explained to him the need for the Japanese themselves to engage in foreign trade, expand their exports, and earn back the gold foreign merchants were taking from the country.

Ichizaemon did not yet have the knowledge himself to go into foreign trade, but he could see opportunities for making money from trade with the Westerners in Japan. He had been surprised to see Westerners in Yokohama selling their foreign goods at roadside shops. It was his first exposure to Western clothes, shoes, woolen blankets, books, modern guns, watches, vases, soap, and the like. Having a keen sense for business, he bought up all the Western goods he could carry back to Edo and in no time had disposed of everything to his chief clients, the hatamoto of the shogunate and the samurai of the domains of Kaga and Tosa. A senior councillor (*karo*) of the Tosa domain became so enamored with Western goods that he appointed Ichizaemon to be his official merchant (*goyo shonin*). The retailing of Western goods became so profitable that Morimura opened a store in Edo to sell them. He also went into another lucrative business when a French military adviser to the shogunate told him that the Japanese needed to produce their own military accouterments instead of importing them. The Frenchman offered to teach Ichizaemon how to make leather saddles for military use. As a result, in the fighting between the imperial forces and the Aizu domain in 1868, Ichizaemon was the sole supplier to Itagaki, the leader of the imperial troops, of all the saddles his forces used and also their blankets, shoes, and Western clothing.

Ichizaemon had kept in mind what Fukuzawa had told him earlier about the need for the Japanese to engage in foreign trade, and, when his adopted brother Toyo, who was fifteen years his junior, became twelve, he enrolled him at Fukuzawa's Keio school, asking the teachers to educate him to become a businessman. Fukuzawa was surprised and remarked that this was the first time he had been asked to educate a boy this way, since most people wished to have their boys prepared to become government officials. When Toyo completed his education at Fukuzawa's school, he found no opening in Japan in foreign trade and worked instead as an assistant teacher at Keio, but Sato's proposal changed the situation. To the great satisfaction of Ichizaemon and with the full endorsement of Fukuzawa, he joined Sato's Oceanic group bound for America.

Before their departure, the Oceanic group assembled at a studio in downtown Tokyo to have their picture taken. Ever since the early 1870s, photographs have been popular in Japan to commemorate special occasions. When Rioichiro graduated from the English School in Yamada in 1874, he and his classmates had posed for a photograph dressed in formal Japanese attire. This time the picture shows the Oceanic group dressed in the latest Western clothing, looking little different from their American or European counterparts whose discards they had purchased. Sato sits in the center, looking the leader he was, surrounded by the five young men he was taking abroad. Rioichiro, the Beau Brummell of the group, sits on his right, his legs crossed, his head turned a little toward Sato, showing his sideburns and looking quite the Western gentleman he aspired to be.

On March 2, 1876, Rioichiro, accompanied by his relatives and schoolfriends, went to the pier in Yokohama. There was a great deal of bowing as he prepared to embark on the small boat that was to take him and his companions to the ship anchored in the harbor. He held firmly onto his precious green and brown carpetbag containing three pounds of silk samples from his brother's mill, which was to be his passport to a future in America. The bag was quite heavy, for it also contained a considerable amount of Mexican silver dollars for his expenses abroad. In 1876 there still were no banking facilities for the transfer of funds from Japan to America, nor was there internationally negotiable paper currency.

The S.S. *Oceanic* was one of four 2000-ton paddlewheel steamships owned by the Pacific Mail and Steamship Company of America, which between them made a Pacific crossing each way every four weeks. Rioichiro climbed up the swaying ship's ladder and walked into the lobby leading to the first-class cabins, but he had paid only 270 yen for steerage passage and was directed down a narrow stairway leading to that area. It consisted of a single large hold with no portholes and with hammocks strung in three tiers. It was sprinkled with red pepper, apparently to counteract the stench, and was swept out once a day. The other steerage passengers were 25 Japanese and 845 Chinese laborers going to work on the railways then under construction in the American West. Weather permitting, meals were cooked on deck in huge pots and dished out to the passengers. The food consisted of buckwheat and pork fat. A record Arai kept of the ship's course and the distance covered each day has been preserved, but the letter he wrote to his parents about the voyage has been lost. One can surmise, however, that the young men were able to tolerate the smell, heat, and other discomforts of their accommodations only because of their excited anticipation of what awaited them on the other side of the Pacific.

A few of Rioichiro's friends were unable to see him off and instead sent their farewells by letter. One written by Sugenoya, his classmate at the Kaisei Gakko, is in quaint English but beautifully written in Spencerian penmanship. It reads:

For Departure of Mr. R. Arai
   Particles cohering together once separate, friends being together, once have a time to separate and finally again unite. Now, my intimate friend, thou, taking departure for America, a sorrowful pen left before you.
   Beautiful country, thou left behind. Upon new world thy feet trace now; Our remaining soul sink in tear, Our graceful mind more covered by darkness; lonely in feeling, after thou gone, but thy mouth-less image never disappear.
   As commerce is thy aim, pursue thy object to the highest pitch; To our home, after thou returned again, let thy polished

199

mind reflect to our eye. Never break thy aim, procure thine with courage and perseverance. As thy and I are not parallel straight-lines, I hope soon produced oblique.

Yours most Sincerely,
M. Sugenoya

In Japanese idiom the figure of two parallel lines implies the fact of never meeting, so the reference to an oblique line was an expression of the hope that they would soon meet again.

———•———

The voyage from Yokohama to San Francisco took three and a half weeks. The group of young Japanese landed on March 26, 1876, and left on March 29 for New York by the Union Pacific Railway, which had been completed only three years earlier. The trip by rail took twelve days. Since direct mail service between the United States and Japan had started in July 1875, less than a year before, Arai had this means of communicating with his family. In late April he wrote them in Japanese about his trip across the continent and his first impressions of New York:

You have already received my letter from San Francisco so you know about our trip. On the 29th of last month we started out from San Francisco by train. We bought a ticket on the lowest class. It was terribly cold in the train, and we passed through places where there were seven to eight feet of snow. Our fellow passengers seemed to be day laborers for the railroad and were extremely unclean and quite unpleasant. We understand that ours is the first Japanese group to travel in this lowest class. The 2000 miles from a place called Reno to a place called Omaha was a desert-like wasteland with no trees to be seen anywhere. This was the so-called Rocky Mountains, which only had brown-colored grass. The inhabitants of this area were blackish red in color and seemed really like savages. They were wearing feathers and skins as clothes and also cotton clothing, and a few spoke a little English.

Up to Omaha there were 21 stops, but from then on there were places like towns, where there were carts and fields. The farm-houses were very pretty, but they are made of wood, unlike in

New York where they are built of brick. But the women were quite beautifully gotten up. Fields are about 1 chobu [2½ acres] in size. The crops are corn. Over three quarters of the land is given over to pasture. All transport is by horse carts, even on hills and mountains, and nothing is carried by back. Sometimes you see women carrying bundles on their heads. But agriculture doesn't seem to be much developed.

Passing St. Louis, Indianapolis, Columbus, Pittsburgh, and Philadelphia, all of them large cities, we arrived here safely at 10 a.m. on the 10th. I haven't found out the conditions of things here in the city yet, but everything looks fine. The water is beautiful, but the weather changes several times a day, and the temperature is very variable. I can't get over how wonderful the buildings are. Maybe it's just because it is such a new world to me that everything seems well worked out and marvelous. Although I don't know anything about Paris, I think it must be much inferior to New York.

As for my activities, since Sato's store is busy, I have for the last two or three weeks been helping out there, and I have not done anything about the samples I brought with me, the silk thread, silk cloth, and hemp.

Tokyo and New York had only one thing in common: both cities had populations of about one million. Almost everything else was quite different, and it was no wonder that Arai wrote, "it is such a new world to me." Compared to the low wooden Japanese buildings, the stone and brick homes of the rich were indeed stately, and the miles of brownstone houses on Fifth Avenue, lined with majestic ailanthus trees, were very impressive. The most eye-boggling building of all must have been the fashionable Fifth Avenue Hotel, a six-story white marble palace, which occupied an entire block and had a half-colonnaded marble facade facing Madison Square, then considered the center of the city.

Accustomed to the narrow, crooked streets of Tokyo, Arai found that the orderly layout of New York made sightseeing easy and a pleasure. He would stare at the buildings, while keeping out of the way of horse-drawn streetcars traveling on rails the length of Fifth Avenue. Telegraph poles lined both sides of Broadway, carrying a maze of wires above the heads of the pedestrians. The future Central Park lay way out in the country, where cows grazed in the meadows. The streets even in the fashionable areas were still unpaved, although some experiments were being made in covering them with asphalt and Belgian blocks, or cobblestones, which had been placed in a haphazard fashion, leaving people to wallow knee deep in mud when it rained. Such inconveniences Arai took for granted, and in his letters he never mentioned the seamy side of New York—the tramps and homeless vagrant youths, who numbered at that time some twenty to thirty thousand, or the urban poor, who were crowded into miserable tenements.

Arai and his friends were jeered at as they walked about. Almost half of New York's population consisted of immigrants, mostly Irish, Germans, Italians, Greeks, Jews, and Chinese, and by far the most disliked by native Americans were the Chinese. These Asiatics, as they were called, were looked down on as being cunning, treacherous, and vicious, but much of the dislike stemmed from their willingness to work long hours at low wages. There were only a handful of Japanese in New York when Arai arrived, consisting largely of students on Japanese government scholarships and a few government officials. So it was natural that Americans assumed any Japanese they saw to be Chinese. The one exception was the group of Japanese acrobats playing at the American Institute Building. They drew large crowds and were loudly applauded for their feats. They had been brought over by a "Professor Riseley," a sometime resident of Yokohama and the joint proprietor of a circus there, who had arranged for the acrobats to perform in P.T. Barnum's show at the Philadelphia Centennial Exhibition.

Despite the hostility directed toward Arai, he seems to have felt no trauma in his sudden move from Japan to New York. At twenty he was vigorous and resilient, and Sato, with his familiarity with the city and fluency in English, helped him over the rough spots. He did, though, have a hard time finding a place to live. With his limited resources, he could afford only a room and a cheap one at that. At some places, when he knocked on the door to ask about a room, the owner slammed the door in his face. He eventually found a boarding house in Brooklyn for $5 a week including breakfast. He was luckier than his friend Morimura Toyo, who had to sleep in a box filled with straw in Sato's store.

To commute to Sato's store, Arai crossed the East River from Brooklyn by the old Wall Street ferry and walked to 97 Front Street in Manhattan. For a nickel he could have ridden the streetcar, but he preferred to walk for reasons of economy and health. For lunch he and his friends usually bought three-penny biscuits from street vendors. For dinner he ate at some nearby restaurant. Not until many years later, when he could afford better eating places, did he realize that not all American meat was tough. He always claimed, however, that if one chews tough meat long enough it becomes tender. Arai's frugal ways became part of his nature. Years later, a millionaire and a member of an exclusive golf club in Connecticut, he would forgo taking a shower after playing in order to save the two cents for a towel.

Although Arai had already studied English for four years, he found that spoken English was difficult to understand, since most of his learning had been through books. To become fluent in speaking, he enrolled for classes after work at the Plymouth Institute in Brooklyn Heights, and he also attended as many lectures as he could to accustom his ear to different types of spoken English. Among those he listened to was the preacher Henry Ward Beecher.

The Philadelphia Centennial Exhibition opened in May 1876, and Arai was anxious to visit it. His classmates back home had written asking him to tell them all about it. There was great interest throughout Japan in the exhibition because of Japan's large-scale participation there. The Japanese government, looking at the exhibition as an opening wedge for exports to the United States, had put up the largest budget of any foreign country. The chief commissioner was the handsome General Saigo Tsugumichi, who was to become one of the elder statesmen together with Matsukata. He was chosen as an expert on the United States, since he had traveled extensively in America as well as Europe while planning for military conscription in Japan. Hayami was responsible for the silk display at the Exhibition, and the beautiful silk brocades attracted much attention. To Arai, however, they were nothing compared to the displays of the American silk manufacturers. In no way did these silk products resemble anything he was familiar with. There were silks for hats, velvets, braids, dress trimmings, and the like.

The Japanese pavilion and a Japanese house constructed beside it made a great impression on the millions of Americans who visited the exhibition. One reporter from the *New York Herald* wrote, "How can an American any longer call a nation that outdoes the French in bronzes and silks, and surpasses the world in carpentry, cabinet making and ceramics 'semi-civilized'?" Ironically many Japanese still did consider themselves uncivilized, as did a friend at the Kaisei Gakko who wrote him on November 9, 1876:

> *My Dear Friend:*
> We received your kind letter dated 23rd Aug. on the last month. Before examining its contents which highly interested us, our minds have already been fulfilled with hope, gratitude and joy, and after examining that our thoughts have been occupied for a long while with a remote idea of that eastern (to us) continent . . .
> I give thousand thanks to you for informing me the condition of the Centennial exhibition at which you have been.
> Oh! How lamentable we feel when we think the condition of our merchants there. Is it the thing which cannot be helped? No. The Japanese people have not yet been civilized so far—the merchants do not know how to earn, how to lead customers . . .
> Here hoping your good health and happiness, I put my pen aside. My Dearest Friend in America, R. Arai Esq.
> > *I remain your forever true friend,*
> > K. Futani

A few years ago, while rummaging through my grandfather's old steamer trunk, I came across a small package wrapped in a faded blue silk handkerchief. In it I found several small leather-covered notebooks. Some were his pocket engagement books and the others, a little larger in size, his account books, which he must have also carried with him in his pocket. Both sets of books covered the period 1877–1880. The engagement books are written in Japanese, the account books in English. Both are in a meticulously careful hand. In those days before the fountain pen, people wrote with pens that had changeable pen points of various thicknesses. Arai must have used the finest of points, for to read some of his figures and writing one must use a magnifying glass.

Arai had been accustomed to relatively mild winters, for in the parts of Japan where he had lived snow was rare and the cold not severe. The first winter in America must have been rather hard for him. Among his first diary entries we read:

January Monday 1, 1877

Cloudy . . . Kagitomi called . . . In the afternoon we took a walk. At four went to Sato's store and his home. Went to pay a sick call on Shimizu. From this time on it started to snow and by the following morning it was three feet deep.

Wednesday 3, 1877

Clear weather. Going to the office the Brooklyn ferry was held up until 10 o'clock by the ice.

The weather was not the only difficult adjustment. Arai felt far from home and missed the usual New Year's festivities. Most of all he was discouraged by having gone several months with only two sales. Of course, he had his friends who had come to New York with him, but what brightened his life more than anything else was to receive letters from home, especially from his former classmates. The news itself, however, was sometimes quite disturbing. A letter he received from his friend at the Kaisei Gakko, dated February 27, 1877, told of the outbreak of the Satsuma Rebellion:

Dear Mr. Arai

It elapsed a little time since I had a great pleasure of receiving your most kind letter that dated 6th February. Every information of your own affairs as well as condition of that country that I had was deep pleasant news to me, and also I had a pleasure of hearing your good health and the busy state of your business. Turning to the point of our affairs, first I should say we (three) are in good health and in diligence; we (except Katsura) pass through the Examination without failing so I hope you will not anxious about it . . .

At 15th instant, the insurrection of Satsuma had arised, the chief is Saigo, Shimowara, Kirino etc. There are many small civil insurrections that occurred in many provinces; and the recent reformation of officers at all departments of Government. I suppose you will get Tokio daily news from Sato, so I do not write precise information of such Civil War . . .

Satsuma talking is heard everywhere, "The news! news!, the

news says" we are only waiting the next day news and vainly we are anxious of knowing Satsuma information, so that at very present we can not turn our attention to our study.

Ah! how foolish Saigo is he! his party about consisting 10,000 . . . divided into three one of that attacked . . . and now they are fighting. My principle is [the rest of the sentence up to the second "peace" is written in Japanese] unless Saigo's head is cut off there will be no peace under heaven; unless Satsuma men are killed our Imperial land will not attain peace but in a few days time will reach to us that Saigo's head will appear to our eye.

Yours truly
M. Sugenoya

Starting the Silk Trade

As soon as Arai was settled in New York, he started making calls on silk traders, armed with letters of introduction from Japanese Consul Tomita. His first visit to one William Skinner turned out to be an unhappy experience, though instructive. It was Skinner's first encounter with a Japanese, although he had imported Japanese silk via London in the past, and he looked at Arai with skepticism. Taking him to the back of his office and pointing to a bundle of silk, which on examination revealed pieces of metal and other extraneous materials mixed in to increase its weight, he shouted angrily, "See here, I don't want this kind of stuff. Young man, you get out!" Dishonest Japanese merchants, exporting through foreign traders in Yokohama, had won a bad reputation through tricks of this sort.

When Iwakura visited the West in 1872, he became aware of the situation and on his return to Japan had initiated a system of strict inspection of export silk in order to prevent such practices. But this was all new to Arai, and he resolved to build his business on a firm foundation of integrity and reliability. In time, William Skinner became one of his best customers and also a friend. Whenever they would meet, Skinner would greet him with, "Hello, '70s," referring to their first encounter. His later esteem for Arai is clearly revealed in a letter he wrote on July 10, 1931:

> Dear Arai:
>
> Yesterday I read in the Japanese American, with great interest the account of what you had accomplished in introducing Japa-

nese Raw Silk to the United States. Just think, 108 bales in 1876 and over 532,000 in 1929. It seems incredible.

I wonder if you remember the dinner given to Gen. Congdon and Col. Homer when they returned from Japan. I think I must be a prophet, for when called upon for a few words, I said *you* were the party who should have received the decorations, for you had done more for Japan than anybody, in introducing Raw Silk to the United States, and I still believe that Japan ought to recognize what you have done.

You and I started on our business careers here in New York the same year. What changes we have seen.

May you continue to enjoy health and happiness for many years to come is the sincere wish of

Your old friend
William Skinner

Despite Skinner's encomium of 1931, it took Arai long hard work in the 1870s to win the confidence of American businessmen but, after four weeks of discouragement, he was able to write a hopeful report to Hoshino on May 6, 1876:

I have seen a silk merchant by the name of Richardson on Mercer Street. In all of New York there are less than twenty silk merchants, and in the U.S. there are only about 30 silk weaving factories, and the silk thread industry is still undeveloped. High quality merchandise is difficult to dispose of. The samples I brought were well received, and I can sell them for $600 or 660 yen (per 100 pounds) immediately, but perhaps I can get more.

Richardson was one of the most prominent silk brokers in New York, and Arai was elated when he received his first order from him. It was for four hundred-pound bales of Hoshino raw silk at $6.50 a pound for delivery in September. The long time lag was necessary since trans-Pacific cable communications were not to start for another two years, and the order alone took several weeks to reach Japan by mail. When Hoshino received his brother's letter in early July, he was shocked to see the low contract price of $6.50. Silk quotations had risen sharply because of another silk blight in France and Italy and resultant heavy demands from Europe. Silk exports from Japan in the latter half of 1876 amounted to 14,000 bales as compared to 4000 bales during the same period in 1875. By July, prices were close to 80 percent higher than Arai's quotation, and fulfilling the order would entail a great loss.

Hoshino wrote Arai asking him to renegotiate the price, but Arai refused to budge from his promise to Richardson, stating that he had staked his honor and the future success of his business on this order. In the end Hoshino had to comply, even though he received much criticism from his fellow merchants and had to pledge his entire family assets to cover the loss. He packed the shipment in four boxes and took them to Yokohama, whence they were shipped to San Francisco on the *City of Peking*, a sister ship of the *Oceanic*. In this one transaction, two historic firsts in Japanese foreign trade were set: this was the first direct shipment of Japanese silk by Japanese merchants to America, and it was the first time Japanese silk was sent across the Pacific (all previous shipments by foreign traders had gone westward through the Indian Ocean and by way of Europe).

In time, as silk exports increased and the Japanese began to carry the silk in their own ships, special holds were constructed to store the precious cargo. Because of the great value and high insurance rates on this expensive commodity, special silk trains were initiated to carry it across the continent at high speed. These silk trains would be at the dock when the ships arrived, and within three hours, even before the passengers had left the port, the silk cargo would be on its way east, usually fifty crates per freight car and ten cars in all. These trains were guarded by special security men and had the right of way, enjoying priority even over express passenger trains. The silk trains usually went from Seattle or San Francisco to a terminal in Hoboken, New Jersey, where the storage warehouses for imported silk were located. The trip took eighty hours, though in 1923, at the height of the silk trade, a record time of seventy-two hours was established. After the Panama Canal was completed in 1914, shipments were also made by this route because the insurance and transportation costs were cheaper—$9.40 per bale as compared to $13.34 on the overland route—but it took two weeks longer. Special fast silk freighters were used for this all-water route. My husband and I at different times both traveled by these ships to New York, and he remembers seeing a silk train in Seattle in the 1920s.

Hoshino's shipment arrived on September 21, 1876, and Arai notified Richardson immediately that he was prepared to deliver his order at the price he had quoted. Richardson had become aware of the great loss Arai was incurring and wrote him in reply on September 26:

Mr. R. Arai
Dear Sir

I have your note of the 21st. I am glad you have filled the order we gave you altho prices advanced on your hand. You have acted like an honest merchant and you will not hereafter be sorry that you did so. After your doing as you have done I beg to assure you that I will do my best to improve the price for you.

Yours faithfully,
B. Richardson

Richardson did increase the price he paid by one dollar per pound. The four boxes contained 368.8 pounds, for which Arai received $2586.82, at $7.50 per pound, minus 5 percent for payment in cash. The loss on this order was more than $2000, but Arai never regretted it, for by this one act he established his reputation as an "honest man" in the silk community of New York.

Arai now faced the problem of how he was going to remit the money to Hoshino, who was anxiously awaiting it to start paying his debts. Arai could not go to a bank in New York and get a bill of exchange to mail to his brother, for no bank at that time would give such assistance to an unknown Japanese without a bank account. Arai's friend Morimura Toyo had faced the same problem when he accumulated funds from the sale of his merchandise. Failing to find a way to transmit the money from New York, he asked his brother to do something about the problem in Japan. Ichizaemon's good friend Fukuzawa came to his assistance and set up a system with officials at the Foreign Office whereby Toyo deposited $1000 monthly at the Japanese consulate in New York, which was the amount the consulate needed for expenses, and mailed the receipt to his brother, who in turn gave it to Fukuzawa for reimbursement to Ichizaemon in Tokyo by the Foreign Office. This system took care of only part of the funds Toyo remitted, but it was a great help nonetheless.

Arai was not so lucky. He finally found a Japanese returning home and entrusted him with the cash for delivery to take back to

Japan. When Hoshino received the money, he wrote Arai, "Don't send silver coins; some of them were defective." Thus, in these early days, even the mechanics of money transfers was a serious hurdle to trade. A regular international postal service did exist, run by Japanese themselves in Japan after the country joined the International Postal Union in 1875. Foreign mail had been in the hands of Western postal systems, as is illustrated by the French stamp on a postcard mailed in Yokohama in 1872, which I bought in 1981 at a Paris bookstall. But it was not until 1879 that the Yokohama Specie Bank was established and began to provide modern financial facilities for Japanese trading abroad.

———— • ————

When Arai first arrived in New York, he found that silk was little used except for ribbons, handkerchiefs, and dress ornaments, but the demand grew rapidly as economic conditions improved and high-speed machinery mills replaced smaller hand-operated ones. Arai regarded it his major responsibility to ensure that his colleagues in Japan would produce silk thread that met the specifications required in America and in sufficient quantity to fill the demand. The problem was not the quality of Japanese silk, but to meet specific requirements for ample quantities of uniform silk thread. It took Arai great efforts to get sufficient silk reeled in Japan of a quality that met American needs, but he managed to do this and became the first Japanese to import into the United States what came to be considered the standard American skein.

During Arai's first two years he worked alone, using as his office a corner of Sato's wholesale store at 97 Front Street. By the spring of 1877 business began to pick up, and by the end of the year he had made six shipments totaling $22,603 in value. This was three times the amount of silk of his 1876 sales but ten times the value, since prices had risen sharply. His problems had become not sales but an adequate source of supply in Japan. Hoshino was responsive to Arai's needs and realized that a larger supply of silk than he could produce in his own mill was required. The other two Western mills in Tomioka and Maebashi produced silk thread similar to the samples Arai had used in obtaining his first order, but most silk thread was still being produced by peasant families or in factories using traditional methods.

Still, traditional technologies were being improved and began to meet part of the new demand.

Three traditional methods of production were used, known as *dokuri, tebiki,* and *zaguri.* The dokuri method was the most primitive, using a reel made either of paulonia or poplar wood 5 inches in diameter and 2 to 3 inches wide. These reels were fixed by their axles on a stand 7 to 8 inches high, and the reelers wound the silk thread on the reels by turning them slowly with their right hands. The tebiki method used a square wooden frame instead of a reel. In 1855 the zaguri method was developed in the silk-producing area of Kozuke. It utilized cog wheels and a belt to turn the reel; this improved the quality of the silk by making it more uniform and thinner. Attempts at mass production were made by linking several zaguri machines together and operating them by water power. By the time Japan was opened to trade in 1860, the more efficient zaguri method had spread widely throughout the silk areas, particularly in Kozuke and a nearby area to the north that was to become Fukushima prefecture. This enabled Japan to meet the sudden demand from abroad in the 1860s.

Hoshino was interested in engineering, and he discovered that he could improve the zaguri method by using certain other parts that moved mechanically rather than by hand power. This new method was called "improved zaguri" (*kairyo zaguri*) and was widely adopted. Since the cost of female labor was cheap, the improved zaguri method, even though labor-intensive, became so widely used that it actually impeded the adoption of Western silk-reeling machinery, especially in the Gumma area. Samples of silk produced by this method were sent to Arai, who reported that the quality was satisfactory.

This encouraged Hoshino to organize a group of about forty dealers in silk thread, named for the local river the Watarase Gumi, which had capital of 5000 yen and 200 shares. The aggregate produce of this organization assured Hoshino of an adequate supply for Arai. Hoshino then went on to establish a larger organization in cooperation with Fukusawa Yuzo, a leading silk merchant in Maebashi, which had developed the largest silk industry in Japan, with the first Western-style mill and, in addition, eleven factories using the improved zaguri method and employing hundreds of impoverished samurai. The new organization, the Seishi Gensha, was established in August 1877 by bringing together six groups of silk dealers and consolidating all aspects of procurement, reeling, packaging, shipping, and quality control. This was the first industrial cooperative in Japan, and its rapid growth proved a major step toward the eventual takeover by Japanese traders of the silk trade from Western merchants.

By the end of 1877 the Japanese government, in line with its policy of promoting direct trade, was subsidizing the Mitsubishi and Nihonmatsu companies in making silk shipments to America. The Nihonmatsu Company of Fukushima had its own machine mills, producing silk thread called *hime,* which had won a high reputation in foreign markets. The entire shipment from this company to America was bought by a mill in Manchester, Connecticut; Mitsubishi made sales in New York, including a small amount to Arai. At the end of the year, Nihonmatsu sent its own representative, Yamada Osamu, to New York. Since Arai had until then been the only Japanese silk merchant in New York, he welcomed Yamada's arrival, and for the next three years the two were close companions. The Nihonmatsu Company, however, did not survive the seriously inflationary times. It was dissolved in 1881, and Yamada returned to Japan.

Because of the increase in his business, Arai felt the need to open a bank account, which he did at the Irving Trust Company. In 1939, after he had been a customer for over sixty years, the bank issued a special poster, which was displayed in all its branches. It read:

Sixty Years in Silk
    In 1877, a progressive young Japanese silk merchant crossed the Pacific in a side-wheeled steamer, came to New York and opened an account with this Company. Since then we have constantly served those engaged in the importation of raw silk. Of the total shipments to this country last year 30 percent were financed by IRVING. The Japanese merchant is still an IRVING CUSTOMER.

In 1878, Arai formed a partnership with Sato, called the Sato-Arai Company, to handle the raw-silk business. Actually Sato was a partner only in name, for he was fully occupied with his own wholesale merchandise store and also a retail outlet, the Hinode Company, which he had organized with Morimura Toyo two years earlier. But these two closest friends of Arai both found it necessary to return to Japan in 1878. Morimura was the first to leave, though only temporarily. He went back in the late spring to assist his older brother Ichizaemon in finding appropriate merchandise to sell in their store. This proved difficult to do. Ichizaemon literally walked the length of Japan in search of goods. Although he collected various different kinds of chinaware, lacquer and metalwork, curios, parasols, fans, scrolls, handicrafts, and silk goods, these did not add up to a staple export of the value of the raw silk Arai was exporting. Morimura Toyo wrote plaintively to Arai on July 13, 1878:

> I tell you, Mr. Arai, it is getting very hard to make money by Jap. business because as you know, in Japan there is not much necessary thing that we can export, except raw silk and I do not know even myself what kind of thing is most saleable or what kind of thing to make. Your business is only business betw. AM. + JAP. that we can call staple article and at the same time we can carry on with profit I think.

Sato was in even more serious trouble. He had started his New York store with merchandise bought on credit. As time passed and he was unable to keep up payments to his creditors, they became uneasy and after two years sent Tachibana, one of their group, to New York to look into the situation and bring Sato back to Japan to account for himself. Sato was forced to hire an assistant, Richard von Briesen, to run the store in his absence. Von Briesen was a German who had emigrated to America during the Civil War and, before coming to New York, had fought under Admiral Farragut on the Mississippi. He and Arai became lifelong friends, developing a close association in both business and private life.

Sato was reluctant to leave New York because he had just married an American girl, Agnes Frankinback, from Philadelphia. He wanted Agnes to accompany him but was concerned for her health and her adjustment to life in Japan. But Agnes as well as Tachibana accompanied him when he left for Japan in September. Sato told Arai that, when he arrived in Tokyo, he would send by telegraph the single word, "Arrived," and he asked Arai to then inform Agnes' mother by mail. On October 10, 1878, Arai noted in his diary, "It is clear in the evening, we have received a teregram from Japan that Mr. Sato and his wife and Tachibana arrived there safely." Then, as now, Japanese had trouble making the distinction between "l" and "r."

Sato communicated with Arai quite often on business matters and also about his personal affairs and feelings on returning to Japan. He wrote of his wife's illness while traveling, of their difficulties in finding adequate housing, and of the long and unpleasant questioning he was subjected to by his creditors. As a result of Sato's return to Japan, a new company was formed, the Sato Gumi. Although it used Sato's name, it was entirely controlled by his creditors. Sato desperately wished to return to New York to manage his store, but his creditors refused to let him go back. He wrote to Arai on November 25, 1878:

> So for my going to New York, my friends do not incline to think advisable, from the reason perhaps that I am too extravagant in living on the other side of the ocean. As I have very little to do in Tokio, I have made up my mind to settle down in Yokohama where I think I can get enough to do to support myself and wife . . . as a broker, interpreter or teacher, so that at any time I was wanted in Tokio I could leave Yokohama at any moment.

Sato's creditors, like other Japanese, had little concept of life in America, and what may have seemed to them extreme extravagance may have been merely a reflection of the higher standard of living. Things may have been difficult for Sato too because marriages between Japanese and foreigners were severely frowned on by both sides. It was difficult for couples like the Satos to live in the society of Tokyo, where Agnes would be treated as a complete outsider. It was for this reason, no doubt, that Sato decided to live in Yokohama, where Agnes and he could make friends among the Americans living in this port city, and life would be more pleasant for them both. Sato's letter to Arai reveals how living in America for a long time had changed his way of life and how difficult he found it to readjust to Japanese ways of thinking. As he wrote in October 1879, "Bear in mind that people here think very different from what you think in America. I have had very hard times to carry what I thought myself when I first came, and even now I have not had my own satisfaction. Still my case and yours are quite different and I have many things to bear."

Hoshino found it helpful to have Sato in Yokohama to take care of shipments. Sato immediately after his arrival also started working on registering a cable address for Arai's company and devising a cable code for its use. The Japanese telegraph office was most uncooperative, regarding foreign cables as a great nuisance. It was almost a year before the cable address of LIGHTSTAR was accepted and Sato had worked out a code and set of ciphers that was approved by the telegraph office. In 1879 Arai was still receiving only piecemeal information about the Yokohama silk market, since Western traders, who still controlled 95 percent of all exports, continued to withhold information about marketing transactions elsewhere in the world as well as the trade journals that included news of the worldwide silk trade. In a letter Sato wrote to Arai dated November 1, 1879, he complained:

> Perhaps you know that it is quite hard thing for Japanese silk man to get good and reliable report from foreigners in Yokohama and what they are doing in way of their business. Even the ablest silkman who is not accustomed in foreigner's way of business can hardly ascertain their full report. I have known this to be the case while I was staying in Yokohama. I have made some friends among the foreigners in Yokohama and shall try my best in procuring as reliable report as possible.

In contrast to Sato's troubles in Japan, Arai was beginning to feel very much at home in New York. The year 1878 proved a most profitable one for him, and he doubled his previous year's sales to $41,000. In this year he also moved to a more respectable boardinghouse in Manhattan at 55 West 9th Street at the corner of Third Avenue. Here he paid $7 for room and breakfast, which was two dollars more than before, but the room was clean and comfortable and the boardinghouse more conveniently located. The atmosphere was definitely more pleasant because there were other Japanese staying there. At that time boardinghouses of this sort were virtually the only lodgings available to foreigners with limited funds. Even the Japanese consul lived in one until as late as 1902, when the fourth man in the position finally rented an official residence for $400 a month on 58th Street near Central Park. Arai's new boardinghouse was owned and operated by a Mrs. Dudley, who was the daughter of an Episcopal minister. She was not only a good housekeeper but a kindhearted and understanding woman who took a sincere interest in her Japanese boarders, becoming much loved by the small Japanese community.

Arai was so happy at Mrs. Dudley's that he remained there for more than ten years.

———•———

By 1879 Arai's business had grown to such an extent that he no longer was able to handle it by himself and asked Sato to find him an assistant who knew English and something about business. When Sato proved unable to find a satisfactory person, Arai decided to go back to Japan himself to attend to this problem and other pressing matters he was unable to solve by mail. He boarded ship in San Francisco in the spring of 1880 for his second Pacific crossing. In all he was to cross the ocean ninety times, which before the days of airplanes was probably close to a record. I estimate that these trips must have added up to a total of about forty months at sea.

In Yokohama Arai was given a hero's welcome by the same large group of friends and relatives who had seen him off four years earlier. The year 1880 was an opportune time for his return. During his four years abroad, Japan had gone through unbelievably rapid social, economic, and political changes, which would have been difficult for him to comprehend without observing them himself. As he stepped ashore in his latest New York clothes, he did not look strange to his friends, since they too were now dressed in Western clothes. It was rather he who was surprised at the total disappearance of sword-bearing samurai, since they had been ordered by the government in 1876 to stop wearing these weapons. He was also astonished at the abundance of imported Western goods in the stores and the cost of everything, which brought home to him the reality of the inflation he had only heard about.

In Gumma Arai found his relatives and friends much interested in all he had to tell about his life in New York, and, when he listened to them talk about events at home, he was amazed to see how involved they had become in politics. As an initial step in the government's long-range program to establish Western political institutions, elections for prefectural assemblies had been held at the end of 1879. At that time, men over twenty-five who paid a certain amount of direct land tax were eligible to vote. Because of their prestige, both Chotaro and his adopted brother Kosaku (1850–1925) had won seats, and

Chotaro had been selected to be the first vice-chairman of the new prefectural assembly of Gumma.

This was the time of the height of the *jiyu minken undo* (the movement for freedom and people's rights). As we have seen, it was started in 1873 by Itagaki, the samurai leader from Tosa whose troops had despoiled the Hoshino house in 1868. Itagaki left the government in a dispute over policy and rallied opposition among his fellow Tosa samurai, but the movement soon found fertile soil among the rich peasants in rural areas like Gumma. One of Arai's relatives, Arai Go (1858–1909), became a leader of the movement in the area. He was three years younger than Rioichiro and had also pursued an education in English, studying for several years with foreigners in Yokohama. Arai Go graduated from Fukuzawa's school, Keio Gijuku, and immediately established an English school of his own, remaining its principal until his enthusiasm for politics led him to become a publisher of the *Yoron Shinsha,* a public-opinion journal, through which he advocated the immediate adoption of universal suffrage, a national assembly, and a constitution. An ardent activist in the movement for freedom and people's rights, he returned to Gumma to organize a political group in Takasaki. Soon it had over three hundred members, most of them ex-samurai, who rallied around this former peasant as their way of showing their dissatisfaction with the new government and its policies.

In September 1880, Arai Go was one of 200,000 signers of a petition sent to Sanjo, the leading minister of state, demanding the establishment of a national assembly and universal suffrage, and sometime after 1881 he toured Japan urging the reduction of political centralization brought about by the new administrative changes and the lowering of local taxes imposed by the Matsukata tax reforms. Arai Go was a successful candidate in the first national election in 1890, becoming a member of the Diet, but he lost his seat in the second election in 1892, when Shinagawa, the home minister in Matsukata's first cabinet, used force, bribery, and every other possible means to suppress the opposition. Arai Go was reelected to the Diet in the third and fourth elections, in 1894, and he became an active member of the party known as the Kokumin Kyokai, or the Citizens' Association.

Among hundreds of old photographs in the Hoshino storehouses, I found a charming photograph of Arai Go taken with Chotaro in

Marseilles in the late fall of 1899. Arai Go had failed in the Diet elections held the previous year, and he and Chotaro took a trip abroad. First they visited Rioichiro in New York and then went on to Europe. The photograph shows Chotaro looking very much the normal tourist of the time, a bowler hat in his hand, wearing an overcoat with a velvet collar, and binoculars held by a strap over his shoulder. But Arai Go cuts a dramatic figure. Unusually tall for a Japanese, he stands with legs spread wide apart, both hands stuffed in the pockets of a huge fur-lined coat reaching down to his shoe tops, and sporting a very tall top hat. His casually opened coat reveals a high buttoned vest and a chain with a gold medallion dangling from it. He appears to have been quite a dandy. One wishes to know more about this "peasant" member of Japan's first Diet and why in 1909 he ended his flamboyant career by jumping overboard from a ship on his way to Kyushu.

In 1880 in Gumma, Rioichiro was also surprised to find Chotaro faithfully reading the Bible every day with his family. A few years earlier the New Testament had been translated into kambun (Japanese-style literary Chinese) by recently converted Christians, who were mostly ex-samurai well versed in kambun. Rioichiro had heard from Chotaro in the summer of 1879 about Chotaro's conversion to Christianity, and he also received a clipping from the local paper dated May 5, 1879, headlined, "Hoshino Chotaro of Minami Seta-gun becomes a Christian." The article telling of the conversion of Hoshino, his wife, and forty of the women workers of his mill concludes with the statement, "Since then all have studied hard to work well."

Chotaro's adopted brother Kosaku had also become a Christian. he was active in the silk-weaving industry, and when he was baptized ninety workers of the Kiryu Textile Factory (Kiryu Orimono Kojo) adopted the faith with him. Conditions for the working girls at the Kiryu mills were as miserable as in all the other textile mills throughout the country, where cheap labor was exploited to the limit. But Kosaku applied the principles of his newfound religion by attempting to give the women more freedom and equality and to improve working conditions. He also was active in the movement to abolish prostitution and to stop the pollution of the Watarase River by the Ashio copper mines.

The Hoshinos were not the only Christian converts in the region.

Hayami, Fukusawa, and practically all of Chotaro's other associates in the silk industry, who constituted a "Who's Who" of Gumma at the time, also became Christians. All took their new religion very seriously, hoping to use it to better not only their home life but also conditions in their places of work. During this period, when silk exports were rising rapidly, Christianity and the silk industry became almost synonymous in Gumma.

Recent research has revealed that the roots of Christianity go far back in this area. Catholicism was already present in the latter decades of the sixteenth century. When the authorities sought to stamp out Christianity in the seventeenth century, groups of "hidden Christians" (*kakure kirishitan*), like those Matsukata dealt with in Nagasaki, went underground. One such group existed in Numata, a small town in Kozuke northwest of Mount Akagi, but most of them were discovered and executed. The Hoshino family has in its possession certificates of merit for persons who revealed such hidden Christians to the authorities. One of the Hoshinos, now in his sixties, remembers that when he was a child a group of older men would gather to gamble secretly in the woods on the border of Mizunuma and would post him as lookout at a square rock set in the ground, which was locally called the shrine of the hidden Christians.

Christianity in Gumma in the 1870s, however, had no connection with these much earlier Christians. It stemmed from the young samurai of the area who, in their disenchantment with Confucianism and their distaste for the new government, eagerly embraced the Western religion. I have already referred to Niijima Jo of Annaka, who was the founder of the Congregational school, Doshisha, in Kyoto, and to Uchimura Kanzo, Rioichiro's classmate at the Takasaki English School, who became a founder of the Christian no-church movement. A Congregational (Kumiai Kyokai) church was founded in Maebashi in 1878, and the same year Ebina Danjo, a graduate of the first class of Doshisha and later a leading churchman, came to Annaka at the age of twenty-two to establish a Congregational church there. In the 1880s, when Christianity had perhaps its greatest influence in Japan in modern times, Gumma ranked next to Tokyo, Kanagawa (where Yokohama is located), and Hokkaido in its number of Christians.

Arai was surprised to find that almost all of his Hoshino relatives had become Christians, and he was even more amazed when he visited his adoptive Arai family in Kazuno to discover that his stepmother Nobuko and her daughter Kikuko were also staunch Christians. Kikuko, then fourteen, was sent to Yokohama for her education and to learn English. After graduating from Ferris Seminary, she served for a while in the Salvation Army before returning to teach at Ferris for many years. Her father had planned a marriage for her with a man of social standing and wealth, but she opted to marry Kaneko, a poor but devout Christian who after graduating from Doshisha became an ordained minister. Today in the Arai graveyard in Kazuno, the gravestones of Nobuko and Kikuko stand side by side, conspicuous among the other stones because of the crosses carved above their names. Rioichiro himself did not become a Christian until some years later, though I have in my possession a Bible printed in 1877 that has his name embossed on its cover.

———— • ————

By 1879 inflation had reached an alarming rate in Japan, because of the cost of the Satsuma Rebellion of 1877, expenditures to pay off the hereditary incomes of the daimyo and samurai, and the multiple expenses of modernization, including the costs of industrialization and the wages of foreign experts. Government expenses far exceeded revenues, and successive issues of unconvertible paper currency proved necessary. Prices soared, and the cost of rice increased over 40 percent. The balance of payments was growing steadily worse because the public had developed a taste for foreign goods, and these could not be excluded by tariffs, which were kept low by the unequal treaties. A heavy burden had fallen on silk exports to make up the balance of payments.

As we have seen, it was in March 1879 that my other grandfather, Matsukata Masayoshi, returned to Japan from a year of study in Europe, where he had acquired the knowledge about national finances that would enable him to become Okuma's successor as finance minister in 1881 and bring inflation under control. He also had taken time to study European agriculture and was much impressed by its efficiency and the backwardness of Japanese farming, which had continued little changed for centuries. He had visited some of the exhibitions for agricultural products held throughout Europe and was convinced that such expositions were essential to encourage agriculture and assist the diffusion of modern techniques. He was particularly struck by the fact that in Europe Japanese silk, because of its inferior quality, was selling for less even than hand-reeled Chinese silk and for only half the price of European silk. He realized that a concentrated effort must be made to improve the quality of Japanese silk, and on his return he persuaded the government to start holding competitive exhibitions for agricultural products, especially for silk and tea.

The first of these exhibits, called Kyoshinkai, was held for tea in October 1879, and it was followed by one for silk and silk cocoons the following month. At this second exhibit Matsukata, as head of the Agricultural Promotion Agency, was one of the main speakers. He started out diplomatically by praising the Nihonmatsu Company because of its outstanding reputation in Europe. "Through its perseverance and diligence," he stated, "it had brought the silk business to where it is today." He went on to say:

> However, as silk is the leading national product for export, every encouragement must be given to increasing it by the cultivation of waste lands for planting mulberry trees and producing cocoons. The outcome of trade is inseparable from the interests of the nation, and it is of greater consequence than the bloodshed and disaster which come from wars . . . In the war of trade, money should serve as our weapons and supplies, and national production must be our generals and soldiers. If production is low, we must use to our advantage our military supplies, scattering silver and gold and using them to start silk industries and increase production . . . At present China's output of silk is four times that of our country. Therefore uncultivated areas must be utilized for the silk industry. In order to promote the industry you must have a definite policy. You must develop it with the purpose of curtailing expenses and producing silk of good quality at low prices. If such is your policy, you will be assured of good business for a long time.

Sato had reported by letter to Arai on November 27, 1879, "The Kiyoshinkai is at the midst of interest. I have been there the other day and was surprised with the varieties of exhibitions. They are very neatly and most beautifully arranged. We hope these exhibitions will furnish the same silk the samples exhibited." The exhibition proved successful, generating great interest and enthusiasm among the silk producers, who for the first time had been brought together and were officially made aware of the importance of their task in improving the faltering Japanese economy.

Matsukata's appeal to develop the silk-export trade inspired the Gumma silk industrialists, Hayami, Hoshino, Fukusawa, and many others, to discuss ways this could be achieved. Their meetings resulted in the founding of a direct export company, the Doshin Kaisha (Company to Progress Together), a jointly owned enterprise capitalized at 300,000 yen. Hayami had been the president of the Tomioka mill, but he resigned to take over the presidency of the new company, and Chotaro became chairman of its board of directors. The company established a main office in Yokohama and built its own warehouse, thus separating itself from the Western exporters of silk. It also by-passed the Japanese wholesale merchants, who had been the collectors of silk for export and the suppliers of the foreign traders. The Doshin Kaisha planned to have branches in New York and Lyons operated by their own representatives, who would not only be in charge of sales but would also report on conditions in the foreign market to the home office by telegraph, which had been extended to Japan in 1877.

The Doshin Kaisha had just been reorganized when Arai returned to Japan, and he was immediately asked to become the company's representative abroad, because of his experience and the confidence Hoshino and Hayami had in his abilities. He was then in partnership with Sato in the Sato-Arai Company and, because of his loyalty to Sato, was reluctant about the new offer. But Sato urged him to accept the position, which would offer Arai a much better opportunity to expand his business, and when Arai returned to New York the Sato-Arai Company was formally dissolved. Sato never did return to America as a businessman, and only many years later did he visit America again briefly for medical treatment.

The Doshin Kaisha was not the only company formed at this time for the direct export of silk. Another was the Boeki Shokai, capitalized at 200,000 yen and founded by Iwasaki Yataro, Fukuzawa Yukichi, and other members of their group. It was to be reorganized as the Yokohama Gomei Kaisha, where Arai was to play an important role, and much later it became the silk department of the Mitsubishi Company.

Arai had found it impossible to convey through his letters to the silk producers in Japan the Americans' requirements for quality and uniformity, and he realized that it was only through direct contact with the people back home that he could do this. The Japanese producers, with no experience of the high-speed machinery now used in America, were simply unable to understand Arai's constant demands. Hoshino had done his best to convey Arai's requests, but even he did not fully understand them. Arai now worked tirelessly with the silk producers, urging them to produce silk according to his specifications, and he continued to return to Japan every few years to keep production in line with American requirements. To assist him, Hoshino and his colleagues finally established a company called Jomo Kairyo Kaisha, specifically designed to work on the improvement of silk thread and the dissemination of information to silk producers all over Japan.

The year before Arai returned to Japan, the Yokohama Specie Bank was established by the government to stimulate foreign trade and assist in the transmission of funds between Japan and foreign countries. The new bank issued documentary bills to exporters, which were actually loans equivalent to 70 percent of the value of the exports at the low interest rate of 7 percent. Through branches abroad, the bank acted as the agent for the exporters and collected the payments from their sales. Since these were in foreign specie, the government was able to obtain the funds for its purchases abroad, such as warships, armaments, and communication equipment, while the silk producers back in Japan received payment in Japanese currency. Matsukata was critical of many decisions made by his predecessor, Okuma, but he heartily endorsed the establishment of the Yokohama Specie Bank: "Theoretically, trade should be left in the hands of the people without interference from the government. Under the present conditions in Japan, however, all informed people acknowledge the necessity of direct export by means of documentary bills."*

Because of the rising demand for silk in the American market, the export trade increased at an amazing rate during the deflationary period brought on by Matsukata's 1881 reforms. In 1880 Japan's exports had amounted to 2.26 million yen, but by 1885 they had risen

---

* Shibusawa Keizo, *Japanese Society in the Meiji Era* (Tokyo: Obunsha, 1958), p. 491.

to 7.8 million, more than a threefold increase. During this period the export of tea, which had been the largest export item from the beginning of foreign trade, remained constant, and it was largely because of silk that Japanese exports grew so rapidly. Aided by a sharp curtailment of imports, silk exports built up a trade surplus of 28 million yen by 1885, and as a result Japanese paper currency regained its value, the yen rising from a low of 58 percent of silver to 105 percent in 1885.

New York Businessman

Arai returned to New York in the autumn of 1880 with high expectations for the future, but even he could not have foreseen how meteoric his rise would be. He was in the right business at the right time and in the right place. It was the heyday of industrial development in the United States, and businesses of every kind were booming. Since before the Civil War there had been a large import trade in silk manufactured goods from France and England to meet the needs of fashionable Americans. After the war, when prices rose because the government imposed for revenue purposes a heavy tariff of from 40 to 60 percent on these manufactured imports, a strong domestic silk industry had an opportunity to develop. Hitherto American manufacturers of silk goods had been unable to compete with European imports because of their use of hand machines requiring much labor, but now concentrated efforts were being made to mechanize the industry, and it developed rapidly. A report prepared by the American Silk Association for the Centennial Exposition claimed that 1875 had been the greatest year in the American silk industry. It made the rosy prediction that, though every farmer would not go to work in silk suits or milkmaids dress in brocades with trains two yards long, America would be exporting instead of importing silk goods by the dawn of the twentieth century. American women engaged in everyday duties, it predicted, would be able to afford silk clothes, and American silks would surpass the products of European looms, which were not being mechanized as fast as those in the United States. The burgeoning demand for silk thread to supply the American manufacturers opened up great possibilities for the Japanese exporters of raw silk.

By the early 1880s high-speed machines had spread throughout the mills on the eastern seaboard, where most silk spinning and weaving were concentrated, especially in the town of Patterson, New Jersey, twenty miles from New York City, which came to be known as the "Lyons of America." One of the most important machines developed at this time was a spinning frame capable of producing silk threads for both sewing and weaving. It operated at a maximum velocity of 10,000 revolutions per minute, permitting one operator to spin as much and better silk than 2,000 workers could have done half a century earlier. The number of such machines increased from 1,605 in 1875 to 5,321 in 1880.

Paralleling this increase in productivity was a great growth in wealth in the United States and a resulting rise in demand for silks of all types. Earlier the use of silk had been restricted to the very rich, but now there was a larger and more affluent class of the "new rich," who unlike the old rich, had only money as their status symbol. They spent their newly acquired wealth ostentatiously on costly homes, jewels, lavish entertainment, and expensive clothing, avidly following fashions, which changed from year to year or even from season to season. Much of the fashion of the time depended on the use of silks, forcing manufacturers to keep up with rapidly changing demands, which in turn kept silk suppliers ever on the alert. Arai was required to maintain close contact with the manufacturers, making frequent trips to the mills in Patterson and almost annual trips to Japan to report on changing demands in America.

As imports of Japanese raw silk rapidly increased, unreliable establishments were able to enter into the business, giving grounds for loud complaints from the American Silk Association. In one report the association stated, "It is an occasion of profound regret that the excellent reputation which had been fairly won in this market for silks of Japan, should be so carelessly impaired."* Even though Arai took every precaution to see that the silk he imported met the standards required, he was deeply concerned for the reputation of the Japanese

* W. C. Wycoff, *Silk Manufacture in the United States: Report of the Silk Association of America* (1883), p. 84.

silk industry as a whole as well as for the future of Japanese trade with America, which was so important for Japan's industrialization. He felt it a patriotic duty to bridge the gap in understanding between the American manufacturers and the Japanese silk producers, who had little concept of the mechanized industry. Reeling any kind of silk is a difficult process, and to reel it for machine use is all the more difficult. The problem is that the filaments in cocoons vary in length, being anywhere from 300 to 1000 yards long, and to make a single thread ordinarily requires 4 to 18 filaments reeled together. It takes 1000 yards of silk thread to produce the warp of a yard of satin, and a single bad filament could lead to a break in the thread and a consequent stoppage of the machine, cutting production by more than half and rendering the satin produced commercially unacceptable.* It was problems like this that Arai had to convey to the Japanese producers, and it took long hours and a great deal of patience and firmness. But his endeavors were rewarded in time, and Japanese silks regained their reputation and eventually won the lion's share of the market.

If Arai had been a short-term resident in the United States, as most Japanese businessmen were, he could never have established a continuous dialogue on problems of mutual concern between Japanese exporters and American buyers; nor could he have assumed personal responsibility for the quality of silk, which was necessary for the development of the trade. His role was essential. During his years in the United States, from 1876 until the 1930s, raw-silk exports financed more than 40 percent of Japan's entire imports of the foreign machinery and raw materials with which Japan built an industrial base for the army and navy that made it a first-class military power and later one of the leading industrial nations in the world.

———•———

When Arai's good reputation in New York became known in Japan, well-to-do families with marriageable daughters began to consider him as a possible son-in-law. By 1885 he was thirty years old and, affluent enough to support a wife, was not averse to the suggestion of his friend Morimura Toyo and his own relatives that he con-

* James Chittick, *Silk Manufacturing and Its Problems* (New York, 1913), p. 21.

sider marriage. In accordance with the Japanese custom of arranged marriages, he left the matter in their hands. His father by adoption, Arai Keisaku, wished to marry him to his own daughter Kikuko, but this he refused to do. Several attractive offers were made but subsequently withdrawn when it became known that the bride would be expected to live permanently in America. Only Ushiba Takuzo made the surprising statement, "Unless my daughter *does* go to America after marriage, I shall not give her in marriage to Arai." Part of Ushiba's eagerness may have been because his daughter Tazu, aged eighteen, had been born in the year of the horse and he felt it would be difficult to marry her off, since it was believed that girls born in that year were unruly. The offer was accepted, and in late 1884 Arai returned to Japan for the wedding, which was held in a restaurant in Shiba Park in Tokyo, with Fukuzawa among those present. Early the following year the young couple went to New York, where Tazu spent the remaining sixty-four years of her life, though she did make some twenty trips back to Japan to visit her family and friends.

Ushiba Takuzo was a progressive man, typical of people in the early years after the Meiji Restoration. He was born in 1848 into a minor samurai family of the outer domain of Tsu in the province of Ise, the present Mie prefecture. Not long after the Restoration, he and his wife Michi were adopted into the Ushiba family, who were from a rich peasant background in Ise but were then in trade in the port city of Kobe. Although older than most students, he went to Fukuzawa's Keio Gijuku and was in the first graduating class. In order to prepare people for popular participation in government, Fukuzawa encouraged the learning of the art of public speaking, and among his first students in this field were Ushiba and the later well-known public figures, Ozaki and Inukai, who became known as the Three Heroes (*San Yushi*) of Mita, the location of Fukuzawa's school in Tokyo.

After graduation, Ushiba became a reporter for the *Yukan Hochi* for a short time before he went into government service, first in the government of Hyogo prefecture and later in the central government, where he held a position under Finance Minister Okuma. When Okuma was ousted from the government by the Satsuma-Choshu clique and replaced by Matsukata, all the young men from Keio, who had been "Okuma's boys," resigned with him. Ozaki and Inukai helped Okuma found the Kaishinto Party, and Ozaki eventually became a famous parliamentarian and mayor of Tokyo and Inukai a prime minister, but Ushiba returned to newspaper work on Fukuzawa's newspaper, the *Jiji Shimpo*. Subsequently he joined the large civil-engineering construction company, the Nihon Doboku Kaisha, of the industrialist Fujita Denzaburo in Osaka, where he acquired experience in an entirely new field. He learned quickly, becoming a key person in the construction of the Sanyo Railroad, which connected Kobe with Shimonoseki in 1884, and serving as the third president of the railway company. He came to be known as the *genkun* (elder statesman) of Japanese railways. He also engaged in various other industrial enterprises and became a leading figure in the economic life of the Kansai area. In 1890 he was a successful candidate in the first elections for the National Diet, running from Mie prefecture, his birthplace. He served only one term, however, preferring business to politics.

Ushiba Takuzo's wife Michi, my great-grandmother, I remember well, since she often visited us in Tokyo. She and Takuzo had become Christians, as had many others of their social class in the early 1870s. The Kobe band of Christians was very active and drew an elite group of people into their church. The members of the Kuki family, the former daimyo of the Sanda domain near Kobe, were among them and were close associates of the Ushibas. Michi was much admired and loved by everyone. One of her grandsons, Ushiba Tomohiko, tells a typical story about her. One day his mother stepped barefoot on a large centipede (*mukade*), and Michi made her lie down at once and started sucking out the poison in her foot, while everyone else concentrated on killing the centipede. Michi excelled in playing the *koto* and in the tea ceremony. Such was her skill that she could break any rule in the rigid tea ceremony and still be considered to have performed outstandingly. She tended to disregard formalities and act according to her own lights. She loved all kinds of foods, but on her visits to us we usually had *soba* (buckwheat noodles) from the Sarashinaya store nearby. This she would slurp down noisely, to the surprise of us children who had been brought up in the Western way not to make noises while eating. She would explain that noisy slurping was the only way to enjoy the taste of soba. She also had a great fondness for butter and loved putting a hand-rolled butter ball in her mouth and savoring it as long as it lasted. Not many people of her age dared try this new foreign food, which was often rancid in those days, being imported and quite aged by the time it reached Japanese tables. Actually *bata kusai* (stinks of butter) was a pejorative term for anyone or anything that was unpleasantly Western.

Takuzo and Michi had two children, Tetsuro, a boy, and Tazu, my grandmother, born in 1867. Tetsuro like his father was educated at Keio Gijuku, and all his life he remained an avid reader of books in English. When Tazu was of highschool age, the Westernization craze was at its peak, and her parents, who both believed in education for women, sent her to Toyo Eiwa Girls School, a Canadian Protestant mission school in Azabu ward in Tokyo, where she too learned English. Tazu told a reporter who interviewed her after World War II, "When I was a young girl, it was the period of the Rokumeikan. I commuted to Toyo Eiwa Girls School wearing Western-style dresses. My mother was very progressive, and in growing up I never wore the *shimada* hair style. At school with me were . . . the mother of the present Mr. Kido [Marquis Kido, the emperor's close adviser before World War II] and the daughter of Prince Ito. Japan at that time was similar to today—it was quite Westernized. Dr. Takaki used to tell us, 'Kimonos for Japanese women are no good. You must eat about a pound of meat a day.' "*

Tazu was an attractive, lively, and independent girl who had many interests and would often spend entire days at the Kabuki Theater, where the Ushiba family had a large box of their own. She was the tallest girl in her class, for which she was nicknamed *denshin bashira* (telegraph pole). This gene was passed on to her children and some of her grandchildren. I too am tall for a Japanese of my generation and, when young, was embarrassed at the way I towered over people in a crowded street car.

The sudden transfer from Tokyo to life as an eighteen-year-old bride in New York must have been quite a shock for Tazu, but she took it well. Many years later she related, "I didn't have a hard time when I first came here. People are quite informal and simple, and social intercourse is much easier here than in Japan. After I arrived in

---

* Suzuki Bunshiro, *Sengo no Amerika daiisshin: Arai-ke yonsei monogatari* (First News from Postwar America: Tales of Four Generations of the Arai Family; Tokyo, 1949), pp. 155–156.

New York, I didn't have to worry too much because I was well taken care of by Mrs. Murai, the wife of my husband's best friend." Tazu had gone with her husband to live at Mrs. Dudley's boarding house, where Murai Yasukata, another Japanese boarder, had an American wife. This was Mrs. Dudley's sister, Caroline Bailey, who had been helping her sister when she met and fell in love with Murai and married him. Since Tazu spoke some English, she was able to communicate with Caroline Murai, who helped her not only in American ways but as a newlywed. The Murais and Arais established a close relationship that lasted throughout their lives.

Murai was born in a samurai family in Kyushu and received his education at Keio Gijuku. When Morimura Toyo needed an assistant in New York to help him in his expanding business, Fukuzawa recommended Murai. Although Toyo had stipulated that the man must speak English, Murai knew very little but Fukuzawa explained that, unlike other students who came to Keio to become politicians, Murai wanted to become a merchant and, because of this as well as his personality and eagerness to work hard, Fukuzawa recommended him for the position. Murai proved to be a good salesman. His original lack of English does not seem to have been a handicap because he won over customers by his charm and amusing efforts to speak English.

Murai followed Fukuzawa's admonition to settle down permanently in America and become a loyal American. Since American law did not permit Asians to become naturalized citizens until after World War II, he did the next best thing by marrying an American. He was short and not at all handsome, while Caroline, or Nenne as she was known to her friends, was a tall, attractive New Englander who towered over him. They made a strange-looking couple, but those who knew them soon found that there was no happier or better-suited pair. And it was Nenne Murai who made Tazu's introduction to life in America so pleasant and easy.

Another factor that aided Tazu in the transition was that her husband now had a good income. His business was prospering and was further stimulated by a favorable exchange rate. Japanese currency was relatively cheap at the time, the silver yen exchanging with the dollar at a ratio of 1:1.25, thus increasing the demand for Japanese silk. Business grew so rapidly that Hoshino sent his adopted son Bunya to New York to assist Arai. Chotaro adopted Bunya when he thought he would have no natural heir, but then he did have a son, Motoji, born in 1873. Since Bunya was no longer needed as Chotaro's heir, he could be dispatched to America, where he lived until his death in 1901. He was buried in Woodlawn Cemetery in New York, although Chotaro erected a stone memorial for him in Mizunuma in the shape of Cleopatra's Needle, seven feet tall, one-tenth the size of the original Egyptian obelisk. Ismail Pasha, the ruler of Egypt, had given one of the original obelisks to England, where it now stands on the Thames embankment; the other had been given to the United States, where it was placed in Central Park in New York.

Despite Bunya's presence, von Briesen served as Arai's chief assistant, in charge of the office whenever Arai was away. Von Briesen, it will be remembered, had been hired by Sato to look after his store when he was called back to Japan in 1878, and he had come into Arai's company through the founding of the partnership between Sato and Arai that same year. Von Briesen took his position very seriously and, when Arai was in Japan, would report on the business in detail by mail, which left San Francisco every two weeks. In a letter dated August 5, 1887, complaining about shipments that fell short of specifications, he wrote:

Japan silks are getting more attention constantly. Hence we cannot be too particular to have our friends in Japan take all possible pains. Surely it stands to reason that if they follow your advice the consumption of raw silk from Japan will largely increase. We want reliability of the goods as the foundation to be able to sell at good price . . .

Do not be afraid to persuade good reelers to send their silk, we can sell it. But be careful you do not make them hope for enormous profits. I am sure (knowing your business principles) that as your reputation is growing here every year, so it will increase in Japan with those who trust their goods to Doshin Kaisha for export to your store. With all the cheating that most other importers carry on here you stand different in the opinion of the manufacturers who deal with you, and as the customers increase in quantity, so the demand for your silk will increase. Therefore be prepared to send more, especially in good filatures.

Von Briesen's letters were long and repetitious, and Arai wrote sparingly in reply, touching only on immediate business matters. In a letter dated July 27, 1887, von Briesen complains:

> Mr. Murai arrived last night (from Japan) but he is so busy kissing his wife, that nobody can get near him for a few days. As soon as he cools off, Mr. Otake and myself prepare visiting him and hope to get some information regarding yourself for which we look in your very short letters in vain.

Ever since Arai had started representing the Doshin Kaisha in New York in 1881, he operated under the name of R. Arai Company because his name was better known in the silk business there than that of the Doshin Kaisha. He conducted his business both in New York and in Lyons on commission from the sales he generated for the company. As business prospered, however, the directors of the company became dissatisfied with the arrangement and in 1893 started negotiations for a reorganization of the R. Arai Company. Essentially they wished to put Arai on a salary basis. He refused and, since he could not come to terms with them, finally decided to resign, even though the prospects were bad for continuing in the silk business without the backing of the Doshin Kaisha.

When Arai took this bold step, his two closest friends, Morimura Toyo and Murai, were greatly concerned. Toyo sent an urgent plea to his older brother Ichizaemon, president of the Morimura Company in Tokyo, to come to Arai's aid. Fortunately, Ichizaemon had become an influential man in the export business and was in a position to respond to Toyo's request. The Boeki Kaisha, which had been established at the same time as the Doshin Kaisha, had grown into an important export company but had fallen into debt and was liquidated. Some directors of the company called on Ichizaemon and others to organize another company to take its place, and just at this time Toyo's pleas to save Arai reached Ichizaemon, who telegraphed Arai to come back to Tokyo at once. Several months of negotiations and planning followed, during which Arai often despaired. In the end, however, Ichizaemon's influence prevailed: in November 1893 the Yokohama Kiito Gomei Kaisha (Yokohama Raw Silk Joint Company) was established with a capitalization of 500,000 yen, a huge sum at that time, and with Toyo as one of the agents in New York in partnership with Arai.

In New York the name Morimura had come to be as well known as Arai. Toyo, who had been one of the original Oceanic group with Arai, had opened a store to sell Japanese merchandise in partnership with Sato Momotaro, and, when Sato returned to Japan for good, Toyo formed the family's own Morimura Company, later called Morimura Brothers when his older brother's son Kaisaku joined him in the business. Although the Morimuras continued their merchandise business with a store in New York and one in fashionable Saratoga Springs, their main business was in wholesaling. As in the case of Arai and Murai, Toyo became a permanent resident of the United States and was able to keep abreast of the fast-changing demands of American consumers. When he found that traditional Japanese unglazed ceramics were appreciated in the United States, but were found to be impractical for everyday use since they could not be washed in very hot water, he had the company study European porcelain making and became the pioneer in the development of modern porcelain exports from Japan. One of the company's innovations that proved most successful was to put handles on Japanese teacups, a technique learned from French makers. Today the company continues to export quality chinaware, known worldwide as Noritake china.

To represent the Yokohama Kiito Gomei Kaisha abroad, Toyo and Arai formed a partnership, naming their company the Morimura Arai Company, and they took in Murai and von Briesen as partners. Morimura and Arai put in $34,000 each and Murai and von Briesen $16,000 each, for a total capitalization of $100,000. Since Arai and von Briesen were to work exclusively for the company, they received a salary of $4,000 and $4,500 respectively. Their office at 29 Mercer Street soon was swamped with orders. In the second year of operation Arai more than doubled the amount of business he had done for the Doshin Kaisha. Three years later Mitsui Bussan entered as a third major competitor in the direct export of silk. My grandmother would complain to her friends that the Mitsui representatives her husband introduced to American silk merchants would end up by stealing his customers, but Arai held his own and his company remained the leader among the three. When the Yokohama Kiito Gomei Kaisha established agencies in Italy, France, Shanghai, and Canton, Arai started handling European and Chinese as well as Japanese silks.

Both Arai and Morimura Toyo held the strong conviction that they were entrusted with a patriotic mission to help Japan build itself into a modern nation by earning specie for its industrialization, and they were always in search of new items for export. In a brief account of his life Arai wrote, "In 1893 I went to Osaka and persuaded some prominent businessmen there to start the Brush Industry. The idea was to stimulate and to increase the export trade with U.S.A." This was when he was apprehensive over his future association with the Doshin Kaisha. He established the Imperial Brush Company with headquarters in New York and contracted with a factory in Osaka to manufacture brushes of all kinds, using Chinese pig bristles. He purchased the latest brush-making machines in Philadelphia and brought over Japanese workers to be trained in their operation. He appointed his brother-in-law Ushiba Tetsuro, just graduated from Keio Gijuku and working with him in New York, to take charge of the brush business. He also organized a distribution network in America and engaged an Englishman to act as the agent in charge of distribution to the British colonies. Despite this preparatory work, the company never had much success. Arai's new position with Yokohama Gomei Kaisha left him no time to develop it, and his brother-in-law proved too much of an intellectual and scholar to have his heart in business.

Arai had other unsuccessful business ventures, including one in gold mining at the Holy Cross Mines in Colorado and an effort to grow rice in Texas, using Japanese immigrant labor. His interest in Texas led him to the discovery of cotton as a profitable export commodity to Japan, where the cotton industry was developing rapidly. Cotton had been introduced to Japan by the Portuguese in the sixteenth century, and domestic production had met most of the country's needs until its opening to trade in 1860; when the British traders in the nineteenth century brought in cheaper Indian cotton, they found a ready market. Cotton yarn and cloth comprised over a third of all Japanese imports by the mid-1870s, making it a heavy drain on Japan's meager supply of specie. Since the unequal treaties prevented the Japanese from curtailing cotton imports, the government embarked on a policy of developing its own domestic industry by building pilot cotton-spinning mills.

Arai's ancestor Hoshino Tomohiro, elevated to quasi-samurai status, 1830

From the Hoshino scroll, 1834, shipping lumber for the reconstruction of the shogun's castle

The Oceanic group in 1876, Rioichiro at far left, before departure for New York

The family of Hoshino Yahei, Rioichiro to the right of his bearded father

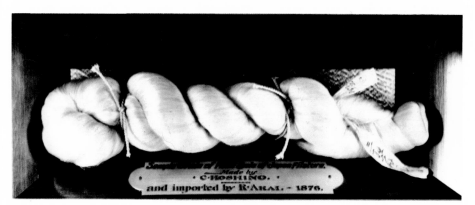

Skein of raw silk, sample of Arai's first shipment, 1877

The Mizunuma silk mill, 1872

Rioichiro's wife, Tazu

Arai in 1899

*The Arais with their son
Yoneo, 1892*

*Hoshino Chotaro and Arai Go,
Marseilles, 1889*

Hoshino Chotaro in 1896, *his mother seated at right, his nephew and niece Yoneo and Miyo Arai at left*

The Arai house at Riverside, Old Greenwich

On the porch at Riverside, Rioichiro and Tazu on far right

Arai and two golfing partners at the Komagawa Golf Club, Tokyo

The Lotus Club dinner, New York, 1915. Arai seated fourth from right along wall

Miyo Arai, Haru's mother

In doing this it was following in the footsteps of Shimazu Naria-kira, the daimyo of Satsuma in the early 1850s, who developed the manufacture by machine of cotton yarn imported from Okinawa as part of his program to increase the wealth of his domain. Matsukata as a young samurai had actively participated in this undertaking, and later it was because of his initiative as an official in the Bureau of Industrial Promotion that a pilot plant was built in Osaka with 2000 spindles he had purchased in England in 1878. From this beginning the cotton industry was developed by private entrepreneurs, and the first great success, as we have seen, was achieved by the Osaka Spinning Mill, built by Shibusawa Eiichi. By the 1890s Japanese mills were producing more cotton goods than were domestically consumed, and exports of cotton yarn commenced. In the 1890s power looms like those used in American mills were introduced, and the rapid development of the cotton industry called for increased imports of raw cotton.

Once again Arai was in the right place at the right time. British merchants had started to buy American cotton for export through Liverpool to Japan, but Arai became the first direct exporter of American cotton to Japan. His cotton exports increased at a tremendous rate, and to handle them he found it necessary to establish in 1903 a separate cotton department in the Morimura Arai Company. By 1910 a quarter of the raw cotton Japan imported came from America.

———•———

With each passing year, Arai sank deeper roots in America. Tazu, attended by a doctor and a nurse, gave birth to her first child on August 26, 1889, in Mrs. Murai's home at 86th Street and Park Avenue, which in those days was not a desirable location since the railroad tracks were still in use. The proud parents named their son Yoneo, using the first character with which America is written in Japanese, followed by "o" to signify a boy's name. Two years later their second child, my mother, was born in Mrs. Dudley's boarding-house and was optimistically named Miyo (beautiful generation). Both children grew up knowing the streets of their neighborhood through daily walks with Tazu. A story is told that one day Yoneo wandered off by himself some blocks away to Fifth Avenue and got lost. Fortunately, a woman who knew of the Japanese boarders at Mrs. Dudley's house saw him and brought him back safely.

As the children grew older, the family needed more room and Arai decided it was time for them to find a place of their own. During the summers he had often gone on picnics to Kaiser Island in Norwalk, Connecticut, and he had become very fond of the beautiful pine trees along the Mianus River, which reminded him of Japan. In 1893 he bought some property nearby at Riverside in Old Greenwich overlooking Long Island Sound, and he started plans for the construction of a house.

Since just then he had to go back to Japan in connection with the crisis in his relations with the Doshin Kaisha, he asked von Briesen to oversee the building. It was a large three-story wooden house, designed in the Victorian style of the time. Given a free hand, von Briesen took it upon himself to construct a tower with a pointed roof, vaguely resembling a castle in his native Germany. The house was situated on a slight rise from the road, and on the west side the terrain sloped down to the Sound, where there was a gazebo and a dock for mooring boats and swimming. The house had all the modern conveniences of gaslight and plumbing, and the bathrooms were the most elegant in the neighborhood. In fact, during the summer months neighbors who did not have bathrooms of their own would come once a week to bathe in the extra bathroom in the basement. On the other side of the driveway were the stables and living apartment for the coachman, surrounded by extensive open fields. Native pine trees and imported Japanese cherry trees and maples gave a touch of home.

The family moved in the fall of 1893 to their new home, where Arai was to live for forty-six years until his death. It housed not only his own family but was a home away from home for many Japanese businessmen, students, and friends. On weekends it was always a lively place. House guests and visitors would play tennis, go fishing in the Mianus River, row boats, and dig for clams. Members of the Hinode Bicycling Club, a group of young Japanese bicycling enthusiasts, would bicycle all the way from New York to spend weekends and enjoy home cooking. The house at Riverside was also my home during vacations while I was attending college in the United States in the 1930s. By then my grandmother, with the help of an extraordinary Japanese gardener, had made part of the open fields into a vegetable garden, and all summer long it supplied us with fresh vegetables. I shall never forget the delicious golden bantam corn she would pick and cook only moments before the family sat down to dinner.

Arai had achieved for himself a solid position in the New York business community, as was shown by his election in 1901 to the board of governors of the American Silk Association, the first Asian to win such recognition in this prestigious body. He took great pride in this and played a prominent role on the board during the remainder of his active business career. He realized, however, that his election was only in recognition of his personal integrity and accomplishments, and he was distressed that Japan itself was still so little respected in the United States.

As my grandmother Tazu later wrote, "When I first came to New York, the general American public knew nothing about Japan." Arai himself had discovered a few years earlier that many Americans could not distinguish between Japanese and Chinese. Any black-haired, "slant-eyed" Oriental was considered Chinese. It was only natural that Americans were more aware of China because there had been a vigorous Sino-American trade since the late eighteenth century, and there were large numbers of Chinese immigrant workers not only on the west coast but also in some eastern cities. But Arai and other proud Japanese, who were determined to have Japan gain equality with the West, found it embarrassing to have their country lumped in the popular mind with China, which was then in a sorry state of disarray. Arai was as much concerned with winning recognition and respect for Japan as he was with achieving personal business success, and he was deeply interested in building social links between Japanese and Americans.

Success in these efforts began to be apparent around the turn of the century. Recognition of Japan's equality as a sovereign power was to come first largely as a result of Japanese victories in its wars with China and Russia. Social acceptance of Japanese as equals came only much later, and they remained under the stigma of being ineligible for naturalization as American citizens until after World War II.

Japan's easy success over China in 1894–95 surprised the world, but even earlier in 1894 Great Britain, recognizing the modernization of Japanese law, had agreed to give up its extraterritorial privileges of trying its citizens resident in Japan under British law. The other Western countries soon followed suit. This gave Japan at last equal legal status with the Western nations, though Japan did not regain full control over its own tariffs until 1911. Needing an ally against Russia on the far side of the world, the British signed in 1902 the Anglo-Japanese Alliance, which was the first military treaty on equal terms between any major Western and non-Western nation. The hard-fought but decisive victory of the Japanese over the Russians in 1905 proved even more surprising to the West than Japan's triumph over a disintegrating China and won for Japan a great deal of admiration.

The opening years of the twentieth century, then, were a hopeful time for Japanese, as their country began to come into its own internationally and attitudes began to change for the better in the United States. As one prominent American informed a Japanese visitor, "The achievements of the Japanese army and navy astonished us and our enthusiasm was keyed to the highest pitch. Every Japanese sailor was a hero and every soldier a samurai, 'devotedly rushing to his foe,' as Bernard Shaw says, 'with shouts of Banzai and brimming over with Bushido, though nobody knew what Banzai meant, or whether Bushido was a liquid or solid.' "* Arai himself wrote in his memoir, "The greatest moment in my life in America was when word came that the Japanese were victorious in the Russo-Japanese War. Then, all Americans were nice to us. There were times when we were thought to be Chinese and American people did not treat us very well."

The new interest in Japan resulted in the publication in 1905 of a tenth revised edition of Nitobe Inazo's book, *Bushido, the Soul of Japan*. Nitobe (1862–1933), the son of a samurai from northern Japan, had been converted to Christianity at the Sapporo Agricultural College (later Hokkaido University), where William S. Clark, president of the Massachusetts Agricultural College (now the University of Massachusetts), had been an influential figure. He later studied in the United States and Europe, marrying an American woman in Philadelphia and becoming a Quaker. His book on Bushido, which more literally means "the way of the warrior," grew out of discussions with his wife in which he tried to answer her questions about Japan. In attempting to clarify such Japanese concepts as courage, loyalty, benevolence, and courtesy, he produced a book that helped to stimulate a veritable

* Tanetaro Megata, *The Japanese in America* (Tokyo, 1926), p. 171.

boom of interest in Japan. President Theodore Roosevelt was so impressed by it that he is said to have purchased sixty copies for distribution to his friends.

The soaring prestige of the nation raised the status of the Japanese community in New York. Japanese consuls had received only scant recognition and lived for the most part in boardinghouses, but in 1902 the consul acquired an official residence in a desirable section of the city. He and the pioneer Japanese residents of New York felt the time had come to develop more formal relations between the Japanese and American residents of the city. In doing this, the leading roles were taken by Takamine Jokichi, Arai, and Murai, who were called "the three genro" in facetious reference to the elder statesmen of Meiji Japan. Takamine was a relatively recent arrival but had already made a large impact because he came as an internationally known scientist. He was famous for his work in fermentation and distillation and particularly as the first person to isolate pure adrenalin in 1901. He was also married to an American, Caroline Hitch, of a prominent New Orleans family. He and his wife had a home at Merriwood near New York, where they erected an authentic Japanese house, brought over from Japan for the St. Louis World Fair, with a Japanese garden around it. They entertained extensively there and at their apartment on Riverside Drive, which was a showcase of Japanese art, both traditional and modern, including early works of Kuniyoshi Yasuo.

The growing number of Japanese in New York made a social club seem desirable, but Arai thought that a place in which they could meet with American friends was even more important. Since most Japanese businessmen came to the United States without their families and lacked homes for entertaining, they needed a club for this purpose. The outcome was the Nippon Club founded in 1905, which met the need of a social club for Japanese and a place where they could entertain American friends. At about this time Americans also began to open their professional clubs to Japanese, who were invited to become members of two social clubs, the Lotus and Manhattan, as well as various athletic clubs. Thus the social relations of Japanese with Americans in New York took a great step forward.

The high point in this development was the founding of the Japan Society in May 1907. It was clearly stimulated by the Japanese victory in the Russo-Japanese War and was founded on the occasion of the visit to New York by two war heroes, General Kuroki Tamesada, who had commanded Japanese forces at the battle of Mukden, and Vice-Admiral Ijuin Goro. The creation of the new society was proposed at a gala welcome dinner for the two men, held at the Hotel Astor and presided over by Admiral George Dewey, the victor at Manila Bay in the Spanish-American War. The society was set up by a group of prominent New York businessmen and other leaders, together with some of the leading members of the Japanese community. The two original vice-presidents were General Fred O. Grant, the son of the former president, and Dr. Takamine. Among the members of the board were the banker August Belmont, Seth Low, a former mayor of New York, Jacob Schiff, who had played a prominent role in floating loans for the Japanese during the Russo-Japanese War, Arai, and Murai. Arai played a prominent role in the early years of the society, which grew rapidly for the next two decades, was revived after World War II, in part with the aid of Arai's son, and is today a fixture in the cultural life of New York.

Americanization of the Arai Family

Arai was fifty years old in 1905, and he had been in the United States for thirty years. Great changes had taken place during that time. He had devoted himself to establishing his business, and now he could survey his accomplishments with satisfaction. The silk trade was firmly established, and earnings from it supplied Japan with the foreign exchange needed for further modernization. He was happy in his private life—his marriage, his family, and his comfortable home. He could relax at last to enjoy these blessings.

He was a handsome, dignified man. Some people said he looked more like a diplomat than a businessman. He was always softspoken and calm, with a twinkle in his eye. He had no vanity and his daily life was simple. Murai, who since the death of Morimura Toyo in 1899 had become his closest friend, called him by the affectionate nickname of "Widie." At home he loved to play with his two children and to read books on American history. He also took great interest in American politics and followed them closely. But he was happiest when he had time to get onto the golf course.

He had been introduced to the game around 1902 when he was at Pinehurst, North Carolina, recuperating from an illness. Golf was just beginning to become popular in the United States. Andrew Carnegie, at a dinner party for my other grandfather in 1902, presented him with a set of clubs and toasted the development of golf in Japan, with Matsukata as its patron. Actually Matsukata never used the clubs, since he was already sixty-five and there were no golf courses in Japan, and it remained for Arai to stimulate interest there in the game.

After taking up golf himself, Arai pestered all his Japanese friends in New York to join him in the sport. Murai was hard to win over. "Why," he asked, "should I get up early in the morning on my vacations and spend the day chasing a silly little ball around the golf course?" He finally agreed to take one swing at a ball if Arai would get down on his knees in front of the ball and bow three times, touching the ground with his forehead. Arai did this and Murai took a swing at the ball, which shot high into the air and landed at some distance. Murai was delighted and thenceforth became Arai's inseparable golf companion. Another Japanese whom Arai converted into a golf enthusiast was Inoue Junnosuke (1869–1932), later a leading financier and politician in Japan and at the time manager of the Yokohama Specie Bank in New York. When Inoue was transferred to Tokyo he took back with him such a love for the game that he got together in 1913 a small group of fellow members of the prestigious Tokyo Club and founded a golf club, with its links at Komazawa in the countryside west of Tokyo. The farmers, whose land he needed for the golf course, were dubious about the whole project, having no idea what golf was, but they were so impressed by the mansion of a former daimyo in which Inoue lived that they agreed to the deal. The golf club at Komazawa was the first in Japan for Japanese, although the English residents of Kobe had earlier built one for their own use on Mt. Rokko behind the city.

Although Arai was not a participant in the organization of the Tokyo Golf Club at Komazawa, he had stimulated the interest that lay behind its founding and he became a charter member. Each time he returned to Japan, one of the first things he did was to play at Komazawa with Inoue and other friends. Because of the growth of the city, the golf course was later moved to Asaka in Saitama prefecture. Inoue never got to play on the new course (he was assassinated by a member of a right-wing organization in 1932), but Arai did play there on his last trip to Japan in 1935. He was then eighty, and to the amazement of his younger partners he played eighteen holes with no signs of fatigue.

When the Arai family first moved to Riverside in 1893, it was a great shock for my grandmother. Tazu had lived all her life in large cities where there was always much to do—theaters, stores to browse in, friends and relatives to visit—and she could not at first get used to living in this remote suburb. The village consisted only of the railroad station, a butcher shop, and a one-man post office, though a fish seller and a vegetable man peddled their wares door to door. She had no friends or neighbors nearby, and it was too far to New York to go visiting there. Her husband left by train for his office in New York early each morning and did not return until evening, so her days were long and lonely, especially in the winter months, when they might be snowed in for days. But there was compensation in her two small children, who at first occupied most of her time.

For the children, Riverside was a wonderful place to grow up. Yoneo, usually called Yone, and Miyo seem to have been the first Japanese children born on the east coast, making them the first nisei, or second-generation Japanese, in that part of the United States and among the earliest in the whole country. The children grew up in a happy home atmosphere and, when they were sent to school, came in contact only with American children. Greenwich was an old community settled by farmers and oystermen in 1640 on land bought from the Indians. It had been a battlefield during the revolution, and landmarks bearing the names of the heroes of that time still remain. In the late nineteenth century, artists and former summer residents began to settle permanently, and by the time Yone started school in 1895 and Miyo two years later it was a typical New England community—all white, Anglo-Saxon, and Protestant—with no blacks, recent European immigrants, or Asians, except the Arais themselves.

Although the children were Americans by birth, their arrival at the public school in Greenwich, with their jet black hair and oriental features, aroused the curiosity of the children. The first day at school, a traumatic experience for many children, was made more so for Miyo by an unfortunate incident. Since she was too young to go by herself, she was accompanied by the cook Katsu, who was quite a dignified man with a small moustache. After school when he came to take Miyo home, the other children innocently asked, "Is he your father?" Miyo was an extremely shy girl and, after bearing all the tensions of the first day at school, found this question so embarrassing that it reduced her to tears. She wept all the way home and told her parents she would never go to the school again. No amount of persuasion could make her change her mind, and finally she was transferred from the public school in Greenwich to a private school, Low Heywood, in the nearby village of Stamford, where her neighbor Toyo Murai went.

By then Arai's best friend, Murai, had built a house next door and moved in with his wife and two adopted children. They made an unusual-looking family. As I have mentioned, Nenne was an American woman about a head taller than Murai. His daughter Toyo, though having a Japanese name, was a blue-eyed blond American (possibly the illegitimate child of Nenne's niece), and his son Taro, a Japanese boy, was the very image of his father (perhaps his illegitimate son). But Nenne was a remarkably strong and loving mother and held the four together as a secure and happy family.

After starting to go to school together, Miyo and Toyo became inseparable friends. Miyo loved her new school and was a good student, with her best grades in arithmetic and Latin. Her favorite pastime was reading—Alcott's *Little Women* and *Little Men* and later Thackeray, Dickens, and Victor Hugo. As a child I reveled in her collection of childhood books. Recently, in recalling those days, she spoke of how these books and Toyo's mother, with whom she spent much time, had been the greatest influences in her life as a girl. Her brother's wedding present to her of the Harvard Classics was very appropriate. After high school Miyo went to Miss Spencer's, a finishing school in New York City, which was considered a suitable final education for girls of good family in those days.

Yone went to Kings School, a private elementary school in Stamford, where he met boys of well-to-do families. He was very anxious to be accepted by them and to be admitted to a prestigious college by going to the right sort of preparatory school. He learned through friends at a summer camp in the Catskills about St. George's in Newport, Rhode Island, and was accepted there. From St. George's he went to Harvard in the class of 1912. He made it his life's ambition to show that Japanese Americans were the equals of other Americans, and he made a concerted effort to win acceptance from the elite. Many of the boys he admired were going out for the baseball team, and, since he was not at all athletic, he became the manager of the team. In his days at Harvard the final clubs dominated the social life and Yone was invited to join the prestigious Fox Club. The friends he made at college were mostly fellow members of this club, and with them he continued lifelong friendships, joining them each year at their annual gatherings, until he became the oldest living member of the club. He was always frank about what he himself called his "social climbing," and he took great pride in having in his circle of friends men with prominent names, such as Vincent Astor, Sinclair Weeks, William Castle (a one-time ambassador to Japan), and T. S. Eliot. He was a typical nisei of the time in his striving to win full acceptance as an American.

But Yone grew up at a time of strong racial prejudice and discrimination against the Japanese. No sooner had Japan's victory in the Russo-Japanese War eradicated some of the inequalities than anti-Japanese feelings flared up against recent immigrants on the west coast. The "yellow peril" was much talked of, and politicians used anti-Japanese propaganda in their election campaigns. On the west coast restrictive measures against Japanese immigrants prevented them from owning land, and they were subjected to all sorts of legislative and judicial discrimination by local and state governments. Finally the federal government declared in 1924 that Japanese as "aliens ineligible for citizenship" were to be totally barred from immigrating to the United States. There was less anti-Japanese feeling on the east coast, since the Japanese there were prosperous businessmen and not poor immigrants, but Yone his whole life felt the anxiety of not being accepted as an equal. He showed this insecurity in what he wrote for the Harvard alumni records sometime after World War II: "As to my deep convictions, the greatest has been that the Japanese as a race, are the equals of any and that they have qualities to emerge from any setbacks . . . The equalization of the races of the world largely through the abolishment of colonialism is a source of much satisfaction." Always Yone was torn between two ambitions—to be accepted by Americans despite his different appearance and to be accepted by Japanese despite his American citizenship and imperfect command of the Japanese language.

———— • ————

The Arai children enjoyed far more privileges than most young Americans. Their summer vacations were happy months, spent at a big hotel at Lake Mohonk in the Catskills or at Moosehead Lake in Maine, where the Arais and Murais rented cottages. Sometimes they took canoe trips led by guides and pitched tents and cooked outdoors. Every few years they accompanied their father and mother on business trips to Japan. These trips were always exciting. Unlike the fast air travel of today, the journeys took close to three weeks. The children loved the four-day train ride in Pullman compartments across the continent. Sometimes they went by way of the Canadian Rockies, taking baskets of food in case there was no dining car. Stopovers in San Francisco before boarding their steamship were always adventures.

By the early 1900s, the Arais traveled exclusively on Japanese ships. Since Arai had made his first crossing, Japan had built its own merchant fleet, which was competing with the long-established British and American lines. Some of the ships of the Nippon Yusen Kaisha and the Toyo Kisen Kaisha were the "silk ships," built with special holds to transport their most valuable cargo. It was no wonder that whenever Arai, the leading silk trader, traveled he was accorded special treatment, given the best cabins, and seated at the captain's table. The leisurely crossing with a stopover in Honolulu allowed him to unwind from his busy New York life. He often boasted to his friends about his large appetite, which sometimes enabled him to "eat right down the menu." During the day he played with the children and took on his friends at go, often playing with Murai, who frequently returned to Japan with his family at the same time.

The children never tired of running up and down the decks, exploring places for hide and seek and playing deck games. In the evenings there was entertainment by magicians, jugglers, acrobats, dancers, and musicians, and on the last evening before reaching port there was always the festive captain's dinner. Docking at Yokohama was a time of great excitement for the children, as they watched the large steamer pull into place and saw the faces of their waving relatives and friends come into focus on shore. On land they would be excited by the unfamiliar sound of geta (wooden clogs).

In Tokyo, the Arais alternated between the Seiyoken, a Western hotel in Tsukiji, and the Yumeikan, a Japanese inn. Tazu's mother would wait at the hotel or inn with Japanese clothes for her to wear. Once they stayed in the Japanese house belonging to Hoshino Chotaro, who lived in Tokyo when he was a member of the Diet. The children loved most to be taken to the Kabuki Theater, where they sat on the floor in boxes and spent the day eating special foods and watching Danjuro and other famous actors. Miyo in particular came at an early age to appreciate good Japanese dancing.

In the early years Arai went to Gumma to visit his foster parents and his original Hoshino family. At such times he was given a returning hero's welcome, since the entire area owed its continuing prosperity to the silk industry. The Hoshino family retained the same prestigious local position it had in feudal days, and it was prominent in the political, social, and civic activities of Gumma prefecture. Chotaro's name had become synonymous with the silk industry of the region, and a monument was erected to him in the park in Maebashi, the capital of the prefecture. Chotaro's half brother Kosaku had been elected to the first prefectural assembly in 1880, and later he became mayor of Kurohone village and held this position for seventeen years. As a member of the committee on education for the prefecture, he was responsible for the establishment of over twenty schools. He was also active in the silk industry, especially through the Kozuke Silk and Cocoon Improvement Company. Chotaro's son Motoji (1873–1955), after his graduation from a Christian school in Yokohama and Meiji Gakuin, a Christian institution in Tokyo, took an active part in both local and prefectural assemblies. He was also prominent in many aspects of the silk industry. Following in the steps of most members of the Hoshino family, who married into families involved in the silk business, he took as his wife the daughter of Machida Kikujiro, the foremost silk industrialist in the prefecture.

About the time Chotaro became involved in national politics and was elected to the Diet in the ninth national election in 1904, relations between him and Arai began to cool. Chotaro took it for granted that his "rich brother" from America would help him out in the diverse activities he had become involved in. This Arai did for some time, even building Chotaro an exceptionally fine house on the family property in Mizunuma. Though in a dilapidated state today, the prefectural authorities hope to preserve the house as a unique architectural landmark. Chotaro made little effort to repay Arai and kept asking him for further support, until Arai decided to put an end to the requests. A rift resulted, and Chotaro died in 1908 before a reconciliation could be achieved. For over twenty years the two families remained completely out of touch, but Chotaro's son, Motoji finally succeeded in arranging a reconciliation with Arai, which took place on

249

Arai's last trip to Japan in 1935. Since then, succeeding generations of the two families have been on good terms.

After the children finished their visits with friends and relatives in the Tokyo area, they would be sent to spend the rest of the summer with their Ushiba grandparents. Their grandfather by then was an important businessman in the Kansai area and president of the Sanyo Railroad. Whenever the family traveled by train he gave them free passes and they went in style. He lived in a beautiful, large house set on a hilltop on the promontory of Shioya, overlooking the Japan Sea just west of Kobe, and the train of his line ran just below the house. During the summers the house would be full of members of the family including their son Tetsuro and his wife and two small boys, with whom Yone and Miyo could play. The Arai children loved their grandmother, who lavished them with affection and prepared delicious Japanese meals with fresh fish from the sea below their home. Miyo also enjoyed the delicious toast made over charcoal fires.

It was not all play for the "American cousins," since their parents insisted they be given lessons in Japanese. In America they had a live-in tutor who taught them Japanese one hour each day after school; outside interests and diversions kept them from concentrating on these lessons. But, when they were with their Ushiba grandparents, they were not allowed to go off to swim and play until the lessons were completed. Although they showed no great aptitude for their studies, in letters I still have both children wrote in Japanese to their parents with traditional Japanese brush and ink which show a certain degree of achievement. These trips back to Japan introduced the children to a more formal and traditional way of life than the one they were accustomed to in America. They learned Japanese social customs, etiquette, attitudes, and styles of living, which later were invaluable to Miyo in helping her adjust to life in Japan after her marriage.

Miyo had hoped to continue on to college after she completed finishing school in New York, but her mother, who herself had been married at eighteen, insisted it was time for her to get married. A suitable young man had been recommended to them. He came from a distinguished family, had been educated at Yale, and was in Washington on the first assignment of a diplomatic career. Tazu felt he was just the right person for Miyo and liked the idea of a diplomatic son-in-law who would be able to include her in the social life she herself longed for. Miyo was less enthusiastic, since she did not care for diplomatic life, but she agreed to meet the young man and look him over in order to placate her mother. She returned from her visit to Washington convinced that she did not want to marry him. This so enraged her mother that she refused to have anything more to do with marriage plans for Miyo.

Before long, another proposal was made. Among the Japanese students Arai came to know in America was Matsukata Kojiro, a graduate of Yale in the class of 1889 and the third son of Matsukata Masayoshi. Kojiro later introduced one of his younger brothers, Shokuma, then attending Yale, and Shokuma often came to spend weekends with the Arais at Riverside. By then Miyo was a teenager and, although she had little to do with her parents' visitors, she remembered Shokuma because of his kindness and gentle manners. Several years later in Japan, when Kojiro was helping his brother to find a wife—Shokuma stipulated that she speak English—he remembered Arai's daughter and sent Arai a proposal by cable. Since her mother refused to play any role, Miyo turned to her brother, then a student at Harvard, asking him to come home and advise her. After much long-distance communication with Tokyo, Miyo agreed and the marriage took place in Japan in 1912.

As we have seen, Miyo on her marriage decided "to do in Rome as the Romans do," but she encountered many situations to which it was difficult to adjust. In particular she found it hard to accept the domineering attitude and apparent coldness of Japanese men, which differed so much from what she had been used to. In a letter to her brother she wrote, "At times (before people) they take no more notice of you than a fly. They assume the air, 'I am everything you are nothing.' Now, I know at heart that is not so (no more than it is with American men), but no one enjoys being made to feel small, and Yone, I have been often scolded for 'being cold hearted,' but I have been petted and loved so I get a queer lonely feeling when I am treated as 'objects taken for granted.' " After a while, when she had become more used to Japan, Miyo wrote on a happier note, "Do you know, I am getting to be quite Japanese? Until of late, I didn't realize what an American I was."

Yone never had the problem of adjusting to life in Japan because he lived permanently in the United States. It was up to his Japanese wife to Americanize herself and make the adjustments. After Yone graduated from Harvard in 1912 and became well established in his father's firm, Arai sent him to Japan to look for a wife. By coincidence he ended up marrying Okabe Mitsu, the younger sister of the young diplomat Miyo had turned down.

Mitsu's father, Nagamoto, had been the last daimyo of Kishiwada, a "house" domain of 53,000 koku. The Okabe were descended from the husband of one of the daughters of Ieyasu, the founder of the line of Tokugawa shoguns, and had been placed by the shogunate south of Osaka to keep an eye on the nearby great collateral domain of Wakayama. Nagamoto was only fifteen years old when he went on horseback to Kyoto in 1869 to return his domain to the new Meiji emperor. Later he was sent by the government to study abroad, attending both Yale and Oxford. He was made a viscount in the new peerage created in 1884 and became a diplomat, posted for a while to the Court of St. James. Subsequently he was appointed governor of Tokyo, and his daughter Mitsu was born at his official residence there in 1898. He was minister of justice in the Katsura cabinet in 1908 and had the distinction of being the only man to have been both a daimyo and a cabinet member in the new system adopted in 1885. He was married to a daughter of the distinguished Maeda family, the former daimyo of Kanazawa, Japan's largest feudal domain.

Mitsu eventually acquired American citizenship when this was made possible after the racist laws against Asians were rescinded after the war. She fitted well into Yone's life and became a prominent resident of Greenwich. She definitely had "class." She had been brought up in style, for her mother's Maeda family was very wealthy and belonged to the highest social circles. Her father's study abroad had also introduced a cosmopolitan note into her upbringing, and she was accustomed to dressing in high Western fashion. Mitsu always took great pride in her ancestry, and Yone all his life basked in her glory, which made him feel the social equal of any of his moneyed and aristocratic American friends.

Mitsu adjusted beautifully to life in America and soon became a popular member of society in both Greenwich and New York. Although her English remained far from perfect, she made up for this by self-confidence, animation, and a cheerful personality, which endeared her to a host of American and Japanese friends. She was an indefatigable worker in many projects. When she started introducing Japanese flower arrangement to her community, she would stay up until the early morning hours preparing her lectures and demonstrations. She needed very little sleep and claimed that some nights she slept only an hour or two in the bathtub. She was a very active member of the Garden Club of America, where her artistic talents and energy were much appreciated. She became well known for her skill in flower arrangement and traveled all over the United States demonstrating this art at a time when it was still little known to Americans. During the war, both she and Yone taught Japanese to American military men at Yale. This was a time when gasoline was scarce and most private citizens were on limited rations, but the town of Greenwich alloted them a special supply to enable them to commute to New Haven each day.

Yone and Mitsu had a son, named Ryo for his grandfather. As a third-generation sansei, he was brought up as a thoroughly American boy, going to the same prep school as his father and then to Harvard. After service in the army during the war, he embarked on a career in book publishing, first in New York and then in the San Francisco area. He did not marry a Japanese wife, and his four sons are typical Californians. One, for example, is an avid hang glider, practicing his sport on the summits of the high Sierra.

My grandfather was much pleased that both his children had married so well—the one into an old daimyo family, the other to a son of a Meiji genro and former prime minister. To a man of peasant stock, this must have seemed quite an achievement. Of course it was only possible because of his own great success as a New York businessman. He was also content to see his family become so completely Americanized. Although Miyo married back into Japan and, in accordance with the laws of that time, lost her American citizenship, she raised an essentially American family and the roots of the whole Arai family were deep in American soil.

———————— • ————————

The last three decades of Arai's business career took place when silk reigned supreme as the "queen of fibers" and was the mainstay of Japanese exports. Silk had come into common use in the United States, and to meet American demand Japanese silk production doubled between 1904 and 1914, from 16.5 million pounds to 31 million pounds. The increase in production was made possible by the development of a process to produce cocoons twice a year, during the usual summer months and again in the fall, and also by the mechanization of reeling, which had been held back earlier by the use of hand-operated machines.

Arai's business increased steadily. In 1876 he sold only four bales, but by 1906 this had increased to 22,773 bales, and the Morimura Arai Company had become the largest exporters of Japanese silk. Its sales alone surpassed the total silk trade still handled by Western merchants. A special spurt in growth came during the 1907 depression in America, when weavers decided to produce medium-quality silk textiles. To do so, they bought less of the more expensive, superior warp threads from Italy and turned instead to Japan and China to supply them with lower-quality silk. Although the Japanese had for many years attempted to improve their warp threads to match the Italians, they failed; but at this time the failure worked to their advantage.

Another period of rapid growth came with the outbreak in August 1914 of World War I. Silk played an important role in the war, as was explained in a report to the Silk Association of America at a meeting held in New York on December 12, 1917:

> On account of its beauty and its former great expense, the idea of silk is almost inextricably interwoven in the public mind with the idea of luxury, and therefore, it is not strange that to many the silk industry might appear to be nonessential. This view of the case, however, is superficial . . . Wool is the only suitable fabric for military wear . . . Cotton is also called for in an unprecedented way . . .
>
> For these two textile fabrics which are of such vital need in conducting the war, there is no substitute so satisfactory and so available as silk . . .
>
> The silk industry is now called upon to do its part in supplying war material, and the Government is calling and will call for enormous quantities of various silk materials for which there are no satisfactory substitutes. Millions upon millions of yards of silk noils cloth is needed for the making of cartridge bag cloth for the

use of artillery of both the army and the navy. Silk cloth is used to an enormous extent in Europe for airplane wings, and it will certainly be so used by America. Sewing silk is largely used both for clothing and for shoes. Silk neckcloths are used by the navy. Silk is the material for our flags and banners.*

The Allies in Europe took strong measures to prevent the importation of silk by Germany and Austria, but their own production fell, creating shortages in both Europe and America and making prices soar. The resulting increased demand for Japanese silk boosted exports from Japan as well as prices, producing a doubling in the value of Japanese exports of silk to the United States from $63 million to $112 million in just two years. When America entered the war in February 1917, the demand became all the greater. Japan had entered the war in November 1914, a few months after its outbreak. Its military operations were insignificant, though it became a major supplier of manufactured goods to its allies and the rest of the world. Japan's export trade boomed as long as the war lasted, and for the first time the country amassed a great trade surplus. Because of the huge increase in the silk trade, the Yokohama Kiito Gomei Kaisha in 1915 became a public corporation, renamed the Yokohama Kiito Kabushiki Kaisha, first capitalized at $5 million and at twice that amount a few years later. Arai was appointed chairman of the board of directors of the new company. Even before the war the United States had consumed more raw silk than France, Germany, Italy, and Switzerland combined. In the single month of July 1917, Arai's agency sold $9 million dollars' worth of raw silk in the United States, from which it received a commission of $40,000. The peak of Arai's career came in 1920, when the volume of silk exports reached its highest point, amounting to a third of Japan's total exports.

The boom of the war years brought huge profits and mounting prices, but by the spring of 1920 a deflationary period had set in. The Yokohama Kiito Kabushiki Kaisha had invested heavily in raw cotton at highly inflated prices, and, when the bottom fell out of the market, the company fell into serious financial difficulties. Through the inter-

---

* *New York Nihonjin hatten shi* (New York: New York Nihonjin Kai, 1921), pp. 77–80.

cession of the Yokohama Specie Bank, however, in 1922, the company tied in with the Mitsubishi Trading Company, established in 1918, which handled the operations of its new affiliate under its subsidiary, the Nihon Kiito Kabushiki Kaisha.

While Japan was still in the doldrums of the postwar economic recession, it suffered another blow. This was the great Kanto earthquake of 1923, which I have already described in the life of Matsukata. Since it occurred at noon, charcoal fires were burning in most homes to cook lunch, and these fires, spreading to the fallen timbers of collapsed houses, engulfed Tokyo and Yokohama in flames. I remember the glow from these fires visible that evening in Kamakura, twenty-five miles from Yokohama.

Arai's latest order of two thousand bales of silk, which was stored in warehouses in Yokohama awaiting shipment, was completely destroyed. The news of the disaster that had befallen Japan and his own losses came as a devastating blow to him. Since silk in storehouses was not covered by fire insurance, his personal losses ran into the millions of dollars. But he had survived many losses before and was determined to surmount the new difficulties, living up to all his commitments as he had in 1876. Since Yokohama had become useless as a port, he made arrangements for silk shipments to be made from Kobe, and, although there were some delays, he delivered all his orders. Still Arai was not able to recover fully from the losses he had suffered, and at sixty-eight he was beginning to feel like retiring. His son Yone had contracted tuberculosis and was sent to Colorado with his family for treatment, but four years later, in 1927, Arai gave control of the Morimura Arai Company to a subsidiary of the Mitsubishi Trading Company. The name of the Morimura Arai Company was retained because of its great prestige in the silk business and also because it was thought to be easier for Americans to pronounce than Mitsubishi. Under the new arrangement, the silk trade continued to grow for a few more years. The high point was reached in 1929 when the United States imported $396 million in raw silk, of which Japan supplied 95 percent. This was the silk-stocking age, and silk imports ranked second only to rubber for automobile tires.

Arai never retired completely. After passing on control of his company, he continued to serve as an adviser and went faithfully several times a week to his office at 2 Park Avenue. Ishii Seitaro, who represented Mitsubishi until 1941, recalls with great affection and appreciation Arai's guidance in his work. But Arai had retired at an opportune time. He was not in charge at the time of the stock crash of 1929 and the resulting great depression. He was a man of the silk age and fortunately did not live to see the collapse of the trade he had devoted his life to building. Soon nylon and other synthetic fibers began to replace silk, and then World War II brought an end to all Japanese-American trade. When trade revived again after the war, silk no longer played an important role.

———— • ————

After his retirement, Arai enjoyed a leisurely life. He liked to visit his New York office but also looked forward to good weather when he could play golf with his friend Murai. He was a member of two golf clubs, one in Stamford and the other in Greenwich, and he would alternate between them. Most evenings he spent quietly at home after dinner, which always ended with a bowl of rice and some Japanese pickles and tea, no matter what the menu had been. Each evening he religiously played two games of *go* with Murai. They always maintained complete silence except for a final "Good night."

The Arais were considered not only a prominent family of the affluent Greenwich community but the first family in the Japanese community of New York. Tazu had helped win that status in her own right. Soon after the Russo-Japanese War, she had taken the lead with the wives of Jacob Schiff and E. H. Harriman in founding a Japanese American Women's Club. She also helped organize the Nihon Fujin Kai (Japanese Women's Club) in 1919 to answer the needs of the growing number of wives in the Japanese business community. She was the founding president of this organization and held the position for many years. As relations between Japan and the United States deepened, economic missions of various sorts were sent from Japan. These missions relieved Arai from being what some had called a "one-man goodwill mission," but he, Takamine, and Murai often took the initiative in organizing elaborate social functions for the visiting missions, invariably held at the Lotus Club. Among the more important missions for which the three men made arrangements in New York was a delegation of prominent industrialists and financiers which came from Japan in 1915 under the leadership of the great entrepreneur,

Shibusawa Eiichi. A sumptuous dinner was held at the Lotus Club, and I have a picture of the occasion in which Arai himself appears prominently and which is redolent of a long-departed era. In place of floral decorations, a three-dimensional Japanese landscape ran the length of the huge dinner table, ingeniously combining mountains, rivers, country houses, and pastoral scenes and culminating in the center with a soaring Mount Fuji.

In the winter of 1939, Arai had patiently waited for the snow to melt so that he could get out on the golf course. One day in early April, though it was still cold, he played eighteen holes and returned home elated with his good score, though somewhat tired. It turned out that he had caught pneumonia and he never recovered, dying on April 9 at the age of eighty-four.

The Japanese government, which had recognized his contributions to Japanese-American trade by conferring on him in 1928 the Order of the Sacred Treasure (Zuiho-sho) Sixth Class, raised the order to Fourth Class. His funeral, held at Woodlawn Cemetery in the Bronx, was conducted by the First Reader of the Christian Science Church of Stamford, since he and his wife had become interested in Christian Science in 1919, not many years after his daughter Miyo had. He was mourned by Japanese and Americans alike, and the American Commodity Exchange paid him the unusual tribute of silence while the funeral was in progress. His good friend, Paolino Gerli, a leading silk merchant and prominent member of the Japan Society of New York, included in his eulogy the following words:

> A young man in your twenties, you came to us from Japan, to bring us tidings of good things to come, of friendships to be made; ambassador of an ancient art to a new industry, and you opened before our eyes the treasure box of silk . . .
>
> As the years passed, we came to know you intimately, and with this knowledge, there grew upon us an increasing appreciation of your great character as a man, of your industriousness, fairness, equity, sympathy and deep understanding . . .
>
> You became the example for the younger generation, of everything that stood for honor, sincerity and straightforwardness . . .
>
> You led in charity, and were always solicitous of the welfare

of this your adopted country, which you loved and served so well . . .

May the sweetness of your nature, the loftiness of your spirit, abide with us.

Arai's life had spanned the years of Japan's transition from a feudal to a modern nation, which had been made financially possible by the silk trade he had done so much to establish. He helped to put Japanese-American relations on a foundation of mutual confidence and trust. But he was spared from seeing the disintegration of the silk trade and the collapse in World War II of the relations between the two countries he loved. Arai faithfully accomplished the mission he had come to perform sixty-three years earlier.

DESCENDANTS AND
RELATIVES

Matsukata Saburo, at Mount Everest base camp, 1970

Matsukata's Sons

Matsukata Masayoshi and Rioichiro Arai, together with other leaders of the Meiji period,
laid solid foundations for the new Japan and its
relations with the outside world. On these foundations their heirs and
successors built a superstructure that is the Japan of today, the second
largest industrial power in the world and one of the acknowledged
leaders in most aspects of human endeavor. No account of the lives of
Matsukata or Arai would be complete without tying them in with
these later developments, especially those in which their own descendants and relatives had a part.

Matsukata's descendants made a greater contribution to the development of Japan than did the descendants of any of the other elder
statesmen, if for no other reason than their number. One encounters in
history books or current life an occasional prominent courtier, businessman, or scholar descended from these other men, but Matsukata's
children, grandchildren, and now great-grandchildren are to be found
in number in a wide variety of fields. At the time of his death in 1924,
sixteen of his twenty-one children were alive, eleven sons and five
daughters. All sixteen lived to ripe old age, ranging from the late
seventies to one who reached ninety. The last of this generation and
their spouses did not die until my mother passed away at the age
of ninety-two in 1984. The next generation numbered over fifty, and
now, if one includes in-laws, there are well over two hundred family
members.

I can keep track of all my cousins only with the aid of a genealogical chart printed by the family. The present family head, Matsukata Mineo of Japan Air Lines, keeps up this chart. He also takes care of the family burial lot, an imposing array of graves in Aoyama Cemetery in Tokyo within a short walk of my mother's recent home. Other duties are to preserve my grandfather's remaining records, personal belongings, and the country estate at Nasuno and to hold the semiannual meetings of the family club, the Kaito Kai (Society of East of the Sea), called after my grandfather's penname. The Kaito Kai is so large that the meetings must be held in public halls, although, when my husband was American ambassador to Japan, he and I once hosted it at our embassy residence—certainly the first occasion of that sort ever held there.

Like the offspring of most great men, none of Matsukata's sons reached the eminence he attained. For one thing, the times no longer called for revolutionaries and nation builders but rather team players and developers. Yet two of the eleven sons who survived Matsukata's death in 1924, Kojiro, the third, and Saburo, the last, did become men of note, and I have devoted separate chapters to each of them. The remainder I have grouped together here.

My grandfather took care to prepare all his sons to participate in the building of the new Japan. He gave them the best education available at the time, just as his father had done for him. As we have seen from Arai's life, schools and universities patterned after Western institutions were being developed by the 1870s, but my grandfather felt that his sons should top off this education by studying abroad. As a result, most of them received a major part of their higher education in the West.

The four oldest of my grandfather's sons were born during the turbulent years of transition from the feudalism of Tokugawa rule to the new emperor-centered system, and his wife and children were not moved to Tokyo until 1877, after their home in Kagoshima had been destroyed in the rebellion led by Matsukata's former mentor and friend, Saigo Takamori. This meant that the older children remained in relatively backward Satsuma during the early years of their education. Iwao, the eldest, who was born in 1862, the year my grandfather joined the higher councils of the Satsuma domain, even went for a while to the same Confucian domain school his father had attended. Once the children came to Tokyo, however, Matsukata enrolled them all, boys and girls alike, in the prestigious Peers School founded in 1847 in Kyoto for children of court nobles. In 1877 it had been reorganized along Western lines for children of the imperial family and the nobility.

In 1883 Matsukata sent Iwao at the age of twenty-one to study in Germany, since by this time Japanese leaders had become great admirers of that militaristic, authoritarian country, which they saw as most akin in spirit to the Japan they wished to build. Iwao spent ten years in Europe, attending the universities of Heidelberg, Berlin, and Leipzig and supplementing his studies with travel throughout the continent. Because of his father's long tenure as finance minister, Iwao became interested in financial matters and chose banking as his career. For three decades after his return to Japan, he held numerous positions in the banking profession. At one time, he was president of the Yokohama Specie Bank, which we have seen from Arai's life was a key institution, and for many years he served as president of the Fifteenth Bank, commonly known as the Peers Bank, since its capital came largely from the bonds with which the new regime had paid off the daimyo when it confiscated their domains.

At the death of his father in 1924, Iwao inherited the title of prince and became a member of the House of Peers in the Diet. He had married Yasuko, the daughter of Nagayo Sensai (1838–1902), the formulator of the laws on vaccination and the founder and first president of the predecessor of the medical faculty of Tokyo Imperial University. For several years he and his wife lived in splendor, but in 1927, just two years before the stock-market crash in New York, there was a financial crisis in Japan in which the Fifteenth Bank and many others went bankrupt. Iwao had resigned from the presidency of the bank some four years before this, but, feeling a deep sense of responsibility, he did his best to save it, selling in its behalf most of his personal assets, including his magnificent residence and the great art collection his father had built up. He also resigned his title of prince as a sign of apology. A rich industrialist, one Muroto of Ise, built him a small house on part of the area now occupied by the annex of the Okura Hotel, across the street from the American embassy residence, but he spent most of his remaining years on his Nasuno estate, where he concentrated on stock breeding. He and his brothers, like their father, all loved horses, and he bred race horses of the highest quality.

Iwao and Yasuko had only one child, a daughter, Takeko, whom they wished to marry a man they could adopt as heir to the headship of the family. My grandfather opposed this on the grounds that there already were too many males in the family, and a son of my grandfather's third son had been designated to be Iwao's successor as head of the family. Takeko married out of the family to Kuroki Sanji, the son of General Kuroki Tamesada, a hero of the Russo-Japanese War, whom we have already met as one of the two Japanese war heroes whose visit to New York in 1907 inspired the founding of the Japan Society.

My grandfather's second son, Shosaku, was born in 1863, the year the British squadron sailed into Kagoshima Bay and bombarded the town. At the age of seventeen, he was sent as an unattached official of the foreign ministry to study in Europe at various places where there were Japanese diplomatic representatives. He eventually became a foreign-service officer, holding posts in London, Brussels, and Paris and becoming minister to Siam. He married Shigeko the oldest daughter of Baron Iwasaki Yataro, founder of the great Mitsubishi conglomerate and one of the richest men in Japan. Shigeko, disliking diplomatic life and not wishing to be away from her beloved Tokyo, persuaded Shosaku to resign his government position, and he spent the rest of his life in virtual retirement. They lived in an elegant house that today serves as the South Korean embassy.

Shosaku was a gentle, cultured man who loved music and art, and he was not well suited to public life. In Europe he developed a deep appreciation for Western art and spent much of his time with Kuroda Kiyoteru (1866–1924), also from Satsuma, who was beginning to win recognition in France as an outstanding Western-style painter. Shosaku was particularly fond of the work of Rubens, and it is said that once he had so set his heart on owning a certain Rubens that he lived on bread and water until he had saved enough to purchase the painting.

Matsukata's fourth son, Masao, was born in 1868, the year of the Meiji Restoration. He graduated from the University of Pennsylvania in the class of 1894 and married the daughter of Admiral Kawahara Yo. Goro, the fifth son, was born in 1871 and graduated from Tokyo Imperial University but did not study abroad. He worked for a while at the Kawasaki Shipyards, which was then run by his older brother

Kojiro. In 1902 he accompanied his father as his secretary during a tour of America and Europe, and he eventually became president of the Tokyo Gas and Electric Company.

My father was the seventh of Matsukata's surviving sons, and the eighth was Yoshisuke, born in 1883. Yoshisuke married the daughter of Viscount Inoue Masaru, originally from Choshu, who accompanied the more famous Inoue Kaoru and Ito Hirobumi when they went surreptitiously to England in 1863. After the Restoration, Inoue Masaru was appointed the superintendent of the Railway Bureau when it was first established in 1871 and was responsible for construction of the Tokyo-Yokohama line in 1872, the Kyoto-Osaka line in 1878, and the Tokaido line in 1890. Matsukata's ninth son was Torakichi, who was adopted by Matsumoto Jutaro, a prominent businessman of the Kansai area, of whom I shall have more to say later. His tenth son, Yoshiyuki, was also adopted out of the family, marrying the daughter of Baron Morimura Ichizaemon and becoming his heir.

———•———

I have reserved Matsukata's sixth son, Otohiko, until last in this short history because, next to Kojiro and Saburo, he is the most interesting. This is not because of any momentous achievement on his part but because of his social grace, which made him a prominent figure as a student at Harvard, and his sincere efforts in the 1930s to utilize his American connections to help ward off war between Japan and America.

Otohiko was born in 1880 and, after completing his education at the Peers School, entered Harvard in 1902. He was the only Japanese in the student body, although a number of fellow countrymen, such as Kaneko Kentaro, preceded him at Harvard. While Otohiko was at Harvard, Arai acted as a sort of guardian, so he naturally saw much of the Arai family. Because of Otohiko's outgoing personality and his prominent family background, he was accepted into the best social circles in Cambridge and Boston, and he became very popular. He was an active member of the Hasty Pudding Club at Harvard, and at this time, when the final clubs played a dominant social role in student life, he was elected to membership in the Delphic Club, of which Franklin Delano Roosevelt was also a member. It was commonly said by other members of the club that, if one wanted champagne or whiskey, Franklin and "Oto" could be counted on to have a supply. In addition to Roosevelt, Otohiko made other enduring friendships with his fellow club members and classmates. Among them were two future American ambassadors to Japan—William Castle and Cameron Forbes. Another classmate was Lyman Delano, a relative of Roosevelt's. The Delano family virtually adopted Otohiko, and he was always deeply grateful for that.

Otohiko's grand social life required a large allowance. For example, when news arrived of the Japanese naval victory over the Russians in 1905, Otohiko organized a great victory party. His father often complained of his lavish ways, saying that they were consuming most of the family income, but his mother Masako defended him, her "baby," the last of her own children. "Leave him alone," she would say to her husband. "He may do something worthwhile some day."

Otohiko was a popular escort at the many dances and social functions at Harvard and in Boston society. When I first came to live in the Boston area in 1956 after my marriage, I encountered in Harvard Square one day an old lady who looked like a typical Boston Brahmin. After eyeing me for some time, she approached and asked if by chance I knew a Japanese by the name of Oto Matsukata. When I said that he was my uncle, she told me that as a young girl she had often attended dancing parties with him. I had heard that this debonair, social uncle of mine had at one time seriously considered marrying an American girl, and I have often wondered whether this woman may not have been the girl in question—but I never found out who she was.

Otohiko's active social life did not help his studies, which were already handicapped by language. As the time for graduation approached, there were grave doubts whether he would receive his diploma. It was only through intensive tutoring in his last semester and the kind intercession of Jerome Greene, the secretary of the Harvard Corporation, that he finally received his diploma a semester late, in February 1907. Jerome was the son of D. C. Greene, who was among the first Congregational missionaries to arrive in Kobe in 1869.

After his years at Harvard, Otohiko always remained a dapper, handsome gentleman with a small mustache. Shortly after he returned to Japan in 1907, he married Tomiko, the daughter of Admiral Yamamoto Gonnohyoe, a man of Satsuma origin who later served twice as prime minister. She had lived fourteen years abroad and spoke excellent English. Otohiko naturally had no problem in obtaining good positions in the business world. The discovery of oil in Niigata on the Japan Sea coast led to the establishment of the Nihon Oil Company, where he became the manager of a branch office in 1910 and in 1915 was promoted to managing director (*jomu torishimari-yaku*). The company prospered, and Otohiko became rich. In 1921 he became managing director of the Tokyo Gas Company, and in 1934 he became president of Nikkatsu, Japan's largest movie company. Throughout his life Otohiko lived in ease and affluence.

Otohiko valued his Harvard friendships and kept them up, particularly with members of the Delano family. When Roosevelt was elected president in 1932, Otohiko wrote him a letter of congratulation and Roosevelt replied personally in a note starting "Dear Oto."

However well Otohiko may have kept up with his American friends, relations between the two countries were deteriorating badly. The Japanese bank crisis of 1927, followed two years later by the American stock-market crash and depression, brought a decline in world commerce, which posed a serious problem for a Japan now crucially dependent on foreign trade. Reactionary elements in Japan, particularly the military, who had not been pleased with the naval limitations imposed by the Washington Conference of 1921–22 and the democratic and internationalist trends in their country after World War I, began to find public sympathy for their demands that the country should strengthen its armaments and return to the task of building an empire.

The turning point came in September 1931, when elements in the Japanese army stationed in Manchuria to protect Japan's South Manchurian Railway suddenly launched the conquest of Manchuria, in what the Japanese euphemistically called the Manchurian Incident. Since the Japanese constitution of 1889 gave the military operational independence of the civil government, the authorities in Tokyo were unable to control the forces in Manchuria, and the public in a great wave of patriotic sentiment gave enthusiastic support to the army's spectacular successes. The League of Nations officially condemned Japan for its actions in Manchuria, but the Japanese government replied by walking out. The United States, which was not a member of the League, enunciated a doctrine of "nonrecognition" of Japan's new military conquests, and public sentiment in America began to turn hostile to Japan.

Japanese who were internationally minded were deeply distressed by these developments, but they found themselves unable to stem the tide. Public opinion in Japan began to divide sharply between the militaristic, expansionist radicals and conservative internationalists, who could see the extreme danger of unbridled nationalism and militarism. The Matsukata family belonged to the conservative internationlist side. I can remember as a young girl listening to endless talk about the crisis that had seized Japan and hopes that each one of the frequent changes of cabinet might produce a government that could somehow bring the military to heel. But the course of history continued to flow in the opposite direction.

Otohiko decided to go to Washington in an attempt to stop the worsening of relations between Japan and the United States through his old friendship with Roosevelt. Whether this was his own idea or the result of urging by friends and political leaders is not clear, but the Japanese newspapers made a great deal of his friendship with the president and his being a "private ambassador." He arrived in New York late in January 1934 together with his twenty-three-year-old son, who was then an employee of General Motors in Tokyo. He stayed at the Waldorf Astoria and established contact with several of his old Harvard friends, some of whom wrote Roosevelt's secretary in order to seek a meeting between Otohiko and the president.

As a result, Roosevelt asked Otohiko to have tea with him and his daughter at the White House on Sunday, February 18, and two days later he met with him alone for almost an hour. Saito Hiroshi, an internationally oriented diplomat, had recently become Japanese ambassador to Washington, and Otohiko wrote in his note of thanks to the president:

> I hope you will find it practicable to send for Mr. Saito and hear what he may have to say on various especific matters which few will deny call for adjustment in the interest of international peace and friendship.
>
> If you permit me to say so, Saito has a great and sincere admiration for you, and thinks that you are perhaps the one American who may give him a fair and sympathetic hearing on

the certain idea which he has cherished for years and which he believes will secure the peace of the Pacific for ages to come.

Otohiko never revealed what Saito's plan for peace was, and he failed to get another meeting with the president before his return to Japan. Roosevelt was at first inclined to see him again but finally refused, at the insistence of the State Department. The department's case was stated forcefully by Stanley Hornbeck, director of the division of Far Eastern affairs:

> I have just been informed by a former American Ambassador to Japan that, in the course of a conversation between himself and the Japanese Ambassador, last evening, after dinner, at the Japanese Embassy, the Japanese Ambassador stated that he was trying to persuade his house guest, Mr. Matsukata, to stay on in Washington "indefinitely." My informant expressed the opinion that this indicated that the Ambassador hopes, relying on the fact of personal friendship between Matsukata and the President, to employ Matsukata as a channel of communication between the Embassy and the President, thus avoiding the Department of State, etc. etc. I concur in that estimate.
>
> If, after what has preceded and in the light of this evidence that Matsukata is working with and presumably under the direction of the Japanese Embassy, the President were to receive him, the President would be giving the Japanese Embassy a special advantage such as is possessed by no other foreign mission in Washington, he would be placing this Department in an embarrassing and hampered position, and he would be exposing himself unnecessarily to special hazards in connection with the conducting of relations between this country and Japan.

Hornbeck was notoriously anti-Japanese as well as a jealous defender of the State Department's prerogatives. Possibly some good would have come from closer contacts between the president and an internationally minded Japanese ambassador like Saito and an influential Japanese businessman like Otohiko. In a farewell note, Otohiko wrote on May 31:

> I consider it most fortunate that I was given the opportunity of talking with you on matters which are close to your heart and

mine. I appreciate more than I can say the friendly thoughts you have expressed for my country. In spite of disquieting views occasionally emanating from both sides of the Pacific, I am confident that peace and friendship between our two countries will remain undisturbed. It cannot be otherwise when statesmen on both sides are of one mind on this point.

I agree with you that intricate international problems can best be adjusted through heart-to-heart talk between responsible leaders. Lack of such friendly exchange of views has been an impediment to international understanding. I wish it were possible to provide more frequent opportunities for America and Japanese statesmen to talk intimately . . .

I trust that the great work you are doing not only for your own country but for better understanding with other countries will be crowned with success. When I am back in my country it will be the greatest pleasure for me to tell my countrymen and particularly my friends that you are deeply interested in the preservation and promotion of the traditional friendship which has bound the two nations together for eighty long years.

Roosevelt replied, "My Dear Oto: Many thanks for your nice note. I wish I could have seen you again before you left. It was grand to have that glimpse of you and I do hope you will come over again soon."

Nothing material came of Otohiko's visit to Roosevelt in 1934, and still less of a second trip in 1937. By then Japanese-American relations had deteriorated even more. Another turning point in Japan had come on February 26, 1936, when an attempted coup by a group of young army officers, though itself unsuccessful, had the effect of putting the central government under the firm control of the military. Meanwhile the Chinese had become determined not to tolerate any more nibbling away of Chinese territory by the Japanese army. When minor hostilities accidentally broke out around Peking in July 1937, they soon escalated into an all-out Sino-Japanese war. Japan, usually victorious on the field of battle, became hopelessly engulfed in the vastness of China and its rising tide of nationalism, and American public opinion turned violently against Japan's military expansionism.

The internationalist elements in Japan, however, kept grasping at straws and working desperately for an understanding with the

United States that would bridle the Japanese militarists. I recall how I, just returned from college in America, was reassured by what I heard that the crisis would soon be settled and peace restored in China. To achieve this end, Otohiko, accompanied by his older brother Kojiro and other prominent businessmen, went as "people's ambassadors" to Washington in November 1939. Roosevelt did see Kojiro briefly, but his old college friend Otohiko had to content himself with sending the president letters and telegrams, to which he received cool answers signed by members of the White House staff.

Otohiko returned from Washington with a very gloomy report on American attitudes. Many Japanese hoped that anti-Japanese feelings in America were superficial and the product of small specific incidents, such as the Japanese attack on the American gunboat *Panay* on the Yangtze River in December 1937, but Otohiko made it clear that anti-Japanese sentiment was deep throughout American society. He also pointed out that American sympathy for Britain was growing and that, if Anglo-Japanese relations should worsen, the United States might very well put economic pressure on Japan.

Otohiko was undoubtedly sincere in his concern over Japanese-American relations and his hopes for a termination of hostilities in China, but he and the many other Japanese like him no longer had any influence on the military men in control of Japan's destiny. Events rushed inexorably toward war, and the Japanese people marched blindly with them. Otohiko had only one more communication with Roosevelt. In September 1941 he sent the president a telegram of condolence on his mother's death and received back a "Dear Oto" note.

After war broke out between Japan and the United States in December 1941, Otohiko moved to Shanghai and spent the remainder of the war years there. Residing in the French Concession, he was able to continue the type of life he enjoyed, surrounded by mountains of books and associating freely with his foreign friends. A later good friend of mine, Inukai Michiko, the granddaughter of the last prewar politician prime minister, who was assassinated by militarists in 1932, happened to live in the same apartment building. Otohiko introduced her to an excellent teacher who soon made her a quite fluent speaker of English. After her morning lesson she would go to Otohiko's eighth-floor apartment, where for an hour and a half each day he would help polish her English by reading Shakespeare with her. After the war Otohiko went back to Japan, where he reestablished contact by letter with some of his American friends; he died in 1952.

While I was at the American embassy in the 1960s, I was reminded one day of Otohiko's wartime stay in Shanghai. A woman official named Mrs. Leavell from the American Department of Labor wished to see me. She was of Chinese origin and informed me that her father, Lo Chih-chien, had been a good friend of my Matsukata grandfather and that during the war my father had saved her from execution by the Japanese military police in Shanghai. I told her that it was not my father but my uncle Otohiko who had saved her life. The act was typical of him. He and his many brothers were all kind and honorable men.

Matsukata Kojiro

My grandfather's third son, Kojiro, was undoubtedly the most remarkable of the lot. Because of their father's eminence, all the sons found doors of opportunity open, but Kojiro was determined to make his own way, free from the domination of his father. He succeeded, achieving renown in a number of fields. Although his place in modern Japanese history falls far short of his father's, his name is better known to the average Japanese today than is my grandfather's.

Kojiro was born in 1865, shortly after his father went from Kagoshima to Nagasaki to study naval matters, and he was eleven when the family moved to Tokyo. Like his brothers he attended the Peers School, and he then entered the Daigaku Yobi Mon, the preparatory branch of Tokyo Imperial University. He was an excellent student but also a leader in extracurricular activities. It was the custom of the school to hold a banquet for the students after graduation ceremonies, but the year he was to graduate the banquet was canceled for reasons of economy. The students were indignant, and Kojiro organized a petition of protest addressed to the school's president. When it was denied, Kojiro organized a student strike. The authorities retaliated by insisting that the students either apologize or face expulsion. My grandfather, who had just become finance minister, pleaded with Kojiro to apologize, but he refused and in the end, in order to save his father further embarrassment, withdrew voluntarily from the school, determined to continue his university education in the United States.

Kojiro crossed the Pacific in 1884 at the age of nineteen, traveling steerage because his two older brothers were studying abroad and his father said he could not support a third son in the same high style. Thus Kojiro led the life of a relatively poor student compared to his brothers, but unlike them he meticulously reported his monthly expenditures to his father. Because his mother worried about his restricted allowance, he wrote her regularly to tell her about his happy life in school and the many friends he was making. Since daughters of samurai families did not have as much education as the sons, he wrote her in kana and in the Kagoshima dialect, instead of in the formal style used by men for letter writing.

At first Kojiro went to Rutgers College because of the close association of the early Meiji leaders with Verbeck and other Dutch Reform missionaries. His cousin Kosuke had gone there in 1871 as one of the students sent with the Iwakura mission. Kojiro, who had a cheerful open personality, adjusted to his new school, becoming a popular member of the Delta Upsilon fraternity and making lifelong friendships.

At Rutgers Kojiro developed an interest in political science and decided to continue his studies at the law school of Yale University. Here he worked under several prominent professors but was most influenced by a fellow Japanese, Katayama Sen, who was then at the Yale Divinity School. Katayama was extremely poor and earned his way through school by working, sometimes as a day laborer. He had been in America much longer than Kojiro and was six years his senior. He was very kind to Kojiro and introduced him to the democratic movement then stirring in Japan and to concepts of socialism. Kojiro, who had been brought up in a conservative and class-conscious environment, was given a new and broader perspective on society and became aware of the bad conditions in which the working classes lived, not only in Japan but also in America.

For his practical education, Kojiro traveled widely in the United States during vacations, visiting factories and observing industrial labor conditions. His father's prominence opened doors to many companies. He was appalled at the discrimination against Japanese laborers discovered when he visited Texas. When Katayama left Yale, he remarked to Kojiro that, even though they had both chosen to go into politics, they would be traveling on different roads, and he doubted if they would ever again be so close. He was quite right. Katayama became the founder and longtime leader of the Communist movement in Japan and Kojiro became a prominent industrialist, but his introduction through Katayama to social justice permanently changed his outlook on life.

During these years Kojiro often went to New York City on holidays to visit friends. Among them was Arai, whose silk business was already well established, although he and Tazu were still living at Mrs. Dudley's boardinghouse in Manhattan. Despite a difference of ten years in age, the two men became good friends. In March 1887, when Arai was leaving New York for a business trip to Japan, Kojiro wrote him a letter in English, requesting him to call on his parents. Kojiro's father was then finance minister in Ito's first cabinet in the new system. Kojiro also asked Arai to remember him to Kuroda Kiyotaka, the Satsuma oligarch who succeeded Ito as the second prime minister. With an American touch of camaraderie, he closed his letter, "Goodbye, old boy. Yours K. Matsugata." (In his and his father's generations, the surname was often pronounced with a "g," whereas today it is pronounced with a "k.")

Kojiro enjoyed his studies in America, but he realized it was still a new country and he wanted to study in Europe, the homeland of Western civilization. After going back to Japan for a while, he went to Paris in 1889, the year the Eiffel Tower was erected, arriving just in time to see its first glorious illumination. He studied at the Sorbonne for a short time, increasing his knowledge of democratic ideas and becoming fascinated with Rousseau and Social Darwinism. In 1890, when he was twenty-five years old, he returned to Japan, with a considerably broadened outlook on life. He had also developed new tastes in clothes and for cigars. His father's repeated efforts to have him stop smoking were in vain. He continued to smoke cigars for the rest of his life, and my memories of Uncle Kojiro have always been associated with the aroma of cigars.

———•———

Kojiro was well placed for a young man wishing to enter a life of politics. The year after his return, his father became prime minister, and Kojiro was plunged into political life as his father's secretary. He made many friends and contacts, one of whom was Hara Takashi, secretary to the Choshu oligarch, Inoue. Hara was to become a major follower of Ito and eventually, in 1918, Japan's first politician prime minister. The Matsukata cabinet lasted a little more than a year, after which Kojiro was given a position in the imperial household ministry to broaden his experience. He proved to be too much of a reformer for the staid household ministry and encountered such stiff opposition that he resigned. He disliked always having to be prim and proper, and he longed for more useful work and a chance to try out the new social ideas he had acquired abroad. His short service in the household ministry was to be his only stint as a government official.

Shortly after Kojiro gave up this position, his father received a caller, Kawasaki Shozo, a Satsuma friend who in the early 1880s had bought the Hyogo Shipyards in Kobe from the government. Kawasaki had done little with his acquisition until the Sino-Japanese War of 1894–95 made him realize the importance of shipbuilding to the nation. He had come to my grandfather, then finance minister in Ito's second cabinet, to tell him of the difficulties he was having in modernizing his shipyard. His chief problem was finding competent people. Kojiro, now without a job, happened to be in the house and my grandfather introduced him to his visitor. Kawasaki was most impressed with Kojiro's education and experiences abroad as well as his outgoing personality. Seeing in him a possible recruit for his shipyard, he invited Kojiro to visit him in Kobe. Kojiro felt this might be a chance not only to have a more active life but to escape the heavy shadow of his father, which touched him everywhere in the capital. His visit to Kobe in 1895 resulted in a permanent move: he made Kobe the base of his activities, until he retired.

Kawasaki Shozo was a leading industrialist in the Kansai, the region centering on Osaka, Kyoto, and Kobe. Kojiro looked over the many enterprises and found himself most attracted by Kawasaki's newspaper, the *Shin Nippo*. Because of the new system of popular elections, newspapers were beginning to play an important role in politics. Working on a newspaper appealed to Kojiro as a good way to air his own ideas, and Kawasaki obliged by appointing him editor of the paper. Kojiro thoroughly enjoyed the work and proved to be very good at it. His democratic spirit made him popular with staff and workers, and his editorials exercised considerable influence.

In one of Kojiro's editorials, "Concerning the Development of

Taiwan," he criticized the government for doing little to develop that newly seized colony, and he called upon Kansai businessmen to take the lead. An important local industrialist, Kaneko Naokichi of Suzuki Shokai, was much impressed with what he had written and called on Kojiro to find out how he had acquired such extensive knowledge of Taiwan. Kojiro had to admit that all he knew was taken from the encyclopedia he had brought back from Paris. An avid reader, he brought back from his studies at the Sorbonne a large store of books on different subjects. Kaneko was not disillusioned by this answer and actually did extend his business activities to Taiwan.

Kojiro also became involved in a second newspaper of more lasting fame, the *Kobe Shimbun,* which is the dominent local newspaper of the city today. In 1896 Kawasaki chose Kojiro to be his own successor as president of the Kawasaki Shipyards (renamed from Hyogo Shipyards). In doing this he passed over his former manager of the shipyard, who had expected the job. Instead he put the man in Kojiro's position as editor of the *Shin Nippo.* The former shipyard manager was deeply embittered but bided his time until he had established a firm grip on the paper. Then he started to change it from a serious organ of information and debate into a scandal sheet full of human-interest stories. The increase in circulation made the paper strong financially, and the former shipyard manager then felt himself secure enough to start a campaign of defamation against Kawasaki and his enterprises and also Kojiro. Kawasaki in great distress consulted Kojiro about the situation. Kojiro replied that nothing could be done about a bird that had flown its cage—the best thing to do was to start another paper to combat the *Shin Nippo*'s influence. The result was the founding of the *Kobe Shimbun* in February 1898, with Kojiro as its editor, a position he held together with the presidency of the shipyard for the next several years.

Kojiro devoted more than thirty years of his life to the Kawasaki Shipyards, until his retirement at the age of sixty-three in 1929. He built it up from an antiquated ship-repair facility, where everything was done by manual labor in a style more than half a century behind comparable Western enterprises, into a modern company on a par with leading shipyards in the West and the forerunner of Kawasaki Heavy Industries, one of Japan's leading enterprises today. It produced battleships, destroyers, cruisers, submarines, locomotives, and airplanes.

Under him its capitalization rose from 2 million to 90 million yen. At first Kojiro knew nothing about shipbuilding, but as a good student he educated himself through direct observation. He visited shipyards in America, Scotland, and elsewhere in Europe and read all the information available. In this way he learned every aspect of the operation of a shipyard until he was able to direct his assistants and workers with confidence.

Kojiro was a hard worker. He arrived daily at the shipyard at the same time as his employees. Work hours at the factory started at 6:00 A.M. in summer and 6:30 in winter. Regularly each morning, before he settled down to his desk work, he toured the entire factory, inspecting operations and taking time to converse with his workers to find out how things were going and whether there were any problems.

In order to have men skilled in up-to-date technology, Kojiro over the years sent several hundred young engineers and technicians for training abroad. But in the beginning he hired Western experts and managers to operate the shipyard. Among the various German technicians he hired, the one most responsible for the development and success of the Kawasaki Shipyards was Camillo Weinberger of Meissen in Saxony. He had come to Japan in the 1880s as the representative of a German machine tool company (DEMAG) and married a Norwegian ship captain's daughter. Kojiro hired him for the Kawasaki Shipyards, where he remained until his death in 1918. I am still in touch with his three granddaughters, born and raised in Japan.

———•———

After Kojiro had established himself as president of the Kawasaki Shipyards, his family was eager to see him married. When this became known, the family received many proposals. Kojiro's background, his education abroad, and his reputation as an upcoming businessman made him a most desirable potential son-in-law. Among the proposals was one for Yoshiko, the daughter of Viscount Kuki Takayoshi, an imperial household official, who served as an attendant to the emperor. Yoshiko had only recently returned from America, where she had studied for several years at Mt. Vernon School outside Washington living with an American family. She was not only fluent in English but was well versed in the Western style of life. She also had a brother studying at the Massachusetts Institute of Technology. Kojiro had always said that his wife would have to speak English, so Yoshiko made an excellent candidate.

Viscount Kuki had been the fifteenth daimyo of Sanda, a fief of 36,000 koku, located a few miles north of Kobe. He was a descendant of Kuki Yoshitaka, the commander of the fleet that accompanied Hideyoshi's army, 150,000 strong, in its invasion of Korea in 1592. The Kuki daimyos had been influenced by Dutch learning and in the 1850s advocated the opening of the ports to foreign trade. After the Restoration in 1868, Takayoshi quickly turned to occidental ways of life, wearing Western clothes and eating meat and bread. In 1872, with the abolishing of the old fiefs, he moved from his rural domain to the port city of Kobe. There he started a business importing medicines and pharmaceutical goods and established a company to handle their distribution. He invested in land around the harbor, which, with the rapid growth of the port city, soon made him a rich and influential businessman. In his circle of friends he came to be known as "the stylish daimyo."

Kuki first met American missionaries in Kobe. In 1869, ten years after the Hepburns and other Presbyterian missionaries established themselves in the port city of Yokohama, the Congregational Church sent out its first missionaries to Japan. D. C. Greene and his wife settled in the Kobe and Osaka area, where they taught English, since the ban on Christianity was still in force. When two years later Z. D. Davis and O. H. Gulick joined them, they all started an English school in Ujinomura. They interspersed discussions of the Bible in their English classes. One day Davis and Gulick received news that their tutor in the Japanese language, Ichikawa Einosuke, had been arrested with his wife on charges that he had in his possession a copy of a handwritten manuscript of Hepburn's translation of the Bible. Their protests to the authorities for the release of the Ichikawas were in vain, and both Ichikawas were imprisoned for over a year until he died in prison on November 26, 1872. He was acclaimed by the missionaries as the first Japanese Protestant martyr, and his death was looked upon as a grave international incident.

The Iwakura mission had left Japan just about a week before Ichikawa's death, so when it arrived in Washington its members were unaware of the repercussions of the incident in America. Iwakura had come to ask for revision of the unequal treaties imposed on Japan during the last days of the Tokugawa shogunate and a new treaty based on equality. This request was sternly dismissed on the grounds that a nation which did not recognize Christianity and persecuted Christians could never be admitted into the comity of civilized nations. Perhaps this was the first time the Japanese fully realized the important role Christianity played in the Western world. Shortly after Iwakura's return to Japan, the ban on Christianity of more than two hundred years' standing was quietly ended, in March 1873.

Free at last to teach Christianity openly, Greene, Davis, and Gulick immediately started public meetings every Sunday. These were not church services but more like Sunday schools where the Bible was taught. The sessions lasted from eight until twelve in the morning. Records show that in the beginning thirty-eight people attended, two-thirds of them Chinese and the rest Western women and Japanese. One was the wife of Ichikawa, who after her husband's death had been released from prison and became a staunch Christian. There were also two prominent Japanese of high social standing who, in contrast to the other Japanese attending, were dressed in Western clothes. They were Kuki and his wife, who brought with them their eldest daughter, Cho.

The Kuki family became converts to Christianity, and when Cho died a few years later Takayoshi asked Davis to hold a Christian funeral service for her, much to the dismay of the Buddhist priests of the Shingetsu-in in Sanda, the family temple, where the long line of Kuki daimyo lay buried. Cho was interred beside her ancestors, but her tombstone bears an inscription in English: "In memory of Cho, the eldest daughter of the Noble Kuki Takayoshi. Born October 15th, 1867. Died May 8, 1878."

Kuki's progressiveness extended to the education of girls. In 1875 two American female missionaries arrived in Kobe, and they were asked by a group of Japanese mothers to start a school to educate their daughters. From the very start, Kuki supported the establishment of the school, and he made the largest contribution of 800 yen to the 6000 yen needed for its construction. It was built at the foot of Mount Suwayama on Yamamoto-dori, appropriately in full view of Kobe harbor where foreign ships could always be seen. The school was a two-story wooden structure with a porch around the front and looked like a small hotel. The first floor was used for classrooms and a dining hall, and the second floor was reserved for the living quarters of the missionary teachers and some dormitory students. The landscaping was distinctively American, with a broad lawn in front and trees. The school was named the Kobe Home, but the local people referred to it as "the girls' school on Yamamoto-dori." Though it was a school to teach English, in the mornings a Japanese curriculum was pursued, with the girls learning Chinese history and writing. In the afternoons the studies were completely devoted to English. At the school's opening there were three girls in the dormitory and twenty-three local commuters, one of them Kuki Yoshiko.

In 1872 the Japanese government had started a program of sending young boys and girls from good families to be educated in America and Europe and, it may be recalled, the Iwakura mission took the first group of 154 boys and girls with it. Among the five girls was a six-year-old, Tsuda Umeko, who, after a second period of study in America and graduation from Bryn Mawr College, returned to Japan to establish the first college for women. Yoshiko and her brother were sent abroad in the third group. When she returned, she hoped she could marry a man with much the same background as hers, since her experience abroad had made her quite different from the girls of her class brought up in the traditional way.

Kojiro and Yoshiko were married in December 1898, and she settled down to live in Kobe not many miles from her place of birth. Kojiro had built a Western house the year before, located at the foot of Suwayama, with a view of the coastline and harbor. They lived in a stylish way, quite uncommon at the time. As their children grew up, Yoshiko spent much of her time teaching them English, and she had a circle of friends who had been abroad and spoke English.

Kojiro had the most elegant carriage in Kobe and each morning went to his office driven by two coachmen dressed in livery, with a footman behind. Townsmen with their children often waited to see the carriage pass in front of their houses, and they could almost set their watches by Kojiro's schedule. When automobiles came into vogue in the early 1900s Kojiro replaced the carriage with the latest models of cars. He was always impeccably dressed in London-made suits, although there were good Chinese tailors in Japan. The only flaw in his appearance was the battered felt hat he wore tilted slightly back. In one hand he carried a cane to support the leg he injured as a little boy falling from a tree, and in the other hand he held a lighted cigar.

———•———

Kojiro by this time had become a prominent leader in Kansai business circles. He was president not only of Kawasaki Shipyards but of many other companies, including the Kobe and Kyoto gas companies and the Kita Kyushu Electric Car Company, and he was the president of the Kobe Chamber of Commerce from its founding, which was even before the Tokyo Chamber of Commerce was established in 1890. The community urged him to run for the eleventh election of the national Diet in May 1912. He joined the Seiyukai Party, founded in 1900 by Prince Ito with the aid of Kojiro's old friend Hara Takashi, who in 1912 was minister of home affairs in the Seiyukai cabinet of Prince Saionji. This put him on a different political side from his father, who had personal connections with the Mitsubishi industrial interests, favoring the opposing Kenseito Party. As we have seen, Matsukata's second son had married the daughter of Iwasaki Yataro, the founder of Mitsubishi, and Iwasaki himself was a friend of long standing. Kojiro was now a rival of Mitsubishi, which in 1905 added to its primary shipyard in Nagasaki a second one in Kobe with the main objective of crushing Kawasaki.

Kojiro won a landslide victory in 1912 and served one term, which lasted until 1915. This was a period of turbulent political development. The Meiji emperor died in July 1912, marking the end of the era in which the old oligarchs had virtually ruled Japan. That winter a parliamentary upheaval, "the Taisho political change," signaled a major transfer of power from court dignitaries and bureaucrats to elected popular representatives in the Diet. Kojiro dropped out of elective politics in 1915 and did not return until 1932, after he had retired from most of his business activities. He was elected again to the Diet that year and three more times, remaining in the Diet until after the end of World War II.

During Kojiro's first term in the Diet, a curious incident occurred. In 1913 Sun Yat-sen sought asylum in Japan, embarrassing the cabinet of Yamamoto Gonnohyoe. For reasons that are not clear, Kojiro took on the task of smuggling Sun from his ship into Japan.

With a launch from his shipyard, he slipped up to the outer side of Sun's ship and took him off, while the Japanese police were looking for him from the other side. Sun hid in Japan several times during his career, and perhaps he was the Chinese of importance I heard about as a child, said to be living somewhere in Tokyo under an assumed Japanese name at the home of a famous pound-cake merchant.

Kojiro went abroad regularly every few years to keep abreast of new technology. The drydock he installed in 1902 was the first in Japan. It enabled him to construct torpedo boats for the Japanese navy from parts he imported from Germany. These played a crucial role in the destruction of the Russian fleet at the battle of Tsushima in the Russo-Japanese War. Later he bought a large crane in England, dismantling it and shipping it to Kobe at great expense. This permitted him to build larger vessels, including the 20,000-ton battle cruiser *Haruna* in 1913 and then a battleship of 31,000 tons. He was the first to replace steam engines with high-pressure turbines and later, when the Germans developed diesel engines, he replaced the turbines with these. Thus Kawasaki Shipyards stayed in the forefront of the industry, a few steps ahead of its nearest competition in Japan, Mitsubishi.

In 1914, when the Austrian crown prince was assassinated in Sarajevo, Kojiro realized this was no localized incident but one that could lead to a major war in Europe. He indicated this in a headline of his *Kobe Shimbun,* when other newspapers reported the assassination as routine news. He also saw that a war would create a great demand for ships, and on the very day he learned of the event he ordered his men to start buying old ships and iron. To pay for these purchases he borrowed heavily from the Fifteenth Bank, where his brother Iwao was president. By the time World War I broke out and his competitors were scrambling to get supplies, Kojiro had already started construction of a fleet. When he completed the ships, he anchored them in the harbor, waiting for customers.

As the war progressed, German submarines began to take a heavy toll on British ships, and the British turned to American shipyards for replacements, causing the United States to ban the export of steel and iron. The Japanese, who had been the largest customers for American iron, were cut off from their supply of raw materials. The shipping industry was hard pressed, and many smaller companies went bankrupt, throwing large numbers of employees out of work. The public clamored for action to lift the embargo, and industrialists and businessmen from all over Japan organized the Alliance Against the Iron Embargo. Among the prime movers was Kojiro and his old associate Kaneko, whom he had earlier persuaded to invest in Taiwan. In March 1916 a committee was chosen to go to Washington to negotiate directly with the Americans. Kojiro was reluctant to join, since he was very much occupied with the construction of the battleship *Ise* and his own "stock of ships." But his familiarity with America and good connections there made the others insist on his going. Hard negotiating induced the Americans to lift the embargo on the condition that two-thirds of the iron exported to Japan would be sold back to America in the form of new ships.

Kojiro decided to proceed from Washington to London to negotiate the sale of his ships. On arriving in England, he held a news conference, announcing the successful agreement he had just completed in Washington, assuring the British that the Japanese would also construct ships for them, and informing them that he already had some under construction. He received a warm welcome because the Matsukata name was well known among the British authorities. The general atmosphere was friendly too, since the Anglo-Japanese Alliance of 1902 had fostered cordial relations between the two countries. If Kojiro had intended to stay only a short time in London, he was mistaken. There was much business to attend to, since the technicians he had sent to England needed supervision, and he accompanied them to France and Italy several times. As the British continued to lose ships, the price of new ones kept rising. By the time Kojiro started to sell his, the price had risen to one hundred pounds a ton, in contrast to the eight pounds per ton they had cost him to construct. His stock of ships made him a very rich man.

In the autumn of 1918 Kojiro returned to Japan by way of America, learning of the end of the war while on the Pacific. He had anticipated this moment some months earlier and had started preparations to develop a new industry at Kawasaki. Knowing that the end of the war would bring a slump in shipbuilding, he had decided to manufacture airplanes. The idea had come to him during German air raids in London. One afternoon as he was walking down Piccadilly, he was almost knocked to the ground by the blast of a bomb that fell nearby. Hearing terrified shrieks for help, he found two young girls huddled together under debris—extricating them he sent them safely home in a cab. From this experience he concluded that the next war would be fought mainly in the air.

The planes of the time were heavy affairs because of their bulky wooden frames, and the small bombs the pilots dropped were thrown out by hand. Kojiro judged that there was much to be done and learned to develop better planes. He immediately started visiting plants in England and France. In Paris he found a group of young Japanese who had come as volunteers to fly planes for the French army. Among them was Hioki Kosaburo, a lieutenant in the Japanese navy, who was a pilot as well as a bright technician at an airplane factory. Kojiro immediately recognized in Hioki the sort of man he would need to operate the airplane factory he planned to build. Before he left Paris, he made an agreement with Hioki to see him as soon as the war ended.

Kojiro found that, during his two and a half years' absence from Japan, many changes had taken place. Industrialization had progressed with great speed, and economic growth resulting from wartime demand for Japanese manufactures had produced a group of rich capitalists. The war, however, had also brought such high inflation that workers and ordinary people were in serious straits. The price of rice had risen to intolerable levels, and angry citizens were rioting against the government. The Terauchi government was forced to resign in the spring of 1918. By the time Kojiro returned, his friend Hara had succeeded Terauchi as prime minister, becoming the first untitled person and professional politician to occupy the post. Hara faced other grave problems, for the success of the Russian revolution had encouraged the spread of Marxism and socialism among intellectuals and the working classes.

Kojiro had built up the Kawasaki Shipyards on the principle that success depends on cooperation between management and labor. He was always concerned with the welfare of his workers and treated them with consideration and respect. His daily tour of the factory and his personal contacts with the workers had built up a reservoir of mutual trust. But the war had turned Kawasaki into a huge company with 15,000 workers, almost double its prewar size. Working conditions needed improvement, and higher wages to keep up with inflation were overdue. Kawasaki workers did nothing when other companies had gone out on strike, but in September 1919 they elected a committee to bargain with management, attracting great public interest.

A large contingent of newsmen attended the meeting arranged between management and labor. The leader of the workers' delegation, a long-time employee at Kawasaki, came forward and bowed low in front of Kojiro and the company officials. He expressed appreciation for Kojiro's concern for his workers in the past and the hope that the demands they were presenting now would receive the same consideration. Kojiro accepted their petition and promised a quick reply. He went on to say that, as he had grown older, he found that some of his ideas had become old and he would have to make changes. Then, to the surprise of everyone, he announced an innovation decided upon just before the meeting. In America and Europe, industries had introduced the eight-hour day for workers, he said, and Kawasaki Shipyards would start doing the same. The reduction of working hours (twelve was the norm) would give the workers time to pursue reading and studying and enable them to do a better job at the shipyard. The newsmen made a mad dash for the door, and before the day was over the big news of an eight-hour workday in Japan had stunned the whole country and surprised much of the rest of the world. It was generally greeted with approbation, though in Japan some of Kojiro's colleagues and friends criticized his action as too early, too rash, or too big a concession to labor. Not many businessmen followed Kojiro's lead, and the postwar economic depression deepened. The suffering of the lower classes increased, and the labor movement flourished and became more radical. In 1920 Japanese workers celebrated their first May Day in conjunction with the working class of other nations.

Kojiro, meanwhile, continued his plans to make aircraft, constructing a factory in Gifu, which Hioki came to manage for him. The Japanese navy wanted to build an air force and encouraged industrialists to enter the field. In the spring of 1921 Kojiro returned to Europe to investigate in Germany the production of a new metal, duralium, which made a good substitute for the bulky wooden frames of the airplanes of World War I.

In the autumn of 1921 Kojiro was asked by the Japanese government to go directly from Europe to America to attend the so-called Washington Conference, which the American government had called to settle various undecided problems of the Far East and to set limits on competitive naval construction among the three leading naval powers in the world, Britain, the United States, and Japan. The principal product of the conference was the 5:5:3 ratio in capital ships. The Japanese, who had already embarked on an ambitious program of naval construction, were not pleased to be limited to three battleships for each five of the British or Americans, but it was difficult to withstand Anglo-American pressure. In compensation the Americans agreed not to build fortifications west of Hawaii and the British east of Singapore, leaving the Japanese navy supreme in the whole Western Pacific. Kojiro had reason to be dissatisfied with the conference's outcome because the Kawasaki Shipyards was an important supplier of Japanese naval vessels. His business was forced into bankruptcy, a few years later.

We have already encountered the great Kanto earthquake of 1923 and the ensuing bank crisis of 1927, which brought the failure of the Fifteenth Bank, of which Iwao, Kojiro's eldest brother, had been president. The bank was the chief supplier of funds to Kojiro's Kawasaki Shipyards and, when the bank failed, it brought the shipyard down with it. The whole Matsukata family voluntarily took personal responsibility for the bank's failure. My own branch of the family gave up, among other things, its large house, which is now the main building of my sister's Nishimachi International School.

Kojiro too gave up most of his assets, and he retired from almost all of his business activities not long after the failure of the bank. One exception was his later involvement in the importation of Soviet oil into Japan. In the 1930s the United States virtually monopolized oil imports to Japan, but in 1933 Kojiro was approached by the Russians to become their agent in selling Soviet oil from Baku to Japan at a lower price than American oil. They had Kojiro in mind because of two previous contacts with him. When a Russian ship had an accident in Japanese waters and no Japanese shipping yard would repair a "Red ship," Kojiro offered to have it repaired and the Russians were very grateful. Kojiro's subsidiary shipping company, the Kokusai Kisen Kaisha, which was a small company compared to the giant Mitsui-Mitsubishi shipping firm, the Nippon Yusen Kaisha, also transported Soviet lumber from Vladivostok. For these reasons the Russians thought first of Kojiro, and he seized the opportunity for a last fling at business, establishing the Japan-Soviet Petroleum Company. When

Kojiro made his last trip to the United States in the autumn of 1937 as a member of a group of prominent private Japanese seeking to soften the indignant reaction of Americans to Japan's invasion of China, he told the American ambassador in Tokyo, Joseph Grew, that he was going on business for his oil company.

The early and mid-1930s were the period in Japan of the *en taku*, or the one-yen taxi, which took a person anywhere in Tokyo for a yen. The cheaper Soviet oil was a big boost to the taxi business. I recall as a highschool student that it was often possible to ride for even less than a yen and that a ride shared with one or two others would be cheaper than going by streetcar. Kojiro became the taxi men's *kami-sama* (god). They all knew about him, and many recognized him. When he happened to go out without his wallet, as he sometimes did, they would be only too happy to take him home free. The era of the *en taku* ended with the outbreak of the Sino-Japanese War in 1937 and the resultant oil shortages, and so too did Kojiro's last venture in business.

————•————

Kojiro is best remembered not as a business magnate or the son of a famous father, but for his collection of Western art, which he started when he was in Europe from 1916 to 1918 and which became the core of the present collection of the National Museum of Western Art in Tokyo. With his usual flair for style, Kojiro during World War I had settled in London in an elegant flat with five large roor in the fashionable Queen Anne's Mansion. During his rare free ..me, he enjoyed browsing through the stores in the city or visited with friends at the Japanese Club. One day as he was walking down St. James Street, he saw in the window of an art gallery a painting of a shipyard with a large red crane. It so reminded him of his own shipyard in Kobe that he walked in and announced his intention of buying it. The art dealer hastily took it out to show him and told him it was by Sir Frank Brangwyn, who was becoming popular in England. Brangwyn was Swiss-born but had become an English subject and a member of the Royal Academy of Art. He and his fellow artists often used this gallery as a social meeting place, and Kojiro was invited to come to meet him. Kojiro's chance acquaintance with Brangwyn was the beginning of a long and close friendship. Brangwyn introduced him to other artists and to dealers as well. Through these contacts Kojiro got the idea of collecting works of art to take back to Japan for the education of Japanese artists and the enjoyment of the public. He made plans with Brangwyn to build a museum in Tokyo to house his collection. Brangwyn offered to make the architectural plans for it and supervise its construction. The name of the museum was to be the Kyo Raku En, meaning the Garden of Shared Enjoyment. About this time Brangwyn painted an oil portrait of Kojiro which now hangs in a museum in Tokyo. It shows him sitting relaxed and in a characteristic pose, smoking a cigar.

Kojiro did not have any special interest in art or knowledge of it, even though his father was a prominent collector of classical Japanese art. His father's associates were also art collectors, and Kojiro sometimes attended their social gatherings, where they would discuss their latest acquisitions. Most of them collected classical Japanese paintings, but, before leaving on his 1916 trip to Europe, Kojiro had attended a gathering of the group where a woodblock print by Kuniyoshi was the focus of attention. This had been his introduction to the essentially modern art form of *ukiyoe,* and he was much impressed.

Kojiro had also learned something about modern art from his long association with Kuroda Kiyoteru, the painter both he and his brother Shosaku had met in France. Kuroda had been sent to France by his father to study law, despite his own preference for art. The son's wishes won out, and he spent his time learning to paint under French teachers. He showed talent and eventually was invited to join several prestigious art societies and made many friends among French artists, including Monet, Manet, and Cézanne. When Kuroda returned to Japan in 1893, he introduced the new school of impressionist painters to eager young Japanese artists. Breaking with traditional artists, he formed his own organization, The White Horse Society (Hakuba Kai), and became the outstanding authority in his time on modern Western painting. He joined the faculty of the Tokyo Bijutsu Gakko (Tokyo School of Fine Arts) and received many honors, including the presidency of the Fine Arts Academy. Kojiro's continued friendship with Kuroda after their return from Paris had brought him in contact with young Japanese artists who were aspiring to learn modern Western art.

The real start of Kojiro's career as a collector started on a day late in 1916 when at the Japanese Club in London he was approached by a young man, Okada Yuji, who introduced himself as the son of a friend of his father's. Okada was the European representative of the Ya-manaka Bijutsu Shokai, which specialized in the sale of oriental art throughout the world. He had just returned to London from wartorn France, where the battle of Verdun, the bloodiest and longest engage-ment of the war, was in progress and Parisians were beginning to fear for their city's safety. He had been approached by Henri Vévér, the famous Parisian jeweler, who wanted desperately to sell his large collection of ukiyoe. Vévér had been buying them for over forty years, and his collection of more than 8000 prints was one of the best in the world, containing all the great woodblock artists: Kaigetsudo, Sharaku, Utamaro, Kiyonobu, Moronobu, Hiroshige, Hokusai.

Vévér told Okada that he could sell the collection by sending a telegram to Ernest Fenollosa or Langdon Warner at the Museum of Fine Arts in Boston, but Vévér wanted to sell it to a Japanese and have it returned to Japan, where there were no outstanding ukiyoe collec-tions. Foreigners had early recognized ukiyoe as a great art form, whereas the Japanese had looked on them as commercial products of little merit, advertising actors or illustrating books. By the time the Japanese came to the realization that ukiyoe was indeed great art, the best of the prints had been collected by foreigners and taken out of the country. Vévér attached three conditions to the sale: that it be made within two weeks; that the payment be made in English pounds; and that the sale be kept secret. The time limitation prevented Okada from contacting Japanese buyers, of whom he knew several, and cer-tainly there would be no buyers in London.

Kojiro listened with much interest to Okada, and he astonished the dealer by offering to buy the entire collection himself. Okada had heard that Kojiro was a rich man but wondered whether he realized the astronomical price being asked. Kojiro assured Okada that he could buy the collection with funds from his own private company, the Matsukata Shosha (Matsukata Commercial Company), which he had established from his private investments in numerous enterprises, in-cluding copper mines in Niigata, gold mines in Kyushu, and even oil fields in Texas. Kojiro declined Okada's invitation to accompany him to look over the collection, since he himself was no authority, but promised Okada he would have the money for him in a few days. Okada made cloth pouches for the money and strapped them around his body, placing the remainder in his false-bottomed suitcase. The trip back to France was filled with danger, for the Germans had started a massive submarine offensive to strangle Britain. The ship zigzagged across the English Channel, taking forty-eight hours. Okada arrived in Paris to find that Vévér had already fled to Bordeaux, with the collection. He followed him there and was able to complete the sale. He succeeded in bringing the prints back to London; Kojiro immediately placed his acquisitions in safekeeping and only at the end of the war did Okada send them to Kobe, in a dozen separate shipments. Kojiro saw his collection for the first time in 1925, when a number of the prints were put on exhibition. This was the first ukiyoe exhibition ever held in Japan. Reproductions were also made of one hundred of the prints. Only a limited number of these copies were made and many were probably destroyed in World War II, but I am fortunate enough to have one of the remaining sets.

Kojiro gave his ukiyoe collection to the Fifteenth Bank at the time of the bank crisis in 1927, but the bank was never able to find a buyer. Mindful of Kojiro's original intention in buying it for the Japanese public, the bank donated it to the National Museum of Art in Tokyo, where it became the core of the museum's print collection. As Kojiro had wished, this made it unnecessary for Japanese to go to Boston or other Western centers to see examples of the best ukiyoe.

———— • ————

Although Kojiro's ukiyoe collection was his chief art acquisition in Europe during World War I, before leaving Europe in 1918 he asked Durand-Ruel, one of the largest art dealers in France, to buy him works of modern art that were selling at a low price. Kojiro left funds for this purpose, and when he returned to Europe in 1921 to look into the manufacture of airplanes, he found that Durand-Ruel had made many purchases for him. He was surprised to be greeted in Paris not as the leading industrialist he had become, but as the "great art collector." Dealers requested him to visit their galleries, and young artists came to his hotel with their paintings.

Kuroki Sanji and his wife, Iwao's daughter Takeko, happened to be in Paris, where Sanji had been an assistant to Makino Nobuaki, one of the Japanese representatives at the Versailles Peace Conference. Learning from the newspapers of Kojiro's visit, they were surprised to find him described as a famous collector. The Kurokis, who themselves were great art lovers, had become good friends of Monet's and invited Kojiro to accompany them on a visit to the master painter. Kojiro was delighted and canceled a scheduled trip to Germany. Monet was then eighty-one years old and, since the death of his wife, was living with his daughter, Blanche-Hoschede Monet. In 1883 the Monets had moved to Giverny and built a new house. It had a Japanese garden with stone lanterns, weeping willows, a typical Japanese wisteria arbor, and an arched wooden bridge over a pond, in which there were lotus flowers. Their home was decorated in Japanese style with woodblock prints hanging on the walls of every room.

Monet's love affair with Japanese woodblock prints had started in 1870 when he was a student in Leiden, where he had gone to study the paintings of Rembrandt. One day he bought some tea and found it wrapped in unusual paper printed with a kind of art he had never seen before. It was a copy of a Japanese woodblock print, which were so common in Holland that they were used for such humble purposes. Monet was fascinated by the print and spent much time studying it. We are all familiar with the influence ukiyoe were to have on Monet and the impressionist style of painting he created.

When Kojiro was introduced to Monet, he told the great man that young artists in Japan were studying his paintings through photographs and were most anxious to see the originals. It pleased Monet that Japanese artists were eager to see his paintings because he felt that Japan was the source of his art. Monet rarely allowed the members of his own family or even close friends like Clemenceau to enter his atelier, but he invited Kojiro in and showed him all his paintings, telling him to choose any he liked. Kojiro purchased sixteen that afternoon. Five months later he went back again, this time accompanied by Yashiro Yukio, a Japanese art historian. He also took with him a present of Napoleon brandy, which Monet loved. On this visit Kojiro purchased eighteen more paintings. Of the thirty-four paintings he acquired on these two occasions, twenty are still in Japan. I have in my possession a rare photograph of Monet taken in 1921 with his daughter, Clemenceau, and Kuroki Takeko in Japanese kimono. Takeko and her husband gave Monet presents of Japanese lotus roots to replenish his pond, which figures in many of his later paintings.

During the war Brangwyn introduced Kojiro to many people in the art world, who gave him advice and helped him make purchases.

One of these was Leonce Benedite, the curator of the Luxembourg Museum in Paris, who in turn introduced him to Auguste Rodin. Kojiro bought many pieces from Rodin, including *The Burghers of Calais, The Three Dancers,* and *The Kiss.* Rodin was in his last days and, like all artists at that time was poor, depending on the government to supply the clay and bronze he required. When the government stopped doing this because of the war, Kojiro promised to pay for these supplies himself, and Rodin in return promised to set aside everything he subsequently made for Kojiro. As a consequence, *The Gates of Hell* and several other late Rodins came into Kojiro's possession. Kojiro's artist friend Kuroda was astonished to learn that Kojiro owned this masterpiece and inquired how he could ship such a huge thing back to Japan. Kojiro assured him that, if he could transport a large crane for his shipyard, he would have no problem with this piece of sculpture.

Most of the art Kojiro purchased during the war was left right where he bought it, either with friends, museums, or dealers, since there was no way to transport it to Japan in wartime. The fact that Kojiro, a good businessman, was unbusinesslike with his art purchases, and kept no real list of what he had bought or where it was, presented difficulties after the war. But when he shipped the ukiyoe collection, Okada also sent back some of Kojiro's other purchases. His list included 700 oil paintings, 66 water colors, 32 pieces of sculpture, 350 pieces of antique furniture, and 17 tapestries. Since no museum had been built to house these treasures, Kojiro stored most of them at his father's country estate in Nasuno, unopened in the crates they arrived in, but some he left with friends or relatives who had houses large enough to give them temporary homes. As a little girl I remember one large oil painting that hung at the end of our front hall. I believe it was one of Eugene Delacroix's paintings, of which Kojiro had several. Unfortunately during the financial panic of 1927, when the Matsukata family lost almost everything, the collection was taken over by the Fifteenth Bank. The bank sold most of it piecemeal to private collectors, business corporations, and galleries. *The Miners* by Edvard Munch is in the Bank of Japan, and one of the tapestries hangs in the Japan Sugar Club, to which my father belonged; other works are in reception halls of insurance companies and other corporations. Seventeen pieces were held for a while by the Bridgestone Collection but in 1984 were returned to Kojiro's heirs and either sold at auction in New York or donated to the National Museum of Western Art.

Between 1921 and 1935 Kojiro continued adding to his collection, buying through dealers all over Europe. In the records of Durand-Ruel, an entry of December 1921 shows the purchase by Kojiro on that day alone of four canvases for 822,000 francs, which in 1850 was about $160,000. His entire collection was worth over $20 million.

Most of the purchases made after 1921 were kept in Europe because the Japanese government was then imposing a 100 percent luxury tax on imported works of art. No exception was made for Kojiro's collection, despite the fact it was to be given to the nation. Kojiro was angered by this and refused to bring back the collection. About the same time, some of the Rodin pieces were prohibited from import to Japan because they were considered pornographic. So the bulk of Kojiro's collection was in France when World War II broke out in 1939, and it became enemy property when Japan joined the war two years later.

When World War II ended, Kojiro was eighty years old and living quietly in retirement in Zushi, a seaside resort thirty miles southwest of Tokyo. He felt sure that his dream would now be realized and his collection permanently housed in Tokyo. The economic destitution and chaos of postwar Japan, however, made this impossible, and he died in 1950, a disheartened man. There was also the continuing problem that the French government, regarding Japan as an enemy country, froze all private Japanese assets in France, with the intention of using them to defray reparation charges. Matsumoto Shigeharu, who was Kojiro's nephew and son-in-law, together with various concerned friends kept working on the problem of getting Kojiro's art treasures to Japan, and they interested Yoshida Shigeru in the project. Yoshida, a former diplomat, was one of Kojiro's oldest friends, having met him in London during World War I, and after World War II he became Japan's most prominent postwar prime minister. Yoshida remembered that, at a farewell banquet the Japanese ambassador to the Court of St. James had given in honor of Kojiro just before his departure in 1918, the ambassador in his toast had congratulated Kojiro on his art collection and had said, "Even though you should fail in business, the works of art you have collected for the

Japanese people will last forever." When Yoshida went to the peace conference in San Francisco in September 1951, he was determined to make arrangements for the transfer of the collection to Japan, even if he could accomplish nothing else. He pleaded with Schumann, the French foreign minister, arguing that Kojiro's collection should be considered "public assets." He even offered to have the Japanese government buy it back.

When the matter of the return of the collection was brought before the French National Assembly, there was strong opposition, especially among the many deputies who had been members of the Resistance. Fortunately, however, there was a former Maquis who was influential with his old comrades in arms but had a very different attitude toward the problem of Kojiro's collection. This was Vadim Elisséeff, a young authority on Chinese and Japanese art. Elisséeff's father Serge was the scion of a wealthy Russian merchant family who took to scholarship and became the first Western graduate of Tokyo Imperial University. After the Russian revolution he fled to Paris, where he became a French citizen and professor at the Sorbonne. In 1952 he transferred to Harvard University, becoming the virtual founder of Japanese studies there and my future husband's mentor. The younger Elisséeff managed to persuade his Maquis associates to support the return of Kojiro's collection to Japan as a gesture of goodwill, on the condition that the Japanese government erect a special museum to house it.

In 1959 the National Museum of Western Art, designed by Le Corbusier, was completed in Ueno Park in Tokyo, near the National Museum of Art, and finally Kojiro's collection came to Japan. But not all of it. The French museums exercised a right of preemption to fill in gaps in their own collections of certain artists. Some fourteen of the most valuable pieces were retained in France. In the catalogue of the Louvre, there are seven paintings, including Van Gogh's painting of his room at Arles in 1889, a portrait of Toulouse-Lautrec, and three paintings by Gaugin, which have the following notation: "Prince Matsukata, Kobe. Taken into the Louvre Museum in 1952, under the terms of the Peace Treaty with Japan."

Kojiro's collection at the National Museum of Western Art in Tokyo consists of 417 paintings, drawings, and pieces of sculpture, representing all the main trends in French art from the 1820s to the

1930s. The collection of impressionists is ranked by some as the fourth best in the world. Orginally Kojiro owned 70 pieces of Rodin's work, but only 54 were returned. Castings were made from the original for some of the missing ones, as in the case of *The Burghers of Calais,* the original of which now stands in front of the Rodin Museum in Paris. Some people consider the Rodin collection in Tokyo the finest in the world. Kojiro's hobby of collecting modern art, which he did not start until he was fifty-two, is what the average Japanese now associates with the name Matsukata, not his outstanding work as an industrialist or his father's even more illustrious career as a statesman. Mention the name Matsukata in Japan today, and the response is likely to concern the "Matsukata collection" or the "Matsukata museum," as the National Museum of Western Art is frequently called.

Matsukata Saburo

Matsukata Saburo, a man of many talents, was my grandfather's youngest surviving son. In terms of age he was more like a grandson and that is what he later became legally, through adoption by his older brother Kojiro. He also became the third family head, inheriting the position from Iwao in 1943.

Saburo was born in Kyoto in August 1899, one of the three children of my grandfather's third concubine, Kita. His original name was Yoshisaburo, but he never liked it and had it legally shortened to Saburo in 1955. At the time of his birth his father was sixty-four, in his seventeenth year as finance minister and only a year away from retirement. His wife Masako at fifty-four had already raised her own eleven children and those of her husband's first two concubines, but for the most part they had already grown up and she felt the raising of Kita's three children too heavy a task to undertake. Saburo therefore was not taken into the family's house in Tokyo but was removed from his mother and put in the care of a wet nurse in a farmer's family at Matsugasaki north of Kyoto, where he remained until the age of four. He was then placed in the home of Matsukata's eldest son Iwao, but he was not treated as a son or the equal of Iwao's own daughter Takeko, a few years his senior, whom we have already met as the wife of Kuroki Sanji and the friend of Kojiro and Monet in Paris. Saburo was even served his meals in a separate room from the rest of the family, and in later life he remarked on having never known the pleasure of eating meals with his parents.

Saburo's cold treatment by Iwao and his wife Yasuko may have been the result of their resentment that they had no son of their own and had been prohibited by my grandfather from adopting Takeko's future husband as their heir, thus keeping the headship of the family and the title in their own blood line. In any case, Yasuko never gave Saburo much love, and he had no one to whom he could *amaeru,* a key concept in Japan, which might best be translated as "to seek to be babied." As a little boy Saburo was frail and cried easily, especially when scolded by Yasuko. His crying obviously irritated her, and she would lock him up in the Western bathroom in the house until he stopped. This denial of a mother's love could have warped his personality in many ways. Obviously it was something he remembered all his life, but others could see only his unusual devotion to others and an extraordinarily sunny disposition.

When Saburo was six he was adopted by his brother Kojiro, twenty-four years his senior, becoming legally his own father's grandson and in due time my cousin rather than my uncle. Since Kojiro was living in Kobe, Saburo continued to live in Iwao's home in order to go on with his education in Tokyo. He had started kindergarten in a school in the precincts of the Zojoji Temple in Shiba Park and then entered the Peers School. At first he was so timid that he was accompanied to school by a servant, but he soon found this too embarrassing and started going alone. At about this time there was a marked change in his health and personality. He enjoyed school and did well. He also became a mischievous activist. One day he slipped some lizards into the chairs of his classmates, causing quite a hubbub, and another time, when the calligraphy teacher bent over the work of the student in front of him, he painted a large circle on the poor man's posterior. At the insistence of Kojiro and his wife, Saburo started learning English early, stopping off for lessons at an English woman's house on his way home from school.

In 1907, when Saburo was in the third grade, General Nogi Maresuke became the head of the Peers School. Nogi was the hero of the Russo-Japanese War and was to be apotheosized when he and his wife committed suicide following the death of the Meiji emperor in 1912. To the public he was an awesome, unapproachable figure, the epitome of a disciplined samurai, whose life style resembled that of a Zen philosopher, but to Saburo he was a wonderfully kind person, even if strict and demanding. Saburo idolized him, and the stern old general seems to have had a special liking for Saburo. Instead of living in the director's residence, Nogi chose to be with the boys in their spartan dormitory, occupying a small room, furnished only with a narrow cot, a plain desk, a few books, and his simple, carefully mended clothing. He was a stickler for cleanliness and each night would wash out his own underwear.

Nogi himself served as the school's instructor in kendo. Each morning the boys would assemble at the *dojo,* the fencing hall, promptly at six and would be put through rigorous kendo exercises by the general. Nogi was always dressed in pure white, including his sturdy mask and armor. Standing erect in the middle of the dojo, he would have each boy charge him and strike him on his mask with a split bamboo sword. The smaller boys had to leap to reach that high. When the boys grew bigger, Nogi had them use real swords to hack at living pigs. One is reminded of my grandfather's schooling seventy years earlier. Nogi was no anachronistic samurai, however. His concepts of character building may have looked to the past, but he had been the leader of a victorious modern army and had a broad international point of view. He introduced his students to the brand-new Boy Scout movement and led them on camping expeditions, living in tents set up on the beach at Katase near Kamakura. He attempted to popularize skiing in Japan and supported the first Japanese antarctic expedition, playing a leading role in assembling the necessary funds and equipment for the undertaking.

Two other teachers greatly influenced Saburo during his years in secondary school between 1911 and 1915. One was Suzuki Daisetsu, the great authority on Zen. Suzuki had spent eleven years in the United States and was the teacher of English, but he was an unorthodox teacher, ignoring the official government textbooks and grammar instruction and using instead Ruskin's *The Crown of Wild Olives.* This he had his students study line by line, only using dictionaries entirely in English. The results fully justified the means. Suzuki was an avid reader with a sizable library of his own, and Saburo acquired a love of books from him. He developed the hobby of browsing through stores in search of interesting books on a wide range of subjects, and he always read himself to sleep at night. On his travels much of his baggage consisted of books, and he habitually went third class on trains to avoid meeting his friends in second class, whose socializing would distract him from his reading.

The other teacher in secondary school who influenced Saburo was a man named Kojima Kikuo, who taught German but was also an art critic. Kojima had written a book on Leonardo da Vinci, and he taught Saburo to appreciate art and how to look at paintings. A later important influence on Saburo was Kuroki Sanji, who was Iwao's son-in-law. Fifteen years Saburo's senior, he was a sort of older brother to him as well as a friend. Kuroki was a cultured man who loved art and music, but he also was devoted to mountain climbing. He passed on all these enthusiasms to Saburo. Because of his interest in art, Saburo played an active role in rounding up Kojiro's scattered collection after World War I and was an insistent advocate of having it transferred to Japan after World War II.

Kuroki also put Saburo in touch with Uchimura Kanzo, the great Christian intellectual, who had a tremendous impact on many young men of the time. Uchimura graduated in 1881 from the Sapporo Agricultural College (later Hokkaido University), where he had been converted to Christianity together with his friend Nitobe Inazo, whom we have already met in connection with Arai's life. After studying at Amherst College and the Hartford Theological Seminary, he returned to Japan, where Kuroki was his student at the First Higher School and was converted to Christianity. It was also at the First Higher School that the insufficient respect Uchimura paid to the Imperial Rescript on Education brought his dismissal, but also nationwide fame and a shift from teaching to writing and lecturing. An ardent though iconoclastic Christian, Uchimura rejected the formal institutions of the church, founding the no-church movement. Kuroki persuaded Saburo during his higher school days (the twelfth through the fourteenth years of formal education) to attend Uchimura's extremely popular Sunday lectures on the Bible and ethics at the Tokyo YMCA. Eventually Saburo became a confirmed Christian of the no-church variety, though on the insistence of his wife, a lifelong Roman Catholic, he received Catholic baptism on his deathbed.

In becoming a disciple of Uchimura, Saburo was proving to be a typical young intellectual of the period of Taisho Democracy, as the 1910s and 1920s are known in Japan. Many young men, dissatisfied with the authoritarian state and rigid ethical concepts of the Japan my grandfather and his generation had created, turned to the universality of Christian ethics as a guide both for their own lives and the nation. Once before, in the 1870s and 1880s, young Japanese had turned away from Confucianism to Christianity and internationalism. After a swing of the pendulum back toward a nationalistic and militaristic brand of Neo-Confucianism in the years surrounding the Sino-Japanese and Russo-Japanese wars, young Japanese intellectuals were again being attracted by liberal Western and Christian ideas.

They were also attracted by British guild socialism and the new British labor movement as well as by Marxism, and in this Saburo too was typical of his generation. After graduating from higher school in 1919, he entered Kyoto Imperial University, where he became a student of the eminent economist, Kawakami Hajime. Kawakami was disturbed by the discrepancy between the poverty of the working classes and the wealth of the leaders of industrial society, which he observed not only in Japan but all over Europe. During World War I he wrote a famous book, *Bimbo monogatari* (Tale of Poverty), and by 1919 was espousing Marxism.

In Kyoto Saburo was lax in attending classes but never missed a lecture by Kawakami, sitting in the front row and taking copious notes. On the side he read the works of Marx and Engels and other socialist writers, often in the original German, and Kawakami would invite Saburo and some other students to his home for long discussions of economic and social problems. Saburo also joined an organization known as the Rogakkai (Society for the Study of Labor), which under Kawakami's sponsorship advocated such causes as the legalizing of labor unions, the right to strike, and freedom of speech and thought. He even went with some of his fellow students to Kobe in 1920 to support the workers in their strike against his adoptive father's Kawasaki Shipyards.

Kawakami continued to move further to the left, being forced to resign from Kyoto Imperial University in 1928 in a cause célèbre of academic freedom; in 1933 he was arrested as a Communist and imprisoned for four years. By then Saburo was no longer close to him, though he continued his interest in socialism. He felt no pressure to embark on a career but drifted along, indulging his varied interests as only a wealthy young man could. On graduating from Kyoto in 1922, he entered Tokyo Imperial University as a graduate student, concentrating on the less controversial field of economic geography. Back in Tokyo he moved into the main family home in Mita, which Iwao had taken over from his father, who had gone after the death of his wife to live at the seashore in Kamakura, with Saburo's real mother as his housekeeper. In Tokyo Saburo lived alone in a little house on the grounds, known as the Yama no Ie (Mountain House), which some of his brothers had used before him. Here he was completely independent and decorated the house with paintings he had collected, including one by William Blake. He surrounded himself with books on art, music, mountain climbing, economics, and the novels of Tolstoy, Dostoevsky, and other Russian writers. He also had a Victrola phonograph and stacks of records, having become deeply interested in Western classical music from his Peers School classmate, Konoe Hidemaro, who was to become one of Japan's leading symphonic conductors. One day at school, when Hidemaro was carrying his violin case with him around the grounds, General Nogi ordered him to go to the dojo and engage in a vigorous series of kendo exercises, but this proved to be a futile effort to shift the young musician's attention to more martial endeavors.

At his little Mountain House, Saburo carefully reviewed the notes he had taken of Kawakami's lectures and even made his own translation of the *Communist Manifesto*. At the end of 1922 he briefly entered the army but was mustered out because of the recurrence of a lung problem from a mountain-climbing accident. (He had slipped, and the rope tying him to his companions crushed one of his lungs.) He was still recovering at my grandfather's home in Kamakura when the great Kanto earthquake struck on September 1, 1923. Saburo was not only thrown out of bed but out of the house from the second story into a nearby pine tree, while the whole building collapsed beside him. He could not move his legs and was bleeding profusely, but a servant managed to get him down to the ground. The next day Kojiro, misinformed that his father had been killed, arrived from Kobe with a coffin on the roof of his car. He found his father in relatively good shape but Saburo in critical condition from loss of blood. The doctor Kojiro brought with him luckily found some American acquaintances who donated blood for transfusions that saved Saburo's life.

After his recovery Saburo joined the staff of a magazine called *Shakai Shiso* (Social Thought), put out by an assortment of Marxists, democratic socialists, and liberals. He also coauthored with the editor, Kaji Ryuichi, a book entitled *Marx and Engels.* Out of consideration for his real father, by then elevated to the highest rank of Prince, he used the penname of Goto Nobuo, which was meant to be an approximation of Godunov in Mussorgsky's opera *Boris Godunov.*

A few months after my grandfather died in July 1924, Saburo left for Europe to continue his studies. The first thing he did in London was to pay his respects at the tomb of Karl Marx. In England, he boarded with families. The person he stayed with longest was Mrs. J. H. Longford, the widow of a former British consul in Nagasaki, who had established a considerable reputation as an authority on Japan. Saburo registered with the London School of Economics but paid little attention to the lectures. Instead he spent most of his time studying, as Marx had before him, in the reading room of the British Museum. The beautiful room with its domed ceiling and many rows of tables filled with absorbed readers was "heaven" to Saburo. There, unlike Japanese libraries, he could get for the asking any books he wished and could read them in undisturbed peace. The high point of the time he spent in the library was when he discovered and held in his own hands a posthumously published book by William Blake, bound by the author himself and containing his last poems charmingly illustrated by Blake and his wife.

Saburo made many trips to the continent, mainly to climb the Alps in Switzerland and France, attaining the goal of all alpinists, the summit of the Matterhorn. In the summer of 1928 he was asked by the imperial household to accompany and guide the emperor's next oldest brother, Prince Chichibu, during a European tour the prince was making before settling down to study at Oxford. Chichibu was an avid sportsman, particularly fond of mountain climbing. He found in sports a chance to be on a level of equality with others, which was denied him in other activities by his high birth. The two young men, accompanied by Saburo's cousin, Matsumoto Shigeharu, climbed a series of mountains that summer, including the Matterhorn.

After Saburo returned to Japan in 1928, he felt that he should take a regular job, though not a very taxing one because he wanted ample time for his other interests. His friend Kuroki found him an ideal position in the East Asia Research Bureau of the South Manchurian Railway. A few afternoon hours a day sufficed for this, and the rest of his time he could devote to browsing in bookstores, visiting museums, helping out on the editorial board of *Shakai Shiso,* and working on an encyclopedia of social science, which had 2500 entries in more than 1000 pages. He himself contributed over a hundred entries on such subjects as Adam Smith, Marx, Engels, and socialism in Scandinavia, using his old penname of Goto Nobuo.

It was during these years that Saburo first became deeply interested in international relations. He was introduced to the field through the Institute of Pacific Relations (IPR), which was organized in Hawaii in 1925 by a group of internationally minded Americans. Its conferences were the first international forums ever held for discussing problems of the Pacific area. The Japan Council of the IPR, known as the Taiheiyo Mondai Chosa Kai, was made up largely of Uchimura's disciples, and when the third international conference of the IRP was held in Kyoto in 1929, it was organized by Takagi Yasaka, professor of American history and diplomacy at Tokyo Imperial University and a member of the no-church movement. Nitobe, who had been serving as an undersecretary of the League of Nations since its inception, returned to Japan just at that time and became chairman of the Japanese IPR.

Among the American participants at the Kyoto conference were Jerome Greene of Harvard, whom we have already met in connection with Otohiko's graduation from Harvard, and Owen Lattimore, the respected and later controversial Central Asian scholar. From the United Kingdom came the historian Arnold Toynbee, and there were also delegates and observers from Canada, China, the Philippines, and France. Saburo and Matsumoto Shigeharu, his nephew by birth and cousin by law, were two of the three young men who acted as assistants for the Japanese delegation.

The 1929 conference centered on the problem of Japanese dominance in Manchuria. Saburo learned how international conferences were organized and saw that delegates with conflicting views could engage in frank and heated arguments but remain friends. He also perceived that there could be a distinction between public stances and inner convictions and that agreeing to disagree was a necessary art.

Much influenced by the IPR conference and concerned over the economic, social, and political problems Japan was experiencing, Saburo, together with his cousin Matsumoto Shigeharu, Kaji, and some other like-minded young men, founded the Tokyo Seiji Keizai Ken-kyukai (Tokyo Institute of Political and Economic Research) under the chairmanship of Professor Royama Masamichi. The group met regularly to discuss current national problems and published a yearbook of Japanese politics and economics. They all were strongly patriotic, but they were more openminded than many of their contemporaries, who had been less influenced by Taisho Democracy and untouched by the Christian universalism of Uchimura. When the Japanese overran Manchuria in 1931, Saburo was among the relatively few Japanese who dared to criticize its acts in print.

Saburo also joined the staff of a magazine published by the long-time liberal critic and journalist, Hasegawa Nyozekan. Originally it had been called *Wareware* (We) but in 1930 was renamed *Hihan* (Criticism), and it published articles advocating political and social democracy to combat the growing fanaticism of the military. In the 1920s *Wareware* had played an important role of protest in the debate over the dismissal of socialist professors, such as Morito Tatsuo from Tokyo University in 1920 and Kawakami Hajime from Kyoto in 1928. Saburo's articles in *Hihan* were largely on European subjects, and he hung back from the radicalism some of his friends were espousing. In this he probably showed the liberal, universalistic teachings of Uchimura, whose influence may have helped to keep most Christian socialists in relatively moderate channels. In any case, the sizable Protestant wing of the socialist movement in Japan always remained on the moderate, democratic side, never drifting over to the dogmatic Marxism and dictatorial communism of many other socialists.

The American Council of the IPR invited Saburo to visit the United States in 1933 to deliver some lectures, and he attended the IPR conference held in Banff, Canada, that year. Unfortunately he did not attend the conference at Yosemite in 1936, when my elder sister and I held the same posts of assistant that he and Matsumoto had occupied in 1929.

———•———

After returning from the United States early in 1934, Saburo finally embarked on his lifetime career. Iwanaga Yukichi, an older disciple of Uchimura's, had long wanted to create a nongovernment news agency in Japan. During World War I, Reuters had been almost the only source of foreign news there, and it so dominated international reporting that the Germans subsequently joked about its having won the war for Britain. Iwanaga started his own Iwanaga News Agency in 1920 and in 1932 founded with some associates the Shimbun Rengo Sha (Japan Associated Press), which was a grouping of newspapers designed to be as independent of the government as possible. He had been favorably impressed by Matsumoto and Saburo at the IPR conference in Kyoto in 1929 and he hired both of them. Since dispatches from abroad were sent in extremely abbreviated form to reduce the expense, they not only had to be translated but fleshed out by someone with adequate knowledge. Saburo was assigned this task, which he performed skillfully for two years, learning in the process a great deal about the news business.

Ever since the 1880s Japanese newspapers had been a major liberal force, agitating for parliamentary government and freedom of expression. In the 1930s reactionary pressures on the press increased and, after the failure of the military coup of February 22, 1936, all the mass media were put under a Board of Information, made up of representatives of the army, navy, and home ministry, which controlled the police. To facilitate the board's supervision of the press, it forced the merger of two hundred and fifty newspapers into fifty, on the pretext of a shortage of newsprint. The Shimbun Rengo Sha was dissolved, and the Domei News Agency was put in its place. Although Iwanaga continued as president of Domei and thought of it at first as having achieved his ideal of an independent news agency, mounting military control forced it in time to become a mouthpiece of the government.

After the troubled aftermath of the Manchurian Incident expanded in 1937 into the Sino-Japanese War, Saburo was given his first overseas assignment, in Tientsin in the part of North China occupied by the Japanese army. A few months later he was transferred to Peking as the chief of the whole North China Bureau. Subsequently he was made chief of the bureau, headquartered in Shanghai, and finally in 1939 chief of the All China Bureau. In 1942 he was transferred out of Domei to become the chief of the Manchukuo News Agency in Hsinking (Shinkyo in Japanese and now known as Ch'ang-ch'un), the capital of the Japanese puppet state of Manchukuo. He stayed there until early August 1945, being shifted by Domei back to Tokyo only a week before the Soviet invasion of Manchuria. The Russians were to keep all Japanese captured in Manchuria imprisoned for several years of hard labor under harsh conditions. Saburo only narrowly escaped this fate.

In all, Saburo was in China and its lost provinces of Manchuria for eight years, living a bachelor's life, but he was very much a family man. He had married Hoshino, the daughter of a businessman, Sato Ichijuro, who had lived many years abroad. Hoshino, as I have mentioned, was a Catholic, and the "Hoshi" in her name, which means star, stood for the Star of Bethlehem. When Saburo was asked what kind of wife he wanted, he answered with typical Japanese male chauvinism, "To be married is as necessary as air or water. All I ask for is someone who will not mind my not taking notice of her." But he was in fact a very attentive husband, and Hoshino was devoted to him. When he left for China they already had four children, and four more were born after his return.

During the war years Hoshino endured many problems because of growing shortages of food and finally the terrible American air raids. Saburo had a much easier time of it in internationalized Shanghai and was under the protection of the victorious Japanese army. He led a relatively austere life by habit, neither smoking nor drinking and certainly not womanizing. He dressed simply in the government uniform decreed for Japanese civilians and, when he arrived in Manchukuo to take up his duties as the head of the Manchukuo News Agency, he astounded his subordinates by turning up unannounced with all his goods carried in a rucksack on his back. His one indulgence was gourmet cooking, which he had plenty of opportunity to satisfy in the fine restaurants of Shanghai and the other Chinese cities. Whenever he discovered a particularly tasty dish, he would take careful notes on its ingredients and where to purchase them. Dining with him came to be known as a special treat, and when he entertained at home he would greet his guests at the door wearing an apron and would himself prepare the meal.

Shortly after Saburo returned to Japan in 1945, the emperor announced the surrender of the country on August 15, and soon General MacArthur arrived with the Allied occupation forces. After a brief period of extreme anxiety, the Japanese realized that the Americans were not going to carry out the atrocities they had expected but would approach their responsibilities in Japan in a businesslike, constructive way. Despite the appalling destruction and near starvation that pervaded Japan, the people were seized by an almost euphoric sense of liberation and hope.

A fresh start necessitated a clearing away of many old institutions, and the top Japanese leaders knew that most of them would be forced to shoulder the blame for past errors by being tried as war criminals or being stripped of their positions. Furuno Inosuke, then the head of the Domei News Agency, was certain that both he and his institution, which had served as a propaganda organ for the military, would be forced to go, and to anticipate this he resigned after dissolving Domei in October 1945 and setting up in its place the private Kyodo News Agency (Kyodo Tsushin Sha), which remains preeminent in the field. As in many other Japanese institutions, the next rank of officers below the top few stepped up to take the place of their departing seniors. Saburo became a director and the managing editor of Kyodo in 1945 and in 1949 its overall head. Since he spent so much time introducing the new agency to its prospective customers among the media, it became known for a while as "Mr. Matsukata's Kyodo."

Japanese newsmen had worked during the war under the strict censorship of the Board of Information in Tokyo and the various military headquarters abroad. MacArthur's occupation immediately decreed freedom of the press and put an end to all Japanese government controls, but there was a basic inconsistency between a truly free press and a military occupation with dictatorial powers. Some press controls actually became tighter under the occupation than they had ever been under the Japanese military. Under the direction of Major Daniel Imboden, chief of the Press Division, who in civilian life had been a smalltown newspaper publisher, a long list of forbidden topics was issued. The Censorship Division exercised close control, first in galleys and then again in page proofs. Only later, after all the rules were clearly understood and carefully adhered to, did the Americans shift to a system of postpublication censorship, which in many ways was even more burdensome. At first, among the forbidden items of news were criticism of any aspect of occupation policy or personnel, criticism of the Japanese government or emperor, expressions of dissatisfaction with existing conditions in Japan, mention of shortages of food, references to friction between the United States and the Soviet

Union, and comments about war criminals before warrants for their arrest had been issued. Most galling, the Japanese had to write about Japan as if the occupation did not exist. Some commented that it was like the fantasy of film making without ever showing the cameras. Despite the rigors of the system, few articles actually had to be censored because Japanese newsmen, who had had a long acquaintance with censorship, quickly adapted to the new limitations.

The occupation's press control extended even to materials from the United States, as in the case of Walter Lippmann's syndicated columns, which were subcribed to by some Japanese papers. Members of the foreign press corps also could run afoul of occupation strictures and be blacklisted, as happened to Gordon Walker, the correspondent of *The Christian Science Monitor.* Since I was partly responsible for Walker's troubles, and Saburo indirectly through me, I might digress briefly to tell about them. During my first visit to Tokyo after the war, I met with Gordon Walker and Robert Peel, who had been my professor in literature at Principia and was in Japan with the Counter Intelligence Corps. To my surprise, both men were dressed in military uniforms with revolvers on their hips. We were standing in front of the Daiichi Hotel, which was being used as an officer's billet, but since I felt embarrassed to be seen talking with armed members of the army of occupation, we withdrew to a bombed-out building to confer under less conspicuous conditions.

Both men offered me jobs with their organizations, but I accepted Gordon's offer as being more likely to permit me to renew my youthful hopes of working for better understanding between Japan and America. Being a neophyte in newspaper work and pathetically uninformed about Japanese politics, I turned to Saburo for assistance, dropping in to talk with him almost daily at his dilapidated office at Kyodo headquarters near the old Radio Tokyo Building in Hibiya. He was extremely helpful, giving me and Gordon introductions to Japanese contacts who provided Gordon with chances to write stories other American correspondents could not get. One such story was Gordon's scoop about the new Japanese constitution, which was announced on March 16, 1946, as the product of the Japanese government but had in fact been written by Americans at the instigation of MacArthur. I remember how nervous I was about passing this information on to Gordon, since I knew MacArthur and his staff would be furious with the contradiction of a fiction the Americans were to maintain stubbornly for years. Despite my fear, I decided to let the cat out of the bag because this was indeed a major falsehood that merited exposure. Such contradictions of the occupation's official "facts" were the reason for Gordon's blacklisting. When he subsequently visited China briefly to report on conditions there, he was at first denied reentry into Japan and it required a great deal of negotiating before he was allowed back in.

Unknown to me at the time was the extension of the blacklist to me as Gordon's assistant and the source of much of his information. One day I ran into British-educated Shirasu Jiro, an old family friend and the vice-director of the Japanese Government Liaison Office with the occupation. Shirasu abruptly said, "I am greatly shocked that you, a granddaughter of Prince Matsukata, are a Communist." I could not fathom what he meant. Subsequently my brother Mako, who had joined the American army in the United States and come to Japan as a member of the Counter Intelligence Corps, clarified the situation. He pointed out that American correspondents who disregarded the occupations censorship rules and were critical of MacArthur were considered dangerous subversives and that I was under a shadow because of my association with them. By this time the cold war was casting a pall over the whole occupation, and I could see that my newspaper activities were proving embarrassing to my whole family. So I severed my connections with the press, taking a position at the Swedish legation until the end of the occupation, when I again resumed my work as a journalist.

Saburo's strong hand built Kyodo into an independent national institution and preserved its integrity and freedom despite the limitations imposed by the occupation. But he had a difficult uphill fight, squeezed between the rigidities of the occupation and an unruly labor movement infiltrated by intransigent Communists and their sympathizers. The occupation at first encouraged the formation of labor unions as a necessary aspect of democracy, but a strike in the spring of 1946 at the *Yomiuri,* one of Japan's largest papers, had revealed the extent of Communist influence in some of the unions, cooling the occupation's enthusiasm for them; efforts were commenced to eliminate unions from the newspapers. In May 1949 Kyodo was reprimanded for releasing a story about rumors of an impending general strike, which the American authorities claimed was based strictly on Communist propaganda and not ascertained facts. Saburo, with his socialistic background as a young man, sympathized with his workers and their union activities, but he felt forced to issue strict orders that no one should take part in political activities as a Kyodo employee and that Kyodo itself should never be associated with any political organization. The outbreak of the Korean War a year later in June 1950 brought stronger pressures from the occupation and the insistence that all Communists and sympathizers be dismissed from newspaper staffs. Saburo found this a trying ordeal, because he had to fire thirty-three of his employees in this "Red purge," some of whom were old colleagues and fine reporters and whose political affiliations were by no means clear.

In the early years of the occupation, Japanese were not permitted to go abroad, but Saburo worked hard to secure status as a true international news agency for Kyodo. Finally in 1949 he won permission to send to America Japan's first postwar foreign correspondent, and in September 1951 he himself led a corps of five Kyodo newsmen to the Japanese peace conference in San Francisco, where they did a fine job of reporting fully and accurately. In January 1952 he was severely criticized by both Japanese and Americans for publishing a New Year's message to Japan from Stalin, but he defended himself by pointing out that he had requested messages from all the major heads of state and only Stalin had responded. Later that same year, after the peace treaty had gone into effect, bringing an end to the occupation, he sent Kyodo's first correspondent to Moscow and in May 1953 followed with a correspondent to Communist China. For this he was reprimanded by the Japanese government on the grounds that Japan did not recognize the People's Republic, but he stood his ground.

Saburo thus won his battle to make Kyodo an independent and reliable news agency, despite external political pressures—but he was finally brought down by an accumulation of economic problems and difficulties with labor. The first blow was when the largest dailies, *Asahi, Mainichi,* and *Yomiuri,* reestablished their own networks of foreign correspondents and in 1952 pulled out of Kyodo. A painful retrenchment became necessary and was exacerbated by bitter labor disputes. At the same time, Kyodo's board of directors, which was made up largely of self-important publishers of minor local newspapers, became dissatisfied with Saburo's unostentatious methods of operation and sought his dismissal. Discouraged by the attack from two sides, Saburo simply resigned, walking quietly out of his office for the last time on December 16, 1959.

———•———

Saburo's career as a newsman lasted only twenty-five years and came at an inhospitable time for good journalism. When he retired in 1959, he was still a vigorous sixty, and his true life's work in a sense only started then. He was friendly and affable by nature, sincerely concerned with the well-being of other people and deeply devoted to the ideal of international understanding. Freed from any regular job, he threw himself for the remainder of his life into a myriad of good causes. In many ways his activities after 1959 were a return to the international and public-spirited interests of his youth, which had been smothered for a quarter of a century by Japan's militarism and the war. He was unable to say no to any worthy proposal, and he became involved in fifty or more organizations. He laughingly described his profession as being that of a *sewa-yaki* (busybody).

Saburo's most notable public service during this period was as the chairman of a commission which in the early 1960s put order into the system of addresses for Tokyo. Most Japanese cities had grown from conglomerations of shops, residences, and unnamed crooked lanes surrounding the central castle of the local lord. In the case of Tokyo, the central moat-enclosed castle grounds were huge, and large areas of the city had been divided up into the spacious estates of the more than 260 feudal lords and the many smaller residences of the lesser vassals—but few roads bore names. Reflecting this confused historical background, prewar addresses had consisted of a modern ward name (*ku*), a traditional district (*cho* or *machi*), ranging from tiny little-known ones to huge sprawling districts, and a number reflecting, not location within a district, but the sequence in which house lots had been established or the process by which larger ones had been broken up. The result was complete chaos. District names and borders were often known only to the local residents, and numbers within a district could be a mystery to everyone but the postman. To direct visitors to one's home, it would be necessary to describe in detail the various corners to be turned in approaching it from some known spot, such as a streetcar stop. When this failed, the visitor would have to seek out a local police substation, where the policeman would try to locate the house on the detailed wall map he had of the area. But even this might fail. My husband remembers a time during our courtship when a policeman in a substation a bare quarter of a mile from my home could not find it because it was across the line in another district.

The task Saburo and his commission faced was herculean in a city that was shooting past the 10 million mark and still resembled for the most part a congeries of tiny villages with narrow unnamed streets. They reduced the number of wards which was the lowest unit of local self-government; they wiped out a vast number of district names, to the loud protests of local residents and traditionalists; they put order into the larger remaining district names by dividing them into geographically ordered subdistricts (*chome*); within these smallest units they put geographic order into the numbering system; and they gave names to the major roads of the city, which the occupation had tried earlier and the Japanese public ignored. Because of Saburo's reforms, you now have at least a fighting chance of finding an address on your own with the aid of a relatively simple map. But he received much more criticism for his efforts than praise. Only as new generations grow up with the more rational system will it be fully appreciated, but its origins will by then be forgotten.

Most of Saburo's public service during these years was limited to Japan, but a number of his endeavors had international aspects. As we have seen, he first became interested in international understanding through the IPR, and he managed to get permission from the occupation authorities to attend the eleventh conference in India in 1950. But after his retirement he found a more important vehicle for internationalism in the Rotary movement. A Tokyo chapter had been established in 1924, but it had been suppressed by the militarists as representing foreign influences, though the members continued to meet secretly under the name of the "Wednesday Club." It was revived after the war, and Saburo became a member in 1950. When the annual convention of Rotary International was held in Tokyo in 1961, Saburo was put in charge of all arrangements.

This was the first time Rotary had met anywhere in East Asia, and it was the largest international conference Japanese had as yet hosted. Some 24,000 members attended, and many stayed on to tour

Japan. Saburo got the Japanese government to take the unprecedented step of waiving visas for all delegates, persuaded the governor of Tokyo to provide special traffic controls for the convention, and arranged for simultaneous translation in Japanese and English of convention proceedings through a shortwave closed-circuit system, which was still something of a novelty at the time. Through a vigorous publicity campaign he educated Japanese about Rotary and its ideal of volunteer service. Rotary was not well known to most Japanese, and the word was associated more with traffic circles than with international relations. The Tokyo convention proved to be a great success, and Rotary as a result became an organization of much greater prestige and influence throughout Japan than it ever was in the United States. Rotary clubs were formed almost everywhere in the country, and the Japanese gained a great deal of experience hosting international get-togethers, which paid off handsomely in the Tokyo Olympics of 1964. Saburo continued his work as an enthusiastic Rotarian and was for some years the governor of the district that includes Tokyo and some neighboring prefectures as well as distant Okinawa.

Mountain climbing remained one of Saburo's great loves. My grandfather had never approved of this activity and contemptuously remarked, "Mountain climbing does no good for the nation." But it did pay off internationally when the first Japanese-American cabinet-level economic conference was held in Japan in 1961, while my husband was American ambassador in Tokyo. Stewart Udall, secretary of the interior, expressed a desire to climb Mount Fuji, and Saburo as the president and one of the founding members of the Japan Alpine Club undertook at age sixty-two to serve as his companion and guide. He was accustomed to climbing the mountain annually, sometimes several times in a single year, and the group of family members and their friends who usually accompanied him were facetiously known as "Mr. Matsukata's Mount Fuji School." The official climbing season terminated at the end of August, but he and Udall had no trouble climbing the snow-covered 12,368-foot peak on November 5th. They were accompanied by two marines from the embassy, American secret-service men, and more than thirty Japanese reporters; Udall held a press interview on top of the mountain.

The ascent of Mount Everest had always been the dream of the Japan Alpine Club, and preparations were started in 1964 under

Saburo's leadership. The Nepalese government, however, banned climbing from 1965 to 1968 and did not give the Japanese permission until the spring of 1970. By then Saburo was seventy, but he led the expedition of thirty-nine persons to the base camp at 17,200 feet, and some of his associates went on to the summit. The next year Saburo received international recognition as an alpinist when he was made an honorary member of the British Alpine Club.

Work for the Boy Scouts was one of Saburo's last major international undertakings. He had been introduced to the movement as a boy in 1910 by General Nogi, but the organization was formally founded in Japan only in 1922 and as an international organization came under the cloud of rising militarism. Plans to hold a world jamboree in Japan in 1971 induced local leaders of the movement to seek Saburo's aid, which he readily gave in his typical fashion. He attended the world conference of the Boy Scout movement held in Helsinki in 1969. Here his name was suggested for the twelve-man world committee. Doubts about having a seventy-year-old member were dispelled by his youthful appearance and demeanor, and he became a most active figure in world scouting and the chairman of the organizing committee for the 1971 jamboree.

The jamboree was held in August on the broad skirts of Mount Fuji, with 25,000 scouts, 13,000 of them from abroad, in attendance and housed in a city of tents. In connection with the jamboree, Saburo participated in his last mountain-climbing venture when he led a large group of foreign scouts to the top of Fuji. The jamboree started well on August 2, but two days later a typhoon struck, flooding out the tents and endangering the scouts. Under Saburo's direction, the emergency was handled with no accidents, the scouts were evacuated, the tent city put up again when the storm passed, and the schedule resumed as if nothing had gone wrong. But Saburo had done too much. At the end of the closing ceremony he suddenly collapsed into a coma. He survived the crisis and was immediately voted the highest Boy Scout award, the Bronze Wolf, which he refused at the time but did accept in 1972 at a ceremony in the presence of the emperor and empress marking the fiftieth anniversary of the founding of the Boy Scouts in Japan. Saburo, however, never fully recovered his health and died the next year at the age of seventy-four.

Saburo in my eyes was an example of a new generation of Japanese, well prepared to build the middle-class society postwar Japan has become. He was no nation builder like his real father and no self-conscious, proud aristocrat or great entrepreneur like Kojiro and his other brothers. He felt himself to be one of the people, following the intellectual vogues of his youth, serving as a regular jobholder during his career, and contributing to the best of his abilities to the betterment of Japan and the world. He was as democratic and unassuming a man as I have ever known, and to me he typified all that is best in the egalitarian society of contemporary Japan.

Matsumoto Shigeharu

Saburo's life was closely paralleled by that of Matsumoto Shigeharu, his nephew by birth and his cousin by law. Born on October 2, 1899, just two months after Saburo, Shigeharu was like him a typical product of Taisho Democracy and a member of that generation which imbibed democratic, international ideals in their youth, struggled unhappily through the years of resurgent Japanese imperialism in midlife, and survived World War II to work again for international order and world understanding.

Shigeharu's mother was Matsukata's fourth daughter, Mitsuko. A very beautiful and dignified lady, she was particularly close to my branch of the family because she and my father had been born of the same concubine mother. He was her favorite younger brother, whom she cared for after a childhood case of typhoid fever. Shigeharu became further linked with the Matsukata family when he married Kojiro's daughter Hanako.

Shigeharu's own Matsumoto family was descended from an extraordinary man named Matsumoto Jutaro, who in age and historical role belonged to the generation of my two grandfathers. Originally called Kamezo, he was born in 1844, the second of four sons of Matsuoka Kameemon. The Matsuokas were peasants in Taiza, a mixed fishing-farming village on the Japan Sea in the province of Tango, now a part of Kyoto prefecture. Kamezo as a younger son had no prospects for any inheritance, and his father urged him to study hard at arithmetic and reading with the local schoolteacher, the village Zen priest, so that he could make his own way in life. At the age of ten he went to

Kyoto and became an apprenticed errand boy in a drapery store called Hishi-ya, which was owned by a friend of his father's. Kyoto was a center of fine silk weaving, but Kamezo soon realized that nearby Osaka was the hub of industry and trade for the Kansai area and that an ambitious man would have more chance there of succeeding in business. He moved to Osaka, finding a position as an errand boy in a store called Watari, which at the time ranked with the now world-famous Mitsui Company and the great department-store chain of Daimaru.

It took decades of hard work to rise in the old apprentice system from errand boy through sales clerk to full-fledged clerk, and few succeeded in going beyond this level to become independent store-owners. But the opening of Japan to foreign trade in 1860 brought turmoil to the old system and opportunities to those who dared seize them. In 1871, Kamezo who by then was a clerk, cut himself off from his old ties and went into business for himself. To emphasize the break, he adopted a new name, Matsumoto Jutaro.

In his new life Jutaro went almost daily to Sakai, a port city on the southern outskirts of Osaka, where Western merchants sold their goods. There he would buy imported cotton fabrics, which he would peddle around the countryside. He also acted as broker for some Chinese merchants. After acquiring some capital, he was able to borrow enough money to open his own shop, which he stocked with imported woolen goods. On the side he engaged in a dubious practice known as "70 percent for the daimyo" (*daimyo no shichi kake*). According to this system, a daimyo would be stocked with goods worth 70 percent of the money he was borrowing and then was expected to sell these at a high enough price to cover his whole loan and perhaps make a small profit. Since daimyo were notoriously inept in matters of trade and some of the merchants dishonest in supplying their 70 percent worth of goods, the profits for the merchants could be big and the financial results for the daimyo disastrous.

When the new government decreed in the summer of 1871 that the samurai cut off their topknots, Matsumoto Jutaro realized that there would be a lot of cold heads that winter and a corresponding demand for wool caps and scarfs. So he took a ship bound for Nagasaki, then the center of Western trade, to try to corner the market on woolen headgear. To his surprise, he found a dozen or more merchants on board with the same idea in mind. To avoid competition that would drive up prices, he got the others to cooperate with him in buying up the supply of woolen headgear surreptitiously at normal prices and then dividing the stock acquired evenly among them. The scheme worked, and Jutaro sold his entire stock at a handsome profit to clamoring customers. One glimpses in this incident the budding commercial skills with which the Japanese would one day astound the world.

Jutaro attempted another such coup in 1874, when a military expedition was sent to Taiwan to chastise the natives for having killed some mariners from Okinawa, which Japan claimed. He bought up all the woolen blankets he could find in the Osaka area and took them to the army supply department in Yokohama for use by the soldiers, but he found that his purchases did not measure up to army standards. Only through good luck was he able to dispose of the blankets to Western merchants. But he was more successful during the Satsuma Rebellion of 1877. Realizing that the government soldiers would require spare uniforms, he bought up all the woolen textiles he could find in the Osaka area and sold them later at a good price to the government.

After the rebellion Jutaro began to branch out into new fields. During the banking boom of the late 1870s, Jutaro founded his own 130th National Bank with 25,000 yen in capital from the two former daimyo of Miyazu and Fukuchiyama in his native area. Later he absorbed the 136th National Bank and three other banks, which together with the 130th Bank, were jointly capitalized at 2,850,000 yen. At the time, Japan was burdened with a heavily unfavorable foreign trade balance, and Jutaro threw himself into attempting to cut imports by manufacturing substitute domestic products. He supported Shibusawa Eiichi in his successful development of the modernized Osaka Spinning Mill in the early 1880s. This mill was followed by a flood of large-scale mechanized spinning plants, which sharply reduced Japan's dependence on imported cotton thread and textiles. Jutaro also founded the Asahi Beer Company and the Japan Sugar Company (Nihon Seito Kaisha), which helped reduce imports in these two products.

Jutaro's greatest industrial undertaking, however, was in an entirely different field. The government had built two short railway lines from Tokyo to Yokohama in 1872 and from Kyoto to Osaka in 1877, and Jutaro added another short line in 1885, from Osaka to Sakai. Extended to Wakayama in 1901, this became the Nankai Railway. He also participated in the construction of the Sanyo railway from Osaka down the Inland Sea to the western tip of Honshu at Shimonoseki, with the innovation of sleeping and dining cars.

Jutaro did not confine his attention to the world of business and took an active interest in education as well, founding kindergartens, building school dormitories, and helping to expand Kansai Law School into Kansai University, which included a faculty of economics and commerce. He also took an active role in developing the *Osaka Mainichi Shimbun,* the predecessor of the *Mainichi Shimbun,* one of Japan's three leading newspapers. In these various ways he became one of the most prosperous entrepreneurs of the whole Kansai area, second in wealth in that part of Japan only to the Sumitomo, one of the four great zaibatsu families of modern Japan. He was sometimes even called "the Shibusawa of the Kansai," which was a flattering comparison to the greatest of all entrepreneurs of the Meiji period.

Matsukata as the longtime finance minister and Jutaro as a leading businessman naturally became acquainted and, as we have seen, Jutaro, lacking children of his own, adopted Matsukata's ninth son, Torakichi. For reasons that are not clear, however, Jutaro did not make Torakichi his heir, adopting for this purpose a youth of seventeen named Inoue Matsuzo, the son of a banker. He sent Matsuzo to the United States, where he remained for eleven years, studying typing and bookkeeping in Poughkeepsie, New York, and then going through Brown University in Providence, Rhode Island. Because of Jutaro's connection with the Matsukata family, Matsuzo came under the charge of the Arai family while in the United States. Immediately after his return to Japan, he married Matsukata's fourth daughter, strengthening the bonds between the two families. Matsukata also persuaded Jutaro to lend him his political support by running for the Diet in the election of February 1892, during Matsukata's first term as prime minister. Jutaro was elected and occupied his seat for one term, until the election of March 1894.

Jutaro made Matsuzo the president of his spinning companies, but the industry was hard hit by the loss of the Chinese market during the Russo-Japanese War. Several companies failed, and the 130th

Bank was forced to close its doors for three weeks. Eventually the bank, because of its importance to industry in the Kansai area, was saved by the Bank of Japan, but Jutaro took full responsibility for its troubles, giving up his personal assets and retiring from his many positions in the business world. He continued to be a highly respected man, however, until his death in 1913, when he was given an elaborate funeral.

Matsuzo gradually recouped the family's fortunes, serving for many years as the managing director of the Kyushu Electric Railway Company (Kyushu Denki Kido Kaisha). He spent most of his time in Kyushu, becoming estranged from his Matsukata wife, Mitsuko, for whom he built a home in her native Tokyo. He lost most of his fortune a second time in the bank crisis of 1927 and, after a prolonged illness, died in Kobe in 1936. A purse found under the mattress of his bed, containing 12.50 yen, was the only inheritance Shigeharu received from him.

———— • ————

Shigeharu lived with his mother in Kobe while he attended primary and middle school. At his father's insistence, he took extra classes in the Chinese classics and in English. After he graduated from middle school, he, his mother, and sister moved to Tokyo, where he attended the prestigious First Higher School (Ichiko). It was at this time that he became a close friend of Saburo and came under the influence of the same men and ideas that played such key roles in Saburo's life. Uchimura Kanzo and Nitobe Inazo in particular loomed large. It is not surprising that the two cousins of almost identical age both drifted into the field of journalism and became lifelong advocates of internationalism.

After graduating from the First Higher School, Shigeharu entered the law faculty of Tokyo Imperial University. Here his most memorable professor was Takayanagi Kenzo, an authority on Anglo-American law, who delivered all his lectures in English. After graduating in 1923, Shigeharu continued as a graduate student, but a few months later the great Kanto earthquake struck, destroying much of Tokyo, including Shigeharu's library of law books, and closing down the law school for a while. Unable to continue his law studies in Japan, Shigeharu decided to go to the United States. Kuroki Sanji introduced him to a young professor we have already met, Takagi Yasaka, who had just returned to Japan from study abroad, and Takagi gave Shigeharu several letters of introduction, including one to Professor Irving Fisher of Yale. Shigeharu attended Fisher's lectures and those of Professor Clive Day, under whom he wrote a thesis on Josiah Child, the seventeenth-century mercantilist. His writing was so good that Day praised it as being superior to that of the American students, though his spoken English of course was far inferior. Shigeharu's explanation of this phenomenon was that he had spent an hour each morning reading Macaulay's *History of England* and had tried to emulate its style.

At Yale Shigeharu became acquainted with a Japanese professor of European medieval history, Asakawa Kanichi. Asakawa, who taught Shigeharu a great deal about American life and Japanese-American relations, was a pioneer in the field of Japanese studies in the United States, producing detailed scholarly studies of Japanese feudalism which were to be much admired by later generations. A highlight of Shigeharu's stay in the United States was the relationship he developed with Charles A. Beard, the well-known historian. Beard took an interest in Shigeharu and invited him to move from Yale to the New School for Social Research in New York, which Beard was running with John Dewey. Shigeharu, though flattered, declined, but he never forgot Beard's insistence, as he later recorded it, that whether a country was large or small the politics of any nation was controlled by a handful of men. In later life Shigeharu seems to have acted in conformity with this dictum, seeking out the elite leaders.

Stimulated by Beard's interest in labor, Shigeharu spent the summer of 1924 studying labor problems at the University of Wisconsin and visiting more than forty factories. He made a point of meeting workers and lunching with them. In a steel plant in Gary, Indiana, the ethnic diversity of the United States was brought home to him when he observed that all notices were written in seven languages: English, German, French, Russian, Serbian, Polish, and Rumanian. He also noted that most of the hard and dirty labor was performed by blacks.

Shortly after Shigeharu arrived at Yale, his father wrote him a letter, advising him to do his best to make friends among Chinese students. (Shigeharu remembers this as being one of the two letters he received from his father during his whole life.) At the time there were hundreds of Chinese students in the United States, at least seventy or eighty at Yale alone, paid for by the Indemnity Fund for the Boxer Uprising in North China in 1898–1900, which the United States had returned to China for educational purposes. Making friends with the Chinese students was not easy because the Twenty-One Demands Japan had forced on China in 1915 had made the Japanese the most hated imperialists in China and the greatest threat to nascent Chinese nationalism. But Shigeharu persevered by various acts of kindness, and he and the Chinese found it easier to talk with each other than with Americans. He eventually made a number of lifelong friends among the Chinese students at Yale, and he was most gratified when they celebrated his birthday with a dinner at a Chinese restaurant.

In the spring of 1925 Shigeharu was asked by the magazine *The Nation* to write an article on the Japanese labor movement. He was delighted to find himself in print and to see his article featured in large letters on the cover of the magazine. He was also surprised to see how much of an impact it seemed to have. The experience inspired him to consider making international journalism his career. The same issue of *The Nation* happened to have an article by Beard on Japanese-American relations, which were in turmoil because of the passage in 1924 of the Exclusion Act, barring Japanese immigrants from the United States in the same way other Asians had already been excluded. The main point Beard made was that the central issue in Japanese-American relations was a conflict of commercial interests in China. This concept, which had some validity at the time, was to loom large in Matsumoto's thinking during most of his life.

In the autumn of 1925 Shigeharu cut short his stay in the United States in order to go to England. He had received word that Kojiro's daughter Hanako had been in London too long and was becoming overly anglicized. Ever since childhood he had hoped to marry Hanako. She was his cousin, though they shared only one common grandparent and, in any case, marriages between cousins of different surnames were not frowned on in Japan. Hanako had been sent to London to study piano and became a piano teacher. What Shigeharu did to counteract her anglicization is not clear. He himself failed in his effort to enter All Souls College at Oxford and spent most of his time traveling around Europe and studying on his own. This continued until the summer of 1927, when the bank crisis in Japan induced

Kojiro to cable Shigeharu to return with Hanako to Japan at once. Immediately on their arrival home, they were married in a small family wedding.

Shigeharu wanted at this time to get started on a career in international journalism but was persuaded to wait a few years in order to gain more experience. Instead he accepted a position as the assistant to Takagi Yasaka, who taught American constitutional law and political history at Tokyo Imperial University, and he also lectured on American politics at Chuo and Nihon universities and at Nihon Women's University.

In the fall of 1929, as we have seen, Shigeharu served with Saburo as an assistant to the Japanese delegation at the third IPR conference in Kyoto. A corresponding position in the American delegation was held by John D. Rockefeller III, who had just graduated from Princeton and was later to play an important role in Shigeharu's life. A fourth IPR conference was scheduled for 1931 in Hangchow in China, but the Manchurian Incident made the Chinese delegates unwilling to attend if the Japanese were there. Jerome Greene, who was the chairman of the international committee, finally worked out a compromise for an informal meeting of the several national committees for the presentation of reports but without any discussion of the situation in Manchuria. The meeting was held in Shanghai, which despite its foreign control seethed with anti-Japanese sentiments. Shigeharu attended the meeting as the youngest of the Japanese delegates and was selected to speak at the closing session as the representative of the younger group. This was his maiden speech before an international audience, but he did well in championing the value of meetings like those of the IPR for the expression of various national interests and the achievement of international understanding. At this meeting he also made useful new friends, such as Hsu Hsin-liu, later an important adviser to Chiang Kai-shek, and Christopher Chancellor, director of the Far Eastern Bureau of Reuters.

Much to the distress of those Japanese who opposed Japanese military expansionism and valued the friendship of the United States, the Manchurian Incident created mounting criticism of Japan in America. Nitobe became convinced that something should be done to counter this rising anti-Japanese feeling, and he and others had proposed that Shigeharu go as a lecturer to the University of California for this purpose. When the plan was vetoed by the university trustees because of the Manchurian invasion, Nitobe decided to go himself on a speaking tour of the United States, breaking the vow he had made that he would not visit America again until the infamous Exclusion Act was rescinded.

On the way back from Yokohama after seeing Nitobe off, Shigeharu was approached by Iwanaga Yukichi, whom we have already encountered in the account of Saburo's life, and was invited by Iwanaga to become the bureau chief in Shanghai of the Shimbun Rengo Sha he was building up. Iwanaga pointed out that there was so much anti-Japanese feeling among Chinese and Westerners in China that the Japanese government authorities and private citizens found it very difficult to make contacts, and he stressed the importance of having a news agency in China that could present the Japanese point of view. Shigeharu accepted the offer, happy to be embarked at last on a career as an international journalist and stationed in a place where he could work for better relations with China.

Shigeharu was in Shanghai from 1932 to 1938, living in the Japanese Concession with Hanako and their three children (one of them was born there). The International Settlement and French Concession, which included the core of the city and its best residential districts, made Shanghai an island of peace in a China torn by war, revolution, and political intrigue. It was a place where Chinese of all stripes could hide and plot in safety and where people from all over China and the world could meet. In other words, it was an ideal place for collecting news. Shigeharu was appalled by the depth of the anti-Japanese sentiment in Shanghai, but he set about learning the operations of the Rengo Agency and making contacts among the Chinese and Westerners.

The Rengo offices, which were located in the Japanese Concession had several secret wireless and telegraph machines, which were actually illegal but had the tacit approval of the local authorities. This permitted the office to receive secretly a steady flow of news from Japan and transmit its information abroad in Japanese, Chinese, and English without censorship. Shigeharu left day-to-day reporting to his staff and concentrated on making contacts with influential or knowledgeable people. He visited the information section of the Japanese embassy twice each day and eventually built up such trust that the

Japanese officials began to show him confidential diplomatic messages. He also developed contacts with many Chinese, some of whom had attended the 1931 IPR conference with him and were influential in the Chinese government. Many of the older Chinese leaders had been educated in Japan and retained a certain degree of friendship for Japan. Shigeharu did not overlook making contacts with Westerners and developed good relations with both Chinese and Westerners by providing them with good information.

Among Westerners the British dominated the scene. Through Chancellor of Reuters, whom Shigeharu had met at the IPR conference, he was able to make useful contacts with the British community, and he eventually was accepted as a member of the exclusive Shanghai Club, made up largely of Britishers, with only a few American, French, and German members and one other Japanese, the managing director of the Federation of Chinese Spinning Companies. To meet more non-British Europeans, he became a member of the French Club, and to meet Americans he joined the local Rotary Club, which included Chinese as well as Americans. Naturally he established close contacts with his fellow newsmen, including even the Russian representative of Tass, though he noted that he could get no information from him. He also developed relations with the diplomatic community, especially the British and, after the Anti-Comintern Pact of 1936, with the Germans and Italians.

Shigeharu's wide contacts and secret transmitting devices led him to a big scoop. In December 1936 he learned from some Chinese friends of the kidnapping of Chiang Kai-shek in North China by the son of the former warlord of Manchuria, and he was able to get the story out to Japan through his own channels. All the other newsmen were frustrated by a Chinese government clampdown on the news, but the correspondent of the *New York Times* came to Shigeharu to ask for aid. Shigeharu obliged, and the *Times* in turn got a big scoop in the United States, though the story had to be transmitted out of China in Japanese and by way of Tokyo.

———•———

The Manchurian Incident had been followed by six years of small but steady Japanese military encroachments in North China, and these smouldering hostilities flared up in all-out warfare in July 1937, when a skirmish near Peking, the Marco Polo Bridge Incident, proved uncontrollable by the local Chinese and Japanese authorities. In August the fighting spread to Shanghai, and my future husband's older brother, a young professor from Princeton, was one of the two American casualties of bombs from Chinese planes. When Chinese refugees started streaming into Shanghai by the thousands, a French priest named Father Jacquino endeavored to create a safety zone for them. Through the correspondent of the *Manchester Guardian,* he approached Shigeharu in an effort to gain Japanese cooperation. Shigeharu brought the matter to the attention of the Japanese embassy, which was able to win the cooperation of the Japanese army, provided all Chinese entering the zone would be disarmed. Through the establishment of this safety zone, it is estimated that the lives of some 250,000 Chinese refugees may have been saved.

Upon the outbreak of the Sino-Japanese War, all of Shigeharu's Chinese friends broke off contact with him, but in September a British friend arranged a dinner meeting for Shigeharu with Hsu Hsin-liu, who had been chairman of the Chinese delegation at the 1931 IPR conference and, as a member of the National Defense Planning Committee, was high in the councils of the Nationalist government. Hsu wished to keep communications open with the Japanese through regular meetings with Shigeharu, though he insisted that these meetings should take place in complete secrecy. For a while the two met in the apartment of their mutual British friend and then later at the home of the American military attaché. In time, Hsu broke with Chiang Kai-shek and became a member of the group seeking peaceful accommodation with the Japanese.

On December 13 the Japanese army captured Nanking, then the capital of China, and the soldiers were permitted such an orgy of pillage and atrocities that the fall of the city became known in the West as the "rape of Nanking." Shigeharu attended the subsequent formal ceremonies marking the capture of Nanking and was moved when, at the end of the regular ceremony, General Matsui, commander of the Japanese forces in China, rose from his seat and delivered a blistering condemnation of the conduct of the Japanese soldiers in Nanking. He said it besmirched the honor of the emperor and nation and, with anger in his voice and tears in his eyes, commanded that henceforth all Japanese troops abide by the rules of war and not harm innocent civilians. Shigeharu was eager to get this speech out to the rest of the world, where it might help to lessen Japan's shame. He won the support of the public relations officer at the Japanese embassy, but the army authorities refused. The public affairs officer continued to back Shigeharu, who after he got back to Shanghai did send out the story of Matsui's impromptu speech on his secret communication channel, and it was published in some Western papers, though not in Japan.

The Chinese Nationalist government had always been divided into factions, and some of the leaders, appalled by the suffering caused by Chiang Kai-shek's "scorched earth" policy, began seeking a speedy compromise to end the war. One of these men was Tung Tao-ning, the chief of the Japan section in the Asia bureau of the foreign ministry, and a former student at the Japanese military academy. Since Tung had learned through Nishi, the chief of the Nanking branch of the Japanese South Manchurian Railway, that there were certain officers on the general staff who were known to favor a compromise settlement, he went secretly to Tokyo to get in touch with them and returned to Shanghai on March 15, 1938 with an encouraging letter from this Japanese group.

In the meantime, Shigeharu had been approached by Kao Tsung-wu, who was Tung's superior in rank. Kao had attended both Kyushu and Tokyo Imperial universities, and he and Shigeharu had become acquainted through one of Shigeharu's Chinese friends from Yale. At the time of the outbreak of the Sino-Japanese War, Kao had been courteous enough to notify Shigeharu formally that he would be breaking off all ties with him. Kao was aware of Tung's initiative, and he and Shigeharu were both encouraged by the message Tung brought back with him. Feeling that Shanghai was somewhat unsafe for the discussions they wished to hold, the three of them, as well as Nishi and another Japanese named Ito, slipped down to Hong Kong on separate ships. For the sake of security, they used code names, selecting the common given names for the first five sons in a Japanese family. Nishi was Taro, Tung was Jiro, Ito was Saburo, Kao was Shiro, and Shigeharu, the youngest, was Goro. The meetings were held in the Repulse Bay Hotel on the far side of Victoria Island from Hong Kong, and Shigeharu found the whole trip, despite its secrecy and code names, a welcome respite from the politically charged atmosphere of Shanghai.

At the first meeting in Hong Kong, Shigeharu asked if any of the top Chinese leaders advocated a compromise settlement of the war, and Kao informed the Japanese that Wang Ching-wei, Chiang Kai-shek's chief rival for leadership of the Nationalist government, did and that another very high official, Chou Fu-hai, leaned in the same direction. During the talks Shigeharu came to realize that the only basis on which a compromise could be worked out would be a ceasefire and a Japanese withdrawal from recently conquered territories, because Chinese nationalism was rising too rapidly to permit anything less. The discussions continued with attempts to outline the details of such a settlement and ended with planning for further efforts at peace.

After the Hong Kong meetings, Kao and Tung returned to the Nationalist government, where the letter from the military group in Japan was simply ignored by Chiang, though Wang Ching-wei learned from it what the Japanese position for a negotiated peace might be. Shigeharu himself got in touch with a group of civilians in Japan favoring peace, including Inukai Ken, a prominent politician and the father of Otohiko's and my friend, the writer Inukai Michiko.

In July Shigeharu learned that, if he approved, Kao planned to visit Japan secretly to establish contact with the group favoring peace. On the night Kao was to sail, he appeared at Shigeharu's apartment, seeking aid in avoiding detection by the Japanese military and police guarding the approaches to the ship. Shigeharu put his own Domei badge and cap on Kao (the change in name from Rengo to Domei had taken place in 1936), and at the checkpoint he stuck his head out of the window of the Domei car, shouting loudly "Matsumoto of Domei News Agency." Shigeharu followed Kao to Japan on another ship and introduced him to Inukai Ken, who thenceforth became the chief figure in the peace movement. Planning continued both in China and Japan, and in December 1938 Wang Ching-wei fled from Nationalist China to Hanoi in French Indochina, where he met with Inukai. Finally in June 1939 Wang came to Japan and in March 1940 became the head of a puppet Chinese government in Nanking, dedicated to making peace with Japan.

The height of Shigeharu's participation in the Sino-Japanese peace movement was between July and September 1938. He had the ear of Prince Konoe Fumimaro, the prime minister, and his advisers and was close to Inukai Ken. In September, however, he came down with a severe case of typhoid fever and was critically ill until December, when he was at last sufficiently recovered to return to Japan. It was at this time that Saburo was moved down from North China to replace him as the head of Domei in Shanghai. Thereafter Shigeharu played only a minor role in the Sino-Japanese peace movement. When Kao called on him at the hospital, Shigeharu was able to warn him to get out of Japan at once because the Japanese military was deeply suspicious of him. Kao fled the next morning and after much wandering ended up in Washington, where after the war he would introduce Shigeharu to his friends as "the man who saved my life."

The peace movement was doomed to failure from the start because there was too wide a gap between Chinese nationalism and Japanese militarism. But Shigeharu sincerely believed in the possibility of accommodation, and it was the greatest disappointment of his life that his strenuous efforts proved fruitless. He did remain influential, however, in the group trying to maintain peace with the United States. Matsuoka Yosuke, who was foreign minister from July 1940 to July 1941, tried to persuade Shigeharu to go to Washington as ambassodor, but Shigeharu refused, realizing that Matsuoka and the whole cabinet were too intransigent to agree to a settlement in China acceptable to the United States. He had become editor-in-chief of Domei after his return to Tokyo in December 1939 and, though he stepped down to the position of managing editor in 1943 because of an attack of pleurisy, he remained with Domei throughout the war.

———— • ————

After the Japanese surrender in 1945, Shigeharu discovered that several of his old IPR friends were members of the headquarters staff of the army of occupation, and he reestablished contact with them. Some of them, however, became suspect to MacArthur and his top staff, who considered them too left-wing and started shipping them back to America. Shigeharu's American friends warned him to be on his guard and, when he gave a farewell party for one of the group, Arthur Bisson, who was decidedly leftist in his sympathies, the occupation authorities reprimanded him severely. As a result, despite his long

The Matsukata and Arai grandparents together at Nasuno, 1915

*Haru (right) with parents, sister Naka, and Matsukata grandfather
at Kamakura, 1918*

Three Matsukata brothers, Brussels, 1889: left to right, Kojiro, Iwao, Masao

Sketch of Matsukata Kojiro, c. 1917, by Sir Frank Brangwyn. National Museum of Western Art, Tokyo

Matsumoto Shigeharu (left) and Ushiba Tomohiko, 1957

Matsukata Otohiko, Shanghai

In Monet's garden at Giverny, 1921: Kuroki Takeko, the Monet family, and President Clemenceau

Kishiwada Castle, the Okabe domain (family of Haru's Aunt Mitsu)

The family of Viscount Okabe Nagamoto, off to a celebration for the emperor, 1912. Nagakage and Mitsu at far right

Four generations, 1917: Miyo with Naka and Haru (on lap),
Grandmother Tazu, Great-grandmother Michi

Top: *Haru (far left) with some relatives, c. 1918. Naka third from left, Nobuhiko Ushiba fourth from left*
Center: *With the Saionji family in front of the Kamakura house, c. 1919. Koichi at far left next to Naka, Haru at far right*
Bottom: *Shokuma and Miyo with all their children in Tokyo, 1926*

Secretaries at Yosemite conference of the Institute of Pacific Relations, 1936. Left to right: Saionji Koichi, Naka, Haru, Konoye Fumitaka

Haru with American occupation officers, Tokyo, 1947

Haru and Ed Reischauer in San Francisco, 1969

Ushiba Nobuhiko (Nobu) with Ed, at Tane's Nishimachi International School, Tokyo

Matsukatas gather at the American Embassy in Tokyo, 1966. Next to the Ambassador are Haru's parents; next to Haru is Yoshisuke, Matsukata's eighth son; Saburo, the eleventh son, is at far right, in white jacket; Matsumoto Shigeharu stands next to him

and close relations with the United States, Shigeharu had little contact with the American occupation.

When Furuno dissolved Domei in October 1945 and replaced it with the Kyodo News Agency, Shigeharu left the organization and founded a small newspaper *Mimpo* (The People's News). He wished it to be an organ that, in the new spirit of democracy, would express popular thinking at a time when party politicians and bureaucrats alike were meekly swallowing all that the occupation told them. He believed that Japan should make a clean sweep of the old order, but he saw no need for Japanese to accept with servility everything the Americans said. At first *Mimpo,* with a circulation of only 10,000 to 15,000, had the blessing of the occupation, but, as Shigeharu began to publish his independent views, it fell into disfavor. He was sharply reproved even for stating that the term "army of occupation" was not being translated correctly by the word *shinchugun,* which might more strictly be rendered "expeditionary force." He was repeatedly lectured for being onesided and not "playing ball."

Mimpo did not last long because of these pressures from the Americans and more specifically because Shigeharu himself was "purged" in the spring of 1946, having been a high Japanese functionary in an area of conquest. This meant that he could occupy no position in government or in public life. Until he was removed from the purge list in 1951, he concentrated on more academic activities, establishing with his former mentor, Takagi Yasaka, the Association of American Studies. The two felt strongly that the war had been caused by shocking ignorance on both sides and that there was a great need to educate the Japanese public about the United States. Together with some other scholars, they published a six-volume documentary history of the United States, which appeared between 1950 and 1958. In order to support himself and his family during this difficult period of food shortages and skyrocketing inflation, Shigeharu practiced law on the side.

In April 1948 Takagi was asked by the American journal *Foreign Affairs* to contribute an article on the future of Japan. He emphasized the importance of education and religion, being himself a sincere Quaker, but at Shigeharu's suggestion he also mentioned that the occupation should not last too long, since it would in time give rise to anti-American sentiments. This was the first article published in

America after the war by any Japanese, and great attention was paid to Takagi's point about the duration of the occupation. MacArthur too had originally favored a short occupation, but the American authorities decided that Takagi's views showed him to be a critic of the occupation and inclined toward communism. In actuality, he was a committed supporter of democracy and a true friend of America. Shigeharu apologized profusely for his advice, which had caused all the trouble, but Takagi made light of it.

In the spring of 1951 John Foster Dulles came to Japan to discuss the impending peace treaty with Japan, and John D. Rockefeller III accompanied him as his adviser on cultural affairs. Shigeharu and Rockefeller renewed their acquaintance started at the IPR conference in 1929 and discussed Rockefeller's idea that intellectual exchanges should be set up between Japan and the United States to broaden their contacts, which, since the end of the war, had been almost exclusively in the hands of military men. Rockefeller assured Shigeharu that the necessary funds would be forthcoming if the Japanese showed sufficient public interest and organized their side of an exchange program. The idea for building an International House of Japan also came up.

Shigeharu was delighted with the proposals because it had always been his ideal to develop sound intellectual contacts between Japan and the United States, and he had been much impressed by the Rockefeller-funded International House in New York, where half of the resident students were foreigners and students from all over the world could mix and exchange ideas. He became Rockefeller's chief lieutenant for the project in Japan, and, after long hard work, the new institution, usually known as "I House," was officially dedicated in June 1955. It had a fine location near the center of the city, with a beautiful garden that had belonged to Baron Iwasaki (I attended ballet lessons there as a child).

Even before the International House building was started, Rockefeller and Shigeharu began two programs for "intellectual exchange" and "distinguished visitors." American opinion makers were invited to Japan to increase Japanese knowledge of the United States and arouse American interest in Japan. Among those who participated in the early years were Eleanor Roosevelt, J. Robert Oppenheimer, the theologian Paul Tillich, Harvard sociologist David Riesman, and the diplomat George Kennan. In return distinguished Japanese went to the United States, such as Hasegawa Nyozekan and Ichikawa Fusae, one of the first women in the Diet and a distinguished leader of the suffragette movement. In time the programs were expanded to include two-way exchanges with other countries in Asia, Europe, and the rest of the world.

International House contained a small but convenient hostelry for visiting scholars and, unlike the New York prototype, became a busy meeting place for all sorts of international meetings and an energetic sponsor of intellectual and cultural exchanges of all types. It also developed into a prestigious private meeting place for Japanese and foreign leaders, and its space became much sought after for receptions, large dinner meetings, weddings, and ceremonies. Shigeharu, aided by his wife Hanako, presided over its multitudinous activities, living in a comfortable residence attached to the main building. The role as head of I House suited Shigeharu, embodying all his ideals and hopes for international understanding, and the House lived up to its original purpose "to promote cultural exchanges and international cooperation between the people of Japan and the peoples of America and other countries."

Japan's position in the postwar world made it clear that, just as in the aftermath of the original opening of Japan to the West, it was imperative for Japanese to learn the English language. With Rockefeller's strong support and the cooperation of some of his friends, including my future husband, Shigeharu founded the English Language Education Council, generally known as ELEC, which introduced new methods for teaching spoken English. At first the new organization had difficulties with the ministry of education, which was devoted to grammatical analysis and the reading of classical English, but these prejudices were gradually overcome and ELEC came to exercise considerable influence in what grew into a veritable explosion of English instruction.

Shigeharu sponsored a large program of translating American books and articles into Japanese, including the works of Charles and Mary Beard, and the speeches of the many foreign leaders his programs brought to Japan. International House also built up a library on Japan in foreign languages, coming in time to have quite a respectable working collection. Shigeharu's activities brought him in touch with great numbers of distinguished visitors from other countries, and he himself wrote extensively and made frequent trips abroad, going not just to the United States and Europe but to the USSR and China. He received several honorary degrees from American universities and was invited to Rutgers for its centennial celebration of the first coming of Japanese students to the university. For this occasion he brought with him the fiftieth-year class badge of his uncle Kojiro. When in 1982 International House celebrated its own thirtieth anniversary with a series of meetings, it was already well established as Japan's leading organ of intellectual and cultural contact with the outside world, and Shigeharu still reigned supreme as its founder and elder statesman, completing in old age a task he had set himself in his youth.

Arai Relatives

In addition to Shigeharu and Saburo, Matsukata's grandchildren included many other interesting people whose lives illustrate the continuing evolution of Japan. My own family is a good case in point. As I mentioned, my next youngest sister, Tane, founded and operated the Nishimachi International School, which became an important feature of Tokyo's growing international society and an educational trailblazer. My brother Makoto, commonly called Mako, during an unusually varied career introduced American styles of ready-made dresses and numbered dress sizes to Japan at a time when the vast majority of Japanese women were shifting from Japanese to Western styles of clothing. The jewelry designs made by my sister Miye in her Janiye atelier in Boston won wide acclaim as "wearable sculpture." My youngest sister, Mari Bruck, attained her childhood ambition of becoming one of the few designated lecturers of the Christian Science Church and still makes tours in this capacity throughout the United States and the world. Even I might be included because of my own modest career as a journalist and writer and my role as the wife of the American ambassador to Japan. If grandchildren-in-law were to be considered, my husband, Edwin O. Reischauer, would of course stand out prominently for his life work of developing Japanese studies in the United States and his highly praised five and a half years as Ambassador to Tokyo.

Limits must be drawn somewhere, however. The Matsukata family is like a wide-branching oak, growing broader and leafier with each new generation. To add more members of my generation or to tell about the next would greatly overburden this account of the family tree. But there are two families related by marriage to the Arais who should be mentioned, since the lives of some of their members fit in well with those of Shigeharu and Saburo in rounding out the picture of the transition from Taisho Democracy through militarism to contemporary Japan.

Two of Yoneo Arai's brothers-in-law had interesting experiences at the end of World War II. Their father, as we have seen, had been both a boy daimyo and a cabinet minister, and they followed him into government service. The youngest one, Okabe Nagaakira, who was born in 1909, attended the Peers School, graduated from Tokyo Imperial University in 1936, and two years later became an imperial chamberlain, a post reserved for members or relatives of the nobility.

After the outbreak of war with China in 1937, an air-raid shelter was built for the imperial family on what had been a nine-hole golf course in the northern part of the palace grounds. The building was called the Obunko, or honorable library, to conceal from the public the fact that it had seemed advisable to build a shelter for the sacred person of the emperor. After the fall of Saipan in July 1944, when American air raids became heavy, the imperial family moved permanently into the Obunko, which was a small structure intended only for brief occupancy. Aside from the imperial quarters, there was only one crowded room for the chamberlains in attendance and another for the ladies-in-waiting. The Obunko lacked kitchen facilities, and food had to be brought in. The food situation had deteriorated severely, and even the meals of the imperial family were meager. Chamberlains and ladies-in-waiting on the night shift often had only a bit of thin rice gruel and seaweed for breakfast. The fare left Nagaakira so weak that the ten-minute walk between the Obunko and the main offices of the chamberlains in the palace would leave him exhausted. The emperor made this same walk each day to his office in order to save on gasoline.

The chief lady-in-waiting, Mrs. Takaki Tatsuo, was a very close friend of my mother's. She was a member of the immensely wealthy Mitsui family and the daughter-in-law of Takaki Kenkan, the physician we met in the story of my Matsukata grandfather's life. Mrs. Takaki normally told us nothing of what went on at the palace, but, when she visited us in Gumma prefecture in July 1945 to see her daughter and two grandsons we had taken under our wing at our mountain retreat, she revealed the sad conditions in which the emperor and empress were living, cooped up for a whole year in a stuffy, damp, and crowded underground shelter and subsisting on a frugal diet. She also told of her shock to find her proud and titled associates stooping to pilfering each other's food. I remember that we spent an afternoon with Mrs. Takaki, roaming the hills to find wildflowers for her to take back to the emperor and empress, who longed for the garden and flowers they could no longer enjoy.

In the course of the war, the military discovered that a ten-ton bomb had been dropped on Hitler's Bavarian hideaway and immediately started the construction of a very strong shelter fifty feet underground to house the Imperial Headquarters (*Daihonei*), which was the supreme organ of the central government during the war. Nagaakira was concerned that this shelter, though close to the Obunko, still was a dangerous five-minute walk away, and he pointed this fact out to the newly appointed grand chamberlain, when he had the duty of showing the new man around. To his relief, work was started almost at once on a connecting tunnel, which was to prove extremely handy in the last few months of the war, when Tokyo suffered heavy air raids. The Japanese did not know that the American airmen were under strict orders not to bomb any part of the palace grounds, though a stray bomb actually did hit the palace and destroyed it.

On the morning of August 6, 1945, the atom bomb was dropped on Hiroshima but, because of the complete disruption of communications, even the army in Tokyo could learn little about what had happened until President Truman announced the event to the world that night, Tokyo time. The Japanese public remained largely in ignorance. On the afternoon of the seventh, a staff officer of the Konoe (Imperial Guards) Division briefed members of the imperial household ministry about the bomb. Nagaakira was not present, but he learned the news when he returned from the Obunko to the headquarters of the chamberlains for his evening meal. That evening, when the air-raid sirens shrieked, in accordance with instructions he requested the imperial couple to go to the shelter by the connecting underground passageway. The emperor was surprised and asked for an explanation. Although chamberlains are not allowed to discuss outside matters with the emperor, Nagaakira felt forced to say that an extremely powerful bomb had been dropped on Hiroshima. The imperial couple then accompanied him, walking on soaking boards down the tunnel to the shelter, and Nagaakira seated himself on a bench outside the door. The empress called him into the room, where he found the emperor highly indignant that he had not been told before about any special bomb. In a voice strengthened by anger, he ordered Nagaakira, "Inform my aide-de-camp the first thing in the morning that I am very displeased."

It was not until the following evening of the 8th, after a party of army officers had gone to Hiroshima to inspect the devastation, that the emperor was officially informed by the foreign minister. At the same time, a vague statement was released to the public about a new type of bomb that caused "considerable damage." On the same day the Soviet Union entered the war, invading Manchuria, and on the following day, the 9th, a second atom bomb was dropped on Nagasaki. In the next few days events rushed rapidly toward Japan's capitulation. The allied powers, having crushed Germany, had issued on July 26 from the Berlin suburb of Potsdam an ultimatum, the Potsdam Proclamation, calling for Japan's immediate surrender. The Japanese government now replied with a tentative acceptance, provided that this would not prejudice the emperor's position as a "sovereign ruler." The allies came back with a somewhat ambiguous answer. This set the stage on the morning of August 14 for a conference in the imperial presence, which was necessary for any major decision. Normally the emperor said nothing at such meetings, but for the first time in modern history the participants presented him with a split decision, leaving it up to him to decide. Those voting were five military men—the army and navy chiefs of staff, the army and navy ministers, the prime minister, himself a retired admiral—and one civilian, the foreign minister. In the voting, the prime minister and navy minister joined the foreign minister in opting for surrender, which the emperor, prepared by his closest advisers, immediately selected as the course Japan was to follow. It was also decided that the emperor would take the unprecedented step of himself informing his people of the decision, speaking to them directly.

Nagaakira, who was on duty at the Obunko that afternoon was startled by a phone call from the palace guard station nearby that an officer of the Konoe Division had arrived and had asked to see the chamberlain on duty. This was a most irregular procedure, reminiscent of similar acts in the 2–2–6 Incident, the attempted military coup d'état of 1936. Nagaakira stepped outside the Obunko to meet the officer, who told him that the Konoe Division had received word that the emperor was to attend an important meeting and wished to know when he would be going. Nagaakira assured him that he knew nothing of such a meeting but would keep the Konoe informed. Because of the tenseness of the situation, Nagaakira offered to spend the night at the Obunko, though it was not his night to be on duty; it was decided that it would be best to adhere to normal schedules. To reassure himself, however, he bicycled around the moat surrounding the palace grounds before returning to his lodgings, noting nothing unusual except the sound of a single pistol shot in the area of the Konoe barracks.

The next morning, with a lunch of soybean pancakes in his rucksack, Nagaakira returned to the palace to discover that a coup d'état by military extremists had been nipped in the bud during his few hours of absence. Technicians from the Japan Broadcasting Corporation had come to the palace to make a recording of the emperor's message of surrender to his people. Because of the emperor's inexperience in such things, the first disc had been botched, but a second one proved more successful; both were carefully hidden away. A group of rebellious officers and soldiers had gotten wind of plans for the imperial recording and broke into the palace grounds. They killed the chief guard officer, intercepted the retiring radio technicians and searched them thoroughly, and, when they found no recording in their possession, spread out through the palace grounds and ransacked all the buildings. They took the precaution of cutting the telephone connections between the palace area and the outside world but were unaware of a secret line installed by the navy for just such an emergency. Through it, the chief of the Eastern Army Command was informed of what was happening and dispatched loyal troops, who subdued the insurgents and suggested that the leaders should commit suicide, which five of them dutifully did.

Getting the emperor's record to the broadcasting office still presented some hazards. The spoiled disc was placed in a lacquer box decorated with an imperial seal, wrapped in a cloth of purple, and taken ceremoniously to the office of the director general of the imperial household ministry. Nagaakira waited a while to see if all went smoothly and then followed nonchalantly on his bicycle with the good disc in his rucksack together with his lunch. Both discs arrived safely, and at Nagaakira's suggestion the first disc in its gorgeous official container was driven by a palace limousine to the broadcasting office, which had been retaken from insurgent officers earlier that morning. A little while later the usable second disc arrived in a battered old Datsun, and that noon the emperor's own voice announced the end of the war to a thunderstruck nation.

Nagaakira continued in his position of chamberlain until April 1946, when the drastic reduction of the emperor's expenses demanded by the American Occupation forced his resignation. He made his adjustment to the postwar world by becoming a professor at Kyoto University of Foreign Languages (Kyoto Gaigo Daigaku).

My Aunt Mitsu's eldest brother, Okabe Nagakage, had a less dramatic but still unusual transition from prewar to postwar days. Born in 1884, he was the young diplomat my mother had refused to marry. He inherited the family title of viscount and had a successful career in government, ending up as minister of education in Tojo's wartime cabinet. Because of this position, he was designated a war criminal at the end of the war and was incarcerated for twenty-two months in Sugamo Prison. However humiliating the experience may have been, he seems to have taken it philosophically, even light-heartedly. He and his friend Aikawa Yoshisuke, the great Manchurian industrialist and founder of Nissan, had the foresight to enter Sugamo one day ahead of schedule, thereby being able to stake out the best cell available in the prison. Comfortably esconced, Nagakage is said to have enjoyed the ample reading matter and the good food supplied the prisoners by the occupation forces. None of these amenities, after all, was readily available in wartorn Japan. Already in his mid-sixties at the time of his release from prison, Nagakage had no need to find a new postwar career.

———•———

Some members of my Arai grandmother's Ushiba family paralleled the lives of the sons and grandsons of Matsukata more closely than did the Okabes. I have already told of the mixed samurai-merchant background of the Ushibas and of my great-grandfather's success as a businessman in the Meiji period. My grandmother's brother Tetsuro was in business with my Arai grandfather. Tetsuro had four sons, two of whom went to Keio University, as had Tetsuro and his father, and two to Tokyo Imperial University. The two who went to Tokyo typically entered public life, while the two Keio graduates found careers in the private sector. Michio, the second son born in 1902, worked for Mitsubishi, and Daizo, the fourth son born in 1913, became a microbiologist at Keio University Hospital and a distinguished dean of the school of medicine.

The eldest son Tomohiko, born in Kyoto in 1901, was raised with his brother Michio largely by their grandparents in Kobe, where they came to know well their older cousins from America, my mother and uncle, who frequently spent long summer visits there. Tomo, as he was called in the family, went to the First Higher School in Tokyo and, after graduating from Tokyo Imperial University, studied at Oxford from 1925 to 1929, reading for honors in philosophy, politics, and economics. At Oxford he perfected his knowledge of English and also became well acquainted with Saburo and Shigeharu, whose stays in England overlapped with his.

Back in Japan in 1929, Tomo taught at a couple of universities and a progressive school called the Jiyu Gakuen (Freedom School), founded in 1921 by the well-known liberal, Mrs. Hani Motoko, on the basis of Protestant Christianity and Confucianism. Mrs. Hani was famous also as Japan's first woman reporter and the founder of the popular women's magazine *Fujin no Tomo* (The Woman's Companion).

Teaching was not to be Tomo's calling. He found his real career through Iwanaga Yukichi, the same man who had steered Saburo and Shigeharu into journalism. Iwanaga recommended Tomo to Prince Konoe Fumimaro as his private secretary and interpreter during a trip to the United States in 1934, and in 1937 Tomo became Konoe's secretary again, serving as his trusted adviser and confidant for the remainder of the prince's turbulent and tragic life. While on their 1934 trip, Konoe and Tomo came to visit my Arai grandparents and uncle and aunt in Greenwich, since my aunt was a second cousin of the prince through her Maeda mother, and gave him a great deal of help during his trip. I was at my grandparents' at the time and remember a

343

rollicking evening we all spent together at the Rye Beach Amusement Park. The reader may wonder about the identity of the prince's name with that of the Imperial Guards Division. The modern Konoe Division had been named for a similar body of soldiers at the court of the emperors in the eighth and ninth centuries, and the Konoe family name was derived from the hereditary position of command they had held in this earlier elite corps.

Konoe Fumimaro was an enigmatic figure. He was a leading member of the old court nobility, which stood at the apex of the peerage. As such he was deeply devoted to the imperial institution. At the same time, he was a product of Taisho Democracy, permeated with concepts of socialism as well as democracy. As a man of great prestige but of somewhat vacillating convictions and will, he was seen as a convenient figure of compromise in an ideologically divided nation heading into a period of crisis. He was selected prime minister in June 1937, bringing Tomo with him to the center of the political stage. But the outbreak of war with China a month later tied his hands, and, after an ineffectual year and a half in office, he resigned in January 1939.

The situation continued to deteriorate, and war with the United States began to threaten. Konoe was brought back as prime minister a second time in July 1940, Tomo still by his side. He attempted to stabilize the domestic situation by founding the Imperial Rule Assistance Association (Taisei Yokusankai) to absorb the old political parties and form a sort of corporate state, rather than a type of one-party rule, but the effort was stillborn. In foreign relations, he feared that Japan would be strangled by American military or economic pressures if some sort of understanding were not reached with the United States to bring an end to the fighting in China. It was his hope to meet Roosevelt in person in order to work out a compromise.

Negotiating with the American ambassador to Japan, Joseph Grew, became difficult when Matsuoka Yosuke, the foreign minister, returned in April 1941 from a trip to Europe and expressed violent opposition to Konoe's ideas. Matsuoka felt that only he himself could deal adequately with the Americans because of his years as a student in the United States. Grew became annoyed at Matsuoka's high-handed style and sought to talk with Konoe directly. One night around midnight, he secretly sent a messenger to Konoe's house to convey this message. Konoe sent for Tomo the next day and had him arrange a meeting between Konoe and Grew on a golf course. But Tomo had been detected going to the American embassy, and Matsuoka was furious, phoning Konoe that he must not have such clandestine meetings with Grew. In June, Japan's ally, Germany, suddenly invaded the Soviet Union, throwing the Japanese government into confusion and making a fool of Matsuoka, who had just negotiated a nonaggression pact with Russia in April. Already regarded as an arrogant troublemaker, Matsuoka was dropped from the government by the strategem of organizing a new Konoe cabinet without Matsuoka.

During the summer of 1941 Konoe had his personal brain trust, including Tomo and Shigeharu, work on a response to a "draft understanding" sent from Washington in April by Ambassador Nomura Kichisaburo. The Japanese government took this to be an official State Department document, but it actually had been drafted largely by an American Catholic Maryknoll missionary and two Japanese. Naturally nothing ever came of the effort.

Tomo continued to try to maintain contacts with the American embassy and to keep alive the possibility of a Konoe-Roosevelt meeting. One evening in August he was the dinner guest of Herbert Norman, a member of the Canadian legation. Present also was John K. Emmerson, a young officer of the American embassy, who later was to serve as my husband's deputy chief of mission. After dinner Tomo informed Emmerson of Konoe's eagerness to continue meeting with Grew and eventually Roosevelt. He also surprised Emmerson by telling him that the Japanese military had broken the American diplomatic codes, except for the most secret one. His motive for making this surprising revelation was to ensure that the Japanese military would not discover Konoe's plans by reading of them in an inadequately secure message from Grew to Washington. This incident is illustrative of the distrust that existed between the civil and military leaders in Tokyo. No meeting ever did take place between Konoe and Roosevelt. Roosevelt himself was at first favorably inclined, but his advisers persuaded him of the futility of such a conference since it was clearly the Japanese military, not Konoe, that was in control of the nation. By autumn, war with the United States seemed inevitable to the Japanese military leaders, and Konoe was forced to resign in October to make way for the wartime cabinet of General Tojo Hideki.

345

Through his friendship with Shigeharu and Saburo, Tomo earlier had become interested in the IPR and attended the Yosemite conference in 1936 where, as I have mentioned, the junior secretaries of the Japanese delegation were my sister and I together with Konoe's son, Fumitaka, and Saionji Koichi, the grandson of the "last genro." Konoe was interested in Koichi as the scion of another distinguished line of the old court nobility, and this made Tomo interested as well. It occurred to him that it would be useful to have Koichi share the same cabin on the voyage and the same room at the conference with a man called Ozaki Hotsumi, who had been a classmate of Tomo's at the First Higher School and had established a reputation as a China expert because of his service from 1928 to 1932 as the Shanghai correspondent of the *Asahi Shimbun*. Tomo did not know that Ozaki had become a secret Communist while in China, and it is possible that Tomo's putting Ozaki and Koichi together at Yosemite started the young Saionji on the road to Communism.

In Shanghai, Ozaki had acquired his Communism from leftist Japanese and Westerners, among them Richard Sorge (then going by the name of Mr. Johnson), who was a Soviet spy. A year after Ozaki returned to Japan in 1932, Sorge turned up in Tokyo in the guise of a German correspondent for a reputable German publication and set about creating a spy ring. Ozaki, now in the Osaka office of the *Asahi,* agreed to help the ring as an informant. After the inauguration of the first Konoe cabinet in 1937, Ozaki was again assigned to Shanghai but Tomo, valuing Ozaki's expertise on China, persuaded Konoe to employ him instead as a temporary consultant to the cabinet. In this position he came in contact again with Saionji Koichi, who was also a temporary consultant.

Meanwhile Sorge established himself as a trusted and valued confidant of German Ambassador Eugen Ott, who made him the editor of the embassy bulletin issued daily for the German community. In this way Sorge became privy to German secrets, which together with the information supplied by Ozaki made the spy ring a rich source of intelligence for the Soviet Union. Sorge was able to give warning of the German invasion of the Soviet Union of June 1941, pinpointing the exact date, and he gave convincing evidence that the Japanese would not join the attack but would direct their military attention southward. This was one of the greatest spying coups in

World War II, because it allowed the Russians to move a great part of their Far Eastern armies to help stem the German onslaught from the west.

Tomo may have unwittingly helped Ozaki in his spying activities in yet another way. After the formation of the first Konoe cabinet, he organized a weekly Breakfast Club (Asameshi Kai), consisting of Konoe brain-trusters and a number of other representative scholars, writers, politicians, and bureaucrats, including Shigeharu, Saburo, and Inukai Ken. Tomo was joined in the organization of this club by the chief cabinet secretary. The group informally discussed current political problems, and the chief cabinet secretary was supposed to relay the results of the discussions to Konoe, but he failed to attend any meetings. The Breakfast Club, nonetheless, was a convenient source of informed opinion for Ozaki and a useful means of spreading his own ideas and information.

The Special Higher Police (Tokkotai) finally uncovered Ozaki and Sorge's spy ring, but only by accident. The police had been conducting a frantic drive against Japanese Communists since 1939, searching especially for Japanese agents who were being trained in the United States. One of these, a struggling artist from Okinawa named Miyagi Yotoku, had returned to Japan from Los Angeles to use his knowledge of English in Sorge's ring. He was traced and apprehended in October 1941, and his confession implicated the whole ring, including Ozaki. The group was held and tried in secret, and Sorge and Ozaki were finally executed in 1944, still in complete secrecy. Twenty years later Moscow gave Sorge the supreme accolade of Hero of the Soviet Union and in 1965 issued a stamp in his honor.

In October 1941, the Ozaki and Sorge incident came as a bombshell to Tomo and Konoe, who had always assumed Ozaki to be a completely loyal and trustworthy colleague. The first inkling that something was amiss only came when Ozaki failed to appear at a Breakfast Club meeting held on the very day of his arrest. The Special Higher Police questioned Konoe at the hospital, where he was suffering from hemorrhoids, and grilled Tomo at their headquarters. The incident contributed to Konoe's willingness to resign from the prime ministership the same month.

Among Miyagi's papers the police found a draft for a secret agreement between Wang Ching-wei and the Japanese government, which Inukai Ken had masterminded and which contained much about long-range Japanese military plans against the Soviet Union. Saionji Koichi made a copy of it, which he showed to Ozaki as a China expert, and Ozaki had it translated by Miyagi to give to Sorge. As a result both Inukai and Saionji were arrested in April 1942 on charges of breaking the Military Secrets Protection Law. Inukai was eventually pronounced innocent, but Saionji was found guilty, though he was given only a suspended sentence of eighteen months on the grounds that his offense was the result of carelessness rather than ill intent.

———————— • ————————

During the four years of war with the United States, Konoe held no public office and tried to remain out of public sight, usually away from Tokyo, because he was viewed with suspicion by the military and feared for his life. Tomo, however, continued to serve as his private secretary, and Konoe, as a former prime minister and the head of one of the most illustrious noble families, continued to be a trusted adviser to the emperor. In February 1945 he presented a memorial, urging the emperor to bring the war to a speedy end because, the longer it lasted, the greater the chances of a Communist revolution at its end. Konoe had become steadily more apprehensive of this, having personally suffered from the penetration of a Communist into his own cabinet advisory group and having learned more recently from Sano Manabu of Communist machinations for a takeover. Sano, a Japanese Communist, had been arrested in Shanghai and sentenced to life imprisonment, but after recanting in prison he had recently been released. However much the emperor may have agreed with Konoe on the desirability of ending the war quickly, he had no chance to act until after the dropping of the atom bomb in August.

When the terms of surrender of the Potsdam Proclamation were accepted, Konoe urged strongly that Prince Higashikuni Naruhiko be appointed prime minister, since his status as a member of the imperial family and a top army general would help gain acceptance of defeat by the military and the people. Higashikuni accepted the assignment, but only if Konoe would serve as deputy prime minister, and the new cabinet was formed on August 17 to supervise the transfer of power to the victorious Americans. This brought Konoe back to the center of the political stage. He held his first meeting with General MacArthur on September 13 in the customs house in Yokohama. Konoe tried to use the occasion to explain to MacArthur the complicated political situation in Japan, but his effort was futile. The American side insisted on using only its own interpreter, who was completely incompetent. Tomo was not permitted to be in the room and was forced to wait outside in frustration. But the foreign correspondents who accompanied the occupation forces showed a great interest in Konoe, and since they were willing to have either Tomo or Shirasu Jiro, the assistant to Foreign Minister Yoshida, do the interpreting for them, their talks with Konoe were far more satisfactory.

When Prime Minister Higashikuni met with MacArthur for the first time late in September, he inquired if there were any members of the government MacArthur felt should resign. MacArthur's reply, "Not one," was very reassuring to both Higashikuni and Konoe. Konoe was further encouraged by a meeting with MacArthur on October 4 in the Daiichi Building in Tokyo, where MacArthur had established his headquarters. Tomo did not attend this meeting, but a good interpreter from the foreign ministry prevented a recurrence of the debacle of misunderstanding at the meeting in Yokohama. MacArthur said that a new constitution must be written and, as Konoe and Tomo understood it, Konoe was to take the lead in doing this and in establishing a new democratic system for Japan. Konoe was only too happy to undertake the task and met on October 8 with George Atcheson, MacArthur's political adviser, to find out American wishes for details of the new constitution. Tomo, Shigeharu, and Takagi Yasaka accompanied Konoe on this occasion, and the three of them continued to meet periodically with Atcheson. Konoe was deeply opposed to any theoretical change in the status of the emperor, but the Japanese side understood that Atcheson was not demanding that the emperor relinquish "sovereignty," only that actual political control be placed in the hands of an elected Diet.

Higashikuni and Konoe were shaken from their dreams that all was proceeding smoothly by two political jolts. Higashikuni was hit first by a sudden demand from MacArthur's staff that the home minister, the chief of the Tokyo metropolitan police, and the chief of the prefectural police be dismissed. Since Higashikuni thought MacArthur had promised to accept his officials, he felt betrayed and resigned on October 5, to be soon replaced by Shidehara Kijuro, a prominent politician and liberal foreign minister of the 1920s.

Konoe received his shock on November 2, when it was announced that he was not to be involved in the revision of the constitution. MacArthur's staff claimed that there had been misunderstandings on this and other matters resulting from mistranslations—an assertion that Tomo has always stoutly denied. What really happened was that Washington had in the meantime decided to treat the top Japanese wartime leaders as war criminals, as had been done with the German leaders, and the Americans had also come to the conclusion that Konoe was simply too devoted to the old status and prerogatives of the Japanese throne to be able to help with a new democratic constitution. Broadcasts from America on November 3 made Konoe realize that, instead of leading the way to democracy, he was likely to be designated a war criminal.

Early in November a large body of American experts, the Strategic Bombing Survey, descended on Japan to examine the effects of the wartime strategic bombing, but on the side they inquired into other matters. A long list of former top leaders were called in for questioning. Konoe's turn came on November 19, when he and Tomo were picked up by an American navy officer and taken to an American warship anchored off Shibaura. After some courteous pleasantries, Konoe and Tomo were taken into another room, where Konoe was subjected to three hours of grueling questioning. The American interpreter was reasonably competent and, when he encountered difficulties, would turn to Tomo for aid. Konoe was questioned on his involvement in the Sino-Japanese War, the Japanese occupation of French Indochina, when he had started his negotiations with the United States, whether he had favored the choice of Tojo as prime minister, what had been discussed at conferences in the imperial presence, what the emperor said, why surrender was delayed until August, and a number of other matters. At the end of the grilling, the interrogator asked if he could conclude that Konoe, as prime minister, did not know how the military would pursue the Sino-Japanese War and that both the prime minister and the emperor were no more than puppets. Konoe answered in an agonized voice with the single word, "Yes." What bothered the interrogator most was the idea that the

Japanese started the war without clear plans for its end. This was indeed the situation, so far as Konoe knew, but the Americans simply could not believe it.

Despite the humiliations of the past few weeks, Konoe continued his work on plans for a new constitution, which he presented to the emperor. He left Tokyo on November 22 for Karuizawa in the mountains, but the members of the Strategic Bombing Survey wanted another interview. Tomo drove up to Karuizawa by jeep with an American navy officer for this second questioning. When the American left, the officer remarked that, no matter what happened, it would not be his responsibility. Konoe took this to mean that it was already decided to prosecute him as a war criminal. He stated simply that he would never go to prison and, when asked by his friends what he would do, replied enigmatically, "There is a way." When the former minister of education committed suicide by poison, Konoe called on his widow and inquired carefully about the details of the minister's death, including the poison used, which was potassium cyanide.

On December 7 Konoe received orders to report as a war criminal to Sugamo Prison on the 16th. Konoe's wife and Tomo drove up to Karuizawa to settle his affairs. On their arrival, the three had a dinner consisting of one egg each, but Konoe stayed in his room. Just before a group of reporters was expected to arrive on December 10, the three of them slipped away by car to Tokyo, where they hid in a friend's house, returning to Konoe's residence only on the 15th, the eve of Konoe's impending imprisonment. That evening friends and relatives came, bringing blankets, sweaters, and other things that would be useful in Sugamo. Before leaving they all drank a solemn toast. Tomo, Shigeharu, and a few others remained to spend the night. While Konoe took his bath, his son unsuccessfully searched his belongings for poison; his wife made no effort to help in the search. In the morning, when Tomo and the others went to Konoe's room, they found him dead of potassium cyanide.

Konoe's suicide brought an end to Tomo's public career, and he subsequently entered the world of business. He served a while as an auditor of the Import Export Bank and finally became part of Japan's postwar economic resurgence as vice-president of the Alaska Pulp Company.

———— • ————

The third of the Ushiba brothers, Nobuhiko, had a more typical career than Tomo. Known to family and friends as Nobu, he was born in Tokyo in 1911. For a while the Ushibas lived next door to my family, and I remember Nobu as an active, rowdy boy. He followed Tomo through the First Higher School and the law faculty of Tokyo Imperial University but was not much touched by the currents of democracy and Marxism, being primarily a sportsman and an enthusiastic member of the rowing team. The Tokyo Imperial University crew was expected to represent Japan at the Los Angeles Olympics of 1932 but lost in the tryouts, and Nobu decided instead to take the examination for the foreign ministry, in which he was successful.

New ministry officials were normally sent abroad for a period of study, and Nobu was dispatched in 1933 to Germany, where he studied at both Berlin and Heidelberg and then served at the Japanese embassy. During this period the 1936 Olympics were held in Berlin, with the Tokyo university team this time representing Japan. The Japanese military attaché, General Oshima Hiroshi, also negotiated with the German foreign minister, Joachim von Ribbentrop, the Anti-Comintern Pact aimed at the Soviet Union, but the Japanese ambassador and his foreign ministry staff were not informed of the pact until just before its signing in November 1936.

In September 1937 Nobu was recalled to Japan. He had not been much impressed in Germany with the brown-shirted stormtroopers of Hitler's movement, but back in Japan he fell in with the nationalistic tides of the time. Konoe had just become prime minister, and Nobu found himself in sympathy with Konoe's call in 1938 for a "new order in East Asia," which aimed at the end of Western colonialism in the region and Japan's replacement of Britain and the United States as the dominant force in the area. Such policies naturally brought Japan together with Germany and Italy as one of the aggressive have-not powers, challenging the status quo. Because he embraced such ideas, Nobu became known as one of the group of pro-German officials in the foreign ministry called the "reformist faction" (*kakushin-ha*).

In September 1939 the military proposed to form a ministry of foreign trade under its own control. There was an uproar of protest in the foreign ministry, but to no avail. The reformist faction was given the primary blame for the violence of the protest, and Nobu was exiled to a post abroad, going to England by way of the United States.

Nobu arrived in London in May 1939, only shortly before the outbreak of World War II in Europe. After the collapse of France in 1940, England was subjected to frequent German air raids, the first of three periods of heavy bombing Nobu was to experience in three different countries. The Japanese embassy was bombed out, and its work had to be shifted to temporary quarters. The British government and people were hostile to Japan as the ally of Germany and a threat to British interests in East Asia. As a consequence, there was not much work to be done at the embassy, and Nobu could spend leisurely weekends playing golf. In September 1941 he received orders to return with the ambassador to Japan, but General Oshima, who in the meantime had become the ambassador in Berlin, suggested that Nobu come there and then proceed to Japan by way of the Soviet Union after Hitler had overrun it.

In Berlin Nobu was with Oshima at the Reichstag when Hitler, much to the relief of the Japanese, declared war on the United States following Japan's attack on Pearl Harbor in December 1941. He also was with Oshima when the ambassador took a tour of inspection of the German conquests in the Ukraine. By 1943 allied air raids had become serious, and Nobu underwent his second experience with heavy bombing in Berlin. Incidentally, Oshima's detailed reports to Tokyo about bomb damage in Germany, which were made available to the allies through the decoding work of the American army, were the best source they had for this vital information.

Nobu was ordered back to Tokyo in November 1943, traveling by way of Turkey and the Soviet Union and reaching Tokyo on January 5, 1944. There he was given notice of his induction into the army but was saved from military service by the head of his bureau in the foreign ministry. By November, American air raids had become frequent and devastating, and from then until the end of the war Nobu experienced more heavy bombing. The family's home in Omori, between Tokyo and Yokohama, was burned to the ground, with the loss of all of the family's papers and treasures. The army planned in April 1945 to move the emperor and empress to safety in the mountains of central Japan, and Nobu was scheduled to accompany them. According to Mrs. Takaki, however, the imperial couple refused to seek safety for themselves while leaving other Japanese in bomb-ravaged cities, and nothing came of the proposal.

After Japan's surrender, General MacArthur was headquartered at first in Yokohama at the Grand Hotel, which had surprisingly survived the bombing. Nobu was made a member of a committee to arrange the transfer of American headquarters to Tokyo. The Americans demanded cars for the move and, when informed there were none, one of them asked in contempt, "How could you ever have waged the war?" Subsequently, Nobu became chief of the Liaison Office for the Termination of the War (Shusen Renraku Jimu Kyoku), where his main task was coordinating plans for the repatriation of surrendered Japanese soldiers from overseas.

During the American occupation, there was little for the foreign ministry to do, since MacArthur and his staff were in control of Japan's relations with the outside world. Yoshida Shigeru, the future prime minister but then foreign minister, planned a drastic reduction of personnel. Since Nobu had been a member of the reformist faction, he was sure he would be dropped and therefore resigned in July 1946. After fourteen years of service his retirement salary, calculated according to prewar monetary values, was only 2118 yen, which would have been $706 before the war but was soon worth only about $6. This miserable settlement seriously affected his eventual retirement salary from the foreign office in 1974, which was a niggardly sum for all his years of service in the top posts of the ministry.

For two and a half years after his resignation, Nobu served as a defense counsel for his old boss, General Oshima, the former ambassador in Berlin, who with twenty-eight others had been designated by the International Tribunal for the Far East as "Class A" war criminals for "crimes against peace." The trial concluded in November 1948, with Tojo and six others condemned to execution and Oshima to a life sentence, though he was released three years later when the occupation came to an end.

Nobu next tried his hand at business, distributing steel for a Swiss importer, but he had no taste for such work and returned to government service in July 1949. He was appointed chief of the secretariat of the Foreign Exchange Control Commission, a body established by the occupation. He had some doubts about taking this post because he lacked financial and economic knowledge, but he was an extremely hard worker and soon mastered the job, preparing himself for a number of important economic positions he was later to occupy. In connection with his work with the commission, Nobu took a one-month trip to the United States, his first trip there of any duration.

In June 1951 Nobu became chief of the International Trade Bureau of the Ministry of International Trade and Industry (MITI). This position made him an important bureaucrat in a key ministry, because MITI was taking the lead in restoring the Japanese economy through international trade, which had only started to revive significantly after the Korean War broke out in June 1950 and began to produce heavy purchases of Japanese industrial goods by the United States. In his MITI position Nobu made an extensive trip through western Europe, making valuable personal contacts that proved useful later and coming to the conclusion that Japanese were not working hard enough but were simply relying on the Americans.

Although Nobu still had some enemies in the foreign ministry, he was reinstated there in July 1954. His first assignment was as a member of a delegation invited to attend a Soviet agricultural exhibition, even though Japan and the Soviet Union still had no formal relations. In December 1954 Nobu was made counselor at the Japanese embassy in Burma, where he supervised negotiations for what was to be Japan's first reparations settlement. In January 1956 he was recalled from Burma and sent to Australia to handle trade negotiations. At the time, Australia exported considerable wool and wheat to Japan but took few Japanese imports because of discriminatory laws. Nobu won much recognition for the trade treaty signed with Australia in July 1957 and was brought back to Tokyo to become chief of the economic section at the foreign ministry, where he oversaw the conclusion of a trade pact with the Soviet Union. Japan had been allowed in 1955 to join GATT, the General Agreement on Tariffs and Trade, and Nobu had his greatest achievements working through that body.

In September 1961 Nobu was appointed ambassador to Canada, remaining there for three years, and then he returned to Tokyo where he took charge of the delicate negotiations for the normalization of relations with South Korea. These had been in progress for some years, but Nobu brought them to a successful conclusion in June 1965.

Nobu attained the apex of his ministry career in April 1967, when he became foreign vice-minister, which in the postwar system is normally the highest post open to a career bureaucrat and is the actual head of the ministry, since the minister, normally a politician, deals for the most part only with high policy and political decisions. After three years as vice-minister, there was only one post of greater prestige left for Nobu, and this was ambassador to the United States. It has become almost a rule for retiring foreign vice-ministers to become ambassadors to Washington, and Nobu made this transition in July 1970.

Previous ambassadors had not cut much of a figure in Washington, but Nobu, consciously or not, followed my husband's strategy in Tokyo by making a special effort to get to know senators and congressmen and to travel all over the country. Because of his good command of English and his outgoing personality, he was very successful in his efforts, setting a new pattern for Japanese ambassadors in the United States, that some of his successors have been able to follow. The only serious problem he encountered during his four years in Washington was when in 1971 President Nixon and Secretary of State Kissinger let him know, only moments before releasing the news to the world, of America's impending rapprochement with the People's Republic of China. Since the Japanese had been urging such a course and the American side had repeatedly promised to consult with them, the Japanese felt humiliated and let down.

After leaving the Washington embassy Nobu, as was customary, retired from the foreign ministry, but his life of public service became more active than ever. Japan had become the second largest industrial power in the democratic world and needed to take its share of international responsibilities. Nobu was among the few who had the requisite broad international experience, knowledge of foreign languages, familiarity with problems of world trade, and ease in dealing with Westerners. His youthful nationalistic expansionism had long since disappeared, and he was known as a sincere friend of the United States and a man of broad vision.

Nobu was tireless in a wide field of activities, but his main achievements were in the area of economics. He was made a member of the cabinet in 1979 as the newly created minister of external economic affairs, serving in this capacity as chief negotiator in many trade negotiations. It is most unusual in the contemporary Japanese system for anyone but members of the Diet to occupy a cabinet post. After leaving the cabinet, Nobu represented Japan in 1979 at the so-called Tokyo Round of the GATT negotiations, and from 1979 to 1981 he served as co-chairman of an officially selected small group of Japanese and American experts, commonly called the "Wisemen," who were assigned the task of surveying the general situation and problems in Japanese–American economic relations. At the same time, he was deputy chairman of the Japanese delegation to the Trilateral Commission, a private body of leaders from the United States and Canada, Europe, and Japan who sought to strengthen cooperation among the major democracies. Despite failing health, Nobu rushed at a frantic pace between meetings all over the world, until he died virtually of exhaustion on the last day of 1984.

Ushiba Nobuhiko is a good person with whom to conclude my book. He was my near contemporary, falling between my husband and me in age. Though an outstanding leader of his generation, his career was far different from those of my two grandfathers. A product of the school and employment examination system, he was an energetic team player through and through, a career bureaucrat albeit a spectacularly successful one. He was a model modern "salary man," as the typical office worker is called. His accomplishments contributed significantly to the fruition of the dreams of my two grandfathers. The uncertain and sometimes timid internationalism of my grandfathers attained full maturity in Nobu's easy participation in world affairs. With my two grandfathers I started back in the feudal age of the Tokugawa shoguns. With Nobu I have reached what Japan is today.

Index

Names of Japanese who became permanent residents of the United States and names of Americans of Japanese origin are distinguished by the use of a comma as in Western style (e.g. Arai, Rioichiro instead of Arai Rioichiro).

Abe family, 159
Agriculture, 69, 70, 87, 88, 104, 118, 149, 221–222. *See also* Meiji Restoration, land reform during
Aikawa Yoshisuke, 342
Aizu domain, 94, 173–174, 197
Amami Oshima, 24
American School in Japan, 3, 15
American Silk Association, 226, 227, 239, 254–255
Anglo-Japanese Alliance, 131, 132, 133, 142, 240, 286
Annaka domain, 162, 170, 220
Arai, Mitsu (daughter of Okabe Nagamoto, wife of Yoneo), 252–253, 342
Arai, Rioichiro (son of Hoshino Yahei, adopted by Arai Keisaku), 1, 10, 12, 155–259; birth, 155–156, 170; early education, 170, 177; in Meiji Restoration, 174, 175; in Tokyo, 175–177, 180, 186; study of English, 177, 178, 179, 180, 184–185, 186, 190, 198, 203; at commercial training school, 187–188, 189, 190; emigration to U.S., 192–206; passage to U.S., 198–199; trip across U.S., 200–201; first impres-

sions of New York, 201–205; early days in New York, 216; Pacific crossings, 217; and Christianity, 221; as representative of Doshin Kaisha, 223; marriage, 228–232; formation of Morimura Arai Company, 235; patriotism, 236; unsuccessful ventures, 236; and cotton industry, 237; and Japan Society, 242; and golf, 243–244, 257, 258; losses in Kanto earthquake, 256; retirement, 256–257; death, 258–259; descendants, 263; and Kojiro, 277; and Ushiba family, 343
Arai, Ryo (son of Yoneo), 195, 253
Arai, Tazu (wife of Rioichiro, daughter of Ushiba Takuzo), 229, 231–232, 235, 237, 239, 244–245, 277; in Japan, 248, 250; and Miyo's marriage, 250–251; and Japanese women's clubs, 257
Arai, Yoneo (Yone, son of Rioichiro), 237, 245, 246–247, 250, 251–252, 253, 256, 338
Arai family, 158, 172, 267, 322, 337–357, 343; Kazuno home, 170–171, 221; Americanization, 243–259; summer vacations, 247–248; trips to Japan, 248–249; in Greenwich home, 1, 4, 12, 238–239, 244–245, 251, 343
Arai Go, 218–219
Arai Keisaku (Denemon; Rioichiro's father by adoption), 170, 171, 229
Arai Kikuko, 221, 229
Arai Nobuko (wife of Keisaku), 171, 172, 221

Arimura brothers, 44–45
Asakawa Kanichi, 324
Ashio copper mines, 156, 161, 219

Bank crisis of 1927, 269, 289, 293, 295, 323, 325
Bank of Japan, 84, 96, 121, 132, 137, 151, 323
Benedite, Leonce, 295
Blake, William, 304, 305
Boeki Shokai, 223, 234. *See also* Mitsubishi Company; Yokohama Gomei Kasha
Boxer Uprising, 128, 137, 325
Boynton, Florence, 3
Brangwyn, Sir Frank, 290, 294
Breakfast Club (Asameshi Kai), 347
Bruck, Mari, 13, 337
Buddhism, 103, 105, 152, 156, 158, 172, 181; Zen, 36, 301, 319
bummei kaika (civilization and enlightenment), 181–182
Bunya, *see* Hoshino, Bunya
Bureau of Industrial Promotion, 79, 82, 87, 237

Carnegie, Andrew, 133, 136, 243
Chancellor, Christopher, 326, 328
Charter Oath of 1868, 175, 181
Chiang Kai-shek, 326, 328, 329, 330, 331
Chikuzen domain, 61, 62, 72
China: Japanese trade with, 23, 24, 125–126, 161, 184; rivalry over Korea, 119–122; and World War I, 142, 143; Japanese relations with, 143–146, 313, 325; laborers from, in U.S., 199; and silk exports, 222; and U.S., 239, 240, 356; Nationalist government of, 329, 330, 331. *See also* Boxer Uprising; Sino-Japanese War
Choshu domain, 45, 52, 58, 59, 63, 176, 278; and Meiji Restoration, 60, 64, 65, 74, 75, 87, 173; men from, in government, 92, 98, 110, 112, 126, 128, 129, 140, 144, 183, 267, 278; samurai of, 194–195. *See also* Satsuma-Choshu oligarchy
Chotaro, *see* Hoshino Chotaro
Chou Fu-hai, 331
Christianity, 97–98, 146, 162, 182, 183, 220, 249, 307, 343; banning of, 23, 24, 70–72, 176, 180, 190, 281; lifting of

ban on, 72, 282; converts to, 182, 187, 219, 230, 240, 302–303. *See also* Missionaries; No-church movement
Christian Science, 3, 258, 337
Christian Science Monitor, 12, 14, 311
Clark, William S., 240
Communism, 146, 287; in Japan, 277, 287, 303, 307, 312–313, 334, 346, 347, 348
Concubinage, 102–103
Conder, Josiah, 105
Confucianism, 26, 35–36, 151, 170, 182, 183, 189, 220, 264, 343
Constitution, Japanese, 65, 82, 97, 98, 111, 114; promulgation of, 80, 98–99; dispute over, 91, 92; of 1946, 311, 349, 350, 351
Cotton industry, 236–237, 255–256, 321
Currency, 88–89, 141, 167, 196, 198; paper, 72, 88–89, 94, 96; and foreign exchange, 197, 199, 224, 232

Daigaku Yobi Mon, 275. *See also* Tokyo Imperial University
Daimyo, 24, 32, 33, 39, 40, 162; and Tokugawa government, 22, 23, 166; and opening of Japan, 42, 43; in Edo, 44, 47, 48, 49, 175; processions of, 49–51, 53; after Meiji Restoration, 64, 65, 73, 89, 96, 98, 175, 221; and agricultural land, 77; and banks, 89, 265; debts of, 163, 168
Dajokan (Council of State), 64, 98
de Blowitz, Henri, 134
Delano, Lyman, 268
Denemon, *see* Arai Keisaku
Diet (national parliament), 111–112, 121, 125, 126, 140, 142, 151, 218–219; House of Representatives, 111; House of Peers, 111, 125, 265; and cabinet, 114–116, 117, 123, 127, 357; special election of 1892, 116; third session, 116–117; and political parties, 124, 126, 127, 129; elections for, 230, 284, 322; postwar, 349
Domei News Agency, 308, 310, 331, 332, 333
Doshin Kaisha (Company to Progress Together), 223, 233, 234, 235, 236, 238
Doshisha University, 94, 162, 220, 221
Dudley, Mrs., 216, 232, 237, 277

Dutch, 24, 25, 40, 57, 117, 161, 184
Dutch learning, 40, 41, 57, 70, 182, 281
Dutch Reformed Church, 75, 191, 276

Earthquake of 1891, 114
Earthquake of 1923, *see* Kanto earthquake
Edo, 22, 42, 43, 44, 45, 47, 52, 61, 64;
    shogun's castle in, 22, 48, 165, 176–
    177, 186; daimyo in, 39; Satsuma resi-
    dence in, 46, 48; march on, 173; West-
    ern goods in, 197. *See also* Tokugawa
    period; Tokyo
Education: of Matsukata's sons, 2, 264,
    266, 267, 275–276, 300–301, 305; re-
    forms in, 70, 74, 135, 151, 178, 184,
    186, 322; of women, 75, 182, 283
ELEC, *see* English Language Education
    Council
Elisséeff, Vadim, 297
Emmerson, John K., 345
Emperor, Meiji, 43, 80, 92, 98, 101, 114;
    and constitution, 91, 92, 98–99; and
    Matsukata, 94, 96, 101–102, 104, 105,
    113, 120, 125, 132, 139, 141; and
    treaties with British, 111; and Diet, 116,
    127; and elder statesmen, 130; and
    Russo-Japanese War, 137, 139; death,
    141, 284, 300
Emperor, Taisho, 118, 142
Emperor Hirohito, 310, 338–339, 348,
    350, 351, 353–354; broadcast of Japa-
    nese surrender, 11, 340, 341–342; as
    crown prince, 147; trip abroad, 147–
    148; postwar status, 349
Empress, Meiji, 98, 100, 101, 102, 105,
    141
Empress, Taisho, 148
Empress Nagako, 147, 339, 353
English Language Education Council
    (ELEC), 335
Europe, 24, 75, 76, 77, 97, 99, 140; Ma-
    tsukata in, 86, 133; study of constitutions
    of, 97, 98; and Japan's gold standard,
    126; racial prejudice in, 134; silk blight in,
    87, 168–169; Matsukata's sons in, 265,
    266, 277, 305. *See also* Iwakura mission
Exclusion Act (1924), 247, 325, 327
Exports, 94–95, 96, 203, 221, 224, 235,
    285; expansion of, 151, 188, 189, 192,
    197, 209, 224, 225; of silk, 177, 221,
    223, 225, 228, 253, 255

Ferris Seminary (Yokohama), 191, 221
Fifteenth Bank (Peers Bank), 89, 106, 265,
    285, 289, 293, 295
Foreign Affairs, 16, 333
Foreign Correspondents Club of Japan, 14
France, 58, 84, 88, 97, 131, 292–294,
    296–297, 353; Matsukata in, 82–87,
    118; and Sino-Japanese War, 121, 122;
    silk industry in, 87, 168–169
"Freedom and people's rights" movement,
    see *jiyu minken undo*
Fukai Eigo, 132, 134
Fukuzawa Yukichi, 125, 182–183, 186,
    195, 210, 229, 232; on foreign trade,
    185, 189, 192, 197, 198; and Maruzen
    Company, 189, 196; founding of Boeki
    Shokai, 223. *See also* Keio Gijuku school
Fukuzawa Yuzo, 212, 220, 223

Geisha, 102–103, 110
General Agreement on Tariffs and Trade
    (GATT), 355, 357
genro (elder statesmen), 2, 65, 117, 127,
    129, 130, 241; and Matsukata, 113,
    116, 124; and Korea, 131, 141; and
    Russo-Japanese War, 137, 140; in Taisho
    period, 142–146, 147, 148; and World
    War I, 142, 143. *See also* Satsuma-
    Choshu oligarchy
Gerli, Paolino, 258–259
Germany, 104, 121, 122, 123, 128; as
    model, 97, 98; and World War I, 142,
    143, 146; Japanese students in, 265,
    352; and Soviet Union, 345, 346–347,
    352
Glover, Thomas, 56, 58, 63, 65
Gneist, Rudolph, 97
Godai Tomoatsu, 56–57
Gogaku, 68, 82, 108
goju (village fraternity), 28–32, 36, 37, 38,
    39. *See also* Samurai, young
Goro, *see* Matsukata Goro
goshi (rural samurai), 23, 24, 25, 26, 32, 46
Goto Nobuo (penname of Matsukata Sa-
    buro), 305, 306
Goto Shojiro, 115, 116
Great Britain, 52, 53–54, 57, 58, 61, 110,
    131; and Matsukata, 58, 62, 104; parlia-
    mentary system of, 91, 97; and Sino-Jap-
    anese War, 120, 121; and extraterrito-
    riality, 127, 239. *See also* Anglo-Japanese

Great Britain (continued)
  Alliance; Richardson affair; Washington
  Conference
Greene, D. C., 268, 282
Greene, Jerome, 268, 306, 326
Grew, Joseph, 290, 344–345

Hanako, see Matsumoto Hanako
harakiri, see seppuku
Hara Takashi: as prime minister, 140, 147,
  148, 277–278, 287; and Seiyukai Party,
  146, 149, 284
Harris, Townsend, 43, 168
Harvard University, 132, 133, 246–247,
  251, 253, 267, 269, 297, 306
hatamoto (standard bearers), 162, 163, 168,
  175, 197
Hayami Kenso, 178, 203, 220; and silk-ex-
  port trade, 185–186, 188, 189, 192,
  223
Hepburn, James C., 190–191, 281
Hideyoshi, 22, 28, 160
Higashikuni Naruhiko, Prince, 348, 349–
  350
Hihan (Criticism), 307
Hinode Company, 213
Hioki Kosaburo, 287, 288
Hirohito, see Emperor Hirohito
Hiroshige, 48, 292
Hiroshima, 11, 122, 339–340, 348
Hisamitsu (Prince Shimazu), 39, 43–44,
  45, 46, 58, 59; and Matsukata, 47, 48,
  49, 51–54, 73; and Richardson affair,
  50–52; and land reform, 78–79; and
  constitution, 98
Hitotsubashi University, 187
Hizen domain, 61, 62, 71, 74, 76, 89, 92
Hokkaido Colonization Agency, 92, 110,
  185
Hokkaido University, 240, 302
Hornbeck, Stanley, 271
Hoshino, Bunya, 232–233
Hoshino, Kosaku, 217, 219, 249
Hoshino Chotaro (oldest brother of
  Rioichiro Arai), 173, 177, 212, 217–
  219, 223, 249; and silk trade, 178, 189,
  192–199, 208, 209, 210, 211,
  215, 223, 224, 249; silk-reeling plant
  of, 185–186, 188; adoption of Bunya,
  232–233; as member of Diet, 248, 249
Hoshino family, 158–169, 170, 172, 249;

in Meiji Restoration, 173, 174, 175,
  176, 179, 218; and Christianity, 219–
  221
Hoshino Hambei, 162
Hoshino Iyabei, 161
Hoshino Kohei, 163–164, 165
Hoshino Motoji, 233, 249–250
Hoshino Seikoin, 159–160
Hoshino Tomohiro, 165–167, 168
Hoshino Ukyonosuke, 159
Hoshino Yahei, 167, 168, 169, 170, 173,
  174, 175, 177
Hoshino Yasushi, 160
Hyogo prefecture, 60, 65, 229
Hyogo Shipyards, 278. See also Kawasaki
  Shipyards

Ichikawa Einosuke, 281, 282
Ii Naosuke, 43, 44, 45, 171, 172
Imperial Rule Assistance Association (Taisei
  Yokusankai), 344
Inflation, 14, 88–89, 93, 96; of 1870s,
  188, 217, 221, 333
Inoue Junnosuke, 244
Inoue Kaoru, 58, 112, 136, 142, 267, 278;
  and Matsukata, 63, 74, 89, 94; and Sat-
  cho clique, 93; and Western customs, 99;
  art collection, 108; resignation, 110; and
  Sino-Japanese War, 121; and adoption of
  gold standard, 125; and Korea, 131,
  141; death, 140
Inoue Masaru, Viscount, 267
Institute of Pacific Relations (IPR), 5; Japan
  Council (Taiheiyo Mondai Chosa Kai),
  306; third conference in Kyoto (1929),
  306, 308, 326, 334; American Council,
  307; conference, Banff (1933), 307; conference, Yosemite (1936), 307, 346; eleventh conference, India, 315; fourth conference, China (1931), 326, 328, 329;
  and Occupation, 332
International House (I House) of Japan,
  334, 335–336
International Tribunal for the Far East, 354
Inukai Ken, 331–332, 347, 348
Inukai Michiko, 273–274, 331
Inukai Tsuyoshi, 126, 183, 229, 230
Iroha uta (Syllabary Poem), 31
Ise Shrines, 179–180
Itagaki Taisuke, 76, 112, 128, 173–174,
  198; and people's rights movement, 78,

80, 91, 218; and Liberal Party, 93, 111; as home minister, 123, 127

Ito Hirobumi, 58, 87, 92, 96, 102, 114, 231, 267, 284; and Japanese constitution, 65, 76, 91, 97, 98, 99; and Iwakura mission, 74–75; and Matsukata, 85–86, 89, 94, 96, 97, 112, 124, 277; and Sat-cho clique, 93; in Europe, 97–98; as prime minister, 98, 101, 110, 112, 114, 117, 124, 126, 128, 129, 130; and Diet, 112, 114, 117, 127; and cabinet, 115, 116, 127, 278; and Korea, 119–120, 131, 140, 141; and Sino-Japanese War, 121–122, 123, 125; and Boxer Uprising, 128; and Seiyukai, 128–129, 136; and title of *genkun*, 130; and Saionji, 131; and Russo-Japanese War, 137; assassination, 140; influence of Yoshida Shoin on, 195

Iwakura mission, 72, 74–76, 78, 80, 147, 191, 276, 281, 283

Iwakura Tomomi, 76, 78, 94, 174, 207

Iwanaga Yukichi, 307–308, 327, 343

Iwao, *see* Matsukata Iwao

Iwasaki Yanosuke, 124

Iwasaki Yataro, 124, 144, 223, 266, 284. *See also* Mitsubishi Company

Japan: war with U.S., 9–12; surrender, 11, 332, 340, 354; postwar, 13–14; U.S. understanding of, 14, 15, 16, 17, 239, 333, 334; treaties with U.S., 42, 43, 119, 334; and Korea, 119–122, 131; militarism, 123, 127, 129, 270, 272, 273, 319, 338, 341, 345; on gold standard, 125–126, 135–136; savings, 135; relations with China, 143–146, 239; economic success, 155; attitude of U.S. to, 240, 247, 270, 272, 273, 290, 326; newspapers, 308–313, 322; exchanges between U.S. and, 334; economic relations with, 357. *See also* Anglo-Japanese Alliance; Occupation, American; Russo-Japanese War; Sino-Japanese War

Japan Alpine Club, 316–317

Japan Broadcasting Corporation, 341–342

Japanese American Women's Club, 257

Japanese Club (London), 290, 291

Japan Society (New York), 241–242, 258, 266

Japan-Soviet Petroleum Company, 289–290

Jiji Shimpo, 230

jiyu minken undo (movement for freedom and people's rights), 80, 218

Jomo Kairyo Kaisha, 224

Juntendo (Sakura), 190

Jutaro, *see* Matsumoto Jutaro

Kagoshima, 21, 23, 24, 25, 26, 28, 29, 39, 40, 44; Matsukata family in, 47, 275; British bombardment of, 52, 54, 56, 58, 63, 266; and Meiji Restoration, 60, 61; destruction of Matsukata's home in, 81, 104, 264; Matsukata's lectures in, 136; dialect of, 276

Kaibara Ekken, *Onna Daigaku,* 26

Kaiseido (Institute of Western Studies), 56

Kaisei Gakko, 184, 199, 204, 205. *See also* Tokyo Imperial University

Kaishinto Party, 229

Kaito Kai (Society of East of the Sea), 264

Kaji Ryuichi, 305, 306

Kamakura, 9, 10, 103, 126, 150–151, 256, 301, 304

Kaneko Naokichi, 279, 286

Kansho nippo, 189

Kanto earthquake (1923), 150–151, 256, 289, 304, 323

Kao Tsung-wu, 330, 331, 332

Katayama Sen, 276–277

Kato Takaaki, 142–144, 149

Kato Tomosaburo, Admiral, 149

Katsu Kaishu, 186–187

Katsura Taro, 102, 129, 131, 136, 137, 140, 141, 142, 252

Kawahara Yo, Admiral, 266

Kawakami Hajime, 303, 304, 307

Kawakami Sukehachiro (father of Matsukata Masako), 33, 46

Kawasaki Heavy Industries, 279

Kawasaki Shipyards, 150, 266, 279–280, 284, 285–286; and labor, 287–288, 303; bankruptcy, 289

Kawasaki Shozo, 278, 279

Keiki, *see* Tokugawa Keiki

Keio Gijuku school, 107, 198, 218, 229, 231, 232, 236. *See also* Keio University

Keio University, 107, 125, 182, 189, 343

Kenseito (Constitutional Party), 126, 284

Kesako, *see* Matsukata Kesako

Kido, Marquis, 231

Kido Koin, 58, 75, 76, 78, 87, 92, 102

Kikuko, *see* Arai Kikuko

Kiryu Textile Factory (Kiryu Orimono Kojo), 219

Kita (3rd concubine of Matsukata, mother of Saburo), 103, 299, 304

Kita Kyushu Electric Car Company, 284

Kiyoura Keigo, 151

Kobe, 65, 136, 150, 229, 230, 244, 250, 281, 284; silk shipments from, 256; missionaries in, 268, 281–283; Kojiro in, 278, 283–284; shipyards in, 278, 284, 303; school for girls (Kobe Home) in, 282–283

Kobe Shimbun, 279, 285

Kohei, *see* Hoshino Kohei

Kojiro, *see* Matsukata Kojiro

Kokumin Kyokai (Citizens' Association), 218

Kokusai Kisen Kaisha, 289

Konoe (Imperial Guards) Division, 339, 341, 344

Konoe Fumimaro, Prince, 5, 332, 343–345, 346, 347, 348–351, 352

Konoe Fumitaka, 5, 346

Konoe Hidemaro, 304

Korea, 28, 31, 80, 90, 119–120, 122, 128, 131, 137, 139, 141. *See also* Korean War; Russo-Japanese War; Sino-Japanese War

Korean War, 14, 313, 355

Kosaku, *see* Hoshino, Kosaku

Koshaku Matsukata Masayoshi Den, 8

Kosuke, *see* Matsukata Kosuke

Kozuke, 156, 162, 164, 165, 177, 220; famine in, 163, 172–173; silk production in, 169, 212

Kozuke Silk and Cocoon Improvement Company, 249

Krantz, Jean Baptiste, 85, 86

Kuki family, 230, 280, 281, 282

Kuki Takayoshi, Viscount, 280, 281, 282

Kuniyoshi Yasuo, 241, 291

Kuroda Kiyotaka, 91, 92, 93, 101, 130, 140; as prime minister, 110, 111, 112, 277

Kuroda Kiyoteru, 266, 291, 295

Kuroki Sanji (husband of Matsukata Takeko), 266, 293–294, 302, 305, 323

Kuroki Takeko (daughter of Iwao, wife of Sanji), 293, 294, 299, 300

Kuroki Tamesada, General, 242, 266

Kyodo News Agency (Kyodo Tsushin Sha), 310, 312–313, 333

Kyoshinkai, 222–223

Kyoto, 22, 49, 60–62, 64, 121, 306; imperial court in, 42, 43, 45, 46, 47, 52, 58; emperor in, 101, 252; attack on Nicholas II in, 113–114, 136; as center of silk production, 157, 320; and Hoshino family, 158, 165

Kyoto Imperial University, 303

Kyushu Electric Railway Company (Kyushu Denki Kido Kaisha), 323

Kyushu University, 330

League of Nations, 269, 306

Le Corbusier, 297. *See also* National Museum of Western Art

Liaison Office for the Termination of the War (Shusen Renreku Jimu Kyoku), 354

Liaotung Peninsula, 122–123, 139

Liberal Democratic Party, 129

Liberal Party, 93, 111, 123, 129

Lotus Club, 241, 257, 258

MacArthur, General Douglas, 14, 309, 310, 311–312, 332, 349, 350, 354

Maebashi, 162–163, 177–178, 179, 211, 212, 220, 249

Maeda family, 252, 343

Mainichi Shimbun, 313, 322

Makino family, 55, 147, 293

Mako, *see* Matsukata, Makoto

Manchukuo News Agency, 308, 309

Manchuria, 122, 137, 139, 140, 143, 306, 307, 309, 328, 340, 342. *See also* Liaotung Peninsula

Manchurian Incident, 269, 308, 326, 328

Marco Polo Bridge Incident, 6, 329

Mari, *see* Bruck, Mari

Maruzen, 189, 196

Marx, Karl, 303, 305, 306, 352; *Communist Manifesto,* 304

Masaki, *see* Matsuda Masaki

Masako, *see* Matsukata Masako

Matsudaira Keiei, 49

Matsudaira Sadanobu, 105

Matsuda Masaki (original name of Matsukata's father, adopted by Matsukata Shichiemon), 23, 24–25

Matsuda Tamemasa (original name of Matsukata's grandfather), 23

Matsukata, *see* Matsukata Masayoshi

Matsukata, Makoto (Mako), 13, 312, 337

Matsukata, Mari, *see* Bruck, Mari

Matsukata, Masao (4th son of Matsukata), 266–267

Matsukata, Miye, 13, 337

Matsukata, Miyo (daughter of Rioichiro Arai, wife of Shokuma), 1–3, 237, 248–249, 250, 258, 263; marriage, 1–2, 250–251, 253; children, 3–4; childhood, 245–246

Matsukata, Tane, 13, 171, 337

Matsukata family, 55, 196, 319, 322, 337; in Kagoshima, 81, 104; residences in Tokyo, 104–107, 138, 141, 304; household, 107–109; at golden wedding celebration, 141; as internationalists, 270. *See also* individual names

Matsukata Goro (5th son of Matsukata), 132

Matsukata Hoshino (wife of Saburo), 302, 309

Matsukata Iwao (eldest son of Matsukata), 55, 264–266, 293, 299–300, 302, 304; birth, 47; as president of Fifteenth Bank, 285, 289

Matsukata jikki, 84, 119, 132

Matsukata Kesako (mother of Matsukata), 25, 26–27, 33, 34

Matsukata Kojiro (3rd son of Matsukata), 251, 264, 273, 275–298, 318; and Kanto earthquake, 150, 304; and shipbuilding in World War I, 266–267, 285–286; and manufacture of airplanes, 286–287, 288; and importation of Soviet oil, 289–290; art collection, 290–298, 302; meeting with Monet, 294; death, 296; adoption of Saburo, 299, 300; and Shigeharu, 325, 326, 336

Matsukata Kosuke, 55, 75, 276

Matsukata Masaki (father of Matsukata), 25, 26, 27, 34. *See also* Matsuda Masaki

Matsukata Masako (wife of Matsukata), 2, 46, 68, 81, 107–109, 149; children, 47, 103, 109, 138, 268, 276; and husband's concubines, 103–104, 108, 299; and Mita residence, 106–107, 138, 141; golden wedding anniversary, 141

Matsukata Masayasu (eldest brother of Matsukata), 55

Matsukata Masayoshi, 1, 21–152; biography, 8; birth, 27–28; youth, 30–41;

calligraphy, 34, 82, 108; as Satsuma official, 42–63, 131; as samurai, 44, 46, 107, 155, 184; in Edo, 47–49; and Richardson affair, 51, 52, 53, 54; in Nagasaki, 57–63, 65, 68, 132, 220, 275; and overthrow of shogunate, 59–60; and Western customs, 63, 86, 100, 243–244; as imperial official, 64–90, 131; as governor of Hita, 65–74, 77, 118; and reforms, 73–74, 77–79, 81, 84, 89, 95, 189, 218, 224; in finance ministry, 74, 76–90, 92; and Satsuma Rebellion, 80–81; at Paris International Exhibition, 81–87; and agriculture, 87, 88, 104, 117–118, 221–222; as finance minister, 91–112, 123–124, 127–128, 185, 229, 265, 275, 278, 299, 322; and constitution, 98; and emperor, 101–102, 131, 140; children, 101, 102, 103, 251, 263–274; concubines, 103; and Diet, 112, 114–116, 123, 126; as prime minister, 112–117, 124–127, 277, 322; and Sino-Japanese War, 119–123; as elder statesman, 130–152; trip abroad (1902), 132–136, 221; on international policy, 143–146; and Hirohito, 148; death, 151–152; and cotton industry, 237; on trade vs. war, 222; on silk industry, 222–223, 224

Matsukata Masayoshi Kyo Jikki (The Authentic Record of Lord Matsukata Masayoshi), 8, 9

Matsukata Mineo, 119, 264

Matsukata-Okuma Cabinet, 125

Matsukata Otohiko (6th son of Matsukata), 133, 142, 267–274, 331

Matsukata Saburo (Yoshisaburo; 11th son of Matsukata, adopted by Kojiro), 264, 267, 299–318, 319, 337, 338, 343, 347; education, 300–304; and Boy Scout movement, 301, 317; in Kanto earthquake, 304; in England, 305; and mountain climbing, 305, 316–317; at IPR conferences, 306, 307, 308, 315, 326, 346; marriage, 309; as newspaperman, 309, 332; as head of Kyodo News Agency, 310, 311, 312–314; in public service, 314–316; and Rotary movement, 315–316

Matsukata Shichiemon (31st generation head of Matsukata family), 25

Matsukata Shigeko (wife of Shosaku), 266

Matsukata Shokuma (7th son of Matsukata), 1, 11, 103, 141, 251, 267, 319
Matsukata Shosaku (2nd son of Matsukata), 55, 124, 133, 266, 291
Matsukata Shosha (Matsukata Commercial Company), 292
Matsukata Takeko (daughter of Iwao, wife of Kuroki Sanji), 266, 293–294
Matsukata Tomiko (wife of Otohiko), 268
Matsukata Torakichi (9th son of Matsukata, adopted by Matsumoto Jutaro), 267, 322
Matsukata Umeko, 138
Matsukata Yasuko (wife of Iwao), 265, 266, 300
Matsukata Yoshiko (wife of Kojiro, daughter of Kuki Takayoshi), 280–281, 283
Matsukata Yoshisuke (8th son of Matsukata), 267
Matsukata Yoshiyuki (10th son of Matsukata), 267
Matsukata zaisei (Matsukata's financial policies), 93
Matsumoto, Shigeharu, 148, 296, 305, 319–336, 337, 338, 343; at IPR conferences, 306, 307, 308, 326, 328, 346; marriage, 319; education, 323; internationalism, 323, 327; and Chinese students, 325; in Shanghai, 327–330; and peace movement, 330–332, 345; and Occupation, 332–333; and International House, 335–336; and Konoe, 345, 347, 349, 351
Matsumoto Hanako (wife of Shigeharu, daughter of Kojiro), 319, 325–326, 327, 335
Matsumoto Jutaro (Kamezo), 267, 319–323
Matsumoto Matsuzo (adopted son of Jutaro, husband of Matsukata's daughter Mitsuko), 322, 323
Matsumoto Mitsuko (4th daughter of Matsukata), 319, 322, 323
Matsuoka Yosuke, 332, 344, 345
Megata Tanetaro, 132
Meiji, *see* Emperor, Meiji
Meiji Gakuin University (Tokyo), 191, 249
Meiji Restoration, 55, 61–81, 159, 266, 281; daimyo domains in, 73–74; reforms during, 74, 77, 94–95, 171; land reform during, 77–78; government in, 98; and the West, 99; disorders during, 173, 264

Meirokusha (Society of the Sixth Year of Meiji), 183
Michi, *see* Ushiba Michi
Military Secrets Protection Law, 348
Mimpo (The People's News), 333
Ministry of International Trade and Industry (MITI), 355
Missionaries, 72, 75, 183, 190, 268, 276, 281–283
Mitsu, *see* Arai, Mitsu
Mitsubishi Company, 105–106, 285, 343; silk exports of, 213, 223, 256, 257; founder of, 124, 144, 266, 284. *See also* Iwasaki Yataro
Mitsui Bussan, 235
Mitsui family, 196, 338
Mitsui firm, 54, 140, 235, 320
Mitsui-Mitsubishi shipping firm, *see* Nippon Yusen Kaisha
Mitsuko, *see* Matsumoto Mitsuko
Miyo, *see* Matsukata, Miyo
Mizunuma, 156, 157, 159, 160, 161, 162, 164, 166, 170, 171; in Meiji Restoration, 173, 174, 175, 176, 177, 188; memorial to Bunya in, 233; Chotaro's house in, 249
Monet, Claude, 291, 294, 299
Mori Arinori, 57, 75, 111, 186
Morimura Arai Company, 235, 237, 254, 256
Morimura Brothers, *see* Morimura Company
Morimura Company (Tokyo), 234, 235
Morimura family, 196
Morimura Ichizaemon VI, 196–198, 210, 214, 234, 267
Morimura Kaisaku, 235
Morimura Yutaka (Toyo), 196, 198, 202, 210, 213–214, 232, 235, 236; and Arai, 228, 234; death, 243. *See also* Hinode Company
Motoji, *see* Hoshino Motoji
Movement to Preserve Parliamentary Government, 142
Murai, Caroline Bailey (Nenne; wife of Yasukata), 232, 234, 237, 246
Murai, Taro, 246
Murai, Toyo, 246
Murai, Yasukata, 235, 241, 242; and Arai, 232, 234, 243, 244, 246, 247, 248, 257
Mutsu Munemitsu, 115, 116, 120, 122, 123

Nagasaki, 56, 61, 67, 92, 132, 171, 275, 320; as Dutch trading post, 24, 25, 40, 57, 161; British in, 57, 58; Christians in, 70–71; Mitsubishi shipyard in, 284; atom bomb, 340
Nagayo Sensai, 265
Naidaijin (Inner Minister), 146
Naka, *see* Rawsthorne, Naka
Nakamura Masanao, 182
Narahara, 46–47, 49, 51, 53
Nariakira, *see* Shimazu Nariakira
Nasuno, 8, 35, 108, 117, 118–119, 264, 265, 295
National Museum of Western Art (Tokyo), 290, 293, 296, 297
New York, 201–202, 233, 245, 258
Nicholas II, Tsar, 113–114, 117, 136
Nihon Fujin Kai (Japanese Women's Club), 257
Nihon Kiito Kabushiki Kaisha, 256. *See also* Mitsubishi Company
Nihonmatsu Company, 213, 222
Nihon Oil Company, 269
Niijima Jo, 162, 183, 220
Nikkatsu (movie company), 269
Nikko, 156
Nippon Club, 241
Nippon Yusen Kaisha (N.Y.K.), 132, 248, 289
Nisei, 245, 247
Nishimachi International School, 13, 171, 289, 337
Nissan, 342
Nitobe Inazo, 302, 306, 323, 326–327; *Bushido,* 240–241
Nobuhiko (Nobu), *see* Ushiba, Nobuhiko
Nobuko, *see* Arai Nobuko
No-church movement, 178–179, 220, 302, 306. *See also* Christianity
Nogi Maresuke, General, 141, 300–301, 304, 317
Norman, Herbert, 345

Occupation, American, 12, 13, 14, 309–310, 342, 354; land reforms, 119; censorship, 310–312; Japanese Government Liaison Office with, 312; and cold war, 312–313, 332–333, 334; and Japanese-American relations, 333–334
Okabe Nagaakira, 338, 339, 340–342

Okabe Nagakage, 342
Okabe Nagamoto, 252
Okada Yuji, 291–293
Okubo Toshimichi, 41, 44, 51, 54, 70, 78, 79, 92; and Matsukata, 39, 49, 67, 71, 72, 73, 74, 78, 79, 81, 82, 147; and Iwakura mission, 75, 76; and Satsuma Rebellion, 80; assassination, 87
Okuma Shigenobu, 71, 74, 76, 78, 92, 111, 184; in finance ministry, 87, 89, 91–92, 94, 229; and Matsukata, 90, 97, 124, 126, 185, 221; memorial on constitution, 91, 92; as founder of Waseda University, 93, 182; as foreign minister, 110, 111, 124; and Progressive Party, 124, 125, 127; as prime minister, 127, 130, 144; and genro, 142–143
130th National Bank, 321, 322–323
Onjo Kendo (father of Nobuko), 171–172
Onna Daigaku (The Great Learning for Women), 26
Osaka, 46, 47, 52, 103, 230, 252, 320; and Sino-Japanese War, 121; uprising in, 166; brush manufacture in, 236; cotton industry in, 237
Osaka Mainichi Shimbun, see Mainichi Shimbun
Osaka Spinning Mill, 88, 95, 237, 321
Oshima Hiroshi, General, 352, 353, 354
Otohiko (Oto), *see* Matsukata Otohiko
Ott, Eugen, 346
Oyama Iwao, 93, 140
Oyomei, *see* Wang Yang-ming
Ozaki Hotsumi, 346, 347, 348
Ozaki Yukio, 179, 229–230

Pacific Mail and Steamship Company, 199
Panay incident, 273
Paris Exhibition of 1867, 81
Paris International Exhibition (1878), 81–83
Parkes, Sir Harry, 58, 71, 90, 94–95
Peace Preservation Regulation, 110
Pearl Harbor, 9, 353
Peers School, 101, 149, 265, 267, 275, 300, 304, 338
Perry, Commodore Matthew C., 40, 42, 155, 168, 170, 195
Philadelphia Centennial Exhibition (1876), 81, 188, 203–204, 226

Potsdam Proclamation, 340, 348
Principia College, 4, 6, 7, 9, 311
Privy Council, 98, 110, 116, 136, 147
Progressive Party, 124, 126

Railroads, 84–85, 117, 140, 230, 267, 321–322. *See also* Silk trains
R. Arai Company, 234
Rawsthorne, Naka, 4–5, 12–13
Red Cross: International, 100; Japanese, 100–101; American, 150
Reischauer, Edwin O., 15, 329, 337; "The Broken Dialogue," 16; as ambassador to Japan, 16–17, 101, 264, 316, 337; at Harvard University, 16, 17, 337
Richardson, B., 208, 209, 210
Richardson affair, 50–54
Rioichiro, *see* Arai, Rioichiro
Rockefeller, John D., III, 326, 334, 335
Rodin, Auguste, 295, 296, 298
Rogakkai (Society for the Study of Labor), 303
Rokumeikan (Pavilion of the Deer's Cry), 99, 100, 105, 109, 231
ronin (masterless samurai), 30, 47, 49, 105
Roosevelt, Franklin Delano, 267–268, 269, 270–272, 273, 344, 345
Roosevelt, Theodore, 133, 139, 241
Russia, 122, 123, 135, 136, 239, 289, 340, 345, 355; and Korea, 120, 128, 131, 137; revolution of 1917, 146, 287, 297; German invasion of, 345, 346–347; spy ring of, 346–348. *See also* Russo-Japanese War
Russo-Japanese War, 137–140, 165, 285, 303, 322; Japanese Red Cross in, 101; financing of, 138–139, 149, 242; heroes of, 141, 242, 266, 300; and attitude of U.S., 239, 240, 241, 247, 257; battle of Mukden in, 242
Rutgers College, 55, 75, 184, 276, 336
Ryukyu Islands, 23, 24, 39, 41, 44, 45, 88, 90

Saburo, *see* Matsukata Saburo
Saigo Takamori, 39, 41, 43, 44, 64, 76; and Satsuma-Choshu alliance, 58, 59, 93; and Satsuma Rebellion, 80–81, 205, 206, 264; suicide, 80, 87
Saigo Tsugumichi, 93, 112, 140, 203
Saionji, *see* Saionji Kimmochi

Saionji Kimmochi, Prince, 6, 140, 142, 148, 284; as last genro, 5, 65, 130–131, 146, 149, 151
Saionji Koichi, 5, 346, 348
Saito Hiroshi, 270–271
Samurai, 2, 21, 23, 24, 26, 44, 49; young, 28–39; code of, 45, 48–49, 114; in Edo, 49, 182; literary skills of, 52; sports of, 54; sent to England, 56, 58, 63, 65, 75; after Meiji Restoration, 64, 79, 94, 96, 98, 320; aid to destitute, 79–80, 90; up-risings of, 80, 89, 166; and banks, 89; values of, 107, 109; and peasants, 160; income of, 162, 163, 167, 175, 221; employment of, in silk industry, 212; and swords, 217. *See also* Satsuma Rebellion
San Francisco, 200, 209, 248, 313
Sanjo, 94, 218
Sanyo Railroad, 230, 250
Sapporo Agricultural College, 240, 302. *See also* Hokkaido University
Sat-cho clique, *see* Satsuma-Choshu oligarchy
Sato-Arai Company, 213, 223
Sato Gumi, 215
Sato Momotaro, 189, 190, 191–192, 193, 194, 215, 235; store in New York, 191, 192, 195, 201, 203, 205, 211, 214, 215, 233; "Oceanic group" of, 196, 198, 202, 235; partnership with Arai, 213, 215, 216, 217, 223, 233; marriage, 214, 215; and silk exhibitions, 222–223
Sato Nobuhiro, 69–70
Satsuma-Choshu oligarchy, 93, 111, 115, 131, 142, 146, 155, 177, 183, 229
Satsuma domain, 21, 44, 45, 46, 88, 102, 155, 160, 176; daimyo of, 22–23, 25, 35, 39, 40, 43, 44, 55–56, 70, 99, 237; samurai education in, 28–38; samurai of, 28, 39, 44, 46, 91, 107, 161, 173; classics of, 31; and Meiji Restoration, 39, 59, 60, 64, 65, 75, 80; technology in, 40–41, 56; and Richardson affair, 52–53; and British, 57–58; alliance with Choshu, 58, 59, 60; and the West, 63, 75; men from, in government, 92, 98, 110, 112, 124, 131, 132, 140, 142, 155, 183, 268. *See also* Samurai, young; Satsuma-Choshu oligarchy
Satsuma jisho (Satsuma Dictionary), 68

Satsuma Rebellion, 55, 80–81, 89, 104, 205–206, 264, 321; cost of, 121, 221
Satsuma ware, 41
Say, Léon, 83–84, 95, 96
Schiff, Jacob, 138–139, 242
Seichu-gumi (spirited and loyal band), 44, 46, 47
Seishi Gensha, 212–213
Seiyo jijo (Conditions in the West; Fukuzawa), 182
Seiyukai party, 128–129, 131, 146, 147, 284
Sekigahara, Battle of, 22
Senbon-matsu (Thousand Pines), 118
seppuku (belly slitting), 44, 45, 51, 62, 141
Sericulture, 87, 157, 162, 164, 189
Shakai Shiso (Social Thought), 304, 306
Shanghai, 273, 274, 309, 326, 327; and Sino-Japanese War of 1937, 329
Sheepraising, 117–118
Shibusawa Eiichi, 88, 89, 95, 186, 237, 258, 321, 322
Shichiemon, *see* Matsukata Shichiemon
Shichiroemon (personal formal name of each head of Hoshino family), 165
Shidehara Kijuro, 350
Shigeharu, *see* Matsumoto, Shigeharu
Shimazu, Prince, *see* Hisamitsu
Shimazu family, 21–22, 23, 25, 31, 55, 72, 147, 161
Shimazu Nariakira, 35, 39, 46, 69, 70, 237; and the West, 39–41, 42, 43, 52, 56
Shimazu Shigehide, 40
Shimazu Tadayoshi, 43, 54
Shimbun Rengo Sha (Japan Associated Press), 308, 327
Shinagawa Yajiro, 115, 116, 218
Shin Nippo, 278, 279
Shinto religion, 36, 37, 111, 151–152, 180
Shirasu Jiro, 312, 349
Shizu (second concubine of Matsukata), 103
Shoguns, 22, 77, 156, 163, 167; and emperor, 36–37, 47, 49, 177; and daimyo, 39, 42, 43, 44; and Western impact, 45; overthrow of, 59–62, 64, 131, 173
Shoho Koshujo (Short-Term Commercial Training School), 187, 193. *See also* Hitotsubashi University

Shokuma, *see* Matsukata Shokuma
Shosaku, *see* Matsukata Shosaku
Silk, 23, 155, 157, 162; export of, 1, 87, 95, 136, 178, 189, 208–209; and European blight, 87, 168–169; demand for, 172, 211–212, 224, 227, 232, 253, 256; and balance of trade, 188, 243; transportation of, 209; quality of, 211, 222, 224, 227–228, 233; supply of, 211, 226, 227; methods of production of, 212, 254
Silk industry, 172, 177, 211–213, 226, 249, 255; and machinery, 178, 185–186, 227; problems of, 228. *See also* Silk
Silk ships, 209
Silk trade, U.S.–Japan, 207–225, 243, 257, 259
Silk trains, 209
Sino-Japanese War: of 1894–95, 6, 119–123, 124, 126, 137–139, 239, 278, 303; of 1937, 272–273, 290, 308, 328–330, 338, 344, 350
Smiles, Samuel, *Self Help* (*Saikoku risshi*), 181, 183
Socialism, 276, 287, 303, 306, 307, 344
sonno joi (honor the emperor, expel the barbarians), 43, 45, 63, 181
Sorge, Richard, 346, 347, 348
South Manchurian Railway, 305, 330
Southwestern Rebellion (Seinan-no-eki), *see* Satsuma Rebellion
Strategic Bombing Survey, 350, 351
Sugenoya, M., 184–185; letters of, 199–200, 205–206
Sun Yat-sen, 284–285

Tadayoshi, *see* Shimazu Tadayoshi
Taisho, *see* Emperor, Taisho
Taisho Democracy, 302, 307, 319, 338, 344
Taisho Political Change, 142, 284
Taiwan (Formosa), 88, 89, 122, 279, 286, 321
Takagi Yasaka, 306, 324, 326, 333–334, 349
Takahashi Korekiyo, Baron, 138, 149
Takaki Kenkan, 104, 113, 231, 338
Takaki Tatsuo, Mrs., 338
Takamine Jokichi, 241, 242, 257
Takasaki Domain English School (Takasaki Han Eigo Gakko), 178, 220

Takayanagi Kenzo, 323
Takeko, *see* Kuroki Takeko
Takuwan, 105
Tariffs, 84, 128, 151, 188, 221, 226, 240
Taxation, 77–79, 89, 111, 161, 167
Tazu, *see* Arai, Tazu
Tempo famines, 166–167
Tempo reforms, 167
Terauchi Masatake, 144, 146, 287
Tetsuro, *see* Ushiba, Tetsuro
Textile industry, 87–88
Togo Heihachiro, Admiral, 60, 140
Tojo Hideki, General, 342, 350, 354
Tokaido (Eastern Sea Route), 47–48, 50, 51, 85
Tokkotai (Special Higher Police), 347
Tokugawa Ieyasu, 22, 252
Tokugawa Keiki, 49, 60
Tokugawa Naval School, 57
Tokugawa period, 29, 58, 59, 98, 155, 161, 172; Neo-Confucianism in, 36; teaching of history in, 37; military strength in, 40, 42, 60; opening of Japan in, 42–44; unequal treaties of, 43, 75, 76, 110; end of, 45, 64, 173; processions in, 49; Christianity in, 70; financial reforms in, 105; money economy in, 161, 162, 163, 167; famine in, 163, 166– 167, 172. *See also* Shoguns
Tokutomi Soho, 8, 9
Tokyo, 7, 9, 10, 12, 13, 15, 201; imperial palace in, 48, 314; change of name from Edo, 64, 175; Matsukata family in, 81, 104, 264; and Sino-Japanese War, 121; Gotokuji temple in, 172; Christians in, 220; Arai family in, 248–249; Chamber of Commerce of, 284; one-yen taxi in, 290; system of addresses, 314–315; Rotary convention in, 315–316; Olympics (1964) in, 316; MacArthur's headquarters in, 349, 354. *See also* Edo; Kanto earthquake
Tokyo Club, 100, 244
Tokyo Gas and Electric Company, 267, 269
Tokyo Imperial University, 184, 297, 303, 306, 307, 330, 338, 343; Matsukata's sons at, 132, 266; medical faculty at, 265; law faculty at, 323, 326, 352
Tokyo Seiji Keizai Kenkyukai (Tokyo Institute of Political and Economic Research), 307

Tokyo University, *see* Tokyo Imperial University
Tomioka, 109; silk factory in, 172, 178, 188, 189, 211, 223
Tomita Tetsunosuke, 186, 188, 191, 207
Tomo, *see* Ushiba, Tomohiko
Tonegawa River, 166
Tonghak insurrection, 119, 120
Toragari monogatari (Tale of the Tiger Hunt), 31
Tosa domain, 61, 62, 76, 80, 98, 173, 197, 218
Toyo, *see* Morimura Yutaka
Toyo Eiwa Girls School, 231
Toyo Kisen Kaisha, 248
Trade Encouragement Bureau (Kansho-kyoku), 189
Transportation, 70, 74, 84–85, 209. *See also* Railroads
Trans-Siberian Railway, 123, 135, 136, 139
Trilateral Commission, 357
Tsuda Umeko, 75, 283
Tsushima, Battle of, 118, 139, 140, 268, 285
Twenty-One Demands, 8, 143, 325
2-2-6 Incident, 5, 341

Uchimura Kanzo, 178, 183, 220, 302, 306, 307, 323
ukiyoe, 291–295
Umeko, *see* Matsukata Umeko
United States, 1, 6–7, 9, 55, 88, 126, 133, 155, 179, 334; war with Japan, 9– 12; Japanese knowledge of, 15, 16, 333, 334; and opening of Japan, 43; samurai students in, 56–57; students in, 75, 132, 133, 186, 325; exclusionist policies of, 123, 247, 325, 327; Matsukata in, 132–133; and Russo-Japanese War, 139; and Twenty-One Demands, 143, 325; silk industry of, 189, 227; commercial treaty with (1860), 196; Chinese in, 199, 200, 202, 324–325; direct mail service to Japan, 200, 211. *See also* Iwakura mission; Washington Conference
Ushiba, Nobuhiko (Nobu), 352–357
Ushiba, Tetsuro (son of Ushiba Tazuzo), 231, 236, 250, 343
Ushiba, Tomohiko (Tomo, eldest son of Tetsuro Ushiba), 230, 343–348, 349, 350, 351, 352

Ushiba Daizo (4th son of Tetsuro), 343
Ushiba family, 342–343
Ushiba Michi (wife of Takuzo), 229, 230, 231, 248, 250
Ushiba Michio (2nd son of Tetsuro), 343
Ushiba Takuzo, 229–231, 250, 343

Verbeck, Guido, 68, 71, 75, 92, 184, 276
Vévér, Henri, 292–293
Vienna exposition of 1873, 81
Volunteer Lady Nurses' Association, 100
von Briesen, Richard, 214, 233–234, 235, 238

Walker, Gordon, 311–312
Wang Ching-wei, 331, 347
Wang Yang-ming (Oyomei), 36, 41
Wareware (We), see *Hihan*
Waseda University, 93, 182
Washington Conference (1921–22), 149, 269, 288–289
Watarase Gumi, 212
Watarase River, 156, 166, 219
White Horse Society (Hakuba Kai), 291
Whitney, Clara, 100, 186, 187
Whitney, William C., 186, 187, 193
Wilmot, Commander, 53
Women, 14, 107, 109, 136, 182, 219, 335, 343
Woodblock prints, see *ukiyoe*
World War I, 118, 142–143, 146, 254–255; and shipbuilding, 285–286; art collecting in, 292–293, 302; foreign news in, 307–308
World War II, 6, 9–12, 157, 171, 273, 296; surrender of Japan, 11, 332, 340; aftermath of, 104, 119, 129, 319, 335, 342; air raids of, 106, 309, 338, 339; and U.S. citizenship, 232, 239; and Japanese-American trade, 257, 259; attempts to ward off, 267, 270–273; Imperial Headquarters (Daihonei) in, 339; bombing in, 353

Yahei, *see* Hoshino Yahei
Yale University, 276, 324, 325

Yamada, 179–180, 198
Yamagata Aritomo, 93, 99, 101, 110–111, 126, 129, 195; as prime minister, 111, 112, 127, 128, 131; resignations of, 112, 128; and Diet, 115, 127; and Boxer Uprising, 128; as genro, 130, 131, 136, 140, 141, 143, 144, 146, 147; and Hirohito, 147, 148; death, 149
Yamaguchi-ya, 171
Yamamoto Gonnohyoe, Admiral, 142, 149, 151, 268–269, 284
Yamamoto Kakuma, 94
Yamanaka Bijutsu Shokai, 292
Yamazaki Anzai, 36
Yasuda Zenjuro, 125
Yoikukan, 67–68
Yokohama, 50, 51, 52, 53, 54, 65; Satsuma students in, 57; sericulture exhibit in (1879), 87; Matsukata's departure from (1902), 132; and Kanto earthquake, 150, 256; study of English in, 180, 182, 190, 221; silk trade in, 185, 186, 209, 216, 223; purchase of Western clothes in, 193, 197; Ame Ichiban (American Number 1) Company in, 196–197; Western merchants in, 197, 207; Arai's family in, 198–200, 217, 248; MacArthur's headquarters in, 354
Yokohama Gomei Kaisha, 223. *See also* Mitsubishi Company
Yokohama Kiito Gomei Kaisha (Yokohama Raw Silk Joint Company), 234–236, 255
Yokohama Specie Bank, 138, 211, 224, 244, 256, 265
Yomiuri, 312, 313
Yone, *see* Arai, Yoneo
Yoron Shinsha, 218
Yoshida Shigeru, 296–297, 349, 354
Yoshida Shoin, 194–195
Yoyoki (record of Matsukata's life), 81
Yukan Hochi, 229

zaibatsu, 54, 95, 124, 125, 140, 235, 320, 322
Zoshikan, 35, 36, 37

Designer	Marianne Perlak
Compositor	Achorn Graphic Services
Printer/Binder	Halliday Lithograph
Text	12/13½ Linotron 202 Garamond No. 49
Display	Michelangelo, hand set by Thomas Todd Printers
Paper	70# Finch Opaque Book Vellum

Library of Congress Cataloging-in-Publication Data

Reischauer, Haru Matsukata, 1915–
　Samurai and silk.

　Includes index.
　1. Matsukata, Masayoshi, 1835–1924.　2. Statesmen—
Japan—Biography.　3. Arai, Ryōichirō, 1855–1939.
4. Businessmen—United States—Biography.　5. Japanese—
United States—Biography.　6. Matsukata family.
7. Arai family.　I. Title.
DS881.97.R44　1986　　952.03'092'4　　85-22006
ISBN 0-674-78801-X (paper)